PERPETRATOR CINEMA

Nonfictions is dedicated to expanding and deepening the range of contemporary documentary studies. It aims to engage in the theoretical conversation about documentaries, open new areas of scholarship, and recover lost or marginalized histories

For a complete list of titles, see page 285

PERPETRATOR CINEMA

CONFRONTING GENOCIDE IN CAMBODIAN DOCUMENTARY

RAYA MORAG

WALLFLOWER

NEW YORK

A Wallflower Press book
Published by
Columbia University Press
Publishers Since 1893
New York   Chichester, West Sussex
cup.columbia.edu

Library of Congress Cataloging-in-Publication Data
Names: Morag, Raya, author.
Title: Perpetrator cinema : confronting genocide in Cambodian documentary.
Description: London ; New York : Wallflower Press, 2020. | Series: Nonfictions |
Includes bibliographical references and index.
Identifiers: LCCN 2019026954 | ISBN 9780231185080 (cloth) | ISBN 9780231185097
(paperback) | ISBN 9780231851176 (ebook)
Subjects: LCSH: Genocide in motion pictures. | Documentary films—Cambodia—
History and criticism. | Genocide—Cambodia. | Mass murderers—Cambodia—
Psychology. | Political atrocities—Cambodia. | Cambodia—In motion pictures. |
Cambodia—Politics and government—1975–1979. |
Cambodia—History—1975–1979.
Classification: LCC PN1995.9.G37 M67 2020 | DDC 791.43/658405318—dc23
LC record available at https://lccn.loc.gov/2019026954

Columbia University Press books are printed on permanent
and durable acid-free paper.

Printed in the United States of America

Cover design: Noah Arlow
The image is taken from Rithy Panh's *The Missing Picture.*
Courtesy of Rithy Panh.

IN MEMORY OF MY FATHER

In Praise of Feeling Bad About Yourself

by Wisława Szymborska (1976)

The buzzard never says it is to blame.

The panther wouldn't know what scruples mean.

When the piranha strikes, it feels no shame.

If snakes had hands, they'd claim their hands were clean.

A jackal doesn't understand remorse.

Lions and lice don't waver in their course.

Why should they, when they know they're right?

Though hearts of killer whales may weigh a ton,

in every other way they're light.

On this third planet of the sun

among the signs of bestiality

a clear conscience is Number One.

Translated from the Polish by

Stanisław Barańczak and Clare Cavanagh

CONTENTS

PREFACE

More than a decade ago, during an international film festival, I watched the Cambodian documentary film *S21: The Khmer Rouge Death Machine* (*S21, la machine de mort Khmère rouge*, Cambodia/France, 2003), which presents the interaction between two survivors of the notorious S-21 execution center in Phnom Penh and their former Khmer Rouge (KR—"Red," Communist, Cambodian) torturers and guards, mediated by the camera of the director, Rithy Panh, himself a survivor of the Cambodian genocide.[1] Soon after I became terrifically amazed by the French-Cambodian director's entire oeuvre. I later learned that during the Pol Pot autogenocidal regime "a greater proportion of the population perished than in any other revolution during the twentieth century,"[2] that the entire strata of the middle and intellectual classes, including directors, actors, actresses, novelists, and technicians, was murdered and the cinema industry demolished. This background made me both more appreciative of and more puzzled over the extraordinary renaissance of the new Cambodian filmmaking, a rare phenomenon in world cinema.

As a cinema trauma scholar, while delving into the Cambodian corpus I found myself in the close but unfamiliar field of genocide and mass murder studies, as well as in a cinematic culture that threatened me, as a Westerner, with being "lost in translation." However, as an Israeli who grew up during the 1950s on Holocaust narratives and after many years of watching globally made second- and third-generation postgenocide cinema, with many of the questions posed in this book accompanying me for years, I felt I owned at least some of the keys to this fascinating "Eastern" corpus.

What do we expect to see on the cinematic screen when watching a postgenocide (mainly documentary) film? Let me put forward at least some of the prevalent expectations: visual-audial representation of the atrocities, portraits of outstanding characters who acted during catastrophic events, survivors' testimonies, stories on top-down reconciliation efforts between previous enemies, revelations of hidden and taboo-ized historical events, descriptions of searching for the traces of dead relatives, autobiographical stories of the return to previous scenes of murder and places of birth, intergenerational dialogue, critique of the genocidal regime, and alternative narration of formal history. Do we expect a thorough depiction of perpetrators, let alone any dialogue initiated from the bottom-up by the directors-survivors between themselves and the perpetrators, as in Panh's film? A direct encounter between Jewish survivor and Nazi perpetrator is unimaginable in post-Holocaust European cinema—thus, *S21: The Khmer Rouge Death Machine* depicts a scene that never happened in the West. Further, do we expect postgenocide cinema to provide nonhegemonic representation of antireconciliation and transitional justice efforts? Post-KR Cambodian cinema proposes new venues in regard to these major questions.

This book completes a trilogy of books on cinema trauma, as it also completes a journey into this unexpected cinematic terrain. The question of how the violent past lives in the psyche of its survivors, both victims and perpetrators, has been a major part of my research for years. In both *Defeated Masculinity: Post-Traumatic Cinema in the Aftermath of War* (2009) and *Waltzing with Bashir: Perpetrator Trauma and Cinema* (2013), the different conceptions of the perpetrator and various relationships between victims/survivors and perpetrators in several cinematic corpora (New German cinema, Vietnam War movies, Israeli and Palestinian cinema) motivate the analysis. In all these corpora the cinema's role in shaping not only a new *lingua trauma* but our understanding of the human condition is decisive. Cambodian cinema, attesting to the failure to prevent the genocides and mass murders that took place globally after the Holocaust (from Darfur, Rwanda, Guatemala, and Indonesia to Serbia and

Phnom Penh was surrounded
by the Khmer Rouge

FIGURE P.1 The Khmer Rouge in Rithy Panh's *The Missing Picture*. Courtesy of Rithy Panh.

Bosnia, to name but a few), provokes new interactions and consequently new questions. Between the cinema's ability to reinvent itself and the survivor's fight for life, is the missing picture that of the perpetrator?

Perpetrator Cinema: Confronting Genocide in Cambodian Documentary discusses what I call the new perpetrator era and perpetrator cinema in this corpus coming out of Southeast Asia, which has not been researched as yet, and the posttraumatic social practices and ideologies that the films represent in the aftermath of the genocidal catastrophe. Striving to undermine the current dominant trend in cinema trauma research by focusing on the underdeveloped topic of the figure of the perpetrator involves exploring diverse forms of working through societal trauma. Though existing studies contribute to the ongoing endeavor to "locate" the traumatic memory (to use Halbawchs's classic terminology), the suggested focalization attempts to expose various conceptions of the societal processes and cinematic strategies for coping with them. In other words, by attempting to expand the "testimony model" established during the 1990s, the book examines how the figure of the perpetrator acquires signification through cinematic-cultural interpretation, and how the film text serves as a site of contestations between social and political agents seeking to promote, challenge, or erase certain meanings, messages, or ideas from public circulation. The missing picture, I finally suggest, is not of the perpetrator, but of the survivor-perpetrator encounter. These exceptional interactions become the heart of the new docu-ethics suggested by this book.

ACKNOWLEDGMENTS

I wish to express my gratitude to the friends, colleagues, and students who have contributed in many generous ways to my work on this project. Most of all I am grateful for their friendship.

I offer my deep appreciation and thanks to Rithy Panh for inspiring dialogue and heartfelt assistance through the years. To Sopheap Chea, the executive director of the Bophana Center, and the staff working at the center for their generous hospitality and assistance during my stay in Phnom Penh in July 2014 and since then: Dararoath Chin, Darong Chour, Huy Hongry, Ratana Lach, and Christoforos Pavlakis.

My deep thanks to Youk Chhang at the Documentation Center of Cambodia (DC-Cam) for his generous hospitality and assistance during my stay in Phnom Penh in July 2014 and since then. Thanks to Dara P. Vanthan, the deputy director, and the staff at DC-Cam: Terith Chy, Khamboly Dy, Kok-Thay Eng, and Savina Sirik.

To Pierre Kogan for his joyful and fantastic hospitality and tireless assistance during my stay in Cambodia and afterwards, and to Sien Meta for his kind advise and help.

My gratitude to my dear colleagues and friends: Shlomo Bekerovich for his continuous help and support; Deirdre Boyle for providing important materials and sharing our love of films; Menahem Blondheim; Dara Kay Cohen for sending me an early version of her book on rape during civil war; Camille Deprez; Ron Eyerman; Kristian Feigelson for kindly and enthusiastically volunteering his assistance; Mihal-Régine Friedman; Michael Reed Hurtado for providing valuable sources; I would particularly like to thank Ben Kiernan for his inspiring work on Cambodian history and for providing rare archival materials; Nurit Kedar; Gertrud Koch; Ifat Maoz, head of the Department of Communication and Journalism at the Hebrew University for her constant help, advice, and wonderful friendship; Kasumi Nakagawa; I am deeply indebted to Bill Nichols for his constant support and generosity; Judith Pernin; Joseph Mai for his unstinting assistance with the films; Sandra Meiri; Alan Rosenthal for legal advice and encouragement; Elad Samorzik; Limor Shifman; Eli Vakil for providing relevant materials on the E-Syndrome; Deane Williams for his kindness and heartfelt assistance in obtaining the films; Brian Winston for his strong support and help whenever it was necessary; Elisabeth Wood; Anat Zuria.

Thank you to the directors who inspired my writing, sent me their films, spent time in conversation, and kindly agreed to provide access to stills from their films: Jutta Brückner, Thomas Weber Carlsen, Bruno Carette, Lida Chan, Bunhom Chhorn, Juan M. Echavarría, Jean-Sébastien Francoeur, Annie Goldson, Neary Adeline Hay, Jan Krogsgaard, Walter Manoschek, Andrew Marchand-Boddy, Sien Meta, Kavich Neang, Matthew Robinson, Kulikar Sotho, and Ian White.

For help in obtaining the films and images, I am grateful to the producers Lucille Artigaud, Christophe Audeguis, Andy Brouwer, Tristan Chytroschek, Edwin Kadri, Lihong Kong, Raphael Millet, Stefanie Nordmann, Anne Reulat, Matthew Robinson, Nick Ray, Justine Smith, Olivier Van Bockstael, and Jessica Zehme.

Thanks to Helene Landau, my ever-extraordinary English editor, for the invaluable editorial help and the thorough assistance she provided in bringing the book to press. Her determined devotion, uncompromising precision, and thoughtfulness were felt every step of the way.

Thanks also to my research assistant David Bertrand for his help in translating the French films. To my graduate and doctoral students for their administrative help, gathering of the materials, and excellent assistance during the years of research: Eedan-Rachel Danhi, Lital Henig, Lior Kraus, Hadar Levy-Landsberg, Yonatan Peleg, Igor Rodin, and Adi Sheffi. And to Gal Yaniv.

I am most grateful to Orit Sen-Gupta, who provided companionship and constant support. And Dina Bitton. For their help, advice, and support throughout the period of writing, my deepest thanks to Alex Volpov and Rafi Yaacobi.

Special and loving thanks go to my family, and particularly to Reout, Snir, Rotem, and Assaf for supporting me and for uncomplainingly putting up with the hours I devoted to this book.

Many thanks to Yoram Allon at Wallflower/Columbia University Press for his competence, energy, and kindness; to Ryan Groendyk at Columbia University Press for his thoughtful and gracious assistance throughout; and to Susan Pensak.

This research was supported by THE ISRAEL SCIENCE FOUNDATION grant no. 467/13. I am truly grateful to the ISF for this funding.

Thanks also the Harry S. Truman Institute for the Advancement of Peace at the Hebrew University, Jerusalem.

Shorter versions of chapters 3 and 4 have appeared in *Post-1990 Documentary: Reconfiguring Independence*,[1] and *Camera Obscura*,[2] respectively.

ABBREVIATIONS

ECCC	Extraordinary Chambers in the Courts of Cambodia for the Prosecution of Crimes Committed During the Period of Democratic Kampuchea. Also known as the KR tribunal.
DK	Democratic Kampuchea
GBV	Gender-Based Violence
ICC	International Criminal Court at the Hague
ICTR	The International Criminal Tribunal for Rwanda
ICTY	The International Criminal Tribunal for former Yugoslavia
KR	Khmer Rouge
NGO	Nongovernmental Organization
TRC	Truth and Reconciliation Commission, South Africa

PERPETRATOR CINEMA

1

DEFINING PERPETRATOR CINEMA

All evil committed by one person . . . is evil undergone by another person. To do evil is to make another person suffer. Violence, in this sense, constantly recreates unity of moral evil and suffering. Hence, any action, whether ethical or political, that diminishes the quantity of violence exercised by some human beings over against other human beings diminishes the amount of suffering in the world. If we were to remove the suffering inflicted by people on other people, we would see what remained of suffering in the world, but to tell the truth, we have no idea of what this would be, to such an extent does human violence impregnate suffering.

—PAUL RICOEUR[1]

While my camera's rolling, his voice is soft. The killer's never far away.

—RITHY PANH[2]

THE ERA OF THE PERPETRATOR

Perpetrator Cinema: Confronting Genocide in Cambodian Documentary recognizes and suggests analyzing the recent social-cultural-psychological shift from the "era of the witness" to the "era of the perpetrator." Studying representations of societal, collective trauma in world cinema through the figure of the perpetrator stands, thus, at the core of this book. How should we define the era of the perpetrator?[3] First, taking into consideration our eternal moral obligation to the victims and their privileged position in the post-Holocaust world, I suggest as a point of departure delineating this era according to the historic—and not the symbolic—end of the era of testimony. With the last survivors of the Holocaust passing away, a new era marked by the end of the first generation's oral (face-to-face) testimonial act is dawning. Nevertheless, it is clear that the global, collective effort to gather archival documents and written testimonies of the Holocaust (as well as all forms of testimony given after each genocide and mass murder event that took place prior to and after the Holocaust)[4] continues.[5] Given the prominence of the Holocaust in the establishment of trauma studies and related fields of research, the "inauguration" of the perpetrator era reflects on the era of testimony as a period that in a particular, timely aspect has come to its end, rather than as an intellectual-cultural-psychological-social process. Standing as a consecutive as well as simultaneous period of coming to terms with the past, the perpetrator era is being defined not only by the timing determined by the traumatic calendar of the almost seventy-five years that have passed since the end of World War II, but also by giving rise to a new twenty-first-century phenomenon, to which, I suggest, it is obliged.

Moreover, it is my contention that during the second half of the twentieth century, genocide studies and related fields of research, overwhelmed by the indecipherability of the Holocaust and continuing difficulties in bringing Nazis to trial, have reproduced one of the major enigmas of the twentieth century, that of the "ordinary perpetrator." "For Lanzmann," Jacques Rancière tells us, "the essential feature of the genocide resides in the gap between the perfect rationality of its organization and the inadequacy of any explanatory reason for that programming."[6] It seems that after Hannah Arendt's works (in the 1960s), Stanley Milgram's work (in the 1970s), Christopher Browning's work (in the 1990s), Daniel Goldhagen's work (in the 1990s and 2000s), and other seminal—or controversial—works, and beyond research's enormous efforts in pointing to a multitude of factors to explain and comprehend the Holocaust, the access to this enigma, especially in relation to "banal evil" but also in relation to "radical evil" (to use Arendt's differentiation), is conceived in research as inherently blocked. Though the question of perpetration triggered a decades-long controversy, the twenty-first century's emergent (Western) field of perpetrator studies has not, as yet, overcome twentieth-century (under)theorization of perpetrators beyond these paradigms and the blocked enigma.

Genocide research (both the old school focusing mainly on the uniqueness of the Holocaust and the new one emphasizing mainly colonialism),[7] human rights studies (devoted to further research and teaching about the nature, causes, and consequences of genocide), and advance policy studies on prevention of genocide do not admit to this enigma as such. It is my premise that in its relentless search to provide adequate responses in the face of the twentieth-century post-Holocaust genocides such as in Guatemala, Rwanda, Darfur, and Indonesia, this research not only provides a multitude of explanations but, perhaps inevitably, and simultaneously, also further accentuates the repression embodied in this enigma and blocks investigation of the perpetrator. Thus, it creates and reproduces an inevitable paradox vis-á-vis this enigma. As Jean Laplanche suggests, "An enigma . . . can only be proposed by someone who does not master the answer, because his message is a compromise-formation in which his unconscious takes part."[8] Mastering our understanding of the totalitarian state of mind, especially the mind of a "follower" and the conditions under which evil is committed, is obstructed. In addition, the concept of the ordinary perpetrator serves as a mask to another, unprovoked matter of contention: It works as a displacement of the death toll. Masking the death toll of the genocides in Cambodia, Rwanda, Indonesia, and other places as inherently uncountable consents to an enduring repetition-compulsion of this enigma.

The reasons for the shift from the era of the witness to the era of the perpetrator are many and varied and attest to deep processes that carry neither similar social-cultural-psychological explanatory forces nor the same causal immediacy: First, there is the "ethical turn," which since the end of the 1980s has recognized the relations of the self with its Others (including representational relations) through validating the continuing power of feminist criticism and theory and the growing influence of multicultural, postcolonial, and queer and LGBT criticism and theory. While maintaining responsibility for the Other without enacting the epistemological violence of the "imperialism of the Same,"[9] it has opened the door for nonhegemonic voices, including the perpetrator's voice. Second, there is the awareness of World War II perpetrators of their final opportunity to be heard directly as they reach the end of their lives and as the events and related atrocities become increasingly distant in time. Third, there is the "discourse of normalization" in contemporary Germany as well as the current "memory battles" in Austria (the Waldheim debate and the questioning of the myth that Austria was a victim of Hitler's Germany and Nazism), Poland (controversy over historian Jan Gross's essay published in 2015 in *Die Welt* saying that during World War II Poles killed more Jews than did Germans, and the publication of his book *Neighbors: The Destruction of the Jewish Community in Jedwabne, Poland*, published in 2001, which explores the massacre of Polish Jews in July 1941 by their non-Jewish neighbors in the village of Jedwabne in Nazi-occupied Poland), and Hungary (the controversy over the Budapest monument commemorating victims of the German Nazi occupation of Hungary and the debate over Hungary's wartime leader Admiral Horthy) over their collaboration with the Nazis vis-à-vis their victimage. Fourth, there are the massive archives containing documentation of the atrocities committed under National Socialism and under Communist regimes that became available for scholars following the end of the Cold War and the collapse of the Soviet Bloc.[10] Fifth, there is the end of Apartheid in South Africa through a series of negotiations between 1990 and 1993 that led to further deliberations on perpetratorhood.[11] Sixth, there is the International Criminal Court (ICC) at the Hague, which adopted the Rome Statute in July 1998, and began its tenure during the same period, in 2003. Seventh, between 1993 and 2017 the International Criminal Tribunal for the former Yugoslavia (ICTY) and between 1994 and 2015 the International Criminal Tribunal for Rwanda (ICTR) worked to try their perpetrators, following recent acts of genocide in the former Yugoslavia and in Rwanda, respectively. Eighth, the 9/11 terrorist attacks on the United States redefined the study of perpetrators and the War on Terror, extended by the question of collateral casualties. Ninth, the exposure of the Abu Ghraib scandal raised anew questions, such as the causes of fetishized conformity, the responsibility of low-level soldiers, US foreign policy and the US policy of torture, and the culture's compulsive visual and aural consumption of risk and threat. Tenth, there is the Guantanamo debate. Eleventh, there was the dominant development of and mass global interest in Al Qaeda and ISIS. Twelfth, there is the brain studies debate over the E-Syndrome (that is, Evil-Syndrome) and new advances in neuropsychiatry in relation to antisocial behavior.[12] Thirteenth, there is the dominance of a reality TV–inspired celeb culture that celebrates an anti-pleasure-able *jouissance* simultaneously with unending trau-mania. Fourteenth, there is the debate over false memoirs embodied in fiction works like *Fragments: Memories of a Wartime Childhood*, by Binjamin Wilkomirski (Bruno Dössekker), published in 1997, on his life as a child during the Holocaust and the trauma envy it triggered.[13] Fifteenth, the enormous critical and commercial success of Jonathan Littell's controversial novel *The Kindly Ones* (2006), which relates the history of the genocide of the Jews in central Europe as recounted by the unrepentant mind of an SS officer. And sixteenth, there are "Public reconstructions of the past according to victim-perpetrator/good-evil absolutes that fail to take account of the more blurred dynamics behind oppressive state rule and acts of atrocity."[14]

GLOBAL PERPETRATOR CINEMA

As a preliminary definition, I suggest that perpetrator cinema is cinema that deals with a genocidal (or other mass killing) event through focusing on the perpetrator (and/or collaborator)[15] figure as the main protagonist/interviewee. Along with the shift from the era of the witness to the era of the perpetrator, we can discern an unprecedented twenty-first-century global boom of films that present perpetrators (and collaborators). It comprises films that relate to three contexts: genocide or mass violence;[16] the War on Terror;[17] and local crime organization killings in the service of various regimes and gang wars.[18] The genocide or mass violence context, which provides the broader framing for this book, includes documentary films such as Malte Ludin's *2 or 3 Things I Know About Him* (*2 oder 3 Dinge, die ich von ihm weiß*, Germany, 2005), in which a second-generation son of a high-ranking member of Hitler's government who was executed for war crimes in 1947 follows his father's and the family history after his mother's death. The film includes interviews with his still-in-denial siblings, members of the third generation, as well as victim testimonies. Anne Aghion's *My Neighbor, My Killer* (*Mon voisin, mon tueur*, USA/France, 2009) stages the Gacaca Community Court Trials, established by the Rwandan government in an attempt to facilitate the return of Hutus suspected of participating in the genocide of 1994 to their homes and encourage rapprochement between the two ethnic communities by meting out justice on the spot, in the small rural village of Gafumba. Christian Karim Chrobog's *War Child* (USA, 2008) is a portrait of London-based black activist and successful hip-hop artist Emmanuel Jar's return to Sudan, where he had been drafted as a child-soldier into the Sudan People's Liberation Army. In Walter Manoschek's *If That's So, Then I'm a Murderer* (. . . *dann bin ich ja ein Mörder!*, Austria, 2012), sixty-three years after some sixty Hungarian Jewish forced laborers were shot dead by three SS men in the village of Deutsch-Schützen in the Austrian province of Burgenland (where a mass grave was found in 1995), the director interviews the former SS junior squad leader Adolf Storms, who denies his deeds, and seven more interviewees, among them two Hitler Youth who assisted with the crime and two Jewish survivors. Vanessa Lapa's *The Decent One* (*Der Anständige*, Austria/Israel/Germany, 2014) follows a chronology based on diary entries, documents, letters that SS leader Heinrich Himmler wrote to his wife, Margarete, her and their daughter's testimonies, his mistress's letters, and his family's letters. Christian Krönes, Olaf S. Müller, Roland Schrotthofer, and Florian Weigensamer's *A German Life* (*Ein deutsches Leben*, Austria, 2016) shows interviews with 104-year-old Brunhilde Pomsel, a secretary who eventually became the stenographer to Nazi propaganda minister Joseph Goebbels, who describes her admiration for him, still totally immersed in the state of mind of a follower and denying any knowledge that the Holocaust took place. Ruth Beckermann's *The Waldheim Waltz* (*Waldheims Walzer*, Austria, 2018) is a biographical portrait of Kurt Josef Waldheim, a former UN secretary general, and the controversy surrounding his participation and role in the Nazi regime during World War II, documenting the demonstrations against Waldheim's fake biographical details covering the war period.[19] And Jonathan Littell's *Wrong Elements* (France/Belgium/Germany, 2016) presents a group of friends who in Uganda during the late 1980s were kidnapped by the LRA (Lord's Resistance Army), an antigovernment guerilla movement that abducted more than sixty thousand teenagers over the course of twenty-five years. In an effort to rebuild their lives, these four men, simultaneously victims and killers, set out to revisit the places that robbed them of their childhoods.

As I have suggested in other forums,[20] during the twentieth century, the perpetrators of major catastrophes, in particular the Holocaust but also those conducted by other totalitarian regimes, did not confess their guilt. In fact, the convoluted and unstable relations the Germans, for instance, have with their past (i.e., the Historian Debate of 1986, the Wehrmacht exhibition of 1995, Goldhagen's book *Willing Execution-ers* [1996],[21] and Oliver Hirschbiegel's film *Downfall* [*Der Untergang*, Germany/Austria/Italy, 2004]) show that in a century dominated by totalitarian regimes, an ethical confession was unimaginable. Dori Laub and Susanna Lee indeed claim, "Memories . . . in perpetrators . . . merely serve a defensive function by replacing unbearable conflict or glaring dissonance with a more tamed and acceptable version of experienced events or perpetrated deeds. Such tamed versions may be concurrent . . . in particular with the perpetrator's evil deeds, as illustrated by the Germans' use of deceptive euphemisms while carrying out mass murder."[22] The case of Albert Speer, which Laub and Lee discuss, is a prime example of the creation of distorted truths in order to mask an extremity of evil.

The perpetrators' confessions[23] become "successful" when they are self-incriminating, ideally capturing the confession's referent, the atrocious deed. When intertwined with the victim's testimony, they are not a truer depiction of the traumatic event, but rather a truer conveyor of total acknowledgment based on appreciation of the historical-traumatic refer-ent, which the victim, immersed in the trauma, could not grasp. Inter-viewing perpetrators is shaped not by enforcing a willful introspection aimed at providing a narrative of selfhood, but by a reassessment of val-ues and affirmation of total transparency regarding the content of their confessions.

These cursory plot lines show that in spite of the differences in the his-torical contexts (most prominently the Holocaust but also the genocides in Darfur, Rwanda, Indonesia, Serbia/former-Yugoslavia, and Uganda), production conditions, specific subject, the local film industry, and cinematic language, among others, these documentaries display the prominent characteristics of perpetrators' representation.

PERPETRATOR CINEMA—CHARACTERISTICS

Perpetrator films share ten prominent, typical characteristics: First, none of them is based on a direct confrontation between the first-generation survivor and the perpetrator, an extraordinary situation with unique ideological overtones revealed in post-KR Cambodian cinema (which I elaborate later). Even films like Laura Waters Hinson's *As We Forgive* (USA, 2010), about Rwanda, and Joshua Oppenheimer's *The Look of Silence* (*Senyap*, Denmark/Indonesia/Finland/Norway/UK/Israel/France/USA/Germany/Netherlands, 2014) (which refers to the mass massacre of 1965–66 of between five hundred thousand and three million alleged communists by paramilitary forces in the service of president Suharto's regime in Indonesia), which attempt to stage this confrontation, eventually refrain from it and/or its representation. *As We Forgive* uses crosscutting to connect the reactions of Rosaria, the survivor, and Saveri, the neighbor who killed her husband and four children. Each speaks to the camera about the question of forgiveness during a workshop for reconciliation established in the village in 2004, but we do not see them meet. The film tells the spectators about the process, but does not show Rosaria and Saveri or other survivors and neighbor-perpetrators reconnecting in real time. The editing serves as a substitute for what is yet unbearable and undoable in reality. Does cinema function to mediate, or does it masquerade this unbearable interaction? In *The Look of Silence*, Adi, the protagonist, a member of the second generation (born in 1968), is afraid to fully confront the commanders of the civilian militia, the village death squad, and the Snake River death squad that operated in his area. Only with the assistance of the director is he able to somewhat confront his own uncle, who, as a prison guard at the time of the massacre, collaborated in the abuse and murder of his nephew, Adi's older brother. These films stand in contrast to the extraordinary phenomenon of the proliferation of new Cambodian films that structure and promote a direct, live survivor-perpetrator encounter.

Second, in contrast to cinema rendered solely through the victims' testimony, which is defined ontologically through the subjective truth of suffering and the testimonial act, perpetrator cinema, directly or indirectly reflecting on the question of guilt, is defined epistemologically through recognition of the deed and accountability. Third, and moreover, we can discern a tension between recollection and the (perpetrator's) recognition. In this regard, and in spite of their significance when taking into consideration the years that have passed since the violent event, memory processes do not exceed the priority of the episteme in shaping the diegesis. Fourth, the films stage anew the twentieth-century paradox of the enigma of the ordinary man: the understanding that the enigma is incomprehensible when it is attributed to Evil, but might be comprehensible in a specific context, revealed through new documents and/or accounts and testimonies. The tension between the philosophical dimension of ethical responsibility and its practical dimension haunts the films.

The fifth characteristic of perpetrator cinema is the tension created by the sudden closeness of both the director and the spectator to the perpetrator (or his or her symbolic "surrogates"—family members, personal items, recorded voice, and so on). This intimidating intimacy might stand in contrast to the attempt (and fantasy) of access to the perpetrator's subjectivity. As James Young suggests, "The taboo on portraying the subjectivity of the perpetrators serves a further function in that it quells the fear that to imagine the crimes from their perspective would somehow 'reperpetrate' them."[24] Sixth, if the film is mainly based on an interview, it is mostly conducted in the format of "talking (heads) with Evil." Seventh, a lacuna is revealed at the heart of most of the films due to the perpetrators' (or the surrogates') denial of their deeds, resulting in a failed confession. The lacuna threatens to erupt and break the usually fragile dialogical or "contractual" surface between the interviewees and the director. Eighth, the narrative that aims at refutation of denials, lies, self-justification, self-deception, evasions, and other strategies typical to perpetrators' reactions is built upon multilayered structures that include a proliferation of strategies like archival materials, illustrations, animation, historical documents, and experts' opinions meant to assist the director in revealing the truth. Ninth, thus, the subject of the Third, usually the dead, is inserted into the narrative, exorcizing the trauma. Tenth, since in most of the cases the perpetrator is nonaccessible, the (real or symbolic) "death-known-in-advance" structure creates a tension with the investigative impulse that typically, following public and political debates or scandals, motivates the making of the film.

Defining perpetrator cinema neither as a genre nor as a global new wave but rather as a phenomenon with certain characteristics demands considering it a symptom of this era. Is it a symptom of Western civilization's failure, transmitted as a twentieth-century "legacy" to resolve the "ordinary perpetrator" enigma? Barbara Harff and Ted Robert Gurr show that genocides and politicides (killings of people in groups targeted because of organized political opposition) between 1945 and 1980 may have caused over twice as many deaths as wars during this period. Such state killings claim up to 2.6 times the number of lives lost in the aftermath of natural disasters between 1967 and 1986.[25] Similarly, Rudolph J. Rummel argues that four times as many people have been killed in democides ("the murder of any person or people by a government, including genocide, politicide, or mass murder") of citizens in the twentieth century than have been killed in wars.[26] Recognizing that the post-Holocaust ethos of "Never Again" has been repetitively violated during the second half of the twentieth century, collapsing the ethical into the political, might attest to Western guilt that is reflected in this new phenomenon: The films (and literature) are cultural products that, in a direct antithesis to past submission of all morality decrees to the political, turn the previous horror, sublimated through the obsessively documented testimonial age, into a new form of global memory, that of the perpetrator (or his or her surrogates). As Andreas Huyssen claims,

> Memory discourses of a new kind first emerged in the West after the 1960s in the wake of decolonization and the new social movements and their search for alternative and revisionist histories. The search for other traditions and the tradition of "others" was accompanied by multiple statements about endings: the end of history, the death of the subject, the end of the work of art, the end of metanarratives. Such claims were frequently understood all too literally, but in their polemical thrust and replication of the ethos of avantgardism, they pointed directly to the ongoing recodification of the past after modernism. Memory discourses accelerated in Europe and the United States in the early 1980s, energized by the broadening debate about the Holocaust (triggered by the network television series *Holocaust* and, somewhat later, the testimony movement) and by media attention paid to the fortieth and fiftieth anniversaries of events in the history of the Third Reich.[27]

In this regard, perpetrator cinema indeed marks the new search for a new Other as well as a new form of a more complex and nuanced interaction between history and memory. In other words, perpetrator cinema's failure to transcend the enigma and directly delve into perpetratorhood might accentuate the tension between epistemology and memory and propose temporary memory redemption as a salvation from guilt.

Two films, one related to the Holocaust and the other to the genocide in former Yugoslavia, exemplify the use of unique cinematic strategies to overcome the tensions typical to perpetrator cinema (memory vs. epistemology, comprehensibility vs. incomprehensibility of the enigma, philosophical vs. practical ethics, intimidating intimacy vs. fantasy access, a death-known-in-advance vs. investigative impulse) as well as the failure of confession described earlier as a constant, immanent threat. Stefan Ruzowitzky, the director (and scriptwriter) of *Radical Evil* (*Das radikal Böse*, Germany/Austria, 2013),[28] who is a member of the third generation (his grandfather was a Nazi), uses three audial sources to reflect on the enigma of the ordinary man, which is the subject of his film: original quotations taken from the diaries and letters of the Nazi death squads, the Einsatzgruppen (who shot about two million Jewish civilians in Eastern Europe during World War II); (excerpts from) head of the SS Heinrich Himmler's Posen speech from early October 1943 (given in Nazi-occupied Poland before officials of the Nazi party);[29] and interviews with psychiatrists, historians, genocide experts, and ninety-three-year-old Benjamin Ferencz, one of the chief prosecutors at the Nuremberg trials.

The Einsatzgruppen quotes are read by well-known German actors (such as Devid Striesow [*The Counterfeiters*[30] and *Downfall*], Alexander Fehling [*Inglourious Basterds* and *Labyrinth of Lies*],[31] and Volker Bruch [*The Baader Meinhof Complex* and *The Reader*]),[32] whose voices are familiar to German, Austrian, as well as global spectators. In contrast, nonfamiliar actors reenact the death squads' lives and deadly acts: watching Nazi propaganda films, vomiting after the first massacre, shaving before the next day of executions begins, and taking pictures together. Their anonymity, symbolizing the faceless Nazi masses, stands in contrast to the familiar voices of the actors who speak "in their place." I suggest that the perpetrator's voice, attached to and based on the enigma, and in contrast to the victim's, is "replaceable" because it symbolizes the nonintegrity of the voice's owner, his denial. Immersed in denial, the perpetrator's disembodied, replaceable voice is not the expression of the speaker's inner essence, a guarantee of the Truth. Thus, it signifies an immanent split between truth and its utterance, the voice being the (failed) mediator. The "exchanged" voice becomes that which radically undermines the possibility of self-expression and self-presence, insofar as it reveals the rupture at the core of the perpetrators' subjectivity. The actors' voices invest the quotations from the diaries and letters with a dramatization that makes them alive but, due to the self-reflexive irony of their immediate identification as cinematic celebs, paradoxically also keep the horror at a distance. Most importantly, I suggest that it is this uncanny combination of the familiar sound with the unfamiliar image, the gap between body and voice, deed and reflection, that calls for the spectators' recognition.

The second audial source, the unmistakable recorded voice of Himmler, is intertwined within the Einsatzgruppen accounts and thus assists in enhancing the sensation of authenticity. The third audial source, interviews with renowned researchers (such as the psychiatrist R. J. Lifton, the author Christopher R. Browning, and the priest Patrick Desbois)[33] who attest to the major insights achieved in research during the last seventy-three years, have an accumulating effect. Thus, when the film represents the results of prominent psychological experiments (of Solomon Asch, Stanley Milgram, and Philip Zimbardo) directed at the topic, the camera is located above the experiments, which are presented through minimal graphic means. Providing a high-angle gaze, it once again raises the question of proximity and distance from Evil and from past events. Ruzowitzky uses a split screen such that a line of boots is juxtaposed with a close-up on the face of one of the soldiers. Benjamin Ferencz closes this complex discussion by emphasizing that out of the three thousand soldiers of the death squads, only twenty-four were put on trial (due to lack of seats at court). Fourteen of them were sentenced to death, but the verdict was carried out in only four cases. All the others served various periods in prison and were released in 1958. According to Ferencz, the court failed in this mission.

In its unique cinematic language, I suggest, *Radical Evil* adheres to Dominick LaCapra's suggestion that there is a "tendency to restrict explanations to two broad, binaristically opposed options: (1) the role of industrialized mass murder, bureaucracy, the machinery of destruction, "desk murder," the banality of evil, and the behavior of ordinary men in extraordinary circumstances and (2) the role of perpetrators as anti-Semitic, cruel, sadistic, gleeful monsters. Moreover, the second option may be criticized solely predominantly in terms of the first."[34]

This is done by juxtaposing these options mainly through the various uses of sound. In this, though the film does not include a victim's testimony and thus its presentation of the trauma is indirect and nonemotional, its multilayered presentation of the perpetrator's figure and symbolic and real voice transcends perpetrator cinema's immanent tensions and paradoxes.

In *Depth Two* (*Dubina dva*, Serbia/Serbia and Montenegro, 2016),[35] seventeen years after the end of the Serbian massacre of the Albanians and the silencing of the investigation into atrocities committed in Kosovo in 1999, the Serbian director (and scriptwriter) Ognjen Glavonić connects two occurrences: the accidental discovery of a freezer truck containing fifty-five corpses of Albanian civilians killed by the Serbian police and army during the Kosovo War that had been dumped into the Danube at the Serbian-Romanian border, and the discovery in 2000–01 of five mass graves with 705 corpses of Kosovars (including seventy-five children) in a Belgrade suburb at the former site of the Serbian Army's Special Anti-Terrorist Forces training center. The corpses from the latter, from the Suva Reka massacre,[36] had later been transported to a secret location during Operation Dubina Dva (Depth Two). In order to establish the link between these two atrocious events, Glavonić watched hundreds of hours of testimonies and accounts presented on various Serbian television channels during the ten years of the trial of Slobodan Milosevic and his subordinates at the International Court for the Former Yugoslavia in The Hague. He based his documentary on ten first-person accounts of the perpetrators and collaborators who had participated in the events, some of whom were also present when the bodies were recovered and reburied: the killers, the policemen, the police officer, the men who had dragged the truck from the river, the truck drivers who moved the corpses, and the workers who buried them. In the midst of their accounts, the sole Albanian survivor of the Suva Reka massacre, who watched the murder of her entire family, relates how she pretended to be dead and jumped out of the truck when the corpses were driven far from her village to the location near Belgrade.

Juxtaposing the perpetrators/collaborators' accounts and the survivor's testimony is enacted on two levels: of sound and of space. *Depth Two* uses the perpetrators' and collaborators' accounts only as acousmêtic voices, disembodied, nonvisualized, and nonconnectable to a face. Film sound theorist Michel Chion claims that acousmêtre has some powers—ubiquity, panopticism, omniscience, and omnipotence[37]—and that at the point of de-acousmatization "the voice loses its virginal acousmatic powers, and reenters the realm of human beings."[38] Glavonić deliberately refrains from deacousmatization, and indeed does not allow the perpetrators' and collaborators' voices to reenter "the realm of human beings." Moreover, this request to give up the gaze and to "see" through the hearing means, in the case of perpetrators' voices, that the spectator cannot establish an illusion built through reconciliation within the imagination. Instead, the spectator sees haunting imagery shots at the locations various parts of the crimes were carried out: from the Danube, through Priština and two small towns in Kosovo, to central Serbia, and finally to Batajnica, where the mass graves were discovered. The filmed crime scene of the river, which opens this documentary thriller, is constantly expanding as the ten acousmatic voices provide more abjecting details. The crime space includes not only the specific locations of the river and the small towns, but also the roads, the pizzeria where the Albanian families were forcefully gathered and shot, the police station, and the surrounding fields. First, the accessible space stands as a replacement for the absence of the perpetrators' and collaborators' bodies. Second, the physical beauty of the environment is disturbing for the spectator, although the demand to mediate between the green meadow and the atrocities committed there is part of the Lanzmannian legacy. The greyness and gloomy, cold weather, reflected in most of the shots of the red roofs and green meadows, do not reduce the Lanzmannian creed. When, as part of the lies and cover-up the spectator hears, including that the victims were not Albanian but rather Kurdish foreign workers who fell into the river, the camera shows stagnant, miring water, a voice says, "I asked the policeman how many are still there because I was pale and threw up, and he said: 'not too many. Another one hundred, one hundred twenty bodies.'" The bald trees, the sound of ravens, and two truck wheels dumped in a field create a space open for projection of the unseen, especially since the camera movements that capture these audio-visual images are slow, their rhythm adhering to the perpetrators' off-screen sound, one that, though complicated with it, does not envelope the image.

By using sound and space, *Depth Two*'s ethical exhumation makes the question of visibility of the perpetrators of ethnic cleansing a collective question. In this regard the film replaces the memorial site, which at the time of screening had not yet been established at the site of the crime.

FROM LITERATURE TO CINEMA: FROM WITNESS TO PERPETRATOR

Part of this global wave, exemplified by *Radical Evil* and *Depth Two*, is an unprecedented, extraordinary phenomenon to which, I suggest, we are particularly obliged. It is revealed in post-KR Cambodian (mainly documentary) films that deal with and present perpetrators through face-to-face encounters between survivor and the perpetrator. Before analyzing the novelty of this Southeast Asian corpus from the 1990s and particularly the 2000s and its contribution to our understanding of the post-Holocaust world in the areas of genocide, trauma, and cinema studies, we should ask if the interaction between the writer and the witness and between literature and testimonial trauma, proposed during the 1990s in the seminal works of Shoshana Felman and Dori Laub and Annette Wieviorka,[39] is being displaced during this century by the interaction between the filmmaker and the perpetrator, the cinema and the (failed) confession. Undoubtedly, despite the prominent contribution of Claude Lanzmann's *Shoah* (France/UK, 1985) to the elaboration of these scholarly works that inaugurated the field (and consequently the era) of witnessing, the literary inclination of trauma studies has been dominating the field for three decades. Moreover, in many respects it has obstructed a complementary understanding of the era through the perspective of the perpetrators, revealed, for example, in literary (and cinematic) works created during the twentieth century.[40]

During the first decades of the twenty-first century, I suggest, it is the perpetrator documentary cinema of Cambodia, and not the global spate of documentaries indicated earlier, that paves the way not only for a retheorization of Raul Hilberg's prevalent "genocidal triad" (victim-collaborator/bystander-perpetrator), but for recognizing the distinctive role of cinema in broadening the current state of trauma studies to contain insights that are essentially cinematic. Thus, delving beyond victimhood into perpetratorhood through the Southeast Asian corpus will be based on a double focus: the cinematic medium (and not just literature) and the perpetrator figure (and not just the victim). Modifying the rigid boundaries of (mostly literary) trauma studies and related fields of research,[41] it is my contention in this book that the Southeast Asian corpus proposes a major change in our understanding of the current conceptualization in trauma and genocide studies, which, consequently, not only contributes to the emerging field of perpetrator studies, as will be elaborated in the following chapters, but sheds a retrospective light on our understanding of the testimony era as well.

Based on a face-to-face direct-encounter-turned-duel between the first-generation survivor and the perpetrator, it is apparent that no media except nonfiction cinema[42] enables a representation of this change-in-the-making of (post)genocidal power relations.[43] In this, the Cambodian nonfiction perpetrator films are entirely distinct from the global "talking (heads) with Evil" nonfiction perpetrator films based on the interview format, from Errol Morris's *The Fog of War: Eleven Lessons from the Life of Robert S. McNamara* (USA, 2003), which follows McNamara's vital role as a secretary of defense under Presidents Kennedy and Johnson during the Vietnam War, to Joshua Oppenheimer, Christine Cynn, and anonymous' *The Act of Killing* (UK/Denmark/Norway, 2012), which stages the paramilitary perpetrators responsible for massacres in Indonesia during the 1960s (let alone representations of interviewing perpetrators in fictional films such as Roland Joffé's *The Forgiven* [UK, 2017], in which the fictional character of the racist death-squad assassin [played by Eric Bana] confronts Forest Whitaker's Archbishop Desmond Tutu in South Africa in the mid-1990s).

REPRODUCING THE ENIGMA:
BEHIND THE GATE AND *THE GATE*

Both Jean Baronnet's documentary film *Behind the Gate* (*Derriere le portail*, France, 2003) and Regis Wargnier's fiction film *The Gate* (*Le temps des aveux*,[44] France/Cambodia/Belgium, 2014) are based on François Bizot's autobiographical memoir *The Gate* (2003) and its elaborated edition, *Facing the Torturer*, published in 2012,[45] respectively. Though they are about Kaing Guek Eav, nicknamed Duch (the former commandant[46] of the notorious torture and execution center Tuol Sleng, codenamed S-21,[47] who was arrested by the Extraordinary Chambers in the Courts of Cambodia for the Prosecution of Crimes Committed during the Period of Democratic Kampuchea[48] [ECCC][49] in 2010), and unfold the Cambodian history, their perspectives embody pure Western fantasy and myth. The discussion later focuses on the earlier made-for-TV documentary film and will reflect briefly on the fiction film. Although both films serve as adaptations of Bizot's autobiography, the documentary film was produced on 2003, the year the United Nations and Cambodia reached agreement to hold a tribunal, while the fiction film was produced close to the final decision in Duch's trial at that tribunal, the ECCC, where, in 2012, he was found guilty of crimes against humanity and grave breaches of the Geneva Convention of 1949 and sentenced to life imprisonment.

The difference in mode of filmmaking (nonfiction vs. fiction) and the time of production is of course apparent. But in both cases, I claim, a fantasy in relation to the enigma of the perpetrator and an unmediated encounter haunts the films. Both concentrate on the protagonist's (as well as the spectator's) difficulty in mediating the psychoethical entanglement embodied by the statement at the beginning of *The Gate* by the character of Bizot, portrayed by the actor Raphaël Personnaz: "I owe my life to a man, Duch, who executed thousands of others. My savior is a torturer, a murderer." That is, life and death, rescue and torture, being a man and being a monster (to use the anthropologist Alexander Laban Hinton's parlance)[50] are the dichotomies that the fantasy of comprehending the perpetrator (while befriending him) is made of. However, both films and both memoirs fail to provide a valuable answer. I suggest that this enigma is irresolvable as such and thus, regardless of the unimagined and unexpected meetings between Bizot and Duch during their life spans, haunts the memoirs and the films based on them in a way that inhibits the development of a novel perspective on Duch that they are so determined to provide.

Behind the Gate begins by showing Cambodian newspaper headlines announcing Duch's forthcoming trial. The voice-over tells us that the estimation is that forty thousand people were murdered under Duch's order, but the prisoners' files found at S-21 attest to between seventeen and twenty thousand dead, and seven survivors. One prisoner, though, the voice-over continues to tell us, managed to escape the slaughter—François Bizot, who in 1971 was working as an ethnologist in Cambodia. He was captured with his two Cambodian assistants and became Duch's prisoner at extermination camp M-13 (the first prison Duch set up in the forests of Amleang, Thpong District). Arrested for espionage, the Frenchman is cast into a vortex of forced confessions, torture, and interrogations, all the while trying to protect his Cambodian wife and daughter. After three months (seventy-seven days), Bizot was released by Duch, who managed to convince Ta Mok (the commander-in-chief of the army and "Brother Number Five")[51] to let him go. Bizot's assistants were executed. The film cuts to a flashback triggered at the plot level by Duch's defense team's request that Bizot testify at the trial. Thus, the film renders his return to Cambodia and his retrospective evaluation of past events in the form of a dark travelogue.

Bizot relives the events after his arrival in Cambodia in 1965 with the objective of assisting in the preservation of monuments and relics of Angkor Watt. He tells the spectators that he was also asked by the École française d'Extrême-Orient (the French School of the Far-East) to investigate the uniqueness of Cambodian Buddhism in the villages. Being an ethnologist who investigates cultures, he decides to become part of the daily life of the peasants and to live in a distant village in the area of Angkor. He describes his life among the peasants, his capture and release, taking refuge on April 17, 1975, in the headquarters of the French Embassy with other foreigners who worked in Phnom Penh,[52] and their later evacuation to Thailand. The next thirty years, in which Bizot continues his scholarly work around Asia, are not described at length. He returns to Cambodia in 1986 and for the first time visits S-21. In 1999, he receives a call from the journalist Nate Thayer, who together with Nic Dunlop found Duch hiding under a false identity.[53] Because Duch talked to them about "*mon amie Bizot*," the confused Bizot decides to write his memoir. Looking for answers, he meets Duch's family (nephew, sister, and daughter) and eventually receives permission to visit him in prison in Phnom Penh.

Instead of providing an answer to the perpetrator enigma, or at least a novel portrayal of Duch, the filmic re-presentations of the literary works, which try to cross "the gate,"[54] follow the chronicle of Bizot's life and his various meetings with Duch (built on some flashbacks to past events in order to produce an effect of immediacy). Providing self-reflection at every stage of his life in Cambodia, past and present, reaffirms Bizot's complex identity and subjectivity while opening an unbridgeable gap between his self-reflection (including his awareness of being both the writer and the subject of his writing) and his reflection on Duch, which hardly transcends the "ordinary man" framing. Though at the camp described in *Behind the Gate* Bizot reflects on the "deviousness he [Duch] had shown" (particularly in regard to Bizot's relationship with his Cambodian assistants, Lay and Son),[55] he later says, "When we look at his childhood and his way we unfortunately notice that he was an ordinary man," and after their conversation in the prison, at the end of the film, he concludes by saying, "I came out of this interview more confused than I have been thirty-five years ago, when Duch was a young revolutionary. In between, there was the horror of Tuol Sleng and what I saw behind the monster that was responsible for this crime was a human being that did not change a lot and is like so many others. When we are aware of this horrific ability within us, we are afraid. Afraid of ourselves."

The fantasy of deciphering the enigma of the perpetrator is embodied first and foremost in the film's narrative. Bizot's autobiographical memoir was written thirty-two years after the events depicted took place. The considerable temporal distance from the narrated facts inevitably anticipates its own ending and closure. Though it was open to self-reflection due to the trauma the protagonist had undergone, as well as a belatedness (*Nachträglichkeit*), I suggest that the roots of the enigma presented in both the literary and the cinematic narrativizations of the Bizot-Duch encounters are to be found in the huge discrepancy between the pure desire of young Bizot to become part of the peasants (he learned the language and established an interethnic marriage and family) and the perversion of this "nativism" by the Cambodian Revolution's horrific insistence that the New People (the KR term describing the new class of civilian Cambodians, including anyone from an urban area and thus corrupted by Western ideas, in contrast to the privileged class of peasants from rural areas, the Old People) learn from and be subjugated to the Old (Base/Ancient) People. Relating to his life in the remote village during the early 1970s, Bizot says that there, for the first time in his life (he was thirty at the time), he met people who became role models for him: the woman who became the

We are the new people.

FIGURE 1.1 The New People in Rithy Panh's *The Missing Picture*. Courtesy of Rithy Panh.

great-grandmother of his daughter, a few pagoda leaders, and some peasants. All made a huge impression on him. Turning from an outside observer into a participant-observer-gone-native, I suggest, intensifies the "perpetrator fantasy."

Though Bizot was a Westerner, of course, and not a Cambodian intellectual, the narrative unfolding in *Behind the Gate* combines this symbolic "inversion" of the Communist ideal with another Western colonial myth—that of becoming a Native. Through the unfolding of his story, from the 1970s until his willingness to testify, the narrative reveals the myth of the Westerner-gone-Native, who, after his assimilation in the society he aspired to be part of, became trapped. The Other (Western, intellectual) who almost became the Self (Native Cambodian) was forced under an extreme situation to be the Other again, marked by the KR Revolution as the Enemy. Because Bizot's becoming native realized the major revolutionary ideal, I suggest that the memoirs and the films were caught in inversed mythicizations that cannot be untied. Thus, in the later film, though Bizot's judgment of Duch was by no means kind ("There is, it seems to me, no forgiveness possible"), his nuanced testimony gave François Roux (Duch's international colawyer at the ECCC) a chance to retrieve his client from beyond the pale. "I felt that [Duch's] crime was the crime of a man," Bizot told the judges, "and that its abomination should be measured not by treating Duch like a monster but by rehabilitating, or rather recognizing in him, the humanity that is his, as much as it is ours." This fantasy stands in complete contrast to the Cambodian cinema's facing of the perpetrator, a phenomenon that will be analyzed later.

PERPETRATOR CINEMA AND THE EXTRAORDINARY CASE OF NEW CAMBODIAN CINEMA

New Cambodian perpetrator cinema, I suggest, is part of the global phenomenon, but in many respects is paradigmatic, due to the number of films produced and its new forms of addressing the perpetrator. As I claimed earlier, interrogating the perpetrator figure in world documentary cinema posits a research perspective aimed at advancing the study of the perpetrator as an inevitably synchronal and thus interconnected, complementary field of research, a central part of current cultural memory in the West. Though the key turning points in the creation and evolution of the testimony movement can be discerned (such as Annette Wieviorka's pointing to the major transformation in the figure of the witness from the period of the ghettos to its current subject position as a survivor, a bearer of history, claiming that "the Eichmann trial marks the advent of the witness,"[56] and the establishment of the Fortunoff Archive at Yale in 1981[57]), the lack of "writings from beyond the grave"[58] and a parallel cultural-sociological-psychological distinctive history of the perpetrator and confessing[59] are obvious. Nevertheless, as I have suggested in other forums,[60] the shift to perpetrator-centric theorization in the West is built on the strong legacy of the victim in current culture and on the West's continued moral obligation to his or her testimony.

Taking the testimony movement and its legacy, as well as the major role that first- and second-generation Holocaust cinema plays in advancing the movement (as well as the inconceivableness of imagining a "confession movement" and the lack of parallel perpetrator studies), as a backdrop to the discussion of the Cambodian context, it is clear that the emergence of perpetrator cinema in Cambodia is exceptional. In the absence of any social-intellectual movement and under the taboo and censorship of the post-KR period, collecting perpetrators' accounts is a process undertaken simultaneously with victims' testimonies and a rebuilding of audio-visual archives.[61] This cinema has emerged despite the Cambodian genocide's relative marginalization in both global politics and trauma and genocide research, which has not regarded it as an immanent part of the testimony era; the blindness of the West to the KR genocide; the censorship inside Cambodia on the KR period and its absence from the education curriculum from 1979 until the early 2000s; American officialdom's continuous ignoring of this history and the burial of its documentation (as Ben Kiernan suggests); the thirty-five years of UN silence on the KR genocide that further encouraged Cambodians to ignore the past; and the demolished film industry. It is only with the beginning of the workings of the ECCC in 2006 that testimonies of survivors (as well as civil parties)[62] and perpetrators' accounts entered more forcefully into the public sphere, with Rithy Panh's cinema of the early 1990s shown mostly abroad. I venture to suggest that despite the ECCC, despite the films and television and radio programs made in the last two decades, and despite the changes caused by the four hundred NGOs working in Cambodia, a thorough process of testimony is still not taking place. With these circumstances taken into account, the renaissance of the new Cambodian cinema, and especially perpetrator films, is indeed remarkable.

Thus, challenging the posttraumatic conventions set during the era of the witness (most prominently, the "effect of belatedness" typical to victims' testimony with its fragile causality, trauma envy, failed testimony, compassion fatigue, vicarious victimhood, distance suffering, and longtime concern about aestheticizing the genocide), Cambodian cinema proposes a new set of non-Western postgenocide perpetrator-oriented conventions. It is endowed with truth-driven ethics that portends, as well as relies upon, the ECCC's legal proceedings. The cinematic activism, supplemented by the legal one, is characterized by naming the dread, advancing institutionalized prosecution through civil party engagement, proclaiming the values of the international legal system, generating additional categories of evidence, and articulating the disavowed. I suggest that beyond victim-related rehabilitation mechanisms such as making justice, creating social context and cultural symbols for mourning, and building the postgenocide self, in transcending post-Holocaust Western epistemology this corpus proposes two interconnected paradigms: the Duel Paradigm and the Moral Resentment Paradigm.

PERPETRATORHOOD PARADIGMS: THE DUEL AND MORAL RESENTMENT

THE DUEL PARADIGM

Far beyond Claude Lanzmann's paradigmatic though inevitably partial and vague representation of Nazi perpetrators in *Shoah*, the Cambodian direct, nonarchival, face-to-face confrontation of the first-generation survivor with the perpetrator as embodied Evil is derived and realized through the directors' activism, which acknowledges and thus breaks the intimacy of the (horrific) neighborhood that is prevalent in post-1979 rural Cambodia, where perpetrators, still exerting power, live among their former victims. Thus, the most conspicuous characteristic of this encounter, which I suggest to regard as a duel, is its (explicit or implicit) transformation of power relations.

Though the difference between this duel and the nineteenth century's spectator-centered violent and illegal ritual of honor is obvious, this metaphor captures dueling, especially when conducted with Big (high-ranking) perpetrators,[63] not as a system for consigning respect or other social capital, but as one that involves two equals in a fight. Such battles with high-ranking perpetrators attest to their unwillingness to accept a person designated a member of the New People as an equal, or at least an equal rival, even after four decades. This is especially illustrated by Duch, who ignored the civil parties and their families, and paid gestures of respect only to the judges at his ECCC trial.[64] The transformation of power relations is discerned in the films along an axis that runs from the moment of disclosure of perpetrators' hiding places to their partial confession. For example, in Cambodian director-survivor Thet Sambath and British codirector Rob Lemkin's *Enemies of the People: A Personal Journey Into the Heart of the Killing Fields* (UK/Cambodia, 2009), after a ten-year quest, in 2001, Sambath found Nuon Chea, the chief ideologist of the KR, prime minister of Democratic Kampuchea (DK), and "Brother Number 2," (second-in-command to KR leader Pol Pot, who was the general secretary of the party during the Cambodian genocide). After three years of developing a relationship and interviewing him, in 2004 Nuon Chea finally admitted to Sambath (and Lemkin) for the first time that he had been involved in Pol Pot's decision to kill compatriots.[65]

As Cambodian perpetrator cinema shows, the search for the perpetrators, or waiting for their approval to be interviewed, or conducting the interview itself could last more than ten years. This exceptional situation is a result not only of postgenocide circumstances in which the whereabouts of (high- as well as low-ranking) perpetrators was unknown, but also of the filmmakers' multiple subject positions: they are survivors of the Pol Pot genocide as well as docu/history-activists and the perpetrator's interviewers. In post-Holocaust activism taken as a paradigm, though a few of the best-known Nazi hunters were concentration camp survivors (most notably, Simon Wiesenthal),[66] they were not filmmakers. The documentarists of the new Cambodian perpetrator cinema are driven by the hunt, the revelation of historical truth, and rewriting it via their confrontation with the "willing" perpetrators, while in most of the films they also feel compelled under the perpetrator's gaze to present their own (partial or full) testimonies.

Moreover, New Cambodian Cinema is a unique phenomenon in world cinema because it is being created out of the almost total absence of *papas kino*, the KR having murdered the entire middle class—including all directors, actors, actresses, and novelists—and having destroyed almost all films made prior to the Revolution during the Golden Age of Cambodian cinema. The cinema created out of this void, a survivors' cinema based on autobiographical quests for the perpetrators and on the first and second generations' desire to expose them, is carried out under very difficult circumstances, mostly as "one-man-projects." In *Enemies of the People*, for example, Thet Sambath tells the spectator that for years he invested all the money he had in his search for Nuon Chea and other low-ranking perpetrators. Thus, during those ten years, he repeatedly left his wife and children in Phnom Penh to travel to rural Cambodia, many times knowing they had no money, even for food. Nevertheless, he felt he must complete this mission, which he owed his murdered parents and siblings. Taking all these historical, political, social, industrial, and personal factors into consideration, it seems, to the best of my knowledge, that the

Cambodian documentarists' challenges in creating the duel, especially with the Big Perpetrators, are different from those of most of directors of perpetrator films in current global cinema.[67]

Thus, and moreover, films like Rithy Panh's *S21: The Khmer Rouge Death Machine* (*S21, la machine de mort Khmère rouge*, Cambodia/France, 2003); Kass Doug's *Behind the Walls of S-21:Oral Histories from Tuol Sleng Prison* (Cambodia, 2007); Socheata Poeuv's *New Year Baby* (USA, 2008); Rob Lemkin and Thet Sambath's *Enemies of the People*; Roshane Saidnattar's *Survive: In the Heart of Khmer Rouge Madness* (*L'important c'est de rester vivant*, France, 2009); Lida Chan and Guillaume P. Suon's *Red Wedding* (*Noces Rouges*, Cambodia/France, 2012); Guillaume P. Suon's *About My Father* (Cambodia, 2010); Rithy Panh's *Duch, Master of the Forges of Hell* (*Duch, le maître des forges de l'enfer*, France/Cambodia, 2011); Andrew Blogg and Tim Purdie's *Camp 32* (Australia/Cambodia, 2014); and Neary Adeline Hay's *Angkar* (France/Cambodia, 2018) mediate the inevitable paradox that emerges in this multi-layered text by which survivors of a genocide breaks their silence. But their singular testimony (as Shoshana Felman calls it), which has no listener, concurrently becomes a tool against the perpetrators' lies and constant denials.[68]

Comprehending this corpus, thus, demands a broad perspective that goes beyond the boundaries of the film text and includes the years of searching, of building relationships with the perpetrators, of editing, as well as of postproduction, as they are expressed in the autobiographical memoirs and other personal documents written by the directors (most notably, Rithy Panh, Thet Sambath, and Youk Chhang). Reflecting on the hundreds of hours of interviewing Duch during the time he served in prison, French-Cambodian director Rithy Panh, for example, writes in his autobiographical memoir five reflections that attest to the complexity of this multiplicity of subject positions enacted during the duel:

> I question Duch tirelessly . . . he never gazes into my camera. Or hardly ever. Is he afraid it will see inside him? . . . He explains his position to me. He makes phrases. I catch him lying. I offer precise information.
>   One day during a dialogue that's turning into a fight, I see the skin of his cheeks grow blotchy. I stare at his irritated, bristling flesh. Then his calm returns, the soldier's calm, the calm of a revolutionary who's had

to face so many cruel committees and endure so many self-criticism sessions. Then I stop filming him and say, "Think about it; take your time."

He smiles and speaks softly to me, "Mr. Rithy, we won't quarrel tomorrow, will we?" . . . he needs to talk to me. To continue the discussion. To win me over.[69]

Twenty years now since the Khmer Rouge fled these broad avenues; but I feel Duch's hand, reaching for my shoulders and the back of my neck. He gropes. I resist. I turn around, shivering. On my way I see a child sleeping in a vegetable cart. The sky is pale. We're saved. (17–19)

I reread these pages. I'd like to erase my childhood. And leave nothing behind: not the words, not the pages, not the trembling hand holding them . . . There would be nothing left except Duch and me: the story of a combat. I've filmed his oversights and his lies. . . . I write and shoot film—in other words I live a little. I'd like to escape this man, my subject, who won't stop telling me about his methods. (200–207)

After hundreds of hours of filming, the truth became cruelly apparent to me: I had become that man's instrument. His adviser in some way. His coach. As I've written, I was searching not for truth but for knowledge, for consciousness. . . . But Duch's words always amounted to the same thing, a game of falsehood. A cruel game. . . . With my questions, I'd helped to prepare him for his trial. So: I had survived the Khmer Rouge, I was investigating the human enigma as humanly personified by Duch, and he was using me? I found this idea intolerable. (17–19)

Duch: Death is with me night and day.
Me: With me too, but we're not on the same side. (146)

Perhaps more than any other posttraumatic oeuvre in post-Holocaust world cinema, Rithy Panh's, highly devoted to the rebuilding of post-KR Cambodian society,[70] paves the way for the cinematic representation of the perpetrator figure. *S21: The Khmer Rouge Death Machine* was the first film representing an encounter between two survivors (Chum Mey, a machine repairman, and Vann Nath, who, after having been interrogated and tortured, was made S-21's official artist because of his ability to paint flattering portraits of Pol Pot) and perpetrators (S-21 guards and other functionaries such as interrogators, a doctor, and a photographer). That, together with the guards' bodily reenactments of their past deeds as part of the filmed encounter (with Panh), paved the way for other films that render these complicated processes of the survivors coming to terms with the past by and large through the encounter with the perpetrator. Released eight years after the completion of *S21*, Panh's *Duch, Master of the Forges of Hell* (analyzed in chapter 3) embodies the "documentary dueling" to its full, while implicitly staging the question of whether it might become a "civilizing" process for the perpetrator.[71]

Panh's autobiographical descriptions in his memoir, *Elimination: A Survivor of the Khmer Rouge Confronts His Past and the Commandant of the Killing Fields*, capture the paradoxical nature of the multilayered survivor-perpetrator duel in the entire corpus. His first description exemplifies the prominent characteristic of the survivor-perpetrator encounter—a dueling dynamic based on escalation of conflicts. However, I suggest that in this corpus the main protagonist is neither the perpetrator nor the survivor, but the duel itself. In this regard, accusations of dishonesty, historically one of the most frequent grounds for dueling, inform the underlying tension between the survivor-interviewer and perpetrator-interviewee. Undoubtedly, the first-generation survivor is aspiring, after years of efforts, to extract the perpetrator's confession of his deeds. However, the films show that, finally, after escalation of the duel, it is a transformation in power relations that is at stake, rather than the (usually failed or partial) confession, unlike in past duels, in which "the point of the duel was more to demonstrate one's status-group membership than to establish dominance over one's opponent. Thus it was less important to win than to display courage."[72] In this corpus, it is the survivor' status and courage that, encountering deep interactional obstacles, shape the flow of the confrontation.

Panh's second autobiographical description exposes the PTSD (posttraumatic stress disorder) symptoms suffered by the survivors and revealed in the films. Shoshana Felman claims, "Holocaust survivors . . . cannot fulfill their task without, in turn, passing through the crisis of experiencing their boundaries, their separateness, their functionality, and indeed their sanity, at risk."[73] Thus, being aware of the enormous difficulty faced by survivors who attempt after the event to narrate their experience as victims and testify, Primo Levi distinguishes between his "camp-self" and his "survivor-self."[74] In the duel, this means that a shattered self in the very act of remembering faces the denial of one's suffering, of oneself, and though the postgenocide self of the survivor motivates the entire process, no assumption of a reconstructive effect that might emerge out of the possibility of a dialogue is rendered. Though Panh as well as Sambath and others testify that relationships were built during the years, the two parties, in contrast to those who participate in a conventional format of interviewer and interviewee, of course do not form a testimonial alliance. As particularly the last quotation from Panh's memoir proves, perpetrators not only represent the indifference of the world of genocide, but with their denials they are still part of this world, making the violence present. The threat that the constant denials, evasions, manipulation, and lying will cause a secondary traumatization of the survivors, although they do not expect the perpetrator to take on the role of a listener, is realized in most of these descriptions, as well as in the films.

Thus, the duels in all these films emphasize shifts from the perpetrator's inhuman behavior to the humanity of the survivor and back. As Geoffrey Hartman argues,

> Every witness, at some level of consciousness, becomes the last—the only remaining—witness. Each account, therefore, tries to reach a less-defined but necessary other, like Paul Celan's ghostly "Thou," who is essentially a listener and soul mate removing the solitariness of those not listened to. The shattered or isolated self of the victim is given a chance to reenter, through the interviewing process and however provisionally, a personal bonding that is also a social bond and which is necessary for the transmission of memory.[75]

In these films, the survivor/interviewer/activist/docu-historian/filmmaker's problem of integrating and communicating his or her own traumatic experiences under conditions that are totally contrasted to Felman's and Hartman's contentions worsens through time. In *Survive: In the Heart of Khmer Rouge Madness*, for example, director-survivor Roshane Saidnattar describes how she awakened in the middle of the night from a nightmare in the house of Khieu Samphan ("Brother Number 4," who had been Cambodia's head of state), where she was staying as his guest-interviewer.

After their long duel of the previous weeks, she became distressed by her failure to establish authority over the contested truth. Thus, she uses the editing in the scenes prior to the nightmare as a major tool of refutation (as do all the directors in this corpus). Describing the hunger, humiliations, and hardship of her life in a labor camp for children during the KR regime, she says: "Our lives were like eggs in the hands of these peasants, to break as they liked." The editing connects her memories (enacted by a young girl who plays her as a child) to the interview with Khieu Samphan, in which, while driving around the area near his house in rural Cambodia, he tells her:

> I'd have liked to have some land near the market. Not for a big business. Just a place to sell soya milk . . . Soy bean milk. We have raised ducks. It wasn't what we had planned, but we didn't know how else to make a living. We started with a few. Not many, two hundred at most. Two hundred ducks. The ducks laid between one hundred to one hundred thirty eggs a day. We sold them . . . that made five hundred or six hundred in all . . . they were underfed. . . . They lay every day. Fifteen were left, but some were stolen. . . . Only three laying ducks left!

His talk about the "difficulty of making a living" is, in fact, a perverse literalization of her metaphoric description of her and her family's life as eggs that might break any minute through the arbitrary violence of the KR and the Old People. In this film (analyzed in chapter 3), because the director does not disclose to Khieu Samphan her true identity as a survivor, the spectator is watching a double duel—one shown in the scenes of the interview and the other rendered through the editing and her voice-over, simultaneously and alternately representing her camp- and survivor-selves. Similar to Panh's, her nightmare, grounded in the suddenness of the shift to anxiety, is the outcome of the emotional field (intertwining fear, anger, tension, hope, dread, grief) to which she has been exposed during the duel.[76]

Moreover, though survivors' symptoms worsen along the length of their interviews with the perpetrators because of the latters' constant denial and lies, the inner paradox of apparently getting closer to the perpetrators—of allegedly getting to know them better while in fact this acquaintance negates itself—becomes more and more unbearable as the relationships develop. The other end of the continuum of this closeness is embodied in Rithy Panh's fourth reflection, attesting to Duch using him to prepare for his trial. During this "round," the duel embodies as well a process of what the French sociologist and philosopher Pierre Bourdieu famously calls "symbolic violence," a battle over domination.

Under these extreme circumstances of months and years of "duel rounds," overcoming the perpetrator's psychological reactions when interviewed, like lying, self-falsification, aporias, projection of guilt, refusal to acknowledge responsibility, and adhering to past indoctrination, while the unspoken and the unspeakable are still felt by the survivor, establishes a unique social process. It leads to constituting the ethics of moral resentment.

THE MORAL RESENTMENT PARADIGM

The notable difference between the Cambodian autogenocide[77]—meaning that the enemy was not a foreign Other but a member of the same imagined community (sharing the same origins, ethnicity, language, and religious belief)—and the other major genocidal catastrophes of the twentieth century (from Rwanda and Sierra Leone to former Yugoslavia) reflects on the extraordinariness of this cinema in terms of its negotiation with perpetration. Thus, in response to the question of the French director Bruno Carette and the Cambodian-survivor codirector Sien Meta in *Bitter Khmer Rouge* (*Khmers Rouges Amers*, France/Cambodia, 2007), Reth, an ex-KR soldier, reflects on the paradoxical and preemptive failure of the ECCC—and, metonymically, the entire Cambodian society—in regard to the issue of bringing low-ranking perpetrators to trial: "Trying KR? But which KR for heaven sake? KR, but who wasn't a KR?"[78]

I suggest that this cinema's acknowledgment of the relationships within Cambodian society regarding the issue of perpetration and collaboration, together with the impracticality of bringing to trial all KRs, generated two historically and ideologically interrelated phenomena: transformation of the spectators' ethical consciousness by defying the twentieth-century legacy of reconciliation and forgiveness and, following the perspective of Holocaust survivor and writer Jean Améry,[79] proposing what I call moral resentment, presented in the films as nonvindictive.[80]

DEFINING PERPETRATOR CINEMA 31

According to the Amérian experience, after a short postwar period in which he felt that Holocaust victims were listened to and respected in Germany and Europe, the politics of forgetting became hegemonic to an extent that the "camp-self"/"victim-self" took over the much-desired "survivor-self." When victimhood was again repressed politically, the camp-self, feeling loneliness and social isolation, prevailed. In 1976, thirty-one years after the end of World War II (and a decade before the "Historians Debate" [*Historikerstreit*] broke out in Germany), Améry writes: "What happened, happened. But *that* it happened cannot be so easily accepted. . . . Nothing has healed, and what perhaps was already on the point of healing in 1964 is bursting open again as an infected wound."[81] At the heart of his thought, Améry stages the political conflict between collective progress and survivors' struggle with the past, between the victims' need for recognition and (both German and European) society's political urge to promote social stability through reconciliation; and, consequently, I maintain, in line with Jacques Derrida's contention on politics' sabotage of pure forgiveness, their need to assure expected political transactions and financial gains.

The victims' immense sense of betrayal harbors Améry's resentment. However, similar to the perpetrator films' mind-set, this is not the Nietzschean (1887) or the Max Schelerian (1914) resentment/*ressentiment*[82] embodying the mental attitude of the weak and powerless—the *schlechtwegekommene*—against their aristocratic masters. Regardless of the difference between Nietzsche's and Scheler's conceptions (elaborated on in chapters 2 and 3), Nietzsche's influential view—that because slaves cannot revolt against noble men openly they try to discredit them and their achievements, leading to a falsification of all genuine sensations and compensating themselves indulgingly with an imaginary revenge—became paradigmatic in Western thought. Opposing both Nietzsche's and Scheler's dominant conceptualization of resentment/*ressentiment*, Améry's innovation lies in his definition of resentment not as an unconscious uncontrollable negative impulse of human nature, but as a highly self-conscious state of personal morality. Enabling an insightful introspection into the humanness of resentment, he defies Nietzsche for despising victims because he regards them as weak, inferior, and cowardly, and elevates the dignity of the victim, having been forced by circumstances beyond their control. Moreover, Améry, in an exceedingly bold move, rejects the entire psychological-moralist tradition that follows the Nietzschean premise by seeing resentment as a kind of sickness that harms the "patient" while repressing its ethics.

As will be elaborated on in the following chapters, this repression, I suggest, is still discerned in post-Amérian criticism by most scholars unable to resist his radicalism to the level of comprising a "reconcilable resentment."[83] However, in Cambodia, a politically sanctioned program of forgiveness guided by commonality such as took place in South Africa's Truth and Reconciliation Commission (TRC)—most famously, Archbishop Desmond Tutu's *No Future Without Forgiveness*—has not been realized.[84] For the victims of violence and torture, the pressure to overcome, repress, or otherwise deny their identity, suggests Améry, is immoral.

In current political-social-psychological thought, in which the discourse of transitional justice and prevention of genocide is embraced more widely than the Amérian radical contemplation, it is important to indicate that two current trends are closer to Amérian ideals: major psychoanalytic theorists of the ethics of democracy and human rights (Alain Badiou, Chantal Mouffe, Alenka Zupančič, and Slavoj Žižek) point out that the prevailing discourse on individual rights is not as natural or as obvious as would seem.[85] They argue that it is used conservatively to mask Western, Christian, and capitalistic values that are the key source of the moral-ideological consensus regarding Good and Evil. Furthermore, care ethics discourse (based on the writings of Joan Tronto, Fiona Robinson, Virginia Held, and Jess Kyle, among others), which grew as part of feminist theory, paves the way, I suggest, for a nonconsensual ethics by framing ethical thought regarding political and global processes of caring.[86] In her book *Moral Boundaries: A Political Argument for an Ethic of Care*, Tronto argues that caring is not only a disposition or stance, but practice based on compassion, attentiveness, responsibility, competence, and responsiveness.[87] Thus, caring relations "form the wider moral framework into which justice should be fitted."[88]

Thirty years earlier than these nonconsensual trends, pointing to the irreconcilable conflict between victims' unreadiness to forget and forgive and a society's privileging of forgiveness, Améry raises a vital conceptualization of time, which, I suggest, is embodied in perpetrator cinema's structuring of time-sense as well:

Natural consciousness of time actually is rooted in the physiological process of wound-healing and became part of the social conception of
reality. But precisely for this reason it is not only extramoral, but also
antimoral in character. Man has the right and the privilege to declare
himself to be in disagreement with every natural occurrence, including
the biological healing that time brings about. What happened, happened. This sentence is just as true as it is hostile to morals and intellect.
The moral power to resist contains the protest, the revolt against reality,
which is rational only as long as it is moral. The moral person demands
annulment of time—in the particular case under question, by nailing the
criminal to his deed.[89]

Aleida Assmann notes that for Améry,

> the political rehabilitation of Germany is accompanied by a new sense
> of time. This sense of time, which Améry calls "natural," "biological" or
> "social" time, is oriented towards forgetting. It is the time in which life
> goes on, wounds are healed and grass eventually covers everything. This
> shape of time enforces the law of life, not of truth. Its opposite is "moral"
> time . . . where there can be . . . only a remorseless return to the crimes
> and the wish for their public acknowledgement.[90]

Reflecting on the affinity between Améry's polemical writing and Cambodian cinema's polemical filmmaking and editing, I suggest that
Amérian-inspired unvindictive epistemology of resentment is embodied
in a new cinematic rendering of time and temporality. As such, it is unique
in world cinema.

What Assmann calls "return to the crimes" is, in fact, a reconstruction of the genocidal time and a remodeling of its dynamics. Based on an
epistemic faith, it is not an act of turning back or a mere reversal but, I
suggest, an act of "Being Then," in the past. In *Duch, Master of the Forges
of Hell* (analyzed at length in chapter 3), Rithy Panh uses three major strategies during his interview-duel with Duch for a rearticulated understanding of the relationship between past, present, and future: The first
strategy is to demand spectators reshape their conception of time by showing very short video clips or still photos that are inserted into the interviewing process. Confronting Duch's responses, these materials reveal his

responses to be lies but also, and simultaneously, incessantly "take" the spectator back to the past. The representation of these materials does not last more than a few seconds; thus, for the spectators, they function as flickers of time-consciousness, marking their difference from the conventional undemanding easiness of cinematic flashbacks. The second strategy is the use of the accumulation of documents and still photographs taken from S-21 that are put on the desk at the center of the mise-en-scène. Through Duch's reading them, pointing at his signature, looking at them, and reflecting on them at Panh's request, he is returned again and again into the past. In contrast to the prison guards' bodily reenactments of their past actions in *S21: The Khmer Rouge Death Machine*, Duch's rereading of these records is not performed automatically. In further contrast to the guards, he is neither possessed by the past nor reliving it. On the contrary, his rereading is saturated with denial and negation. Thus, Panh's constant and relentless use of these materials has major significance in terms of constituting moral resentment through remodeling of cinematic time. The third strategy that transforms the perception of time for both Duch and the spectator is Panh's avoidance of a corporeal appearance before the camera such that the conjuring act, which makes the dead play the Third, meaningful Other during the interview, is at the center, while repeatedly reflecting on the "time of the dead." (Thus, in *The Missing Picture* [*L'image manquante*, Cambodia/France, 2013], a film that represents his autobiography, Panh says that mourning is impossible. This is embodied in the repeated image of the figurine representing his father being buried, though each time this happens his head remains uncovered. This repetitiveness of the "time of the dead" is a reflection of moral resentment as well.)[91]

The use of these strategies to build a polemical narrative through counterediting of course aims at refuting, contradicting, opposing, and disproving the Big Perpetrator's lies. Its major significance, however, lies in reconstructing the genocidal time into a form of resentment. It is not only the refusal of future reconciliation and the disordering of temporality in order to bring the perpetrator back to his past deeds that are the major component of Panh's ideology of resentment. Returning into the past as an act of resentment also means rupturing the everlasting now that is rooted in denial. The Now in *Duch*, I claim, is the time of denial realized as a continuous mind-set of tactics and manipulations. After all, the "willing executioner" unfolds his denial of the past in the present, while blocking out the past. In this regard, rupturing the attachment between denial and the Now as its dominant temporalization elevates resentment's value. About this, Panh says: "I think about those four years . . . which I'll never forgive. For me, forgiveness is something very private. Only politicians arrogate to themselves the right to grant reprieves or pardons in the name of all—a right unimaginable when mass crimes or genocides are concerned. I don't believe in reconciliation by decree."[92]

ANGKAR

Neary Adeline Hay's *Angkar* constitutes as well the epistemology of unvindictive moral resentment. In this 1.5/second-generation documentary film,[93] the filmmaker, who was born out of a forced marriage (marriage between total strangers enforced on the New People in order to increase the number of KRs as well as to control the family unit),[94] accompanies her father, Khonsaly Hay, the only survivor of his family, to the village of Ta Saeng (in North Cambodia), where he was subjected to four years of forced labor. After over forty years living in France (where the family fled after staying a few years in a refugee camp on the Thai border), they also visit the old family house and Khonsaly's pharmacy in Phnom Penh. In

FIGURE 1.2 Meeting with the perpetrators in Neary Adeline Hay's *Angkar*. Courtesy of Christophe Audeguis (The Cup of Tea Productions).

Ta Saeng, he meets the Old People who were his torturers, the guards, the camp's perpetrators and collaborators (who participated in the criticism sessions, who supervised the hard labor in the rice fields, and so on), and the collaborator-spies (*chhlop*).

Although other films (such as *S21: The Khmer Rouge Death Machine* and *Enemies of the People*) present low-ranking perpetrators, *Angkar* is exceptional. *S21* focuses on the prison guards in the execution center in Phnom Penh; although they are representative of the KR's cruel violence, their world at S-21 is an enclosed one, very different from the labor camps in rural Cambodia. *Enemies* focuses on the duel with the Big Perpetrator, Nuon Chea, and (as the analysis of the film in chapter 2 shows), though many scenes depict low-ranking perpetrators of rural Cambodia as well as their confessions, they are not connected to Sambath's personal story. In contrast, *Angkar* is the first documentary film that renders the suffering caused by low-ranking perpetrators in rural Cambodia through a personal story. Thus, the duel's "rules of the game" are presented in an entirely different way from the other films included in this corpus. Neary Hay, being Khonsaly's daughter, received the perpetrators' permission to film the sequences of the meetings with her father. Thus, the heart of the film is built on sheer verité scenes that she shot as the cinematographer, creating an unnatural eerie "home-movie-with-the-perpetrators" film.[95]

The film's title, *Angkar*, means literally in Khmer "The Organization."[96] Only in 1977 were Cambodians finally told that Angkar, which was running the country, was in fact Cambodia's Communist Party.[97] The opening scene takes place in almost total darkness, where a blurred figure of a man shot from behind is seen walking, his white shirt illuminated from time to time by a ray of light (probably from a flashlight he is holding). His voice-over in Khmer is heard: "It was chaos. There were no ID papers any more, no legal system, no doctors, no property ownership, no intellectuals, no currency, no memories. The village was called Ta Saeng. I thought I would live there forever. It was year zero. The beginning of a new era." Following a cut, the film's title, *Angkar*, written in huge red bold letters, appears on the entire cinematic screen. This design, I suggest, is an act of naming that stands against the supreme stratagem of the Communist Party to propagate its omnipresent terror by concealing the identity of its leaders.[98] Reflecting on the invisible leadership, this is also a metareflection on cinema's power to disrupt the invisible. Since Angkar had no face and there were no posters of Pol Pot on village or town walls, the emphasis of the huge letters of "Angkar" is also preemptive of the film's strategy of naming the perpetrators (especially those not seen in the film but known to be in the village, like the cannibals [who removed human livers and regularly drank the gallbladder bile of their victims],[99] the cut-throat Khmer, and the executioners). In this, the film metareflexively declares cinema's powers in establishing a visual duel with Evil. The red color refers of course to danger; thus, together with the act of naming, it serves to break Angkar's terror, still felt in the village: in one of the first scenes, for example, the following conversation takes place between the father and an old-aged perpetrator:

> KHONSALY HAY: I heard you were a collaborationist spy.
> PERPETRATOR: Yes. I was with Chorm.
> KHONSALY HAY: Is the throat-cutter still alive? . . . What's his name?
> PERPETRATOR: Moeung San. The executions took place in the next village.
> KHONSALY HAY: Yes. That's right . . . Is the executioner still alive?
> PERPETRATOR: Yes, today he is deputy head of the village.
> KHONSALY HAY: Right now?
> PERPETRATOR: Yes. But he is illiterate . . .
> KHONSALY HAY: His name is Mei Sang, isn't it?
> PERPETRATOR: Moeung Sang.
> KHONSALY HAY: Hmmm . . . Moeung Sang
> PERPETRATOR: No one must know I told you.
> KHONSALY HAY: Of course not.[100]

In contrast to the duels in the films that interview the Big Perpetrators (like Nuon Chea and Duch), in this film the talks take place in the presence of many people, over food, drink, the sharing of memories, and laughter. Simultaneously, as the perpetrator's last comment proves, fear and uneasiness are still prevalent.[101]

After the film's title appears, we hear the father's question ("What am I doing here?"), still in the darkness, and the cut leads to a fast track on the road to and inside the village, in daylight, while a woman's voice-over says in French: "I was three months old when we left Cambodia. I grew up in France, in your silence . . ."

FIGURE 1.3 Khonsaly Hay at the execution site in Neary Adeline Hay's *Angkar.* Courtesy of Christophe Audeguis (The Cup of Tea Productions).

In analyzing Lanzmann's *Shoah* as part of the "ethical turn," Jacques Rancière differentiates between "an art of the unrepresentable" and "an art of representation."[102] Considering the unrepresentable as the central category of the ethical turn in aesthetic reflection means, for Rancière, as for Adorno, cutting any form of salvation to come. In its adherence to the Rancièrian definition of ethics as "the kind of thinking in which identity is established between an environment, a way of being and a principle of action,"[103] *Angkar*'s poetics, alternately shifting between the art of the unrepresentable and the art of representation, is grounded in both constituting moral nonvindictive resentment and the protagonists' identities-of-return. Two cinematic strategies are conspicuous: First, as the description shows, the film structures two parallel narratives: of the father, heard in the voice-over in Khmer, and of the daughter/filmmaker, heard in the voice-over in French. These nonlinear narratives intertwine throughout the film, combining inner monologues; her reflections on the environment, on her and her father's identities, and the actions in the village (meetings, a walk in the rice fields, a local wedding); his painful recollections; and their shared and distinct memories. The double narrativization is a major strategy for the filmmaker/daughter to honorably oppose her father's reconciled behavior as well as strictly oppose the perpetrators' refusal to be engaged with questions regarding their deeds. The duel, in other words, is taking place through the film's cinematic language not less than through the father's encounters with the perpetrators. Thus, for example, Neary Hay uses silence during the first meeting with the perpetrators so that we do not hear what they say to one another. Instead, we hear a soundtrack built on a shout mixed with a sound of elegy, symbolizing the horror and the dead (the entire family of the father, eleven people who were murdered, as well as the other millions).

In another scene, her narration intervenes and presents the option of resentment even more directly. In this scene, the spectator just hears the voice of a perpetrator who sits behind a curtain. The only person shown during the entire talk is the father:

THE PERPETRATOR: Ask your questions, I am not afraid. I am not scared of anything. There is no blood on my hands. My hands are clean. And I was only a spy for a year.

THE FATHER: You were told what to do and you did it? You had to report on what people were saying?

THE PERPETRATOR: I know there was a spy under the house.

THE FATHER: Ma Nol used to say, "especially at night, don't talk."

THE PERPETRATOR: It's true, it was so hard back then. . . . Sorry to interrupt, but even we Old People. . . . Couldn't the Old People speak? But if we said something bad . . . you were finished. I understand.

THE FATHER: A word too many . . .

THE PERPETRATOR: Better to say nothing! I couldn't even eat my own chickens! Yes, I ate them in secret.

THE FATHER: Did you realize you had rice? Did you think about the New People when you were eating? As a spy, you were better off than we were, though.

THE PERPETRATOR: Seriously, no. I promise you, it was worse for us.

THE FATHER: Worse for spies than for the New People?

At this absurdist stage, the editing cuts without further presenting the perpetrator's response. The next scene shows the father in a barbershop getting a shave. The close-up on the old, huge razor on his neck, which opens this scene, symbolizes the hidden violence of the previous dialogue, as well as serves as a visual reminder of the throat-cutting prevalent in the past. The filmmaker's voice-over is heard over the shaving scene, honorably subverting the last meeting: "There was still a fearful respect when you spoke of them. As if the victim you'd been had never entirely left you." The double-narrative structure not only presents the daughter-father and second-first generation relationships, but, through the editing, also contrasts the perpetrators' reactions of evasion, lying, indifference, and denial with a woman's voice, and with her objection revealed through her film.

The second strategy that builds moral resentment is Hay's insertion of very short (two-second) close-ups of the faces of the perpetrators into various scenes. In this way she uses the editing to stress both her perspective on her father's consciousness/memory/subconscious, still haunted and partially obsessed by the perpetrators despite all his efforts to reconcile and be redeemed by avoiding feelings of vindictiveness. It is as if he is reminded of them: his camp-self takes over her own postmemorial reflection; the exposure of the perpetrators' faces engraved on the cinematic screen stand against their unrepentant anonymity; and, most importantly, the brief close-ups, bringing the past again and again through the killer's face, stress her objection to reconciliation and support of Amérian moral resentment. Through these insertions she expresses her disagreement with her father's declaration to the perpetrators that, although he lived and suffered in the village, he is not interested in revenge and he believes in Dharma and is happy to see the Old People again. The frightening close-ups, I suggest, are a form of dueling that constitutes for the spectator the obligation to not reconcile and to remember. Even when the father sadly reflects on what seems to be survivor's guilt, with which his daughter identifies ("I'm a survivor among millions of dead"), the editing cuts to a two-second close-up of one of the perpetrator's faces, emphasizing once again the time shift.

Finally, the verité style that dominates the survivor-perpetrators encounters is combined with highly designed scenes shot from a bird's-eye angle (from a drone) showing the Cambodian landscape, which, serving as a background to both her father's and her voice-over, stands in contrast to the meetings, and thus subverts their content as well. In this, Hay's taking the spectators back to the past is unlike Panh's acts with Duch. Duch refuses to relate to the genocide and Panh's various means force him, through the duel, to do just that, while it simultaneously constitutes a new epistemology for the spectators. Hay's strategies of remodeling the cinematic time through narration and editing are not oriented toward the perpetrators, but toward the spectators. Using the commentary she wrote for the entire film (as the scriptwriter) and the editing, she advances the epistemology of moral resentment. In one of the last scenes of the film, over a landscape of the village at night, her father's memories are heard in the voice-over, describing how he left his family during the deportation and after just five days in the jungle was caught by the soldiers of Angkar: "They took us to a village in the middle of the jungle. The village was called Ta Saeng. That day I was confronted by . . ." With a series of cuts, the next shots present the faces of the perpetrators and collaborators on the cinematic screen. Their roles are printed with big red letters over their faces while her father's voice mentions their names and roles: "Chief of District, Ta So; Pat, Bourreau, executioner; Égorgeur, Moeung San, Throat Cutter; Ta San, Collabo, collaborator." The spectators, who were not familiar with their names or with their specific roles until this scene, and who got to know them partially through the filmed meetings, are now confronted not only with the naming, but with their total exposure. The faces that were part of semifriendly talks or appear for a few seconds, flickering as a brief nightmare, are bestowed through this noticeable infographic with the responsibility they mostly refused to accept. This intertwining of the father's narration and the daughter's cinematic language gives, thus, extra weight to her "tagging" of the perpetrators as such.

FIGURE 1.4 Horrific intimacy in *Angkar*. Courtesy of Christophe Audeguis (The Cup of Tea Productions).

ARGUMENT AND OUTLINE OF THE BOOK

In *Perpetrator Cinema: Confronting Genocide in Cambodian Documentary,* I put forward perpetrator cinema as a new phenomenon in world cinema that in many respects, I suggest, sheds light on the twenty-first-century emergence of the new psychological-social-political era of the perpetrator, and—resting upon the remarkable achievements of twentieth-century scholarship in regard to witnessing—a new perpetrator-oriented discourse to be considered by genocide studies, trauma studies, human rights studies, and perpetrator studies as well as cinema studies. I suggest that current post-KR Cambodian cinema (as yet almost unexplored), which has been unprecedentedly reestablished after the void caused by the KR's murder of the entire population of cinema creators and its total demolition of the cinema industry, is a unique and highly important case of perpetrator cinema. Motivated by the epistemophilic urge to find the truth about the autogenocide, this corpus proposes for the first time in the history of cinema a direct confrontation between the (first-generation) survivor and the perpetrator. This extraordinary form of what I call documentary dueling has managed paradoxically, due to the autogenocide, to offer new conceptions in regard to the major questions that still haunt post-Holocaust research and practice and have become part of the legacy of the twentieth century. Although the question of accountability and responsibility is addressed over and again during the Cambodian survivor-perpetrator encounter (with both high- and low-ranking perpetrators), the intimate horror of the autogenocide enables a Cambodian cinema that advances confrontational tension and the transformation in power relations to shift the twentieth-century "ordinary man" enigma and, instead, based on a lengthy interaction, to pose a new question: Will the dueling become a "civilizing" process for the perpetrator?

This corpus proposes as well new conceptions in relation to the major thinking in the West that shaped the discourse and practice surrounding the enormous conflicts that were (and still are) ubiquitous in the era of post-Holocaust colonial genocide and mass killings. The films' analysis proposes this new thinking along five major intertwining extremities: East-West, survivor-perpetrator, testimony-confession, cinema-literature, and forgiveness-nonforgiveness. Through analysis of both the films and the relevant proceedings of the ECCC (the KR tribunal), I discuss

Cambodian cinema's insights not only in relation to the definition of perpetratorhood, but also in relation to reconciliation and forgiveness. Simultaneously, I suggest thinking outside the conceptualizations that have promoted these extremities as such: namely, the Nietzschean (and Schelerian) rejection of resentment that became paradigmatic not only in philosophical and historical-cultural-social thinking, but also in psychological thinking and practice. Cambodian cinema blocks the conception of resentment as an unconscious negative impulse of human nature that is impossible to suppress. Instead, it is positioned as a highly self-conscious state of personal morality, enabling deep insight into reconciliation not as a tendency antithetical to resentment, but as complementary to it. The films constitute moral resentment as ethics while demanding the perpetrator's accountability and objecting to and fundamentally disrupting the political view that reconciliation is the only legitimate response to the atrocious past.

Moreover, though the insights provided by some exemplary fiction films are taken into consideration, it is only documentary cinema, I suggest, that is capable of providing this era's new epistemic tools. The dueling documentaries also point to current genocide research's widespread concern for identification with the perpetrator (mostly provoked by literary works such as Jonathan Littell's *The Kindly Ones*) as irrelevant to this corpus due to the perpetrator's lengthy and detailed exposure, the incessant refutation of his or her perspective, and elevation of the survivors' subjectivity. The high- and low-ranking perpetrator's point of view is revealed only in the course of direct confrontation with the survivor.

In discussing Derrida's conceptualization of forgiveness and Améry's conceptualization of resentment, the new approach I call "unvindictive moral resentment" has implications in regard to cinema's ability to forge nonhegemonic and nonconsensual ethics. The films' analysis shows how the temporality of resentment enforces on the perpetrator as well as the spectator a new relation to the past, which I term "Being Then": This new time-sense brings the perpetrator back to his past deeds, rupturing the everlasting "Now" that is rooted in denial. Finally, I suggest delaying what is considered an urgent need for prevention in favor of care ethics embodied in moral resentment that puts forth both the survivors and the victims, the dead. Resentment as a precategorial experience becomes, thus, a way to distinguish how evil might be experienced, symbolized, judged, and finally incorporated into a system of ethics.

In chapter 2, "Post–Khmer Rouges Cambodian Cinema and the Big Perpetrators: Reconciliation or Resentment?," I propose the necessary background to the analysis and discussion of the cinema that renders the survivor/Big Perpetrator duel in both chapters 2 and 3; the genealogy of *ressentiment*/resentment from Nietzsche through Scheler and Améry, to post-Amérian conceptions, as well as Derrida's deconstruction of forgiveness, and the reconciliation paradigm. I suggest, first, questioning in what ways Big Perpetrator cinema represents "Pol Potism" vis-à-vis the reconciliation/resentment issue and, second, if the spectators' juridical imaginary enables the ECCC to function as an imaginary replacement for the vast number of low-ranking perpetrators who will never be tried.

Further, I deal with the unique conception of "post"-genocide in Cambodia and, finally, analyze Bruno Carette and Sien Meta's Big Perpetrator film (*Bitter Khmer Rouge*), in which the codirector, who is a survivor, refrains from direct confrontation with the high-ranking perpetrators presented. Thus, this film raises questions in regard to the problematics of interviewing the Big Perpetrators without confrontation, as well as the chaos emanating from a postgenocide era unacknowledged as such by the perpetrators.

Chapter 3, "Perpetratorhood Paradigms: The Duel and Moral Resentment," continues the discussion of unvindictive resentment and proposes an analysis of Rob Lemkin and Thet Sambath's *Enemies of the People*'s complex text and its surrounding discourse. Moreover, pointing to the affinity between the Cambodian-French director Rithy Panh and the Holocaust survivor and writer Améry's viewpoints, I analyze Panh's *Duch, Master of the Forges of Hell* as a paradigmatic film that, in contrast to *Bitter Khmer Rouge*, portrays the duel. The analysis leads to my suggestion that perpetrator cinema is neither a transitional justice cinema nor a reconciliatory one, but—being the voice of the dead by giving voice to the perpetrators—a corpus that above all foregrounds a new epistemology based on moral resentment, particularly unprone to conservative manipulation and repressive panaceas. This chapter also includes analysis of two other films that deal with the Big Perpetrators (Duch, Nuon Chea, and Khieu Samphan): Guillaume P. Suon's *About My Father* and Roshane Saidnattar's *Survive: In the Heart of Khmer Rouge Madness*. Taking them together, the conclusions are compared to Kulikar Sotho's fiction film *The Last Reel* (Cambodia, 2014), which deals with low-ranking perpetrators as an exemplar of the problematics of presenting both low-ranking perpetrators and inside-the-family betrayal, as well as the fictionalization of KR cadres.

Chapter 4, "Gendered Genocide: The Female Perpetrator, Forced Marriage, and Rape," discloses through Cambodian documentary cinema a new form of gendered genocide unknown in world cinema: the KR's forced marriage and rape policy, which, I suggest, epitomizes the perverse unconscious of the Cambodian revolution. The chapter begins with a discussion of the relationship between trauma and revolution through what I regard as the KR regime's enforcement of three consecutive revolutionary displacements: from gender to class, from bourgeois people to the "New People" (that is, from class to classless), and from a civilian to a KR revolutionary/ cadre. I examine the ways these class-dominated displacements transform the conventional definition of victimhood. Further, I submit the background for the films' analysis: the concept of KR forced marriage, Code No. 6, and a brief history of the ECCC proceedings on forced marriage. The analysis of Lida Chan and Guillaume P. Suon's *Red Wedding* proves, first, the exceptional case of forced marriage and rape among other global, more known forms of gendered genocidal crimes. Second, it proves the contribution of docu-activism to the survivors' confrontations with various female perpetrators, as well as the process of becoming a civil party in the ECCC. Analyzing the film's contribution to the ECCC hearings and the complexity of West-East intermingling during the legal proceedings reflects on the relationship between this corpus and the legal processes. Third, the film proposes new ethics based on symbolic necrophagia (eating the flesh of the dead). The chapter concludes with a comparison to Kavich Neang's *Three Wheels* (*Kong Bei*, Cambodia/France, 2015), a short autobiographical drama that presents the male point of view on forced marriage, as well as a brief discussion of the television miniseries *Time to Speak Out* (UK/Cambodia, 2016). Finally, I discuss gender crimes as crimes against humanity and the contribution of Cambodian cinema to legal recognition of this form of gendered genocide.

In the epilogue, "The Era of the Perpetrator Ethics," I briefly consider the most prominent Holocaust ethical decrees in relation to the perpetrator corpus and present a new form of testimony: the duel. Finally, I discuss the challenges faced by the spectator of the perpetrator era.

2

POST-KHMER ROUGE CAMBODIAN
CINEMA AND THE BIG PERPETRATORS

Reconciliation or Resentment?

In Cambodian folk religion one of the main mythological figures is known as the King of Death. He is a judge, the one who assigns souls to heaven or hell, and he knows all about everyone's good and bad deeds. Nothing is hidden from him. The souls he sends to hell become pret, *spirits of the damned, the victims of gory and everlasting tortures brought upon them by their misdeeds. Looking around the room at our room of eighteen prisoners, all of us afraid, dressed in ragged, stinking clothes, I decided that we were already* pret; *our fates had already been decided. The Khmer Rouge . . . who sat smiling at us now—he was the King of Death.*

—HAING S NGOR[1]

BIG PERPETRATOR CINEMA

The renaissance of the Cambodian film industry in the 1990s is remarkable given the mass murder of the previous generation of filmmakers, actors, actresses, novelists, scriptwriters, cinematographers, and film technicians by the Khmer Rouge (KR) regime. The total obliteration of the Cambodian film industry included the destruction of four hundred films (both negative and prints) made during the "Golden Age" of Cambodian cinema in the 1960s, as well as the filmmaking equipment and the thirty movie theaters that were active in Phnom Penh before its evacuation on April 17, 1975. In contrast to the blossoming of the industry prior to the KR revolution, the only films made during the revolution were propaganda films. With the invasion of Cambodia by Vietnam in 1979, the fall of the KR, and the installation of the Vietnam-backed government of the People's Republic of Kampuchea, a few movie theaters in Phnom Penh were reopened, but there was no domestic film industry.[2] Undoubtedly, this total elimination of the cinematic tradition, history, and culture that constituted Cambodia's cinematic "Year Zero" is a rare phenomenon in world cinema.[3] Overcoming the Year Zero through the unprecedented renaissance of the New Cambodian Cinema enables rendering the major unconscious collective transformations still hidden beneath the surface of post-KR social-political as well as psychomemorial processes.

I suggest that during the first decade of the twenty-first century, the new post-KR (mainly documentary) cinema constituted two exceptional phenomena, rare in world cinema: first, a new documentary genre based on the survivor-perpetrator duel; and second, and consequently through this encounter, exposure of an irresolvable tension between two different attitudes toward Cambodia's yet unassimilated genocidal past—reconciliation and resentment[4]—with an inclination toward what will be described later as moral resentment. The scale of the Cambodian autogenocide reminds us of the magnitude of this profound tension and the significance of the perspective and project of resentment:

Democratic Kampuchea was one of the worst human tragedies of the 20th century. Nearly two million Cambodians died from diseases due to a lack of medicines and medical services, starvation, execution, or exhaustion from overwork. Tens of thousands were made widows and orphans, and those who lived through the regime were severely traumatized by their experiences. Several hundred thousand Cambodians fled their country and became refugees. Millions of mines were laid by the KR and government forces, which have led to thousands of deaths and disabilities since the 1980s. A large proportion of the Cambodian people have mental problems because their family members were lost and their spirits damaged. These factors are one of the major causes of the poverty that plagues Cambodia today.[5]

During the new social age, dominated by the ECCC, also known as the KR tribunal,[6] this inclination toward resentment enables not only a rethinking of the postgenocide theoretical conceptualizations meant to comprehend the Cambodian context, including the huge change that has taken place in the legal system, but also a rethinking of the postgenocide conceptualizations prevalent since World War II in genocide studies, trauma studies, and memory studies, and in transitional justice and human-rights discourses. In other words, despite the contextual particularities, I suggest that the theoretical paradigm of moral resentment emanating from the post-autogenocide survivor-perpetrator duel might pave the way for a new understanding of the aftermath of genocide and of perpetratorhood in prolonged conflicts, tribal wars, racial and ethnic cleansing and policing, and other genocidal forms beyond the Cambodian case, especially in regard to how studying perpetratorhood might transform the current prevalent conceptualizations in genocide studies and related fields of research. However, it is the shift, I claim, from the post-Holocaust recognition of the "Hitler in Us" and the "Murderers are among Us" to the Cambodian predetermined "Hitler is Us" that will validate the lesson that this exceptional postgenocide Cambodian genre so strongly carries.[7]

The term *autogenocide* has been rejected by the French-Cambodian director Rithy Panh. In his autobiographical memoir *The Elimination: A Survivor of the Khmer Rouge Confronts His Past and the Commandant of the Killing Fields*, Panh writes:

How can we qualify those 1.7 million deaths in four years, a total reached without the means of mass extermination? A dictatorship by terror? A crime against humanity? The suicide of a nation? Behind those crimes there were a small handful of intellectuals, a powerful ideology, a rigorous organization, an obsession with control and therefore with secrecy, total contempt for the individual, and the status of death as an absolute recourse. Yes, there was a human project. This is the reason why I dislike the expressions "suicide of a nation" and "autogenocide" and "politicide" so profoundly. . . . A nation that commits suicide is a unique body, a body cut off from the greater body of nations. Such a nation is enigmatic, impenetrable. It's a sick nation, maybe even an insane one. And the world remains innocent. The crimes committed by Democratic Kampuchea, and the intention behind those crimes, were incontrovertible human; they involved man in his universality, man in his entirety, man in his history and in his politics. No one can consider those crimes as a geographical peculiarity or a historical oddity; on the contrary the twentieth century reached its fulfillment in that place; the crimes of Cambodia can even be taken to represent the whole twentieth century. . . . It was in the Enlightenment that those crimes took place. At the same time I don't believe that. Not everyone is Saint-Just. And taking everything literally is also a crime.[8]

Despite, or even because of, the disclaimer in Panh's last sentence, it is important to point out that my use of the term *autogenocide* henceforth is not evaluative. Comprehending the Cambodian genocide through its cinema, I suggest, exposes its uniqueness beyond the catastrophe as well as, as this chapter suggests, its contribution to an understanding of the twentieth century that does not exist in other corpora. Thus, using the concept *autogenocide* means addressing the *Condition Inhumane* of the extermination of the Other who prerevolution was myself.

In autogenocide, those whom we wish to eliminate are not Others whose strangeness makes us wary, but those we know best: our family members and closest neighbors as well as those who, like ourselves, belong to the same imagined community. Autogenocide, thus, is an intimate and erotic crime, inspired not by estrangement or ignorance, but by the closest possible relations and confidential knowledge. The victims—especially when naive, passive, and easily overpowered—arouse not empathy but revulsion and the perpetrator's impulse is to first exclude and then to extirpate them, similar to what one feels toward one's abjectness or disease. At a certain camouflaged—and fantasized—level, killing the enemy within stands for all previous failures of conquering the enemy without. It is particularly in relation to these processes that the New Cambodian Cinema's survivor-perpetrator duel documentaries, so exceptional in world cinema, might assist in deciphering the hidden "logics" of genocides.

The main contention of this chapter is that the Cambodian cinema's refusal to propose or represent reconciliation and its inclination toward resentment are derived from this exceptional context of post-autogenocide, in which for the first time in the history of post-Holocaust cinema we find a direct confrontation between the (first-generation) survivor and the perpetrator. The posttraumatic (mainly German and European) cinema that emerged and developed during the decades following the end of World War II did not include this kind of encounter because of the difference between these two periods in terms of social-political circumstances. In contrast to the Cambodian context, the basic situation, which is the foundation of this genre, could not have been realized: the wide majority of Jewish survivors did not return to their homes in Germany (and all over Europe) and the option of confronting the Nazi perpetrators was unimaginable and indescribable.

Due to the processes undergone mainly by German society, which defined the Era of the Witness, post-Holocaust witnessing triggered the rethinking of various genocide studies', trauma studies', and memory studies' conceptualizations, such as mourning, coming to terms with the past, working-through, acting-out, the negative sublime, the crisis of witnessing, postmemory, and vicarious trauma (developed by Shoshana Felman and Dori Laub, Cathy Caruth, Annette Wieviorka, Dominick LaCapra, and Marianne Hirsch, among others).[9] The age starting after the Truth and Reconciliation Commission (TRC) added new debates on reconciliation, apology, forgiveness, and mercy based on the confluence of the subject positions of perpetrator and victim.[10] Data from former Yugoslavia to Rwanda gave rise to the political, social, and legal dynamics of retroactive or transitional justice.[11] Though some research criticized various projects of reconciliation, mainly in regard to the TRC, none of these genocidal contexts gave rise to a cinematic survivor-perpetrator direct encounter or to moral resentment.

In defining the new Cambodian cinematic paradigm of moral resentment and the ethics it entails, I regard reconciliation not as its opposite tendency, but as a complementary one. Thus, the discussion of these cinematic tendencies and the analysis of the films will be based on two frames of thought, while pointing to their common denominator: the French philosopher Jacques Derrida's conceptualization of pure forgiveness, unsuccumbed to social politics, and the French Auschwitz survivor and writer Jean Améry's contemplation on resentment. Améry claims,

My resentments are there in order that the crime become a moral reality for the criminal, in order that he be swept into the truth of his atrocity. . . . In the two decades of contemplating what happened to me, I believe to have recognized that a forgiving and forgetting induced by social pressure is immoral. . . . The moral person demands annulment of time—in the particular case under question, by nailing the criminal to his deed. Thereby, and through a moral turning-back of the clock, the latter can join his victim as a fellow human being.[12]

As will be elaborated later, through the survivor-perpetrator confrontation, Cambodian (mainly documentary) cinema builds moral resentment as an ethics that elevates the survivor's subjectivity while demanding the perpetrator's accountability.

First, I propose that the new post-KR cinema stages this new paradigm of moral resentment based on the films' epistemophilic quest, which has the quality and force of *seeking* an often-intolerable truth in regard to the Cambodian autogenocide. As the ECCC hearings, debates in the public sphere, NGO reports, and new cinema prove, after forty years, the historical truth of the genocide is still under dispute and major events are not all known and acknowledged. For example, the crimes of sexual violence committed during the KR regime (described in the chapter 4) were legally recognized as crimes against humanity only in 2016, ten years after the ECCC began its work; and even then, as both the ECCC reports and documentary films like Lov Sophea's *Breaking the Silence—Sexual Violence Under the Khmer Rouge* (Cambodia, 2017) tell us, only the marital rapes committed under KR forced marriages are dealt with and not those committed in detention centers and work camps. In a culture saturated with silence, taboo, and impunity, it is not surprising, thus, that the first history book on the period meant to be studied in schools and universities—*A History of Democratic Kampuchea (1975–1979)*[13]—was written only in 2007, breaking thirty-two years of taboo in the Cambodian historiography and education curriculum.

Second, I claim that the films' unique negotiation with the past, propelled by their epistemophilic quest, is based on an aporetic reconciliation (one saturated with inner paradoxes) that receives its power and endurance from the seemingly opposite attitude of unvindictive resentment (an Amérian moral resentment). The exceptionality of the Cambodian genocide as an autogenocide, namely, one based on intimate intranational violence, inevitably enables this unusual affinity between these two otherwise radically different perspectives and projects. However, the sheer importance of the representation of these attitudes in the

Cambodian cinematic psyche lies in the cinematic emphasis on the genocidal context as determining both the inconclusiveness and the nondia-
lectical nature of the tension built on and through them. Moreover,
because of this epistemophilic quest, both reconciliation and resentment
are cinematically directed toward Cambodia's as yet unacknowledged history and not toward a presumed national reunion: that is, toward the
past and not the future.

Third, and consequently, taking into consideration this new wave's differentiation between its attitudes toward KR history and its attitudes
toward the post-KR nation, one of the first questions to be asked is how
we assess the prefix "post" in relation to the postgenocide. The prefix
denotes "after" and implies that the genocidal past has been overcome.
However, although the regime was removed from power on January 7,
1979, when Vietnam invaded Cambodia and destroyed most of the KR
army, the KR fled to Thailand and continued to fight the Vietnamese and
the new People's Republic of Kampuchea government during the
Cambodian-Vietnamese War, which only ended in 1991. In 1994, thousands of KR guerrillas surrendered themselves in a government amnesty,
and in 1996, Ieng Sary was granted amnesty for his role as the deputy
leader of the KR.[14] But it was only in 1999 that the last KR surrendered
completely to Prime Minister Hun Sen's government,[15] following the capture of General Ta Mok, the KR's chief of staff, in March 1999 by Cambodian government forces while on the run.[16] Undoubtedly, this twenty-year
period (1979–99) points to a problematic temporality in regard to the
notion of "post."

However, most importantly, following the demand to try lower-ranking
perpetrators (Cases 003 and 004 against Meas Muth, Yim Tith, and Ao
An),[17] in 2010, Prime Minister Hun Sen expressed his disapproval of the
notion that the court's remit extended beyond Case 002 (against Nuon
Chea and Khieu Samphan),[18] which has raised the threatening option of
the inevitable breakout of a civil war. This threat reflects the ailments that
are an inescapable part of the current regime due, among other reasons,
to its being populated by many former KR officials, including Hun Sen
himself. Their powerful presence in the current government renders this
postgenocide temporality not only problematic, but also ambiguous.
Thus, we can ask, when exactly does the "postgenocide" begin, and what
are the relationships between these diverse beginnings (1979, 1991, 1994,

1996, and 1999)? Does the ECCC verdict in 2014 against the two KR leaders Nuon Chea and Khieu Samphan, who were found guilty of crimes
against humanity for their roles in the KR genocide and sentenced to life
imprisonment, contribute to a further ambiguity of this temporality?[19]
Beyond recognition that the justice process for crimes against humanity
has no expiration date, these various factors (army defeat, guerrilla fighting, stages of surrenders, fall of the KR movement, trial and punishment
of high-ranking KR leaders, and KR status in the current regime) make
both the starting point of the "postgenocide" period and its related major
differentiation (pre- and post-KR) vague and destined to slippage.

Fourth, the convergence of the chronological and nonchronological
meanings included in the conceptualization of "post"-genocide marks the
public debates following the ECCC hearings and the transitional justice
period. Cambodian cinema's unique representation of the simultaneous
presence of reconciliation and resentment as the major tension embodied in the survivor-perpetrator confrontation adheres to this nonlinear,
vague, and ambiguous temporality and conceptualization. Both the
fiction and nonfiction films analyzed later avoid any suggestion of
future-oriented national reconciliation or forgiveness, and by this, despite
the end of the genocide, they clearly accentuate the blurred difference
between the pre- and post-KR periods, which, reflecting the inability to
differentiate, becomes a schism between "Cambodia's historical genocide" and "the Cambodian nation." Based on previous massive deception, secrecy and misinformation, and the earlier-mentioned contemporary crushing debates that took place after the ECCC hearings, it also
reflects both the self-deception and "innerism" ("a pathological alienation from self and society" at the heart of collective consciousness) that
the films structure as well as undermine.[20]

Fifth, and above all, I claim, the tension between reconciliation and
resentment and the emphasis on moral resentment are embodied in the
films dealing with high-ranking KR perpetrators: Bruno Carette and Sien
Meta's *Bitter Khmer Rouge* (*Khmers Rouges Amers*, France/Cambodia,
2007); Rob Lemkin and Thet Sambath's *Enemies of the People: A Personal
Journey Into the Heart of the Killing Fields* (UK/Cambodia, 2009); Roshane
Saidnattar's *Survive: In the Heart of Khmer Rouge Madness* (*L'important
c'est de rester vivant*, France, 2009); Guillaume P. Suon's *About My Father*;
and Rithy Panh's *Duch, Master of the Forges of Hell* (*Duch, le maître des*

forges de l'enfer, France/Cambodia, 2011).[21] Mostly made between 2007 and 2011, these documentary films establish the cinematic phenomenon I term Big Perpetrator Cinema, a corpus that at its best focuses on understanding and comprehending the Cambodian genocide through the high-ranking perpetrator's point of view as it is revealed in the course of direct confrontation with a survivor.[22] The detailed voice of the Big Perpetrator is mediated by this unique corpus and is heard against the proceedings of the ECCC, which, since its establishment in 2006, I argue, serves as a backdrop to and a focal point of reference for perpetrator cinema.

As the New Cambodian documentary cinema shows, the twentieth-century enigma concerning the perpetrator's monstrosity needs to be recontextualized in relation to the autogenocidal nature of the Cambodian genocide. Under the unprecedented circumstances of the complicity of most of the Cambodian people with the Pol Pot regime (whether voluntarily when, often as young people following the KR propaganda against Vietnam, King Norodom Sihanouk's support of the KR, and US carpet bombing during the early 1970s, they joined the movement, or involuntarily under the regime's terror and suppression), defining the corpus of Big Perpetrator Cinema means direct reference to the high-ranking perpetrators.[23] However, it entails an additional, symbolic layer of reference both to the huge number of (mostly hidden) low-ranking perpetrators and to bystander-perpetrators (being everywhere and nowhere).[24] Interviewing the Big Brothers and simultaneously reflecting on the entire community of KR cadres, this corpus touches on the all-encompassing problematic of the Cambodian postgenocide human condition—threatened by a potentially massive indictment of a huge population—which is crucial to Cambodia's psychosocial and political as well as cine-cultural and postmemorial future.

Finally, as a result of these exceptional circumstances, the tension between resentment and reconciliation embodied in this corpus reflects as well on ongoing social unrest. As mentioned earlier, although forty years have passed since the liberation of Phnom Penh by the Vietnamese in 1979, it was only twenty years later, in 1999, after the death of Pol Pot and the defection of the last KR militant to Hun Sen's government, that the KR movement ceased to exist. That is, current Cambodian society, militaristically reunified for only twenty years (1999–2019), still faces unsettling events that enhance the tension between resentment and reconciliation revealed in the cinema, as well as in the ECCC proceedings and the public sphere. Prior to the films' analysis, I will briefly describe two such events as background: the Jarvis and the Roux scandals.

The Jarvis scandal first broke out when it was publicized that Helen Jarvis, who is Western, i.e., non-Cambodian, was appointed to serve as head of the Victims Support Section of the ECCC. It was alleged both that she has a longtime Communist affiliation (she is a member of the Democratic Socialist Perspective's Leninist Party Faction) and, thus, is distrusted by the victims,[25] and that she was close to Sok An, a member of Hun Sen's administration (who died in 2017).[26] The French journalist Thierry Cruvellier (who has attended all the international tribunals of the post–Cold War era) claims in his book on the ECCC, "The Cambodian government closely monitors the tribunal. . . . Nothing illustrates the atmosphere of hushed tension and ambiguity hanging over the court better than the 'Jarvis Affair.' . . . The victims of Cambodia's Communist dictatorship . . . carry very little weight. The storm passes. Ideas and Ideology, we're told, aren't relevant. Jarvis keeps her job."[27]

The second unsettling event exemplary of the tension between resentment and reconciliation, the Roux scandal, refers to the dispute between Kaing Guek Eav (Duch)'s Cambodian and international colawyers (Kar Savuth and François Roux, respectively) over Duch's final statement at the ECCC.[28] As Bernard Mangiante's documentary film *The Khmer Rouge and the Man of Non-Violence* (*Le Khmer rouge et le non-violent*, France/Cambodia, 2011), which portrays the dramatic upheavals in these relationships, shows, for Roux, the cathartic moment of Duch admitting to his guilt was what he was working toward during the entire trial. Opposing Roux, after six months of evidentiary hearings (on November 27, 2009), Kar Savuth, the Cambodian lawyer, requested acquittal on war crimes and crimes against humanity charges, and Duch's release.[29] This unanticipated precipitous request raised serious doubts about Duch's true acknowledgment of responsibility and sincere repentance.[30] The film emphasizes that Duch's request six months later (on June 9, 2010) to dismiss Roux as his defense colawyer, much to Roux's frustration and disillusionment, also raises questions in regard to Kar Savuth's secret connections with Prime Minister Hun Sen.[31]

These scandals are not just prominent examples of the inevitable dynamics entailed in the court's proceedings due to its hybridity, "based on fusing national and international laws, procedures, personnel, and political interests,"[32] or conflicting defense strategies. They are, in fact, symptoms of the social-political reality in Cambodia during the ECCC years, in which the battle over Cambodia's historical past and social-political future continues. These symptoms also embody the burden of the time passed since the establishment of the ECCC (from 2003 to 2019): The survivor and perpetrator populations in Cambodia are aging and their numbers are decreasing with each passing year. (In 2017, the seventy-five to eighty-nine age group comprised around 1.3 percent of the population—208,966 out of 16,076,370—90,266 of whom are over eighty years old. The forty-five to seventy-four age group comprised 18.65 percent of the population.)[33] That is, the majority of the Cambodian population was born after the KR's demise. This means that the challenge faced by New Cambodian interview-based Big Perpetrator Cinema is urgent and pressing.

The following analysis will focus on Bruno Carette and Sien Meta's documentary film *Bitter Khmer Rouge*, made in the pre-ECCC period. Through its uncommon perspective, presenting the perpetrator's uninterrupted point of view culminating in the perpetrators' resentment (rather than the survivor's possible resentment emanating from his or her encounter with the perpetrator's unaccountability), *Bitter Khmer Rouge* raises questions in regard to the problematics of interviewing the Big Perpetrators without confrontation, as well as the chaos emanating from a postgenocide era unacknowledged as such by the perpetrators. The film's analysis will serve, thus, as background to the analysis of the autobiographical films in the next chapter, in which the survivor puts forth an upfront, direct confrontation with the high-ranking perpetrator.

In contrast to *Bitter Khmer Rouge*, two films discussed in chapter 3, both made by first-generation survivors, embody the survivor-perpetrator confrontation to its fullest and present the two major paradigms discussed—the duel and moral resentment: In *Enemies of the People: A Personal Journey Into the Heart of the Killing Fields*, Thet Sambath (and Rob Lemkin) confront Nuon Chea, and in *Duch, Master of the Forges of Hell*, Rithy Panh confronts Kaing Guek Eve (Duch).[34] Staging the reconciliation paradigm and Derrida's elaborations on forgiveness as a background to discussing the moral resentment paradigm, the first part of the next chapter will analyze *Enemies of the People* and its surrounding public discourse. Based on the Derridean philosophy on forgiveness, I suggest that *Enemies of the People*, which ends with the arrest of Nuon Chea by the ECCC in 2007, proposes a unique epistemology moving between aporetic reconciliation and resentment.

Depicting the genealogy of resentment, and especially Jean Améry's intervention, the second part of the next chapter will analyze Rithy Panh's *Duch*. Based on interviews Panh conducted with Duch during the eight pretrial years during which Duch was imprisoned, I suggest that the film proposes an unvindictive resentment. The second part will also analyze Guillaume P. Suon's film *About My Father*, which follows for several years the journey of Phung-Guth Sunthary, a second-generation civil party in Duch's trial.[35] To conclude, Roshane Saidnattar's film *Survive: In the Heart of Khmer Rouge Madness*, in which a second-generation survivor confronts Khieu Samphan,[36] will lead to a final reflection on the role of this corpus against the backdrop of the ECCC proceedings. As a comparison, the conclusion will relate to Kulikar Sotho's fiction film *The Last Reel* (Cambodia, 2016), which, discussing low-ranking perpetrators, proposes a different perspective on the question of reconciliation vis-à-vis resentment and the postgenocide collective unconscious.

Most research on the ECCC refers to the tribunal's uniqueness:[37] its hybridity, its majority of domestic judges, the side role of the United Nations, the inclusion of victims in the proceedings as civil parties,[38] and the development of an innovative victim outreach and participation program. This research also refers to the ECCC's apparent failings beyond the key structural flaws caused by its hybridity, like its acute vulnerability to political interference.[39] However, most of these scholars did not refer to a major characteristic—the ECCC being the first international tribunal to address the crimes of Communism. The twentieth-century courts from Nuremberg (1945–49) and Tokyo (1946–48) to Rwanda (1994–2012) and former Yugoslavia (1993–2013) dealt with crimes of ultra-nationalist regimes, identified as ideologies of the Right. Among the major tribunals that dealt with crimes against humanity only the Cambodian tribunal has addressed the crimes of the Left. As Thierry Cruvellier claims, at the Cambodian tribunal a surprising number of Westerners who did not come from the far Left showed a level of sympathy for the "good intentions" of the Communist project. As a result, the trial was a trial not of Communism as a political philosophy, but of "Pol

Potism," circumscribed and vilified as a despicable betrayal of a genuine revolutionary ideal.[40]

Thus, two questions will be addressed at the conclusion of these chapters: First, in what ways does the Big Perpetrator cinema represent "Pol Potism" vis-à-vis the reconciliation/resentment issue? Second, does the spectators' juridical imaginary enable the ECCC to function as an imaginary replacement for the vast number of low-ranking perpetrators who would never be tried?

Finally, I will try to draw some general implications that will enhance the resonance of Cambodian cinema and create new understandings in regard to the contribution of perpetratorhood and the two perpetratorhood paradigms for both trauma studies and genocide studies.

THE BIG PERPETRATOR'S UNINTERRUPTED VOICE: BRUNO CARETTE AND SIEN META'S *BITTER KHMER ROUGE*

Codirected by the French scriptwriter and producer Bruno Carette and the Cambodian director Sien Meta, the documentary film *Bitter Khmer Rouge* depicts the history of the KR movement from 1970 to 2006 from the point of view of KR leaders, cadres, soldiers, and collaborators,[41] but (though the codirector Sien Meta, who conducts part of the interviews, is a survivor)[42] it does not stage any confrontation between Big Perpetrators and survivors. The film is centered on a double act of mourning: it begins and ends with representation of the funerals of two major KR figures—Pol Pot's first wife, Khieu Ponnary,[43] who died in 2003 at the age of eighty-three (one month after the United Nations and the Cambodian government signed an agreement to establish the ECCC), and the last KR military leader, Ta Mok, the commander in chief of the army and "Brother Number Five,"[44] who died in 2006 at the age of eighty-two, before he was tried. This structure—portraying the history of the KR movement in between the two funerals—reflects on both the demise of the movement and its still effervescent spirit.

Representing the funerary ritual, arguably the most important one in Buddhist practice,[45] has a special significance at the site of Khieu

Ponnary's funeral, the small town of Pailin. Located in the foothills of the Kardamom Mountains in northwestern Cambodia,[46] and bordering on Thailand to the west, Pailin was an ill-famed KR stronghold. In the opening scene of *Bitter Khmer Rouge*, an extreme long shot of the afforested town emphasizes the binary of field and forest, raising well-known connotations: the Khmer words *srok* and *prei* are traditionally paired and translatable variously as "field and forest," "civilized and savage," "domesticated and wild."[47] This representation of Pailin's landscape further establishes the contrast between the New People,[48] whose identity was attached to their enslavement as workers in the rice fields, and KR leaders and cadres, whose identity became more powerful because of their secretive hiding in the Pailin (and Anlong Veng) forests.

As Henri Lefebvre claims, space is produced via competing discursive claims, usages, and material practices.[49] The spatial "ensembles" created by the presence of high-ranking KR leaders (Ieng Sary, Ieng Thirith, Nuon Chea, and Khieu Samphan) at Khieu Ponnary's funeral rebuild Pailin beyond its function as a site of death and remembrance. During the funeral, Pailin is once again rendered as a dominant social space "closely bound up with the forces of production."[50] While the camera identifies the high-ranking KR leaders among the crowd, the narrator's voice-of-God commentary reflects on both the event and its symbolic meaning, thus questioning the inconsolability and irreconcilability of this moment of mourning: "Pol Pot's first wife Kieu Ponnary clearly succumbed to madness. As early as 1975, it is said, at the very moment the KR imposed the totalitarian dictatorship of Democratic Kampuchea. Like her, the new political leaders, some of them relatives, lost all reason . . . [and] inflicted agrarian revolution on the entire country, leading to one of the twentieth-century's most devastating tragedies."

Using Ponnary's madness, with its uncanny timing, as a symbol for the madness of the regime, it becomes apparent that the funeral scenes speak about mourning but are not "themselves texts *of* or *in* mourning."[51] When the camera follows the path of hundreds of mourners participating in the funeral parade and shows the decorated coffin covered with the national flag, we hear the narrator's voice saying, "And yet, on July 2003, homage is paid to 'The Mother of the Revolution.'" The fact that Khieu Ponnary was a prominent member of the movement in its early days but was last seen in public in 1978, and, incapacitated by mental illness since the KR victory in 1975, spent her last twenty-eight years in seclusion further accentuates the film's depiction of Pailin as an undefeated KR social space and the revolution as a major part of the KR imaginary, even after all of its leaders had defected to the Royal Government of Cambodia, been arrested, or had died.[52]

The cross-cutting from Khieu Ponnary's funeral after the second moving of the corpse to the neglected and unpopulated site of Pol Pot's grave (where he was buried five years previously, in 1998) and back to the funeral emphasizes the contrast between the Mother and the Father of the revolution.[53] In other words, the detailed representation of Khieu Ponnary's funeral pays tribute to, and reflects on, the apparently innocent and pure KR utopian-Communist ideology before its rise to power (i.e., before April 17, 1975). In this regard, Khieu Ponnary's uncontaminated image enables mourning that does not immediately evoke the 1.7 million dead who, marked as ungrievable, were not entitled to be buried during the Pol Pot years.

After the prologue, which presents the funeral, Carette and Meta's rendering of the movement's history is based on 250 hours of interviews,[54] complemented by voice-over commentary (written by Carette) and archive materials. As mentioned earlier, Reth, an ex-KR soldier who was interviewed in Pailin, sets the postfuneral tone for the entire film through his reflection on the paradoxical and preemptive failure of the ECCC—and, metonymically, the entire Cambodian society—in regard to the issue of trying low-ranking perpetrators: "Trying KR? But which KR for heaven sake? KR, but who wasn't a KR?" Following this reaction, though they emphasize firsthand testimony about the happenings, most of the directors' questions address the interviewees' participation in crucial historical events (such as the Paris-based friendship during the 1950s that led to the establishment of the inner circle of the Communist Party and King Norodom Sihanouk's support of the KR after Lon Nol's defeat)[55] and their current personal, economic, and familial situation, rather than focusing on the issues of accountability and responsibility, justice, and the ECCC. Even when the directors relate to a retrospective assessment of the past, as they do while interviewing Khieu Samphan, an ideology of "KR heterogeneity" eclipses ethical exigency.[56]

As the editing repeatedly goes back to the interview with Khieu Samphan,[57] exposing the spectator to the denial, self-justification, self-deception, and ostensible obfuscation of this prominent KR leader, the question of voice-over, of "who speaks," becomes highly problematic. This is made worse by the film's constant oscillation between insider-KR and outsider-KR points of view: Presenting the KR low-ranking stories through very short interviews (based on only few shots) raises on one hand an immediate identification (for instance, with an ex-soldier who lost his legs while fighting far away in the forest, unaware of the tragedy taking place in other areas). On the other, however, the film's deliberate nonreflexive style and adherence to the conventions of investigative journalism position the spectator as alternating between distance from the ambiguous worldview revealed and complicity with the ideology of heterogeneity, which, I suggest, entails avoidance of an ethical stand toward all that has been said.

In the midst of this ambiguous ideology, two interviews, one with Ta Mok's niece, Ven Dara, and one with Laurence Picq, stand in conspicuous contrast to each other. Ven Dara, a councilor of the opposition Cambodia National Rescue Party (CNRP) in Pailin,[58] represents a reactionary attitude to the Cambodian genocide. Showing Ven Dara during a local election campaign through empowering low-angle shots, the film's voice-over adds, "Sam Rainsy, the head of the opposition in parliament who for years has called for an international tribunal even came here to support Ra [Ven Dara], his party's representative, and to congratulate the valorized KR patriots." Then, the editing cuts to Ven Dara, who says to her supporters (all dressed in white shirts with the party slogan):

> Journalists came to ask us what we felt about the announcement of a trial to try our leaders, and does this possibility worry us. I told them that we do not fear the trial of the KR. You have to understand that when our president Sam Rainsy asks for international trial for the KR, it's to find justice. It's to find the ones who are truly guilty, and to avoid that the patriots who fought for the country be considered the assassins of the Khmer people. *Other than the Vietnamese, who else wants to kill the Cambodians?* You know very well that *the desire to bring grief and to kill the Cambodian people can only come from the Vietnamese.*[59]

During this ultrareactionary speech, the editing reveals more than a few reaction shots of members of the "valorized KR patriots," but, in contrast to Ven Dara's passion, their faces are emotionless. Undoubtedly her highly selective rendering of history discloses some of the anxiety that the (then) future tribunal might hold for her audience, but even more it discloses a society committed to a reversal of its own genocidal history. Fostered by a political agenda that deepens central conflicts and enforces contested relations, this reversal means first and foremost a conception of the genocide as not having been committed by the Cambodians themselves: i.e., as a non-autogenocide. The patterns revealed in the campaign scene (and in some of the interviews to follow) have a larger significance, as this reactionary attitude toward history (hardly acknowledged as such by the commentary or the film style) promotes old hostilities and extreme racism toward Cambodia's "eternal" enemy, the Vietnamese, as well as a KR-inclined nationalism. Staging racial antipathies as an implicit outcry against the tribunal set them as an alternative solution. Indeed, Ven Dara's speech should be seen as one of *Bitter Khmer Rouge*'s defining elements of the reactionary dimension embedded in an ideology of heterogeneity, enlarged under the mantle of "the people."

The reactionary resolution proposed by this highly contentious milieu with its escalated hostility toward justice is totally undermined by Laurence Picq's interview. The French ex-wife of Sikoeun Suong (a KR high-ranking officer) who was forced to live in Cambodia during the KR regime, Picq worked as a translator for Ieng Sary's Ministry of Foreign Affairs in the B1 compound inside evacuated Phnom Penh.[60] The editing connects between Khieu Samphan, who claims he did not know what was happening, and Picq's critique of the KR's untruth. When asked by the directors during an interview in Paris, "And when Khieu Samphan claims that he wasn't aware [of the massive killings], do you think that it's possible?" she responds:

With difficulty . . . slightly possible. . . . And that he didn't become aware. . . . This question will pertain to all the KR: the question of awareness. It is true that from the start the KR used a Buddhist concept for awareness. Awareness should be clear and straightforward. Otherwise, it is muddled. . . . There were many illusions around this idea of clear consciousness because this type of consciousness is *a consciousness without thoughts*. Thoughts are completely wiped out. Do we have a consciousness that is emerging or not? That is: do we see what is there or do we see

what we know? Take Ieng Thirith for example. She knows there are traitors everywhere, but she doesn't see the disorganization, the famine, and
that everything is going wrong. She only sees traitors. I suppose that
Khieu Samphan . . . with the help of Sihanouk . . . probably saw "paradise
on earth." . . . But we didn't see the reality.[61]

In this observation, Picq proposes a distinctive Eastern-Cambodian
form unrelated, for example, to Stanley Cohen's definition of (Western)
"cognitive errors." Backed by advances in cognitive science, neuropsychology, artificial intelligence, and brain functioning, Cohen suggests
that perception without awareness appears in three forms: negative hal-
lucinations, blindsight, and subliminal perception.[62] In contrast, Picq
reflects on an abuse of Buddhist meditative habits.

In her memoir, Picq uses a compelling metaphor that refers to the historical events she has been witness to in order to express her feelings of
loss of control and impending chaos: "The long march with death."[63] However, what distinguishes her testimony in this film the most is her total
lack of revolutionary rhetoric, which was prevalent to various degrees in
every other interviewee's discourse. She convincingly counters the reactionary history declared by Ta Mok's niece with a critical perspective of
the historical events committed to the truth. Nevertheless, being one voice
among many, as the film's linear portrayal of Cambodian history is
expanded to include the period from the final years of the civil war till
the last of the KR cadres joined the government army (that is, ongoing
KR violence for another twenty years), the commentary's tone lacks any
hint of condemnation.

I claim that although the film follows a linear narrative and the commentary covers the events that led to the KR surrendering to Hun Sen's
government, the narrative structure is not based on a "rise and fall" pattern. Rather, it emphasizes the KR's domination despite the circumstances
and, most importantly, generally avoids any critical reflection. Thus, the
last stages of the movement (beginning with Ieng Sary's defection in 1996)
are described by the voice-over as follows:

It was a Khmer-style reconciliation. . . . Ieng Sary was allowed to maintain the autonomy of his stronghold in Pailin, and was granted a
royal amnesty. . . . In the north, isolated in Anlong Veng, the KR was

weakened by infighting and could no longer resist Hun Sen's offensives. After the death of Pol Pot in 1998, Khieu Samphan and Nuon Chea . . . supported Hun Sen in exchange for their freedom. A few weeks later, in February 1999, the last KR surrendered. The only man missing was their leader, General Ta Mok.

The camera, which previously showed hundreds of Ieng Sary disciples and a long line of the KR soldiers walking back to the jungle, depicts the surrender ceremony by emphasizing that although Ta Mok was not present, it was led by the minister of defense, an ex-KR himself. The film shows the KR soldiers changing their clothes to government uniforms, and the voice-over states: "After thirty years of war, the Khmer Royal Armed Forces was finally at full strength."

Then, the editing cuts from the scene of the hundreds of (old and new) Royal soldiers waving their hands in the air to an interview with Prime Minister Hun Sen, an ex-KR, it is said, for whom national reconciliation was preferred to reawakening the past. The camera depicts Hun Sen showing a video clip of Ta Mok and declaring that capturing him marks the end of the KR movement. However, the editing, which cut short all previous events, cuts immediately to Hun Sen's worrying about the international tribunal requested by the king: "If we want the KR to die," he declares, "they'll die. . . . If we act like certain foreign countries, the KR will be back."

Hun Sen's reflections on what might be seen as the national paranoia (the "return" of the KR) are heard out loud because, avoiding any reflection on either Ta Mok's image or Hun Sen's hidden threat, the camera cuts to the Royal Palace, where the sound of the gong marks the swearing in of the ECCC judicial officers on July 3, 2006. It is only now that the commentary includes an evaluative interpretation when it says that the four years of the KR regime that will be dealt with by the tribunal are "notably absent from Cambodia school history books." Once again, however, the ambiguous tone takes over when, with the prayers of the monks and their celebratory rituals, the editing cuts back to three figures, Ven Dara, Nuon Chea, and Khieu Samphan: Ven Dara, who declares that she does not see how the current government "can try the KR," and asks "Why?" (that is, Why try them?); Nuon Chea, who once again declares, "it was a national, democratic, and independent revolution"; and Khieu Samphan, who repeats his previous statements about Vietnam as the cause of all evil. *Bitter Khmer Rouge*'s return to these voices at the end of its portrayal of KR history again strengthens heterogeneity ideology as a political worldview that, together with avoidance of a critical perspective, though it does not totally exempt the leaders from responsibility, still grants the KR movement power.

This problematic framing is emphasized by the last scene of the film, which, as mentioned earlier, presents the funeral of General Ta Mok (who was buried on July 24, 2006, in Anlong Veng, a jungle town that lies at the foot of the Dangrek Mountains on the northern Cambodian border, together with two of the most famous KR leaders, Pol Pot and Son Sen).[64] Known also as a significant KR stronghold, and as where the last KR surrendered to the government in 1999,[65] prior to the coverage of the funeral, Anlong Veng is presented by the camera and the interviewees as a disaster zone filled with mines and populated by aging KR soldiers almost starving to death, hardly making a living, and some gold miners hopefully looking for bits of gold left behind by the mining companies that had robbed and drained the area of its natural resources.

However, as Cruvellier suggests,

> Anlong Veng was the last bastion of the Big Brothers of the Revolution before they all died or surrendered. It's where Pol Pot and his most faithful associates lived out the last decade of the war, from 1988 until 1998. But Anlong Veng's true master was Ta Mok. Known within the Politburo first as Brother Number Five, then, with each successive purge or defection, as Brother Number Four, then Number Three, Ta Mok gained a reputation for being the most ruthless member of a cohort in which competition was fierce.[66]

In accordance with the presentation of Khieu Ponnary's funeral as a first act of mourning, *Bitter Khmer Rouge* presents Ta Mok's funerary rituals as a last act of mourning, once again failing to reflect on the horrendous gap between this meticulous funeral ceremony and the scattering of millions who were left unburied in the killing fields. The close-up of Ta Mok's body reveals that in keeping with ritual, it was washed. As Erik Davis, based on Li's descriptions and his own extensive ethnographic fieldwork, claims, the water used to wash the body should have been thoroughly boiled and then allowed to cool completely. The symbolism here, according to Li Sovira and other Acarya (instructors in Buddhist religious matters),[67] is that the water must be both pure and cool (calm). As the next close-up shows, once cleaned, the "doors of the body"—"mouth, eyes, ears, nose, body, and navel"[68]—were closed with pure beeswax. Li states that this is done to close "the roads of *akusala* (unskillfulness) and not let the dead person be born in *akusala*."[69] Then the body was dressed (usually the shirt is put onto the body backwards, literally, with the "buttons facing the rear"). According to religious belief, these practices help confuse the corpse and prevent it from returning home.

Davis stresses that beyond this type of preparation, the corpse is arranged into a position of homage; items of symbolic or real value are placed in or with the body. An extreme close-up shows that a bunch of one hundred-riel notes (the currency of Cambodia) carrying the picture of King Norodom Sihanouk were rolled up and put on Ta Mok's body and a collection of ritual offerings was placed in the hands of the corpse: candles, incense, betel shoots, flowers, and a betel nut knife. "These are clasped by the hands of the corpse, which were then bound together in the position of *Anjali*, or homage, on top of the chest."[70]

The camera's detailed record of these funerary rituals—including purification of body, participation of monks, and the parade route of mourners, mostly dressed in white, holding flowers, performing music, and hitting the gong—is seen simultaneously with the narrator's voice-over, which adjusts to the local perspective:

> The KR warlord Ta Mok was suspected of massive assassinations and widely known as "the butcher," but here nobody believes he is guilty of such crimes. . . . Ta Mok was popular here. There is a school, a hospital, roads and dams for irrigation. . . . He was a good leader, a patriot too, they say. . . . In Anlong Veng or Pailin, and even in the corridors of power at Phnom Penh the idea of justice and crimes against humanity is far from a unanimous approval.

The film ends with a scene in which the coffin is covered with the national flag and a close-up on the symbol of Angkor Wat, reflecting on the possible return not only of the Cambodian glorified Angkorian past (which occurred between the ninth century and the fifteenth) but, inevitably, of Angkar, Cambodia's Communist Party.[71]

Does this funeral depiction consolidate the very power of the context? In other words, is it a (last) tribute to "the butcher"? Undoubtedly, the presentation of the two funerals contributes to a regeneration of the distinctive culture of the KR, its unique belief system and the characteristic behavior of its followers without questioning their postgenocide affiliation as such. Moreover, as its title suggests, *Bitter Khmer Rouge* emphasizes the enmity that lurks beneath the apparently homogenous surface of the surrender after 1999 of the last KR cadres to the Hun Sen government while simultaneously reflecting with skepticism on the ECCC's promise of rendering justice. Most importantly, although it presents the point of view of dozens of former ex-KR soldiers, mid-ranking KR officials, significant figures who were directly connected to the revolution's elite, leaders (especially Nuon Chea and Khieu Samphan), and the current prime minister, Hun Sen—the film fails to reflect on the KR's powerful appeal and hold, and thus, I claim, becomes complicit with the prevalent point of view it depicts.

Made in the pre-ECCC period and rendered from the perpetrators' uninterrupted point of view, the film does not present the tension embodied in a direct duel with a survivor (as will be described in the following chapter). *Bitter Khmer Rouge* also avoids negotiation with the question of reconciliation embodied within the KR surrender. Rather, apparently breaching Cambodia's illusioned democratic forms,[72] the film breaks the prevailing conceptualization of the KR as a homogenous body and presents its heterogeneity as well as its still violent-by-spirit diversity. The perpetrators (particularly the Big Perpetrators, but also other elite cadres) are reintroduced by the film into the shared moral sphere, although, paradoxically, they pretend to never have left it. Thus, the question of presenting the perpetrators' voices (as a miswritten history that raises major questions of responsibility and accountability) shifts the focus from a purely cognitive or epistemological question—a problem of knowing and not-knowing—to a question of communicating *to others*: a problem of address. Together with offering various voices that mostly confirm the movement's power (and undermine the ECCC's objectives for justice) rather than introducing new insights into the movement's history, this attitude characterizes *Bitter Khmer Rouge* as an exceptional reactionary document among the Cambodian (and Cambodian-French) films that present the perpetrators or the tribunal.

BACKGROUND: RECONCILIATION
AND FORGIVENESS

Before analyzing the representation of the survivor-perpetrator duel in the Big Perpetrator films, I will discuss the major theoretical writings that contribute to the evolution of the concepts of reconciliation and forgiveness.[73]

The evolution of the reconciliation paradigm, developed mainly during and after the South African Truth and Reconciliation Commission work[74] (for example, Ervin Staub, John Bornerman, Ernesto Verdeja, Damien Short, Andrew Schaap, Jens Meierhenrich, Jeffrey K. Olick, Ann Rigney, and Eve Monique Zucker),[75] reveals that the conceptualization of reconciliation continues to be a source of great perplexity.

John Paul Lederach, who has developed one of the few theoretical conceptualizations of reconciliation, suggests that as a peacemaking paradigm, reconciliation involves "the creation of a 'social space' where truth, justice, mercy, and forgiveness are validated and joined together, rather than being forced into a confrontation where one must win out over the other."[76] As Robert I. Roteberg claims, in its early stages, the underlying goal of reconciliation was prevention through understanding. In order to fully come to terms with their brutal pasts, societies had to uncover, in precise detail, who did what to whom and why, and under whose orders. This was done through establishment of an investigative tribunal, a truth commission. By attempting to acknowledge and atone for past injustices in novel ways and focusing on restoring and rebuilding relationships, these reconciliation initiatives foster state legitimacy, forgiveness, and social stability.[77] Fueled by examples such as the TRC, Damien Short suggests as well that the reconciliation paradigm as a means for social stability has identified and appropriately addressed the multiple sources of the "conflict," moving away from prosecutions and embracing "an ideal of *restorative justice.*"[78]

In other words, the reconciliation paradigm as a process that leads to social stability seeks to repair injustice and to effect changes both in the present and in the future. If indeed truth and reconciliation commissions typically operate in certain historical contexts, that of transitions from authoritarian or totalitarian regimes to more democratic ones (as in the case in South Africa after forty-three years of Apartheid), the "transitional justice" they establish becomes, as Short suggests, a cornerstone for a founding of a legitimate political order from the ashes of an illegitimate prior regime. However, these conceptualizations, which emerged from varied postgenocide and transitional justice contexts, are not suitable to the Cambodian case, in which the current regime, though not totalitarian, it is still authoritarian and led by former KRs. Thus, although the ECCC was established after the South African TRC was over, it could not apply the latter's seven years of experience and embrace its societal-legal conclusions because of the immense differences in both past and current contexts.

Are other conceptualizations of reconciliation relevant to the Cambodian context? John Borneman's definition of reconciliation, for example, is based neither on a permanent peace or harmony nor on an *ideal moral community* that is prior to (and so transcends) any actually existing political community, as most of the research cited earlier claims. Rather, he defines reconciliation as a project of *departure from violence* based on a solid conception of temporality.[79] This perspective, I suggest, adds to the reasons why the TRC lesson is irrelevant to the Cambodian case. Referring to ethnic cleansing, Borneman suggests,

> To reconcile is an intersubjective process, an agreement to settle accounts that involves at least two subjects who are related in time. They are related in a temporal sense not in that they necessarily have a shared past or even think of themselves as sharing a concrete future. Rather, to reconcile, different subjects must agree only "to render no longer opposed," which means sharing a present, a present that is non-repetitive. . . . To agree to a present that does not repeat requires both to create a "sense of ending"—a radical break or rupture from existing relations—and to create a "sense of beginning"—a departure into new relations of affinity marked not by cyclical violence but by trust and care. (282)

Moreover, according to Borneman, "Legal accounting is never capable of redressing all of the wrongs perpetrated. . . . But its significance derives not from the efficiency and comprehensiveness of its prosecutions but rather from the political efficacy of prosecuting select, symbolically significant cases—what might be called a *ritual purification of the center*—and thus creating a sense of end to the set of injustices" (298, emphasis in the original).

However, after thirteen years of activity, since 2006, the ECCC, which tried Duch, Nuon Chea, and Khieu Samphan (Case Nos. 001 and 002), faces political pressures aimed to block this "purified center," to use Borneman's term, and to prevent the trying of Case Nos. 003 and 004. It seems, thus, that the Cambodian case, marked by both its ambiguous temporality and the ECCC proceedings, defies these reconciliatory characterizations.

In contrast to Borneman's emphasis on symbolization, Ann Rigney, for example, claims,

> Trials, apologies, gestures are perceived as a means to effect new social relations or reactivate old ones . . . though it is apparent . . . that symbolic measures are often initially welcomed, but subsequently perceived as insufficient in themselves. . . . At times, the reconciliation scenario itself may help obfuscate the fact that past injustices have persisted into the present and that a radical change in the present, and not just symbolic gestures towards the past, may be required.[80]

Thus, she adds, "The very desire to 'move on' from the past is often in the interest of the perpetrators of violence, including states, who have been adept in using the rhetoric of reconciliation and the politics of regret to obfuscate current injustice."[81] Indeed, the Cambodian case proves this scenario true, with the Hun Sen regime embracing the Bornemanian symbolic temporality by which the court reaffirms, with the authority of the state behind it, the fiction of "an end."

Expanding Rigney's critical perspective, Andrew Schaap claims, "Since Marx's critique of Hegel, reconciliation has often been suspected of being an inherently conservative concept because it casts social conflict as always in the service of the unity of the state."[82] Consequently, following popular and academic debates about reconciliation in the 1990s, he discusses six objections to the framing of politics in terms of reconciliation:

The concept of reconciliation stands accused of being too *vague* to form a coherent political project; *illiberal* because it looks forward to an ideal of community that is not compatible with the pluralism of modern societies; *question-begging* since it aims to restore a prior state of harmony that never actually existed; *assimilative* in that it represents the political claims of the ruled only in terms commensurate with the interests of the rulers; *quietist* insofar as it demands resignation to the injustices of the past and forgoing resentment of their continuing legacy; and *exculpatory* in that it provides an opportunity to redeem the good conscience of the nation primarily through symbolic gestures.[83]

The Cambodian context, it seems, is highly susceptible to Schaap's critique.

As even this cursory review suggests, the conceptualization of reconciliation continues to be a source of great perplexity, and in the Cambodian case, I claim, is revealed to be repressive as well. Part of this perplexity has to do with another objection (not mentioned by Schaap) to the framing of politics in terms of reconciliation. Following Schaap's parlance, I suggest that the concept of reconciliation might stand accused of being *universalized*: the various conceptualizations of reconciliation stem from specific historical situations and are highly context-dependent, but they pretend to reflect a context-transcendent universal truth. On a similar line, Jeffrey K. Olick claims that forgiveness is a concept with a history of its own, one that at different historical moments has different meanings. In contrast to contemporary philosophical discourses, which address forgiveness as a general principle rather than as a product of history, Olick proposes "the politics of regret," a new political accountability based on the ethics of responsibility. Its "hallmark feature . . . is the propensity toward, and advocacy of, forgiveness not simply between persons . . . but within and between collectivities as well."[84] The politics of regret strives to overcome forgiveness as a noncontextual concept that, grounded in historical context, will expand beyond the "superhuman request for forgiveness" (91). Though the Cambodian films analyzed later show that historical contextualizing is indeed crucial, they do not propose a response to the difficulty pointed to by Olick (which in itself stems from the World War II German context), who says, "The question is . . . whether there can ever be an ethically responsible politics of regret or whether all such calls are ultimately expressions of an irrational moralism, perhaps well motivated but blind to reality."[85]

In his seminal work "On Forgiveness," Derrida opposes the underlying premises of the reconciliation paradigm described earlier and goes beyond the horizon it suggests and against the "ceremony of culpability." He elucidates the tensions in the relation between ethics and politics (and by this reflects more extensively on the problematic aspects raised by the major works on reconciliation),[86] proposing a sharp differentiation between forgiveness and all related themes such as regret, excuse, reconciliation, and amnesty. Expressing his dissatisfaction with existing models, he put forth a notion of forgiveness based on a radical purity.

In order to unfold this radical perception, Derrida discusses an essay by the French philosopher Vladimir Jankélévitch written in 1967 ("Should We Pardon Them?"). Referring to the Germans, Jankélévtich passionately argues that the terrible deeds committed during the Holocaust are irreparable, inexpiable, and unforgivable. Derrida agrees with Jankélévitch that forgiveness is impossible; however, unlike with Jankélévitch's claims (and Hannah Arendt's in *The Human Condition*), he defines the paradox of forgiveness: for Derrida, "forgiveness forgives only the unforgivable" and "forgiveness must announce itself as impossibility itself."[87]

Striving to avoid the useful mystification, abusive rhetoric, inauthenticity, corruption, and trivialization of forgiveness, and the (mostly made by the nation-state) calculated transactions of reconciliation that inevitably entail conditions agreed to in advance, Derrida emphasizes the contrast between responsible ethics and irresponsible politics that stands at the heart of his thought:

> Each time forgiveness is at the service of a finality, be it noble and spiritual (atonement or redemption, reconciliation, salvation), each time that it aims to re-establish a normality (social, national, political, psychological) by a work of mourning, by some therapy or ecology of memory, then the "forgiveness" is not pure—nor is its concept. Forgiveness is not, it *should not be*, normal, normative, normalising. It *should* remain exceptional and extraordinary, in the face of the impossible: as if it interrupted the ordinary course of historical temporality. (31–32, emphases in the original)

Foregrounding what he perceives as the Abrahamic language (which brings together Judaism, the Christianities, and the Islams) for discussing forgiveness, Derrida stages the aporia between a conditional forgiveness, which he associates with reconciliation, and a pure forgiveness arising from a Levinasian unconditional ethical injunction. He stresses that pure forgiveness is an effect of relations and differences based on these poles, the unconditional and the conditional, and that these poles are heterogeneous, irreducible, and indissociable. Thus, "Forgiveness is mad . . . a madness of the impossible" (39).

Can Derrida's deconstructive rearticulation of forgiveness and his hyperbolic ethics, which "carries itself beyond laws, norms, or any obligation. Ethics beyond ethics" (35–36), pave the way in a world in which "the proliferation of scenes of repentance, or of asking 'forgiveness,' signifies, no doubt, a *universal urgency* of memory?" And, if "*it is necessary* to turn toward the past; and *it is necessary* to take this act of memory, of self-accusation, of 'repentance,' of appearance [*comparution*] at the same time beyond the juridical instance, or that of the Nation-State" (28, emphases in the original), how will this act be carried out?

Given that "the concept of the 'crime against humanity' remains on the horizon of the entire geopolitics of forgiveness" (30), Derrida claims that "forgiveness must engage two singularities: the guilty (the 'perpetrator' as they say in South Africa) and the victim. As soon as a third party intervenes, one can again speak of amnesty, reconciliation, reparation, etc., but certainly not of pure forgiveness" (42). Elaborating and repeating this creed, Derrida contends, "if anyone has the right to forgive, it is only the victim, and not a tertiary institution. For, in addition, even if this spouse is also a victim, well, the absolute victim, if one can say that, remains her dead husband. Only the dead man could legitimately consider forgiveness. The survivor is not ready to substitute herself, abusively, for the dead" (44).

The imperative against the Third, which usually means an affirmation of sovereignty, closes Derrida's essay on forgiveness: "What I dream of, what I try to think as the 'purity' of a forgiveness worthy of its name, would be a forgiveness without power: *unconditional but without sovereignty*. The most difficult task, at once necessary and apparently impossible, would be to dissociate *unconditionality* and *sovereignty*" (52). Breaking what he regards as a dangerous cathexis, Derrida uses the metaphor of the abyss to indicate the site of responsibility. I suggest that this radical reworking of this basic Levinasian term, finally described as metaphor, is highly pertinent to the Cambodian autogenocide:

> There could be, in effect, all sorts of proximity (where the crime is between people who know each other): language, neighbourhood, familiarity, even family, etc. But in order for evil to emerge, "radical evil" and perhaps worse again, the unforgivable evil, the only one which would make the question of forgiveness emerge, it is necessary that at the most intimate of that intimacy an absolute hatred would come to interrupt the peace. This destructive hostility can only aim at what Levinas calls the "face" of the Other, the similar other, the closest neighbour, between the Bosnians and Serbs, for example, within the same quarter, the same house, sometimes in the same family. Must forgiveness saturate the abyss? (49–50)[88]

The conceptions of aporetic reconciliation and un-vindictive resentment, which will be presented later as characterizing the New Cambodian Big Perpetrator cinema, are derived from Derrida's argumentation in regard to the aporia that stands at the heart of the concept of pure forgiveness and from Améry's intervention into traditional and prevalent philosophical and psychological conceptions of resentment. Since for Derrida ethics makes unconditional demands, he argues that in politics the negotiation of the nonnegotiable will lead to ethical responsibility. In other words, the aporia is the *experience* of responsibility. Thus, what looks like an impasse hanging over an abyss in relation to both the aporia-based reconciliation and resentment in this corpus in fact provokes thinking along new paths. As will be elaborated on in the next chapter, Améry's novelty lies in opposing resentment as an attitude based, among other negative emotions, on direct or sublimated revenge.

3

PERPETRATORHOOD PARADIGMS

The Duel and Moral Resentment

Where the violations are brutal, severe, and intimate, it can be a new assault to expect the victims to forgive.

—MARTHA MINOW[1]

You're a liar.
You can't deny knowing about the killings, everybody knew about the killings, "A dead elephant could never be covered with a flat basket."

—ANNEMARIE PRINS[2]

A DIRECT SURVIVOR-PERPETRATOR CONFRONTATION, APORETIC RECONCILIATION, AND UNVINDICTIVE RESENTMENT

ROB LEMKIN AND THET SAMBATH'S *ENEMIES OF THE PEOPLE: A PERSONAL JOURNEY INTO THE HEART OF THE KILLING FIELDS*

As a supra-docu-activist film, Rob Lemkin and Thet Sambath's *Enemies of the People: A Personal Journey Into the Heart of the Killing Fields* (UK/Cambodia, 2009) charts the ten-year quest of first-generation codirector

Thet Sambath to find truth in regard to the genocide and its victims.[3] Sambath, who tells the story of his quest through the voice-over, began his project in 1998, while he was still working as a journalist at the *Phnom Penh Post*.[4] Motivated by the murder of his mother, father, and brother, and a deep incomprehension of why the Khmer Rouge (KR) unleashed such violence on its compatriots, he decides to seek explanations from former KR officials. In 2001, he met Nuon Chea, who was then living in Prum, a small town on the Thai-Cambodian border. For around three years, Sambath continued visiting and interviewing him without telling him of his own family's fate during the years of Democratic Kampuchea (DK). In 2004, Nuon Chea first admitted to Sambath that he had made decisions with Pol Pot to kill compatriots. Encouraged by this turning point in their relationship, for three more years Sambath continued to interview him on his role in the genocide. Using a video camera, he later kept all the hundreds of tapes in a locked chest in his home in Phnom Penh.

During the same period, Sambath also built a network of less senior KR officials and cadres who were prepared to acknowledge and relate in detail their role in the genocide. The film focuses on two perpetrators in the northwest of Cambodia, Khoun (who admits to overseeing the killing of over thirty-five hundred people during KR rule) and Suon (who admits to killing between 1976 and 1978 over two hundred Cambodians designated "enemies of the people").[5] Khoun and Suon take Sambath to the scenes of their massacres, where they describe their deeds in graphic detail, and later introduce him to their superior officer, a woman known as "Sister Em."[6]

During Sambath's last meeting with Khoun and Suon, they light a number of torches in a former killing field, partially reenacting their past preparation for the killings, which took place at night. While the sound of thunder is heard, an extreme long shot of the field shows the lightning above the torches. However, these symbolic marks of a storm hardly prepare the spectator for the confessions soon to be heard. Attached to Sambath's point of view (and voice-over), the spectator is exposed to unexpected horror. Suon, a KR militia commander, confesses that when they finished the killings, "Comrade Kouch offered me something to taste. . . . He said it was human gallbladder [bile]. I got used to the taste and drank it often. It was bitter but it tasted good. So I always carried a human gall-bladder to sip." Responding to Sambath's following question, if this was thought to have some medicinal benefit, they relate that the people from the social affairs office said, "Drinking human gallbladder [bile] could cure dengue fever." They added, "We believed it made the body cool down. So sometimes when you eat your body becomes hot but you can cool yourself down with human gall. Your skin became much cooler." Then Suon says, "Now I don't want to do it anymore. Now I am completely normal. Now I am appalled by the idea of smashing people to get gallbladders."

The entire confession scene is filmed as if flooded with the red light of the fire. The camera gazes at both Khoun's and Suon's faces lit in red, emphasizing their red faces and red eyeballs through extreme close-ups. In this way, Sambath and Lemkin's camera symbolically visualizes the victims' blood, the disembowelment, and the executioners' everlasting contamination by their crimes against humanity.[7] The color stresses that because of their obscene, desecrated, and atrocious behavior, they are still immersed in blood. Since this scene appears toward the end of the film, after Sambath has built close relationships with the perpetrators, cannibalism alters in retrospect the film's view of the perpetrators, preventing any option of inclination toward reconciliation.

I suggest that despite Khoun's and Suon's admissions, *Enemies of the People* stages the exposure of gallbladder (*brâmat*) cannibalism as an irresolvable irredeemable act, committed not outside the bounds of the social rules of the period, not as a prohibited action, but, on the contrary, as a relatively widespread and regular practice of the KR's society of cruelty.[8] Moreover, this gruesome taboo-ized violence stands as a metaphor for the entire autogenocide because the figure of the perpetrator-cannibal confounds the distinction between self and other: not only before the cannibalism are they the same, part of the same people, but they are even more perversely so after the cannibalism. Thus, though the Cambodian perpetrators attempt to devour their enemies, they become self-contradictory, self-consuming figures. As is well known, according to Freud's *Totem and Taboo*, totemism became a "substitute" for killing and eating the father, a kind of "endocannibalism" (to be explained later), and the model for social rules.[9] In contrast to the conventional taxonomy found in anthropological and cultural research on cannibalism, which stresses the difference between endocannibalism ("the volitional eating of someone from within the group") and exocannibalism ("eating someone from outside the group"),[10] the Cambodian cannibal-ism, both endo- and exo-, was a form of bodily nontotemized aggres-sion that induced terror. However, I suggest that above all, this visceral embodiment of the enemy affirms again and again the "dark bond"[11] of interconnectedness between aggressor and victim. Through this hor-rific self-contradictory act, incorporation, assimilation, and digestion made both of them "one flesh" once again, in total contrast to the KR's classicide[12] policy of total elimination by smashing (kamtech)[13] those labeled an enemy.

The cannibalism scene is connected through the editing to the final scenes of the film. Sambath discloses his personal story to Chea only at the end of the film, just before, in 2007, Chea was arrested by the Extraor-dinary Chambers in the Courts of Cambodia for the Prosecution of Crimes Committed during the Period of Democratic Kampuchea (ECCC) and charged with war crimes and crimes against humanity.[14] They spend the night before Chea's arrest together. The morning after, the scene of the arrest is conveyed in the film through the media coverage, as if Sambath (and Lemkin) are unwilling to record what has been transformed at once from a highly personal (and secretive) event to a collective (and publicized) one. At the end of the official media report of the historical moment of Chea's arrest, Sambath is seen and his voice (in a sound bridge) is heard, admitting, "When he [Chea] was taken into the aircraft, that made me very sad . . . not to say he's a good man . . . but because we had worked together for almost ten years . . . I am sad, yeah."

The film's ethical attitude toward Chea is revealed close to its conclu-sion, which is the end of the quest for the truth, and, I suggest, is embodied in the editing and use of archival material: After the words "I am sad, yeah," the close-up on Sambath's gloomy face changes to black and white; then, through establishing a color association, the editing cuts to the black-and-white final scenes of the film: the archival clips of Tuol Sleng (S-21) filmed by the Vietnamese when they first entered the rooms of the execution center. These clips include the horrific picture of a corpse chained to an iron bed with shackles on its ankles, a vulture walking by its side; an oven full of skulls and bones; a huge number of skulls and corpses interspersed, some of the mouths open in a cry. The skulls and bones fill the entire frame while the sound of the countryside is heard. Then the black and white changes back to color and the editing cuts to

Sambath, standing in the green countryside. We hear his voice saying, "I have bought some land along the border. I must stop researching the past. . . . I plan to plant some fruit trees . . . Now the project is finished, I plan to stop and take a rest." As he walks up a hill his figure gradually disappears and we hear once again (through a sound bridge) his self-reflective decision: "I need to stop researching the past. I would like to spend more time with my family, my children, my wife . . . and concentrate on farming the land." Then, a series of close-ups on the mucky water of a swamp (a previous killing field) is followed by a last extreme long shot of the swamp.

The psychosocial logics and processes culminating in Sambath's final statement and embodied in his pledge to stop the search, consciously adhering to traumatic nonrepetition, rest on the recuperation of losses that are, in fact, unrecoupable. Consequently, a question that sheds light on the entire corpus of the Big Perpetrator Cinema arises: Do the editing and imagery point to another (and perhaps also different) inclination, that of resentment? The achievements of the film in terms of investigative journalism of perpetratorhood include its breakthrough on multiple levels: the establishment of a continuing dialogue with the perpetrators; the disclosure of the truth through Nuon Chea's admission of the killing; revealing methods of killing used by low-ranking perpetrators like Suon and Khoun, especially through reenactments of murder scenes; disclosure of the fear existing among low- and mid-level perpetrators like Sister Em, still preferring to hide in rural Cambodia (combined with their denial of responsibility); and the uncovering of atrocious tabooized acts like cannibalism and murder-meant-for-cannibalism. However, it is clear that these achievements do not include Chea's full accountability, proposed directly and symbolically under the prodding of the survivor's questions.

I suggest, therefore, that the Tuol Sleng clips, which appear just after Sambath's expression of sadness over Chea's arrest, are a replacement for what Chea did not acknowledge, a final step that demonstrates the film's acknowledgment of Chea's failed accountability and truth-telling. Moreover, the bubbling turbid swamps that were filled with unburied bodies speak again for the dead, who motivated the entire quest. Thus, following Sambath's last self-reflective resolution, an ethical stand of unvindictive resentment is revealed through the film's final imagery and editing.

APORETIC RECONCILIATION:
ENEMIES OF THE PEOPLE AND ITS POLITICS

This resentment toward the past and the film's avoidance of any hint of reconciliation stands in contrast to the conciliatory mood that dominates *Enemies of the People*'s surrounding discourse. This discourse combines Sambath's and Lemkin's public statements and interviews,[15] their refusal to hand over the interview tapes to the ECCC as evidence of Nuon Chea's admission of the mass killing,[16] Sambath's book with Korean journalist Gina Chon, *Behind the Killing Fields: A Khmer Rouge Leader and One of His Victims* (2010),[17] the film's promotion in festival circuits, information on the film website, and extra features on the DVD. This discourse reveals a complex attitude in regard to both the portrait of Nuon Chea and the issue of reconciliation.[18] Mostly developed after the film's release, it not only calls for forgiveness and reconciliation, but also assists in promoting them in every way possible,[19] culminating in organizing a dialogue between the perpetrators and their victims.

For example, Sambath and Chon's book *Behind the Killing Fields*, based on more than one thousand hours of interviews obtained over a six-year period, unfolds Sambath's and Chea's life chronologies. On the final pages, Sambath quotes Chea saying,

> Now all the blame is put on Democratic Kampuchea leaders. But we are not cruel. We are compatriots. . . . The court could not try my heart but my heart already tried me. So don't accuse me of being cruel. The court could only imprison my body but not my heart. Even if the court says I am not guilty, I already tried myself and have remorse because I gave up my self to serve my nation and the people since I was young but it was not fruitful. I think the court is a hot battlefield for me. I have to struggle with the court to find justice for Cambodia, the victims, and the KR.[20]

Indirectly relating to Chea's denial of his genocidal crimes, Sambath concludes the book by saying, "Revenge and hatred are big mistakes that caused many innocent people to be killed. . . . That's why finding out the truth and understanding are better. I let go of my feelings to find out the truth for the Cambodian people and the victims. Now I understand everything and my search is over."[21]

This conciliatory mood stands in sharp contrast to the horrific annihilation embodied in the archival footage and the repeated filming of
the still-boiling swamps presented at the end of *Enemies of the People*,
which are "replacements," as I suggested earlier, for Nuon Chea's refusal
to admit accountability and responsibility. I claim that the ethical complexity of Sambath's (and Lemkin's) overall discourse, with its internal
contradictions, points to what I term *aporetic reconciliation*. This term,
which combines Derrida's critique of the politics of reconciliation and
his open-ended conceptualization of aporia as a radical mechanism of
intervention, captures the complex relationships between the film and
its surrounding postproduction, distributive, and docu-activist politics
and discourse.

Moreover, the film's main title—*Enemies of the People*—reflects as well
on this complexity and contradiction, unanticipated by the major writings on reconciliation mentioned earlier. The title is, in fact, a direct quotation from Nuon Chea heard during the turning point in the interviews
in 2004, when for the first time in three years he admits that the massive
killings, previously denied, were committed. Chea refers to those the
regime considered traitors, who conducted "treacherous activities," by
saying, "They were categorized as criminals." In response to Sambath's
following question—"What did you do to those 'criminals'?"—Chea says,
"They were killed and destroyed. . . . They were enemies of the people."
However, this expression has a double-edged meaning, referring not only
to the Cambodians murdered by the regime, but also to the KR leaders
and cadres who after the fall of the regime were considered enemies of
the Cambodian people.

In addition, the film's secondary title—*A Personal Journey Into the
Heart of the Killing Fields*—refers both to Sambath's journey and to
Roland Joffé's *The Killing Fields* (UK, 1984), the first international fiction
film to present Pol Pot's horrors to the West, albeit from a Western journalist's point of view.[22] Thus, it signifies a reappropriation of this cinematic historiography by a Cambodian point of view and by the documentary mode as the preferred ethical mode for addressing the genocide.[23]
Even more, it stresses the profound ethical challenge of presenting an
autogenocide while strongly presenting the perpetrators' perspective
without falling into the (Western) "heart-of-darkness" Orientalist Sava-
gism of the Pol Pot regime. I suggest that the main title's ambiguity (which

stands in contrast to the secondary title's reappropriation) makes this ethical complexity less clear.

Thus, unvindictive resentment based on the unredemptive dynamics of the autogenocide entails ramifications in relation to both the personal and the collective levels embodied in the film's attitude toward the past (and not only toward Nuon Chea). If mercy indeed embodies the public dimension and forgiveness embodies its private one,[24] we should ask: Is forgiveness, referred to through Sambath's (and Lemkin's) surrounding discourse, an individual act or a social one intended to unite the community-to-be-reconciled? I suggest that Sambath's momentary conciliatory mode, which he declares in the film as the end of his quest, embodies this fictional construct of "an end." However, regardless of this moment of conciliatory feeling, *Enemies of the People* as a whole is based on an unvindictive resentment. Directed toward both the end-of-quest and posttraumatic repetition and the bubbling killing fields, it serves as a symbol of the opposite—the unburied dead, the buried accountability of truth.

These internal ethical contradictions, embodied in the relationship between the film and its postproduction discourse and constructing aporetic reconciliation, are not meant to be resolved. Devoid of aura, the momentarily conciliatory mode represented at the end of *Enemies of the People* entails a terminal aporia, which, expressed in the entire film, does not call for integration of thought (epistemophilic truth-revealing, transitional justice contemplating), action (a ten-year quest, interviewing, acting-out, memorialization), and emotion (sorrow for the dead, obsession, dread, mourning, nonrepetition, distanciation).[25] It is to this aporia that action and the catharsis of feelings and emotions are called upon not to provide a solution, but instead, unvindictive resentment as a response.

BACKGROUND: *RESSENTIMENT*/RESENTMENT

Ressentiment is the French word for "resentment" (from the Latin intensive prefix *re*, and *sentir*, "to feel"—*resentir* means "to re-sent," to feel again). Manfred Frings, the editor of the German editions of the German philosopher Max Scheler's works, says that "the French word possesses a peculiar strong nuance of a lingering hate that our English word 'resentment' does not always carry."[26] To his claim that the German language does not even have a word for *ressentiment,* Scheler adds the German word *Groll* (grudge, rancor), which covers a basic component of the meaning of the vernacular French use of the noun *ressentiment* (21). Frings emphasizes two initial forms of *ressentiment* mentioned by Scheler that have a particular meaning in German: *Scheelsucht* ("which refers to an uninterrupted blind impulse to detract, 'cross-eyed,' a very strong need to look askance at others, to disparage") and *Schadenfreude* ("reveling in someone else's bad luck and misfortune") (17–18). Thomas Brudholm, who follows the genealogy of *ressentiment,* proposes that the noun *ressentiment* has been found in French literature since the sixteenth century and that the strongly negative connotation it acquired appeared only later.[27]

As most of the scholars dealing with the subject point out,[28] even before Nietzsche spread the word *ressentiment* as a *terminus technicus* in his philosophy, the Danish philosopher Søren Kierkegaard said in *The Present Age* (1846) that his own time was marked by the rise of *ressentiment as a particular* envy. The connotation of malice appeared later in Nietzsche's and Scheler's philosophy. Nietzsche explains in *The Genealogy of Morals* (1887) that *ressentiment* is a dark passion caused by affects like anger, pathological vulnerability, and impotent desire for revenge.[29] He portrays psychologically the type of person who harbors *ressentiment* as embodying the mental attitude of the weak and powerless—the *schelechtwegekommene*—against their aristocratic masters. As slaves cannot revolt against noble men openly, they try to discredit them and their achievements, leading to a falsification of all genuine sensations and compensating themselves indulgingly with an "imaginary revenge."[30]

In his introduction to the fifth edition of Max Scheler's *Ressentiment* (2010, originally published in 1914), Manfred Frings regards Scheler's investigation into resentment as a work that marks the modern era because of its intrigue dealing with the nonrational and emotional depth of being human. In contrast to the tradition of Descartes, ruling since the seventeenth century, which recognized reason as the essence of being human, Frings praises Scheler's delving into the "darkest spheres of human feelings" through an explicit acknowledgment that "the human heart has its *own* reasons."[31] Describing Scheler's contribution, Frings points to a three-fold definition of *ressentiment*:

> 1. Ressentiment is an incurable, persistent feeling of hating and despising which occurs in certain individuals and groups. It takes its root in equally incurable *impotencies* or weaknesses that those subjects constantly suffer from, . . . 2. Any feeling of ressentiment stemming from impotency in a ressentiment-subject is accompanied by hidden feelings of self-disvalue over against others, . . . 3. The constant state of ressentiment is distinguished sharply from furious reactions or outbursts of anger.[32]

Analyzing resentment, Brudholm, more than any of the other scholars mentioned earlier, highlights the repetition typical to the process of becoming "a man of *ressentiment*." He suggests that in *ressentiment*, according to Scheler, a particular negative or hostile emotional reaction to someone or something is repeatedly relived, and that through this repeated experiencing "the emotion in question might become a deep-seated character trait of the person: a gloomy and engrained hostility—perhaps, one may add, generalized and directed toward all sorts of things or persons. . . . 'Ressentiment' . . . finally takes shape through the repeated reliving of intentionalities of hatred or other hostile emotions." Thus, suggests Brudholm,

> "Ressentiment" is a more theorized and complex condition than "the grudging," and given the prominence of the Nietzschean picture of the man of ressentiment, the degrading and pathological connotations are probably exaggerated when a person is considered a *Ressentimenttrager* (a person who harbors ressentiment). . . . Drawing on Scheler, I suggest that neither ressentiment nor grudging is accurately seen as involving a single, specific emotion. Rather, a range of emotions are involved.[33]

Though Scheler begins his discussion of *ressentiment* by praising Nietzsche for his "most profound" discovery of *ressentiment* as a source of value judgment, in contrast to his predecessor's argumentative philosophy of "external"-determined morals ("In order to arise, slave morality always needs a hostile external world"), he characterizes *res-sentiment* phenomenologically:

> *Ressentiment* is a self-poisoning of the mind. . . . It is a lasting mental atti-tude, caused by the systematic repression of certain emotions and affects, which, as such, are normal components of human nature. Their repression leads to the constant tendency to indulge in certain kinds of value delusions and corresponding value judgments. The emotions and affects primarily concerned are revenge, hatred, malice, envy, the impulse to detract, and spite. . . . Thirst for revenge is the most important source of ressentiment.[34]

Thus, while for Nietzsche *ressentiment* was definitively a pathological dis-position associated with a particular psychological type (the slave revolt and the weak mentality, which eventually developed into Christian val-ues), Scheler understands its emergence as a typical modern phenomenon. He sees *ressentiment* as a particular emotional attitude that describes the sociological type of the "common man" who feels profound insecurity and weakness as a permanent condition of his existence, and thus becomes the "man of *ressentiment*" (32): "*Ressentiment* can only arise if these emo-tions are particularly powerful and yet must be suppressed because they are coupled with the feeling that one is unable to act them out—either because of weakness, physical or mental, or because of fear" (26–27).[35] Being constantly divided between his object of desire, an existential envy, and his powerless nature, unable to penetrate the world, the "affects become fixed attitudes, detached from all determinate objects. . . . The first result of this inner process is a *falsification* of the *world view*" (46–47, emphases in the original). Concluding his analysis of the sociology and phenomenology of *ressentiment*, Scheler claims:

> *Ressentiment* has brought deliverance from the inner torment of these affects. . . . *Ressentiment* man . . . is delivered from hatred, from the tormenting desire of an impossible revenge, though deep down his poi-soned sense of life and the true values may still shine through the illusory ones. . . . Beyond all conscious lying and falsifying, there is a deeper "organic mendacity." Here the falsification is not formed in consciousness, but at the same stage of the mental process as the

impressions and value feelings themselves: *on the road of* experience into consciousness. . . . The value judgment is based on this original "falsification." (48–49, emphases in the original)

JEAN AMÉRY AND RITHY PANH:
UNVINDICTIVE RESENTMENT

Jean Améry's collection of essays from 1966, *At the Mind's Limits: Contemplations by a Survivor on Auschwitz and Its Realities*, especially the essay titled "Resentments," paves the way, I claim, to a new perspective on the tension between reconciliation and resentment embodied in Rithy Panh's film *Duch*, as well as the other Big Perpetrator films. The affinity revealed through Améry's and Panh's creative works—Améry's contemplation on resentment as well as some of his other writings,[36] and Panh's film *Duch, Master of the Forges of Hell* (*Duch, le maître des forges de l'enfer*, France/Cambodia, 2011) and his entire oeuvre (and his memoir *Elimination*)—attest to Panh's perspective on survival as having been deeply inspired by Améry.

"I will no longer eat animal food.

FIGURE 3.1 Rithy Panh's father—a refusal to eat. *The Missing Picture*. Courtesy of Rithy Panh.

A brief description of their biographies will enrich our understanding of this affinity: Rithy Panh was born in a suburb close to Phnom Penh in 1962, to a family of nine children. His father, to whom he devotes *Duch*, was a longtime undersecretary at the Ministry of Education, a senator, a schoolteacher, and inspector of primary schools. After the KR entered the capital on April 17, 1975 (when Panh was thirteen years old), the family was designated as New People and deported to the countryside in northwest Cambodia. He saw his parents, siblings, and other relatives suffer and slowly die from "reeducation," overwork, disease, or famine. At one stage, his father refused to eat "anything that doesn't resemble food fit for human beings,"[37] and little by little stopped feeding himself till he died. First working in several labor camps during these years, Rithy Panh was later assigned to be a cleaning person in a hospital and then a gravedigger, in charge of burying the hospital's dead. In 1979, Panh escaped to the jungle and finally reached a refugee camp at Mai Rut, Thailand. In Paris, he was reunited with two of his siblings who were studying abroad, became interested in filmmaking, and graduated from the Institut des hautes études cinématographiques (Institute for the Advanced Cinematographic Studies). In 1989, *Site 2*, his first documentary (on Cambodian refugees), won several international awards. Since then, Panh has created a unique body of work consisting of both nonfiction and fiction films that mostly deal with the traumatic history of the KR regime, established the Bophana Audiovisual Centre in Phnom Penh, and, as a cinema activist, established various postgenocide projects, including the founding and mentoring of the young generation of Cambodian filmmakers.[38]

Jean Améry was born Hanns Chaim Mayer, in Vienna, Austria, in 1912, to a Jewish father and a Catholic mother. The family was estranged from its Jewish origins and assimilated. His father, a Tyrolean Imperial Rifleman, was killed in action in 1916 during World War I, and Améry was raised Roman Catholic by his mother. In Vienna, he enrolled in university to study literature and philosophy, but economic necessity kept him from the regular pursuit of his studies. After the *Anschluss* in March 1938, Améry fled with his Jewish wife first to France and then to Belgium. He was initially deported back to France by the Belgians as a German foreigner and wound up interned in the south of France. After escaping from the camp at Gurs, he returned to Belgium where he joined the Resistance. In July 1943 he was arrested by the Gestapo for distributing anti-Nazi propaganda among the German occupation forces in Belgium, was tortured, and then sent to Auschwitz. Améry endured a year in Auschwitz III, the Buna-Monowitz labor camp, where he was assigned to a labor detail: digging dirt, laying cables, lugging sacks of cement and iron crossbeams. He was evacuated first to Buchenwald and then to Bergen-Belsen ahead of the advancing Red Army and was liberated from Belsen in April 1945.

After the war, the former Hanns Mayer changed his name to Jean Améry in order to symbolize his dissociation from German and his alliance with French culture. He lived in Brussels and worked as a culture journalist for German-language newspapers in Switzerland. He refused to publish in Germany or Austria for many years. As he writes in the preface to the first edition of *Jenseits von Schuld und Sühne* (*Beyond Guilt and Atonement*, translated into English in 1966 as *At the Mind's Limits: Contemplations by a Survivor on Auschwitz and Its Realities*): "When the big Auschwitz trial began in Frankfurt in 1964, I wrote the first essay on my experiences in the Third Reich, after twenty years of silence."[39] He broke his silence in Germany when he delivered a radio address on the intellectual in Auschwitz, which became the opening essay of *At the Mind's Limits* and made him one of the most highly regarded of Holocaust writers. During his lifetime, Améry published over twenty works and novels. On October 17, 1978, he took his own life and was buried in Vienna.[40]

Opposing both Nietzsche's and Scheler's influential conceptualization of *ressentiment*/resentment, Améry's innovation lies in his definition of resentment not as an unconscious incontrollable negative impulse of human nature, but as a highly self-conscious state of personal morality. Enabling a "deep insight into the humanness of resentment,"[41] he defies Nietzsche, who despises victims because he regards them as weak, inferior, and cowardly, and elevates the dignity of the victim, having been forced by circumstances beyond one's control. Moreover, Améry does not regard resentment as an emotional disturbance: "My personal task is to justify a psychic condition that has been condemned by moralists and psychologists alike. The former regard it as a taint, the latter as a kind of sickness."[42] Embodying and living with resentment do not make Améry a "man of *ressentiment*" in either the Nietzschean or the Schelerian sense. On the contrary. Resentment, being simultaneously psychologically required and morally justified, is not a private condition for Améry, but rather a way to provoke collective moral consciousness, a political demand for responsible recognition in a "Century of Barbarism" (80):

> Only I possessed, and still possess, the moral truth of the blows that even today roar in my skull, and for that reason I am more entitled to judge, not only more than the culprit but also more than society—which thinks only about its continued existence. The social body is occupied merely with safeguarding itself and could not care less about a life that has been damaged. At the very best, it looks forward, so that such things don't happen again. But my resentments are there in order that the crime become a moral reality for the criminal, in order that he be swept into the truth of his atrocity. (70)

For Améry, resentment originated in his Holocaust victimization and his experience of torture and involuntary exile.[43] After a short postwar period, during which, being respected as a Holocaust victim, he felt "one with the world," his resentment intensified due to Germany's "most grandiose resurrection of might" (66), rituals of "easy atonement," less and less talk of remorse, and public amnesia that were gradually institutionalized in postwar West Germany till they became all pervasive in the 1970s. In the preface to the edition of *Mind's Limits* from 1977, Améry declares his right to resentment, objecting and fundamentally disrupting the political view that reconciliation is the only legitimate response to the atrocious past: "For nothing is resolved, no conflict is settled, no remembering has become a mere memory. . . . I rebel: against my past, against history, and against a present that places the incomprehensible in the cold storage of history and thus falsifies it in a revolting way. Nothing has healed" (xxi).

Moreover, we should notice that this collection of essays was not written according to the chronology of events, but in the order of their writing, enabling the reader to "accompany me . . . through the darkness that I illuminated step by step" (xiv). In this regard, *Mind's Limits* is a metareflection on time-consciousness not through biological time, but through the gradual breakings of what Améry conceives a "mental intoxication" (9). Thus, "Resentments" appears before the last essay (titled "On the Necessity and Impossibility of Being a Jew") and embodies the climax of his thought.

unvindictive
ressent [handwritten marginalia]

Reflecting on the affinity between Améry's polemical writing and Panh's polemical filmmaking and editing, I suggest that Panh's Amérian-inspired epistemology, which I term unvindictive resentment, is based on a new cinematic rendering of time and temporality. As such, it is unique in world cinema.

UNVINDICTIVENESS

Although Amérian resentment is not based on, or immersed in, negative attitudes,[44] and is not future-oriented, given the situation of autogenocide and social phenomena such as the launching in 1984 of the national day of remembrance (on May 20) in Cambodia as the "Day to Remain Tied in Anger," it is important to emphasize that the films' resentment is unvindictive. The ethnographer Alexander Laban Hinton suggests that Cambodian cultural traditions require that bad deeds, like good ones, must be repaid. Differentiating between begrudgement (*kum*), and revenge (*sangsoek*), he further points to the specific Cambodian trait of uneven revenge, termed *kum*:

> The Khmer Buddhist Dictionary . . . defines *kum* as "the desire to do something bad or harm another person, to be tied in a grudge (*châng kumnum*)" that leads one to "prepare oneself to take disproportionate revenge (*sangsoek*)." . . . A *kumkuon* . . . is a *kum* that is "long-lasting and can't be forgotten." . . . Moreover, the injured party's obligation to repay an enemy for whatever the latter has done creates a bond between them. A Cambodian bearing malice is often said to be "tied/linked" (*châng*) to an enemy by anger or a grudge (*châng komhoeng, châng kumnum*). . . . A grudge thus contains an element of latent potentiality and is frequently long-lasting.[45]

Although the following analysis of the films differentiates between aporetic reconciliation and unvindictive resentment, the films' major inclination, whether they represent high-ranking or low-ranking KR (or both), is toward unvindictive resentment, and not toward latent or explicit *kum*. As will be described later, the films protest against the "antimoral natural process of healing that time brings about" and propose an acceleration of the time-sense in serving a new morality, and not a regression to dehumanizing choices.[46] The constitution of this new time-sense moral epistemology proves, thus, the reciprocity between these two trends and their mutual interdependence.

RITHY PANH'S *DUCH, MASTER OF THE FORGES OF HELL*

Duch, Master of the Forges of Hell (and to a lesser degree Panh's earlier film *S21: The Khmer Rouge Death Machine* [*S21: la machine de mort Khmère rouge*, Cambodia/France, 2003]) is a distinctive case of perpetrator documentary because of the posttraumatic ways by which the director, a survivor of the Cambodian genocide, identifies his major missions: to confront the perpetrator and through this confrontation to constitute an epistemology of an unvindictive resentment that demands an ethical response from both the perpetrator and the spectator. In other words, I claim that Panh's concrete and constant battle with Duch aims not only to overcome the perpetrator's psychological reactions, inner mind-structures, propaganda techniques, explicit and implicit strategies, and dynamics of argumentations and language—all of which have been described by genocide scholars from Leo Kuper[47] to Israel Charny[48] and others—but also to embody resentment.

Most scholars who advocate reconciliation (described earlier) stress social stability, which according to prevailing views relates to, and should impact, society's postgenocide present and future. Thus, they promote justice, mercy, and forgiveness,[49] the end of the past and the marking of a new beginning,[50] a radical change in the present,[51] and so on. Derrida, "torn," as he calls it, between the politics of forgiveness and ethics and between the nation's present and transcendence, strives for transcendence. According to his conceptualization, forgiveness interferes with the ordinary course of historical temporality.[52] In contrast to both the reconciliation paradigm and project, and in line with the Derridean perspective on forgiveness, Panh, not less than Améry, proposes resentment as a radical conceptualization of survival morality based on a new relation to the past. Améry believes that time must be disordered to become moral: "I hope that my resentment—which is my personal protest against the anti-moral natural process of healing that time brings about, and by which I make the genuinely humane and absurd demand that time be turned back—will also perform a historical function."[53] Thus, during the survivor-perpetrator encounter, Panh's resentment, I claim, has a threefold inter-related embodiment: as a constitution of the victim's position vis-á-vis the perpetrator; as an act of conjuring the dead, who are transformed into the meaningful Other; and as a reconstruction of the genocidal time and a remodeling of its dynamics.

In *S21*, made after years of searching for perpetrators in hiding in rural Cambodia, Panh interviews ten low-ranking perpetrators who worked at the Phnom Penh torture and execution center Tuol Sleng, code-named S-21:[54] former guards, an interrogator, a torturer, a photographer, a doctor, a security deputy, the head of registers, and a driver.[55] Panh, together with former prisoner Vann Nath, whose paintings of Pol Pot enabled him to survive S-21, questions the former guards about their part in Tuol Sleng's technologies of death. *S21* stages the survivor-perpetrator confrontation in a series of interviews mixed with the former guards' reenactments of their daily routine in Tuol Sleng. In a few remarkable scenes, when asked by Rithy Panh to demonstrate their methods, the former guards reenact their deeds in the now empty cells of Tuol Sleng as if they were once again in the past: shouting at imaginary prisoners, kicking and cursing them, checking the locks, and so on.[56] The bodily demonstration, based on reflexes, attests to the power of the realistic reenactment to uncover a secretive and unknowable past, as well as the perpetrators' susceptibility to indoctrination, still embodied after twenty-four years. Contrasting perpetration with acknowledgment, the perpetrators' verbal confessions for "crimes of obedience" are thus combined with—and grapple with—their bodily reflexes.[57]

When discussing perpetrator documentaries in general and confrontation scenes in particular, the use of the term *confession* is highly problematic. We should recall that in totalitarian regimes like Pol Pot's, victims were frequently forced to write accounts ("confessions") before their execution in order to justify it. Once the regime proved through these forced accounts that the prisoners were traitors, in an inversion of cause and effect, the "confession" itself became the excuse for execution. I regard the pervasiveness of the term in this context in genocide and trauma studies a regrettable misuse of a term taken from perpetrators' discourse, perhaps further proof of the power of the perpetrators and their forged rhetoric to pave their way into even the most critical discourse. Moreover, the use of the term *confession* when referring to what I suggest should be regarded as the prisoners' "execution account" is evidence of another inversion: in fact, it is the perpetrators who should confess their crimes.[58] Using the term *confession* in relation to the prisoners and not to themselves masks the perpetrators' constant refusal to acknowledge their responsibility, to confess.

As I have argued in other forums,[59] the term *confession* is more appropriate than the term *testimony* to define the perpetrators' acknowledgment of their deeds and should be used to differentiate between the victim and the perpetrator. We are, undoubtedly, morally committed to listen to the victims' testimony and, as an imaginary supportive community, to ease their suffering. In the post-Holocaust era, we have learned to accept their "emotional testimony" as truth, as described by Dori Laub in the famous case of the Holocaust survivor who testified about the Auschwitz uprising, stating that "four chimneys [were] going up in flames" where, "historically, only one chimney was blown up, not all four."[60] However, our acceptance and the connotations ascribed to testimony in the post-Holocaust era as a result of the huge scholarly effort to comprehend the Holocaust should not be taken into consideration in regard to perpetrators' confessions. In the case of genocide, the perpetrators' confessions should be based not on the psychological register (as is the victims' testimony, grounded in their personal feelings, reflections, projections, and so on), but on the ethical register: that is, they should be based on an uncathartic, accurate, unconvoluted, cognitive acknowledgment of their crimes.[61]

Thus, Panh's perpetrator documentary renders two confessional modes—one that is forced, verbal, partially self-incriminatory, and mostly disavowed; and one that is automatic, out-of-habit, and inscribed-on-the-body. The first is revealed finally as a failed confession (as Duch says in the film, "I tend to regard myself as innocent. I belonged to the police force of Democratic Kampuchea . . . so the government is responsible for this crime. . . . I admit that I was held hostage by the KR regime from April 17, 1975, to January 6, 1979");[62] the second, highly uncontrolled, embodies the option for a confession as a mode to paradoxically acknowledge some, mostly unconscious, part of the truth. As Panh writes in his memoir:

> Often, during the filming of *S21: The Khmer Rouge Killing Machine*, I ask the "comrade guards" to "make the gestures" of the period for my camera. I specify that I'm not asking them to "act," but "to make the gestures"—a way of extending their words. If necessary they start, stop, and start again ten or twenty times. Their reflexes return; I see what really happened. Or what's impossible. The method and the truth of the extermination appear.[63]

The bodily mode is thus but another form of the failed confession since the body "confesses" despite the perpetrators' verbal efforts to deny their responsibility. However, this is a limited, undeciphered confession. Unable to reflect the broader context of the scale of the genocide (for example, the number of deaths), it is eventually just partial evidence in comparison to what is required from a full accountability.

In contrast to the group of perpetrators interviewed in *S21*, the only interviewee in *Duch* is the former commandant of Tuol Sleng, Kaing Guek Eav, nicknamed Duch. Between 1975 and 1979, "at least 12,380 people were tortured"[64] and approximately seventeen thousand were executed under his orders.[65] In his eerie memoir *Elimination*, Panh describes the making of the film *Duch* as crucial to him because Duch does not appear in *S21*, a film that "is almost entirely an indictment of the man."[66]

The historical-political circumstances that enabled the making of *Duch* are worth mentioning: It was only in 1999, after the last of the KR had surrendered to the government and the civil war had come to an end, that while on a visit to the district of Samlaut, often considered the birthplace of the KR revolution, the American photojournalist Nic Dunlop (together with Nate Thayer) identified Duch. Duch, who had disappeared twenty years before, had taken on the identity of Hang Pin, presented himself as a schoolteacher, and was working with American refugee aid organizations. Shortly after the story of his discovery appeared in the Western media Duch gave himself up to the authorities.[67]

For the making of *Duch*, nine years after *S21*, Panh spent hundreds of hours interviewing him during the period of his arrest and trial.[68] The film's mise-en-scène is built around Duch's desk, a major trope that symbolizes the bureaucrat's mind-set, his devotion to the seg-mented, routinized, and depersonalized bureaucratic and administra-tive aspects of the extermination process. Because in some scenes Duch sits near a desk in an empty court hall, this trope, empowered by the Q and A format, also symbolizes an imaginary trial.[69] As the camera repeatedly shows, the desk—much like the one Duch had in the past—is covered with piles of documents found in Tuol Sleng and rep-resenting the dead.

Panh asks Duch to read from them out loud: slogans of Angkar (includ-ing "Only the newborn child is pure!" and "If we protect you, we earn nothing. If we cast you out, we lose nothing!"),[70] prisoner accounts, his own contemporaneous comments written on the accounts, interrogators' reports, and rules written for the guards. Panh also asks Duch to look at photo prints taken of prisoners before their executions and at Vann Nath's paintings of scenes of torture and suffering in S-21, and to listen to video testimonies describing the atrocities carried out under his command.

FIGURE 3.2 Proliferation of materials, the duel in *Duch, Master of the Forges of Hell.* Courtesy of Rithy Panh.

As will be described later, this proliferation of materials and elements Panh made use of in the film of course aims at refuting, contradicting, opposing, and disproving Duch's lies, but its major significance lies in reconstructing the genocidal time into a form of resentment. Shaping time-consciousness[71] (which Améry calls "time-sense")[72] through this proliferation of means, the staging of the mise-en-scène, and the editing becomes the instrumental acts for a rearticulated understanding of the relationship between past, present, and future, moving, as Améry strongly states, "out of the biological and social sphere into the moral sphere."[73] In his memoir, Panh attests to the same act:

> The archives are alive. Nothing in them is silent. A photograph. A sheet of paper marked with red ink. I think about the woman who refused to be photographed from the front when she entered S-21. She was a professor. She faced away, holding herself obliquely to the camera, and almost smiled. In one of her handwritten confessions, she evoked Cuba, which was also on the revolutionary road, but where the revolutionaries "aren't killing everybody or starving the people." Thirty years later her message reaches us. It's often combative. Sometimes despairing, but not always. We should listen for those words, listen to that murmur, and we should recall Taing Siv Leang—I write her name—so that she may remain among us, she and her smile.[74]

Modifying our perception of time as it chains us to a permanent past, in *Duch* Panh uses three major strategies repetitively and alternately. All three strategies, built on editing, follow Améry's decree on the annulment of time. Based on an epistemic faith, this annulment of the genocidal past is, thus, not an act of turning back or a mere reversal but an act of "Being Then," in the past. These strategies demonstrate the profoundly affective power of resentment during the survivor-perpetrator battle. I suggest that Améry and Panh share the subjective state of the victim in a world that is mostly dominated by those Améry calls "nonvictims,"[75] embodied to its extreme in this battle.

Projecting resentment, these strategies construct the representation of the Cambodian past as a moral time for Duch. The first strategy is to demand spectators remodel their conception of time by showing very short video clips or still photos that are inserted into the interviewing process. Confronting Duch's responses, these materials reveal his responses to be lies but also, and simultaneously, incessantly take the spectator back to the past. The representation of these materials does not last more than a few seconds (as will be described later in regard to a typical scene). Thus, for the spectators, they function as flickers of time-consciousness, marking their difference from the conventional unde-manding easiness of cinematic flashbacks. Flickering sometimes so quickly (for instance, a four-second shot of hands examining a button taken from a pile of dead prisoners' clothes), as if almost ungraspable, they are nevertheless engraved on the spectators' consciousness due to their contrasting content and the repetition of this technique.

Epistemologically, this means also calling the spectators' attention to the various—even contradictory—ways by which images might be engraved onto one's consciousness or memory. Thus, as a metalanguage, they call into question the subconscious or unconscious component of the memorial process, as well as cinema and visual images' ability to create new associations of atrocity in order to reshape mental processes.

The second strategy of modifying our perception of time as a major component of expressing moral resentment toward Cambodia's past is the use of the accumulation of materials that are put on the desk at the center of the mise-en-scène. These materials, mostly comprising written documents and still photographs taken from S-21, are orchestrated on Duch's desk such that some are alternately noticeable more than others. Through Duch's reading them, pointing at his signature, looking at them, and reflecting on them, he is returned again and again into the past. Since Duch had read these execution accounts[76] while he was the director of S-21 and regarded them as true confessions,[77] Panh's requirement that he reread them becomes a form of reenactment of Duch's deeds through the speech act. Duch's rereading thus becomes a substitute for his unperformed confession, for his obstinate refusal to acknowl-edge responsibility for his crimes. The rereading is also a substitute for—and, ironically, also refutes—Duch's lies. In contrast to the bodily reenactments in *S21*, Duch's rereading of these records is not performed automatically. In further contrast to the guards, he is neither pos-sessed by the past nor reliving it. On the contrary, his rereading is satu-rated with denial and negation, using Angkar rhetoric as a major tool of his determined confrontation with Rithy Panh.[78] Thus, Panh's constant and relentless use of these materials has major significance in terms of the new epistemology.

Whenever Duch refrains from looking, the camera's gaze forces the spectators to gaze at a document, Duch's signature, comments in red ink ("Exterminate!"), or the looks of the soon-to-be-dead-prisoners in the mug shots. As Panh writes: "Duch asks me why I'm always showing him photographs. 'What's the point?' he asks, in that tone of his. I answer, 'But the thing is . . . they're listening to you. Koy Thourn is here. Bophana's here.[79] Taing Siv Leang too. I believe they're listening to you.'"[80] It is not only the refusal of future reconciliation and the disordering of temporality in order to bring the perpetrator back to his past deeds that are the major component of Panh's ideology of resentment. Returning into the past as an act of resentment also means rupturing the moment of *nunc-stans* (the everlasting now) that is rooted in denial.[81] The Now in *Duch*, I claim, is the time of denial realized as a continuous mind-set of tactics and manipulations. After all, the "willing executioner" unfolds his denial of the past in the present. The "twilight state of knowing and not-knowing," as Stanley Cohen calls it,[82] happens in the present, while blocking out the past. In this regard, rupturing the attachment between denial and the Now as its dominant temporalization elevates resentment's value and makes it more coherent than Améry suggests:

> Resentment is not only unnatural but also a logically inconsistent condition. It nails every one of us onto the cross of his ruined past. Absurdly, it demands that the irreversible be turned around, that the event be undone. Resentment blocks the exit to the genuine human dimension, the future. I know that the time-sense of the person trapped in resentment is twisted around, dis-ordered, if you wish, for it desires two impossible things: regression into the past and nullification of what happened.[83]

In contrast to Améry, who presents his retrospection through writing, Panh realizes his perspective in the very acts of both filmmaking and his incessant duel with Duch.

The third strategy that transforms the perception of time for both Duch and the spectator is the present absentee Panh, whose "documentary voice" is heard in every way possible except as a physical voice.[84] Panh avoids a corporeal appearance before the camera, and together with his physical "muteness," his representation of the dead becomes more total. The interview-based encounter between Panh and Duch is built on the conjuring act, which makes the dead play the Third, meaningful Other. But the dead are more than ghost-participants. Ceaselessly presented through both the accounts and the photos, they become a third participant.

This embodying of the dead reflects as well on a unique form of mourning described by Derrida in *The Work of Mourning*, in which he invokes "the unbearable paradox of fidelity" to the dead,[85] according to which the source of our responsibility is the impossibility of the interiorization of the dead, who is "living in me" (42). Thus, if the dead is revealed to us through his image, and the "image looks at us," "We are all looked at. . . . He looks at us. *In us.* He looks in us. And from now on more than ever" (160, emphases in the original). In Derridean mourning, conceived as a healthy process of attachment to the dead (unlike Freudian-influenced schools), we honor the Otherness of the dead and our continuous engagement with them. This conception, which is dominant in Panh's position as a survivor, is elaborated in Derrida's earlier work, *The Gift of Death*, in which he argues that death is the place of one's irreplaceability and responsibility, which in Levinasian terms is always oriented toward the Other.[86] Keeping the singularity and the presence of the dead "in me," as Derrida conceives it, becomes, thus, the only way to mourn. The absence of Panh's corporeal figure from the duel allows his voice to be the voice of the many dead whose mourning, which accentuates their presentness, becomes part of the new temporality.

Moreover, in Panh's *The Missing Picture* (Cambodia/France, 2013), it is through the voice-over of the actor Randal Douc[87] that we hear Panh's memories being recited as if it were a first-person narration.[88] Panh's disembodied voice and physical absence in *S21*, *Duch*, and *Missing Picture* are used as a strategy that reflects on subject/object positions, constantly evoking self-reflexive questions in regard to these positions: What makes one a subject? Or object, for that matter? What is the meaning of having a voice or being deprived of one? Of having a body or—out of torture, hunger, or hard labor—becoming body-less? As Hannah Arendt suggests, to deprive men of their humanity is a powerful instrument belonging to the arsenal of the extermination process.[89] It has to do with the strategy of denying the reality of extermination by hiding any traces of mass murder, while at the same time asserting, in this case, that the "New People" are no longer human beings.[90] This murderous utopia created its own language of extermination, including assimilation of the dead and the survivor: that is, it related to the living as if they were already dead. The regime's ideology destroyed the symbolic boundary between life and death, which establishes the human condition. Under this "ideocide,"[91] the dead and the living become identical and are destined to disappear without leaving either trace or memory. Opposing the KR's logic of elimination, Panh creates a cinema that holds past traces and, thereby, through this conjuring confrontation, reconstitutes the symbolic space between the perpetrator, the survivor, and the dead victim. Furthermore, and most importantly, Panh's disembodied voice means deliberately avoiding any comparison between the survivor and the perpetrator.

In the following, a description of one of the striking confrontation scenes will serve as an example of the strategies of resentment put forward by Panh against the "immensity and monstrosity of the natural time-sense."[92] As is seen throughout *Duch*, in this confrontation scene as well, Duch's desk is at the heart of the mise-en-scène.

Duch is shown sitting near the desk. Bophana's photo is noticeable;[93] however, the desk is loaded with many piles of documents and a computer. Duch is holding a photograph of a tortured prisoner, the camera follows his gaze. In the background, a propaganda song is heard. Panh presents Duch's following monologue:

DUCH. Let's talk about hitting intelligently. Mam Nay aka Chan could beat someone while thinking about what he was doing because he was not hungry for recognition. He was a very good interrogator. He behaved according to the answer he got. He hit very hard. He would deliver a very strong blow from time to time if it was necessary. He would strike one, two, three blows [*Cut to a four-second illustration shot of a blow that lasts the time the blow itself takes. The last words of the sentence are heard as a sound bridge over the inserted shot.*] and almost never reached five!

Those who hit without thinking were like Comrade Touy. He wanted the same power as Comrade Pon but he never reached Pon's level because I hadn't had much time to train him. Thus, he had only one method:

One, two, three blows
and hardly ever five blows!

FIGURE 3.3 A shot of a blow, "Being Then," in *Duch, Master of the Forges of Hell.* Courtesy of Rithy Panh.

torture. Biff! Boom! He controlled his blows so that the prisoner wouldn't die. He wanted to compete with Pon. [*Cut. The camera reveals an image that soon will be comprehended as video testimony, which Panh shows to Duch (and the viewers) in order to refute Duch's previous statement. Duch watches the video on his computer.*]

[*The one who speaks in the video shows a still picture and, pointing to it he says:*] I met Mam Nay aka Chan in 1973 in the secret prison M13. I saw him use an AK47 to execute someone. [*The video's frame is enlarged and we see him on the entire film screen.*]

There was a place there that we called the winner's podium. When a person was tied to it, he was to be executed. Every prisoner knew what it meant (execution). On that day, the prisoners were gathered around the podium. Chan killed one of them with his rifle. Blood splattered all over the prisoners standing around, on everyone who was there. It was terrifying. He wanted to scare us with this behavior.

[*Close-up on Duch. He laughs.*]

[*On the soundtrack we hear the propaganda songs. Duch is seen sitting behind his desk. The noticeable documents are others than those shown at the beginning of the scene*]

DUCH. You can put it that way. But if you do, you will make me acknowledge lies. I will not accept this. My officers knew how to hit and all the rest. But to say that Mam Nay was the one who shot is not true. Not true. I wouldn't say Mam Nay never hit anyone. [*His last words are heard over a four-second video archive of a b/w propaganda film of KR cadres walking with their weapons in a line in the countryside.*] He had beaten prisoners in the past. Sometimes he interrogated with his eyes closed. From time to time he would get up and pick up his long stick to hit with. [*Duch shows the presumed length of the stick on his stretched arm. The desk is shown from another angle with Bophana's photo once again on top of one pile of documents.*] Then he would go to sleep. [*A two-second shot (in color) of a tortured skinny prisoner tied to the podium is seen bending his head.*] Then he would come back to interrogate the prisoner. Mr. Witness may keep talking, there's nothing I can do. There's nothing to document this. . . . Mr. Witness is speaking up, but he has no documents either. So he can keep talking all he wants.

As this description shows, this typical scene, which lasts about three and a half minutes, includes insertions of four still photographs, two "flickering" short clips, and two archive clips presented as videos. This meticulous work of editing attests to Panh's commitment to a moral regression to the past, creating a resentment that "blocks the exit to the genuine human dimension, the future. . . . For this reason the man of resentment cannot join in the unisonous peace chorus all around him, which cheerfully proposes: not backward let us look but forward, to a better, common future!"[94] The belief in being somewhat fundamentally conditioned by the past, shared by Panh and Améry, stands in contrast to Duch's constant denials declared repetitively in this scene. His reaction to the proliferation of materials presented by Panh reveals itself to be rooted in the total unacknowledgment that has characterized all the years Panh spent shooting the film. Thus, it is obvious that Panh refrains from anchoring the confrontation in the discourse of reconciliation, forgiveness, and similitude, and that his objection to this discourse is revealed through embracing the discourse of responsibility, accountability, justice, and difference as part of the Amérian philosophy of resentment.

Moreover, as Panh describes, in shooting Duch he uses only two kinds of shots: head-on or from a slight angle;[95] however, despite the fact that we experience an abundance of head-on shots in close-up, Duch almost never gazes at the camera. His unlooking, I suggest, means he considers himself someone not willing to be gazed at, as if objectified. His horrific pride in mastering torture, training his officers to "hit intelligently," as he calls it, culminates in the moment in this scene when instead of confessing the beating as a crime, he smugly laughs and then addresses "Mr. Witness" as a liar. Duch's laugh is not an expression of embarrassment or confusion in the face of contradictory evidence, but rather a mark of sadistic violence. As the psychoanalytic research claims, "In *sadistic lying*, the intent is to attack and triumph. . . . The object needs to be controlled and humiliated for the self's gratification, often to reverse an earlier experience of humiliation."[96]

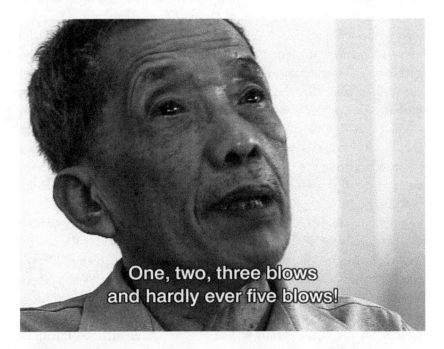

One, two, three blows and hardly ever five blows!

FIGURE 3.4 Duch in close-up: never gazes at the camera, in *Duch, Master of the Forges of Hell*. Courtesy of Rithy Panh.

Moreover, as described earlier, the battle against both the perpetrator's lies and the perseverance of self-image as the "master of torture" is built on juxtaposition of voices. Panh, who is not only the writer and director of this film but also its coeditor, establishes a polemical narrative through counterediting. Reemphasizing the evidentiary status of archival representation and empowering the referential grounding by repeating the same images over and over, the clips taken from propaganda films and the video testimony stand, of course, in total contrast to Duch's reaction. As Panh says: "Thanks to the cinema, the truth comes out: montage versus mendacity,"[97] and "Duch reinvents his truth in order to survive. . . . I edit my film, therefore, against Duch. The only morality is the editing, the montage."[98]

Using the camera's constant showing of documents and counterediting, through the duel, Panh constitutes what I term a "truth archive." On the same line of reasoning as in the debate on the use of "confession" vs. "testimony" summed up earlier in this text, and in reference to the status of the victims' "emotional testimony" as truth, I use the word *truth* to emphasize Panh's efforts to expose Duch's lies in regard to the Cambodian genocide. In many respects, this use transcends traditional debates over documentary truth that take place in documentary research. Panh's perpetrator documentaries take the truth-value of the evidence they present while confronting the perpetrators' lies as an ideal, rather than as grounds for a post–*cinéma vérité* or postmodern controversy. In other words, the traditional questions of objectivity, authenticity, transparency, the nature of evidence, accuracy, and so on become irrelevant in the face of lies concerning the 1.7 million dead. The scale of the historical event demands putting aside any discussion that might impede the revelation of truth.

Simultaneously exposing the mode of production, Panh's cinema both provides the basis for the evidence it presents and stands for the spectators' cognitive engagement with the value of truth as a necessary ideal in post-KR Cambodian society and culture. Put another way, Panh's perpetrator documentary cinema is built on transforming the perpetrator's constant denial of his responsibility as attested to by these documents, testimonies, photos, notes, paintings, and slogans into an archive of truth. A cinema of refuting, it uses the duel not only for establishing a new epistemology of resentment but also to put forward a new collective imagery.

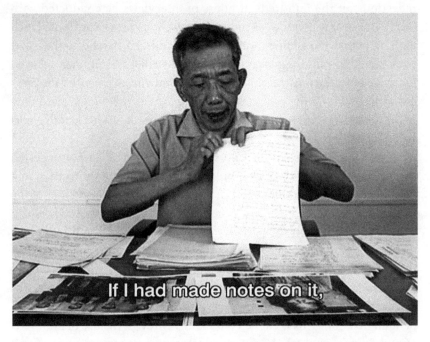

If I had made notes on it,

FIGURE 3.5 S-21 files in *Duch, Master of the Forges of Hell*. Courtesy of Rithy Panh.

Reconstituting the symbolic space while conjuring the dead and transforming every visual, audial, and bodily detail disclosed about Tuol Sleng's death machine into a chronicle of truth anchored in the past means distinguishing between the subject positions entailed in the battle. The evolution of Panh's three films (*S21, Duch, Missing Picture*) in terms of subject positions is intriguing. His struggle against the ideology of elimination entails concealing his own traumatic past. Reconstitution of the distinction between life and death, survivor and victim, humanity and elimination becomes symbolically central through this present absence, his appearance or lack of it, detailing his personal memories or refraining from doing so. Playing with the object/subject dialectic—one that was fulfilled so harrowingly by the KR terror—Panh uses these diverse ghostly positions to confront the perpetrator's mind-set and rhetoric of utmost objectification.

In *Elimination*, Panh's memories of the horrific experiences he underwent as a young child under the Pol Pot regime are interwoven with his reflections on the hundreds of hours of interviews he conducted with Duch. But in this memoir, as in his film *Duch*, he never confronts Duch with his own personal memories. In other words, Panh renders the battle with this high-ranking perpetrator, Pol Pot's chief executioner, by leaving aside both the posttraumatic reactions and affects invading his present while recalling the past and the psychological crises (expressed only in the book) he went through during—and as a result of—his lengthy talks with Duch.

According to Panh's perpetrator documentary cinema, as suggested earlier, the perpetrator's story should be told in different terms than that of the survivor (or of the victim). In other words, the necropolitics of the Cambodian genocide are transformed through the perpetrator's perspective of time, in which the perpetrator is called to imagine himself as a member of a response-able community.[99] Thus, it is only in *Missing Picture*, after Duch was sentenced to life imprisonment by the ECCC, that Panh discloses his personal memories. However, in this documentary as well he is reflecting on subject/object relationships, on objectification and dehumanization. This is carried out mainly through the use of hundreds of clay figurines, which, by nature silent, represent the ontology of creation and destruction in a material, close-to-earth manner. The fully manipulated clay bodies are placed in elaborate dioramas or superimposed by deliberately rough-edged visual effects that highlight the gap between the deeds and rhetoric of the Pol Pot regime and the suffering of the Khmer people.

Three major spectatorial positions, I suggest, are revealed in Panh's perpetrator cinema. First, objecthood—tasting the impossible status of being an object in the web of the Other. Second, self-Othering—imagining the Other who does not resemble the self or the Otherness within the self. This position includes acknowledging direct or indirect symbolic collaboration with different degrees of perpetration, mainly through state terror. The third spectatorial position is subjecthood—regaining self-identity, a post-genocide self, through participation in "truth-archiving" processes and the temporalization of resentment. These complex processes include opposition to the KR regime (which is relevant for many KR families),[100] acknowledgment of (various levels) of responsibility, rebuilding of the historical past, and participating in commemoration of the dead. In proposing these spectatorial positions (and their linear or simultaneous adoption), Panh's cinema demands not only the emotional investment of the viewers, but their ethical one as well.

In Rithy Panh's perpetrator cinema, resentment transcends its earlier philosophical definitions as an embodiment of a damaged morality and—based on the survivors' reclaiming of their subjectivity vis-à-vis the perpetrators'—becomes a major perspective for addressing the Cambodian genocide. Under the specific uniqueness of the Cambodian autogenocide, in which the KR murdered their own people, and under the cinematic-cultural phenomenon of post-KR perpetrator cinema, Panh's *Duch* stresses the unvindictive resentment as unavoidable, crucial epistemology. In his memoir, Rithy Panh says:

> I think about those four years, which aren't a nightmare, which are neither dream nor nightmare, even though I still have plenty of nightmares. Let's call it a complicated chapter in my life. And one which I'll never forgive. For me, forgiveness is something very private.
>
> Only politicians arrogate to themselves the right to grant reprieves or pardons in the name of all—a right unimaginable when mass crimes or genocides are concerned. I don't believe in reconciliation by decree. And whatever's too quickly resolved scares me. It's peace of soul that brings about reconciliation and not the reverse.[101]

A VICARIOUS SURVIVOR-PERPETRATOR ENCOUNTER THROUGH THE ECCC: *ABOUT MY FATHER*

Guillaume P. Suon's *About My Father* (Cambodia, 2010), a documentary film about Duch, represents a direct survivor-perpetrator confrontation. However, it renders a unique case of the vicarious, legally mediated encounter: It tells the story of a daughter's search for the traces of her dead father, who was sentenced to death at S-21. At the end of her quest, she appears as a civil party in Duch's trial and confronts him. The film presents a survivor-perpetrator duel through the ECCC, thus expanding the juridical imaginary mediated by the cinema. The survivor "faced" the torturer and executioner in her daily life years prior to their final meeting at the ECCC, where she testifies. The film shows how, despite the failure of testimony to rupture Duch's denials, encounters with the Big Perpetrator contribute to the survivor's belief in an inevitable unforgiveness, and thus to the film's constitution of the ethics of resentment.

About My Father (written and directed by Guillaume P. Suon, who is also coeditor and cocinematographer) follows the journey of Phung-Guth Sunthary, who spent the KR years in a labor camp for young girls, lost many members of her family, and for four years before the film was shot conducted a search for her father, who—as she found out by accident during a visit to Phnom Penh—had been imprisoned and executed in S-21 in 1977.[102] Phung Ton, her father, a professor of international public law and a university dean (whose students included Kar Savuth, the ECCC colawyer for Duch), was close to Ieng Sary and Son Sen (who at that time was in charge of the security centers, including S-21). However, upon his return to Cambodia from abroad in 1975, her father disappeared. Tenaciously searching for the truth about her father's death, Phung-Guth looks at the photos and files at S-21 and meets and confronts the S-21 interrogator Prak Khan and the guard and executioner Him Houy (fifty-four and fifty-three years old, respectively), as well as the S-21 survivor and painter Vann Nath, before she testifies at the ECCC.

About My Father, which follows the narrative of a quest for the Big Perpetrator, previously constituted in the post-KR Cambodian culture by Nic Dunlop, Thet Sambath and Rob Lemkin, and Rithy Panh (among others), is unique in its staging upfront the question of reconciliation and forgiveness through the protagonist's dialogue with low-ranking S-21 perpetrators. During her visit to the irrigation site she worked in until the fall of the regime, Phung-Guth does not speak with a woman whom she meets there and who was a cadre in 1976. Devoted to her father's story, it is only in S-21 that she confronts Prak Khan and Him Houy. Walking inside S-21, the two are willing to talk about their past deeds; however, they do not hold themselves accountable. In contrast to Duch's total denial and refusal to disclose details, they talk with Phung-Guth about the "chewing group" and their methods of torture (including removing prisoners' blood until they died, a crime Rithy Panh put upfront in *Duch* because of Duch's constant denial that it was committed in S-21) and killing.

Houy describes the method of killing, first at S-21 and later at Choeung Ek ("Crow's Feet Pond"—a killing field south of Phnom Penh),[103] saying, "They were taken to be killed. We united their hands like that. Their strings were that long. They were blindfolded, hands tied behind their backs. They walked to the pit where they were knelt down. And then we hit them from behind. We hit them and they fell back. Then we slit their throat." Houy embodies the prisoner-victim's bodyliness by demonstrating with his hands the tying and immediately illustrates the image of the length of the strings from the perpetrator's point of view. However, both his and Khan's resistance to acknowledging their responsibility, despite this precise description, becomes, I suggest, a resistance to the imaginary image of the killing itself.

The director, Suon, uses editing to bridge the gap between the detailed description of the killing and their refusal to account for it as a crime. Thus, after the description, the editing cuts to archival footage of a killing field, a naked horror, in which the bodies, dumped into a swamp, move between its deep water and surface, sinking and floating, seen and unseen. Despite the camera's closeness to the bodies as it tracks the small swampy pond—the clothes and the body parts, object and abject, can be recognized as such, in separation, only to a certain extent. Then, moving from the swamp to what looks like a pit, the camera's track exposes skulls and bones, though it is hard to decipher their number.

I suggest that this archival black-and-white image of the killing field unaccompanied by sound is what Georges Didi-Huberman calls a *tear image* (*image-déchirure*—pulled apart). Referring to Holocaust images, he suggests,

> Georges Bataille . . . tried to uncover . . . the essential "violence" that the image is capable of *evoking*. After Bataille, Maurice Blanchot said that it was correct, but incomplete, to speak of the image as that which "denies nothingness": what also needed to be recognized was the moment when the image becomes, reciprocally, "the gaze of nothingness upon us." . . . A little later, in a few superb pages echoing the style of Bataille, Lacan analyzed the "sudden appearance of the terrifying image." . . . Where "all words stop and all categories fail"—where theses, refutable or not, are literally stunned—that is where an image can suddenly appear. Not a

veil-image of the fetish, but the *tear-image* from which a fragment of the real escapes.[104]

The *tear effect* thus becomes the embodiment of the *ethical moment of the gaze* imposed on the spectator.[105] However, the tear image not only proposes an exorcising perspective, but constitutes an ethics based on an essential tearing apart of the survivor-perpetrator relationship. Beyond the unimaginable, the formlessness of the killing field image becomes an opposition to Khan and Houy's refusal to take responsibility, working against their making the image an *empty image*. Khan and Houy's resistance to meaning-making through constant refusal of accountability and culpability is displaced onto the excessive realm of the killing field image (much as Thet Sambath's editing in *Enemies of the People* renders the corpse chained to the iron bed at S-21 as a replacement for what Nuon Chea refused to say, described earlier). In other words, this excessive nightmarish image negates the perpetrators' engagement with detailing and demonstrations as a convenient displacement of confessing.

This cinematic version of Didi-Huberman's "in spite of all" theses marks the Cambodian image of the killing field not as an image that invokes memory, but as one that in the absence of accountability tears the fabric of the survivor-perpetrator encounter and proposes unforgiveness. The gaze of nothingness upon us, the terrifying image, permits moral resentment. It is the degree of the corpses' nonrecognizability that embodies the "disastrous logic" of replacement.[106] The director's reflection on the status of the image and on the role of the archive in mobilizing a new epistemology of "knowing" transcends the contrast between confession and archive, attesting to that which was perpetrated.

Inevitably, the next cut leads to Phung-Guth's question, addressed to Khan and Houy: "What do you think? . . . We, the victims, and you, the executioners, is it possible to make up?" First avoiding her question, after prodding, Houy responds: "I don't know. Up to you." After they walk through the corridors of S-21, the camera at their back imitating the reenactment scenes in Rithy Panh's *S21* that showed how they took a prisoner to interrogation, they sit around a desk on which Phung-Guth's late father's photo serves as a *lived archive*. But it is not only her father's photo that serves as such. The entire mise-en-scène still carries the traces that caused shock when S-21 was first seen by the Vietnamese upon their victorious invasion of Phnom Penh in 1979: the camera shows the dusty files containing the "confessions" of hundreds of prisoners, an open box filled with bones and skulls, and the instruments of torture. In this mise-en-scène, in the background, in between the three protagonists, we see the chair that was used when mug shots of the prisoners were taken upon their arrival, embodying the exterminatory violence soon to be inflicted. The imaginary walk through the corridors, the chair, and her father's photo all mark different ghostly phases in the happenings of the past that Phung-Guth so desperately wants to expose.

As a response to Phung-Guth's question about possible reconciliation, both Khan and Houy again refuse to take personal responsibility ("Because what I did here was against my will," says Khan). Though they don't claim blindness and "not-knowing," as Nuon Chea and Duch incessantly claim in Sambath and Lemkin's *Enemies of the People* and Panh's *Duch* (respectively), their self-deception reflects what the research (e.g., Robert Jay Lifton and Stanley Cohen), deciphering the pathologization of perpetrators, calls obedience, "splitting," compartmentalization, and distancing.[107] They evade her question as to the scale of their crimes ("How many people did you kill?") as well as any emotional or specific response toward Phung-Guth and her family. However, while keeping up an ambiguous nongenuine rhetoric, both propose to ask forgiveness from the dead and the victims' families. Phung-Guth responds: "I can't speak of reconciliation yet because nobody in my family was on the KR side. They were all victims, both rural and urban. . . . I can't hurt anyone. . . . So don't be afraid of me. I am not going to hire someone to hurt you. Never. . . . But about reconciliation I am not capable." Although Phung-Guth assures Khan and Houy she has no intention of *kum* (revenge), it becomes clear that her—and the spectators'—incremental processes of knowing how the death machine at S-21 worked are intermingled with the perpetrators' refusal to accept culpability. The film's reflection on the crime of obedience and "unanchored responsibility" in the encounter scenes emphasizes its negation of reconciliation and forgiveness and its making way for (yet undeclared) unvindictive moral resentment.

In the following scene, watching Vann Nath's horrifying paintings of S-21 (the guards dragging a group of blindfolded prisoners tied together by their necks with their pictures being taken, a skinny half-conscious family with nothing to eat) and of Choeung Ek (a mother torn from her baby watching a guard throw her infant against the infamous tree trunk, prisoners taken to interrogation), sometimes enlarged by the camera to fill the entire cinematic screen, we hear in the soundtrack the KR anthem ("Bright red blood / that covers cities and plains / of Kampuchea, our motherland. / Sublime blood / of valiant workers and peasants / blood of warriors"). The celebratory nationalist "materiality" of this nondiegetic background propaganda music further exacerbates the critical tone of the film toward the perpetrators' unreflective apology. Sharing their experience in regard to Khan and Houy's refusal to take full responsibility, both survivors, Phung-Guth and Vann Nath (who, after been interrogated and tortured, was made S-21's official painter), agree on their shared attitude of unforgiveness.

In many respects, Phung-Guth's irresolvable and unreconcilable survivor-perpetrator encounter with these low-ranking perpetrators serves as a portent of her encounter with Duch as a civil party.[108] Duch's account at court in regard to Phung Ton—asserting Phung Ton was not tortured and claiming he does not know where "his professor" died and where his ashes are buried—reflects both the perpetrator's and the KR regime's massive deception, secrecy, and misinformation. Suon's film presents this encounter through the computer screen Phung-Guth watches after the encounter took place. She is seen listening to Duch testifying, "There was no torture," and weeping. Then, as a multilayered sound we hear her reflection that "the accused is lying. I stopped believing him. He tries to see if I watch him or not. When you weep sincerely, you don't wonder if people see you crying." While she talks to Suon's camera, we see Duch both weeping and looking aside, as she describes. The cinematic "doubling" of the event and the upfront medium shot of Duch that, unfolding on the entire cinematic screen, erases the glass of the booth in which he sits in court expose the drama of deception defined in cinematic bodily terms. In this way, the staged court of cinema both enables a transcendence of the limits of legal procedures, especially in regard to the civil party, and self-reflectively uses the vicarious encounter as a way to project on cinema and law as two vocabularies of ethics.

The cut to the next (very short) scene with Mam Nai (Chan), the leader of the interrogation unit at S-21 who assisted Duch, shows him crying and expressing his regret in court. It occurred on July 14, 2009, about halfway through the trial (after two and half months), when Mam Nai was called to testify about the torture of Phung Ton (his former professor). However, as the streaming of the court's proceedings proves, he spent a day and a half not remembering, equivocating, and lying in the face of incontrovertible documents and his own earlier statements, carefully avoiding incriminating himself.[109] In the scene depicted in the film, the camera follows Duch, who rises from his chair and addresses Mam Nai, asking him to remember when "our professor" died: "Speak! don't be afraid! Tell the truth!" In between Mam Nai's response to Duch, the editing cuts to Phung-Guth's reflection on Duch's call as a manipulative tactic because at that stage it was already clear that low-ranking perpetrators would probably not be tried. The next cut, back to the film's representation of the court, leads to Mam Nai's response to both Duch and the court's president, as he declares that he did his best. He finally states: "If you ask me further information, I am lost in the night."

As the research and even the weekly Cambodian TV show *Duch on Trial*,[110] which followed the development of the trial from 2009 onward, state, for the first time in an international criminal trial, survivors of mass atrocity were included as civil parties rather than as mere witnesses and were permitted to question witnesses, experts, and the accused. *About My Father*, focusing on the survivor-perpetrator encounter and on Mam Nai, one of the trial's most important witnesses, re-presents the Duch/Mam Nai scene while showing the painful and difficult processes of international court proceedings, especially that of the ECCC as a hybrid court, for the civil parties. The cinematic screen as an alternative complementary stage in contrast to the legal one enables Phung-Guth to painfully state that without indicating any reason, the courts refrained from a further investigation of Mam Nai, thus blocking any future option for revealing the truth about her father's death.[111]

Thus, in her final statement (on August 19, 2009), depicted at the end of the film, she says: "The accused knows very well the answers to my questions. If he claims to know nothing, then he is not the great chief of the secret police as described. . . . He's just a puppet, a coward." Repeating her significant questions ("Who killed my father? What tortures did my father suffer?"), and hearing Duch's repeatedly "not knowing" responses, she reads her statement: "Under these conditions, the accused may not speak to me with remorse or ask forgiveness or offer condolences to my family ever again. I have not come here for revenge but to find the truth. But if the accused refuses to answer my questions, I shut the door forever to forgiveness. The accused may lie and hide the truth for several reasons. But he can't deceive the soul of my father."[112]

Repeating the survivor' story and historically creating it in its entirety for the first time, this Big Perpetrator film proposes a vision of both the victim (the survivor) and the perpetrator that undoes the inaccessibility of the civil party to the court. As the confrontation scenes show, as the proceedings evolved, Phung-Guth became a prosecution witness within the trial, a change that proposes a new moral perception. Her historical authority, emerging through the obstacles of giving testimony and addressing the accused and other witnesses to perpetratorhood, has changed into an ethical authority.

In its re-presentation of the Phung-Guth/Mam Nai/Duch confrontation, *About My Father* goes beyond the themes that have accompanied the multiple legal explanations relating to Duch during the court's proceedings: state of mind vs. morality, passive vs. active role, personal vs. lack of personal involvement, knowing vs. not knowing, accountability vs. remorse, lie vs. truth, responsibility vs. irresponsibility, realization of facts vs. reduction, manipulation of court vs. genuineness.[113] Through stressing the survivor-perpetrator encounter beyond the concepts and the logic of the legal, and by including "moments of rupture of the legal framework,"[114] the film supports resentment as the main subject position, constituted through epistemophilic truth-revealing.

SURVIVE: IN THE HEART OF THE KHMER ROUGE MADNESS

Roshane Saidnattar's *Survive: In the Heart of Khmer Rouge Madness* (*L'important c'est de rester vivant*, France, 2009) is a survivor's autobiographical film presenting her lengthy interview with Khieu Samphan,[115] which took place over several days in his house near the Thai frontier. The uniqueness of Saidnattar's duel with Samphan lies in the way she deals with his various forms of denial (particularly his denial of knowledge and of responsibility, but also moral indifference, means-end dissociation, and denial of the victims).[116] First, in terms of the narrative, after introductory historical scenes based on voice-over commentary and archival footage of US president Nixon's bombing of Cambodia, she begins with her testimony:

> In 1974, I was five years old. I lived in Phnom Penh with my family. I remember the day my uncle grabbed me from school under the bombs. He swept me away, holding me close to protect me from the heat. . . . The first new year I remember was that of 1975. . . . My parents, my grandparents, my aunts, and my uncles. We took to the road with all the others. . . . I cried so hard. I was scared I'd never see my father again. For a long time I thought he was dead.

Setting the testimonial urge and the personal tone endowed the testimonial mode with a significance that attempts to both create an incessant conflict with the perpetrator's "story" (which is, in fact, a failed account) and reduce the latter's significance in terms of the narrativization of the history the film aspires to portray.

Second, and consequently, the uniqueness of Saidnattar's encounter with Samphan lies in the multiple perspectives built into the structure of the narrative, which constitute the film's ethics of moral resentment with which the spectator needs to negotiate: Since Saidnattar presents through reenactments the voice of the five- and seven-year-old girl that she was, it is through their perspective that she as an adult tells her story. However, there is also the perspective of the interviewer who listens to the unprotected child inside her and to herself hearing their traumatically broken narrative. There is the perspective of the adult who shares posttraumatic experiences with her cosurvivor mother and young daughter, accompanying them to the scene of the crime—the labor camp and the last village she lived in with her mother. And there is the perspective of the filmmaker who is making the film, reflecting both on what she heard and on what she came to comprehend through the memorial process. Thus, personal testimony, reenactments, dreams (nightmares), remembrances through archival materials and Voice-of-God historical commentary, a return to the scenes of crimes, three generations of posttraumatic sharing, and three generations of mother-daughter mirror-relations provide the scaffolding along which the cinematic narrative unfolds.

Third, regardless of Samphan's incessant denials and highly disturbing evasion of past horrors, Saidnattar as an interviewer keeps asking him mainly "naturalized" questions typical of low-profile investigative journalism, as if he had answered her in a moral, accountable way. This gradually reveals the film's total negation of his version of history and the mechanism of the official discourse of denial, resting on "*literal* (nothing happened), *interpretive* (what happened is really something else), and *implicatory* (what happened is justified)" denial.[117] For instance,

ROSHANE SAIDNATTAR: What were your daily tasks at that time? What did you do?

KHIEU SAMPHAN: My daily work . . . I didn't do much. Like when I was in the resistance. I was president, but it was just a title. I worked in Centre 870. In this centre, I ensured good relations with His Majesty and princess. Secondly, I divided up items collected in the Phnom Penh, like fabric, clothes, household goods, sugar, medicine, etc. There was no one left in Phnom Penh, and more stores. Everything was abandoned. The KR stocked it all in warehouses. And my job was to manage and guard these stocks. In fact, I had subordinates to do it. I had the title of the president, but I was president of warehouse security. And that's exactly what I did! I shared out the goods by sector according to the decisions of the Party's Permanent Committee. Apart from that I kept the registers. I had to list and price all the production of the cooperatives. But I couldn't do it, because there was no commercial exchange.

Samphan relates a "whitewashed" description of the office for enforcing mass killing known by the code name "870," and of the horror of the Phnom Penh evacuation. He speaks using the same devoid-of-emotion, cold tone, and so does she, presenting her questions in a naturalized tone. Even when she poses more critical questions, she neither discloses her attitude nor her emotional reaction:

ROSHANE SAIDNATTAR: Do you think those who massacred the population overstepped the orders of the party leaders? You said that the hierarchy didn't order any massacres. Yet those accused of illegal sentimentality were removed. Those accused of lacking discipline were reeducated. Reeducated, under the KR between 1975 and 1979, meant killed. Love brought death. Were your orders overstepped? Or were they ill interpreted?

KHIEU SAMPHAN: For me, reeducating doesn't mean killing. Reeducating means persuading someone to do the right thing, not the wrong thing. To mend their ways. I didn't know about these executions. So . . . at every meeting, we gave directives. Were they ill interpreted or did our subordinates overstep their orders? I prefer not to say. I can't comment on this. Some of those who applied our directives in the field also belonged to the upper hierarchy. It is difficult to measure each person's responsibility. I can't tell you. From what I saw and heard, I thought everything was going as it should.

Following this encounter, addressed to the spectator, the film constantly builds a contrast between the archival materials and the testimony the filmmaker inserts, which reflects the same events to which Samphan refers. This refuting editing is made more complex due to the multiple perspectives that make the spectator an active listener. For instance, showing a reenactment of a little girl collecting dung in the field, we hear the perspective of Saidnattar, the adult, reflecting on herself and then giving body and voice to herself as the little girl who was forced to be a laborer in a children's camp (and to survive alone, far from her mother, who worked in a unit building a dam): "Children had to collect dung to serve as fertilizer, five kilograms a day per child. Each person also had to provide a pound of excrement and a liter of urine a day but we didn't eat enough to give the required quantity. When we didn't meet standards, self-criticism was imposed. We were deprived of food, given even worse jobs, and we had to work to the point of collapse. In the end, their favorite fertilizer was bodies."

The editing cuts from first-person testimony intermingled with the commentary of the narrator, the filmmaker, to reenacting the first-person testimony of a little girl returning from the field (followed by pictures of the director and her daughter in the present, laughing in a field). The little girl says: "Often in the evening, I returned to my hut crying because I was all covered in dung. During work, the peasant kids played at making me fall so I'd get dirty. They were the children of the Old People. They were taught to despise us, those of April the 17th children of the New People."

The editing creates a contrast when, in the next scene, we hear Khieu Samphan's reflection on labor:

> I only visited the work sites when I escorted King Sihanouk and the princess. It was an honor for me. I did it to entertain them. . . . I tried to explain to them what they were seeing. . . . The sites were prepared for the official visits. Like in His Majesty's time, when for every inauguration, palm trees would be planted. . . . That's how these things were. In truth, I didn't know it was all staged. I'd never thought about it. I knew our comrades were tired. They maintained their enthusiasm and their fervor by working to the rhythm of revolutionary songs. I thought they worked willingly. The proof was in the results. They worked hard . . . but it resulted in many dams, which allowed us to irrigate our rice fields.[118]

Fourth, and most importantly, *Survive*'s uniqueness in terms of the survivor-perpetrator encounter lies in the shift presented when Saidnattar declares in the midst of this "naturalized" interview that she is reexperiencing the genocide not only because of the internal pressure to bear witness, but because of the nightmarish presence of the perpetrator. As she says,

> It took me years to get this interview. I didn't say that I lived here in the time of Democratic Kampuchea. I simply said I wanted to understand their motivations, their ideals, the reasons for their fight. He said to me, "I am going to tell you the real story of Cambodia." Now I had to win his trust but I no longer really knew what I expected from this encounter. Since I had arrived at his home, a flood of memories were coming back to me.

The scene that embodies this turning point begins with a series of reenactments (a little girl awakens because she hears someone screaming when taken away in the middle of the night, a girl breaks the camp's rules and runs to look for her mother and finds herself stepping into a killing field). A cut to the little girl, showing her hiding in the forest and hearing someone beg the KR cadre not to kill him and a shadow theater presenting a scene in which the cadre grabs a baby from his mother and throws him against a tree to smash his skull, is revealed in retrospect to be Saidnattar's nightmare. This nightmare takes place in Khieu Samphan's home, where she, as his guest, sleeps. The camera shows her as she awakens to an unrecognized noise and the sound of the monsoon. She takes the camera and films him sleeping. She is then seen on the stairs outside of the house, all wet from the heavy rain. The impulse to record Samphan's uninterrupted sleep as another reflection on his non-posttraumatic life is enhanced by her need to cleanse herself in the rain and by the soundtrack, in which we hear the lullaby of a mother to her child. The next scene is a reenactment of the director with a line of girls planting rice during a heavy rain, eating from a bowl full of the rainy water, shivering.

In the next scene, the next morning, we hear her adult voice-over telling us: "With each passing day my anxiety and fear intensified. I didn't yet tell Khieu Samphan what I had seen and heard. I survived KR massacres while he was president."

I suggest that the nightmares and the voices of the dead begging to come back, which she hears, stand for what Samphan does not say. Thus, not only combining (through the editing) Samphan's monologues of denial and her posttraumatic memories but also understanding her own story and reconstructing her testimony are produced as well in relation to his genocidal personality. As the narrative deepens, the beneath-the-surface encounter gains a life of its own, unlike the polite and formal discourse of the interview. In this, it is the unspoken dimension of the survivor-perpetrator encounter, revealed to the survivor in a horrific, painful way, that makes trauma-induced fragmented memories and psychic disruption, "what has been left deeply wounded,"[119] a major way for rejecting the perpetrator and self-healing.

This total rejection is embodied in the painful visit that Saidnattar with her mother and daughter made to the last village they had lived in. The camera shows the poor condition of the peasants as another indication of the failure of the revolution. The shift from black and white to color and the people they meet are reminiscent of the past. But, the last scene, inside a Buddhist temple, reflects faith, inner silence, a family bonding, and Saidnattar's reconciliation-within-herself. As Dori Laub suggests in regard to the testimonial act,

> There is an internal unrelenting pressure to convey it. . . . She or he is less helplessly prey to its devastating impact. The internal cauldron of sensations and affects has been put into the frame of a sequential narrative. . . .

Such narrative, however, is never complete and highly charged blank spots of the inexpressible (almost unimaginable) experience persist, exerting their magnetic power on the survivor, who feels compelled to endlessly revisit them while at the same time she or he constantly flees their proximity.[120]

Survive: In the Heart of Khmer Rouge Madness proves that this complex process of testimony, triggered by a survivor-perpetrator duel, constitutes an ethics of survival that first and foremost establishes the truth and the women's ability to constitute internal mirror-relations as a way for self-healing.

The film ends with titles that inform the viewers about Khieu Samphan's arrest and future trial. In that, it marks an undeniable attitude toward the past.

CONCLUSION—MORAL RESENTMENT

Stanley Cohen convincingly argues,

> The voice of reconciliation starts with the tone of gentle reason: "Why live in the past? . . . You have to draw a line somewhere. . . . Close the book on the past. . . . We must learn to live with each other. . . . Let's look forward to a new future for our children instead of looking backwards." This voice, however—especially under the slogan of "national reconciliation"—may be bogus and self-serving, a strategy to evade accountability and perpetuate historical denial. . . . When the rhetoric of reconciliation is genuine, it looks for tolerance, forgiveness, social reconstruction and solution of social conflicts in ways other than punishment. . . . Victims and survivors cannot be expected to forgive without full knowledge. . . . Reconciliation is a radical way of confronting the past. It demands the greatest struggle in the personal lives of victims, survivors, and their families, especially if coupled with a demand for forgiveness.[121]

While the basic premise of this chapter is that beyond the victim's personal testimony, only the survivor-perpetrator documentary duel, staged at the heart of perpetrator cinema and interconnected to the ECCC, can tell us what lurks beneath the surface of Cambodia's relation to its past, this is a complex premise. Perpetrator cinema fulfills a major role in confronting the Big Perpetrators and exposing the taboo-ized history of the genocide while constituting a "truth archive," untold and mostly unseen for the last forty years. With ex-KR still holding prominent positions in Prime Minister Hun Sen's government and Sen's constant pressures on the ECCC, the questions immanent to the autogenocide (causes of eruption, comprehension in the present, future vulnerabilities) and to perpetrators' responsibility, intrastate guilt, national (urban vs. rural) identity, remorse, reparations, and justice are positioned again and again in the public sphere vis-à-vis the "principle of evil."[122] In contrast to the Nuremberg Trials, which took place after World War II, the South African Truth and Reconciliation Commission (TRC) focused on social reconciliation rather than punitive justice. In Cambodia, in light of the ECCC's verdicts on one hand and lengthy hearings on the other, the judicial enterprise and the momentum that Duch's trial created have been decisive in allowing, for the first time, a national public debate on the KR era.[123] However, I suggest, it is the cinema that paves the way for spectators to discover a new ethics, one that emanates from the exceptionality of the autogenocide and the political-social-psychological and cultural situation in identity-torn Cambodia in the post-autogenocide age.

As the earlier analysis of prominent perpetrator films shows, during the first decade of the twenty-first century the new post-KR documentary cinema has constituted two exceptional phenomena, rare in world genocide cinema: First, the new documentary focuses on understanding and comprehending the Cambodian genocide through a direct survivor-Big Perpetrator confrontation. Second, and consequently, through this duel, an irresolvable tension between two different attitudes toward Cambodia's as yet unintegrated genocidal past, reconciliation and resentment, is revealed, with an inclination toward moral resentment. The chapter proposes to bring Jean Améry into the debate, and to revive his distinction of resentment as a conceptual term, attitude, and praxis. Thus, most importantly, perpetrator cinema, I suggest, taking a part in this social process and based on duel documentaries, is neither a transitional justice cinema nor a reconciliatory one, but—being the voice of the dead by giving voice to the perpetrators—a corpus that above all foregrounds a new epistemology based on moral resentment, particularly unprone to conservative manipulation and repressive panaceas.

In defining the Cambodian new cinematic paradigm of moral resentment ethics, I suggest that the films scrutinize the form of aporetic reconciliation (reconciliation saturated with inner paradoxes). The analysis shows that the two trends can only be described at different levels—and not as consecutive stages—of the post-autogenocide Cambodian psychic life. That is to say, referring to complex intensities, they are not positioned along the axis of linear temporality and progress. Under the circumstances of the vague and ambiguous "post"-autogenocide, described earlier, their logic is nonseparative. The exceptionality of the Cambodian genocide as an autogenocide, namely, one based on intimate intranational violence, inevitably enables this unusual affinity between these two perspectives and projects. As the films, motivated by the epistemophilic quest, prove, both aporetic reconciliation and unvindictive resentment are cinematically directed toward Cambodia's as yet repressed history and painful past, toward "Pol Potism," and not toward an imaginary national reunion set in the future.

The detailed voice of the Big Perpetrator mediated by this unique corpus is heard against the proceedings of the ECCC, which serves as background to and focal point of reference for perpetrator cinema. Thus, it is conspicuous that the films re-present the trial (especially of Duch, who as Pol Pot's chief executioner became the symbol of the regime) while using cinema aesthetics and the cinematic apparatus (for example, by enlarging the trial session into the entire cinematic screen) to both undermine and complete what was shown and heard outside the range and focus of the cameras in court (i.e., Duch's body language in the Phung Ton case). In other words, structuring the spectator's juridical imaginary through cinema enables perpetrator cinema to function as an imaginary replacement, proposing another staged court and, when needed, compensating for the ECCC's failures.

Moreover, the *live archive* assists in the ethical rejection of "presentism," the perpetrators' Now being, as I suggest, the time of denial realized as a continuous mind-set of tactics and manipulations. While Shoshana Felman understands the relationship between trauma and the law as a highly unstable *dynamic*, stating that the Eichmann trial tried to put an end to trauma but inadvertently performs an acting out of it,[124] the Cambodian case, I suggest, marked by both its ambiguous temporality and the ECCC proceedings, is based on a new cinematic rendering of time and temporality, an act of "Being Then." Far beyond Felman's concern, as well as beyond the dialectics between acting-out and working-through proposed by LaCapra,[125] the moral resentment structured by the new Cambodian cinema should be seen as both a new attitude and an active praxis.

In its tenacious epistemophilic impulse and its aspiring to establish moral resentment, this corpus uses a major metaphor for the autogenocide—the figure of the perpetrator-cannibal. The perpetrator-cannibal confounds the distinction between self and Other, which—previous to the cannibalism—are, in fact, the same, deeply sharing the same consanguinity, ethnic origins, ancestral heritage, language, religion, body politic, and fellowship. Thus, as I claimed earlier, though the Cambodian perpetrators attempt to devour their (internal) enemies, their genocidal act becomes self-contradictory and they are transformed into self-consuming figures.

Moreover, both inside Tuol Sleng and in the archival videos shown in these perpetrator films, the camera incessantly displays skulls. Although they are probably the most iconic image of the Cambodian genocide, the films return obsessively to the skulls' imagery. I suggest that this is a cinematic obsession with the nonlook. In fact, theirs is an empty gaze not due only to the lack of materiality and the victims' unburied abjected "mode." The ghastly skulls that stare at the spectator from their empty sockets symbolize the nonlooking of the perpetrators. They gaze at nothingness, a void that is once again open to appropriation and meaning-making through the encounter. As this corpus constantly demonstrates, the films challenge the perpetrators' denial, refusal to accept accountability, and other forms of evasion through the unique visualization of the genocide's horrific images. These images function as a replacement for the unsaid and unconfessed, as a lived archive of the past that assists in building this corpus' new ethics.

In contrast to perceptions of transitional justice prevalent in genocide studies and related fields of research, and although the scholarship written in light of the ECCC is gradually expanding in this direction,[126] it should be taken into consideration that perpetrator cinema, as a docu-activist cinema, has taken upon itself both searching for the Big Perpetrators and establishing a confrontational and aesthetic "intervention" in regard to the ECCC.[127] Thus, its suggestion of moral resentment ethics should not be regarded as promoting an unreconciled aftermath of the Cambodian autogenocide. Cambodia's various intensities reveal moral resentment as an active, demanding ethics.

While defining the corpus of Big Perpetrator Cinema means a direct reference to the high-ranking perpetrators, the question still to be asked is to what level it entails an additional, symbolic layer of reference to the huge number of (mostly hidden) low-ranking perpetrators. In Cambodia during the ECCC period, there are undoubtedly "other Duchs": men and women who ran the prisons and torture chambers, supervised mass murder, used slave labor, and are still free and undetected.

The last section of the conclusion will analyze a fiction film that presents a confrontation with low-ranking perpetrators, symbolizing the vast number who will never be tried, and, most importantly, reflects on the unconscious trends typical of fiction filmmaking.

THE LAST REEL: THE LOW-RANKING PERPETRATOR, THE CAMBODIAN FAMILY, AND THE FICTIONAL ENCOUNTER

Kulikar Sotho's fiction film *The Last Reel* (Cambodia, 2016) is a postgenocide melodrama that presents a within-the-family encounter with the KR perpetrator.[128] As such, the following analysis aims to question and demonstrate the different ways by which this new Cambodian fiction film, which stages the ECCC in the background, presents the tension between reconciliation and resentment typical of the nonfiction corpus. Moving beyond the domestic sphere, how does *The Last Reel* provide an imaginary dramatic resonance to the wide range of interconnected psychosocial taboos that, inevitably, are not accessible to nonfiction filmmaking? Does its ethics promote an adaptable social mode?

Melodrama and cinema melodrama research during the 1970s and 1980s (from, for example, Thomas Elsaesser, Peter Brooks, and Linda Wlliams to Christian Gledhill and Ann Kaplan and, more recently, Ben Singer) points to the (American) genre's traditional cinematic codes: imploding and dysfunctional families, suffering women, overwrought emotion, sensationalism, hysteria and pathos, and moral polarization.[129]

Though it is interesting that the origin of the melodrama as a genre in the West was implicated in the class struggle, a thorough analysis of the difference between Western and Cambodian melodrama is beyond the scope of this chapter. However, acknowledging the intense and expressive forms of realism and affect in Cambodian melodrama, two major, interconnected differences that are crucial to defining the corpus' relation to the past are immediately discerned: first, *The Last Reel*'s presentation of morality ruptures the Western melodrama's moral polarization and defies a clear characterization of good and evil; second, the film undermines the definition of victimhood. The film's obsession lies in examining the contradictions that animated the manipulable, producible postgenocidal morality conceived as such by the new, young generation. Struggling with the contradictions inherent in the Cambodian post-autogenocide period, exacerbated by the intergenerational knowledge gap in relation to Cambodia's history, *The Last Reel* aspires to provide not closure or cathartic relief, but—based on the "hysterical" text of excess in the film-within-the-film and melodramatic spectacle—a necessary historical truth. By establishing a more nuanced understanding of the genocide's evils, totally unknown to the young generation, it transcends the horrific situation of revealing a KR perpetrator within the family, thus producing and sustaining the contradictions that keep the fragile normalcy of the future. Focusing on actual as well as imaginary survivor-perpetrator encounters, and redefining the triad of perpetrators, victims, and collaborators, *The Last Reel* proposes a melodramatic ethics that goes beyond victimhood and the spectators' emotional identification with the victim.

The plot of *The Last Reel* presents Sophoun (Ma Rynet), the rebellious daughter of a tough army colonel, who, ignorant of her country's past, lives her life for the moment, hanging out with a local gang and the "big brother" of the gang, Veasna (Rous Mony).[130] When her father, Colonel Bora (Hun Sophy), returns home with another proposal for an arranged marriage, to a general's son, Sophoun flees her home and seeks refuge in a derelict cinema.[131] There, she is shocked to discover an incomplete melodrama from 1974, from pre-KR times, starring her mother (Dy Saveth).[132] The cinema's elderly projectionist, Vichea (Sok Sothun), tells her that the film, titled *The Long Way Home*, is about a prince who falls in love with a beautiful peasant girl, Sothea. On the day before their wedding, she is kidnapped by the evil brother of the prince, but a peasant wearing a mask saves her. The evil prince uses black magic to impede their long trip back home. Overcoming all kind of dangers and obstacles, the girl and the masked peasant fall for each other, but as they near her home, she understands that she must choose between the peasant who saved her life and the prince. She chooses the prince. Sothea is played by Sophoun's mother, who was a film star during the pre-KR period but now suffers from posttraumatic stress disorder and is desperately ill (she is seen lying in bed incessantly repeating KR slogans like "Do not speak, do not listen, do not know, do not ask. . . . We are the youth, we are liberated, and on a bright road, the road of Revolutionary Communism!"). The projectionist, whom Sophoun mistakenly refers to as the director of the film, tells her that the last reel of the film is missing. Aware of her striking physical resemblance to her mother at her age, Sophoun is convinced that she can save her mother by re-creating her on the screen. She insists on reprising her mother's role and entices her close friend, Veasna, to play the masked peasant. With the help of Vichea, Sophoun remakes the missing last reel of the film.

The original film was shot at Tonle Bati, a lakeside site about thirty kilometers south of Phnom Penh. At home, her mother for the first time tells her what happened later in Tonle Bati, which during the KR period was a labor camp they had been deported to. She and the director of the film, Sokha, were in love, but someone informed the KR cadres that he was a film director and he was sent for reeducation. "Everybody knew he would be killed and Sothea died at the same moment," she tells her daughter. "Your father saved my life. He was a KR cadre at the camp." To protect her, he gave her a new name, Srey Mom. Sophoun, who thinks that Vichea is Sokha, her mother's beloved, tells her that he is alive, but the mother recognizes Vichea as Sokha's brother, who, by informing on Sokha to the KR, sent him to his death. At the cinema, Vichea confesses to Sophoun that the missing reel is in fact not missing. Confirming her mother's tale, he tells her that his brother was the director, that he was the scriptwriter, and that both were in love with Sothea. His brother played the prince and he played the masked peasant, and when he first saw Sophoun he thought it might be "a chance to remake the ending in the way I'd always wanted" (i.e., Sothea would prefer the masked peasant over the prince). He tells Sophoun that in Tonle Bati he was tortured until he informed on his brother, Sokha, to the KR, but after his brother's death he could not win Sothea's love. At Tonle Bati, where they reenact the last scene with Sothea/Srey Mom, Sophoun's father (Colonel Bora) tells Sophoun the truth. Near the memorial *stupa* in Tonle Bati,[133] he confesses that when it was revealed that Sokha was a film director, he was ordered to kill him: "I killed the one person, the only person, your mother ever loved and she does not know." They both cry and Sophoun says: "Dad, it's the past. Maybe she doesn't need to know."

At the premiere of *The Long Way Home*, in 2014, after forty years, Sophoun tells the audience that they shot a new ending and that the film is a tribute to both the director, Sokha, who was murdered during the KR period, and the scriptwriter, Vichea (who is not present). A cut to Vichea shows him in the Buddhist temple he recently joined, where his hair is shaved before he prays at the *stupa*. The next shot shows Srey Mom dressed as Sothea, looking at him and silently participating in the ceremony. Then she is shown sitting in a canoe on the lake where in the past she used to sing. This new final scene is being screened while the camera shows the entire family, including the father, who finally joins them. They sit together and with tears watch the mother playing her role and hear the applause of the audience as the film ends.

As this detailed description of the melodramatic plot and its narrative trajectories reveals,[134] *The Last Reel*, a film made by a 1.5-/first-generation director as a tribute to her mother,[135] proposes reconciliation with the past. However, I suggest that it is aporetic reconciliation based on irresolvable aporias. Negotiated through encounters with the perpetrators after thirty-five years, some of the past's secrets are disclosed (i.e., that the father, Colonel Bora, was a KR soldier and that Vichea betrayed his brother to the KR), while other secrets are kept (that the father murdered the man his wife loved). In order to negotiate the interdiegetic tensions that affectively and emotionally engage the spectator in the film's ethics of aporetic reconciliation, *The Last Reel* constitutes a distinction between the two perpetrator figures—Vichea, who is defined as a one-time-event collaborator-perpetrator, and Colonel Bora, who, regardless of his remorse in relation to his family, expresses no repentance toward other victims and thus is represented as a KR perpetrator.

This distinction between the two perpetrator figures is set through flashbacks to the scenes of perpetration, which, similar to the entire film, are shot on location. Vichea's torture is rendered in hyperbolic visual and emotional intensity that unavoidably evokes the spectators'

FIGURE 3.6 The projectionist/collaborator in Kulikar Sotho's *The Last Reel*. Courtesy of Andy Brouwer (Hanuman Films).

identification and thus, subverting previous conceptualization, emphasizes collaboration as an enforced subject position. Thus, Sothea/Srey Mom's presence at his initiation into Buddhism, after he revealed the secret of betrayal and murder, signifies the choice made by the "one-time collaborator" as a form of individual salvation. In contrast, the flashback to Sokha's murder by the colonel shows him sitting near a desk, busy with his notes and indifferent to the prisoner being beaten. Though he says, "I was ordered to kill him," the next scene presents him at the killing field, at night. The anonymity of the victims and the routinization of emotionless murder (hitting the kneeling, blindfolded, and handcuffed prisoners from behind and leaving the place without looking back) characterize the colonel as a heartless perpetrator who committed crimes en masse.

Thus, keeping the secret of murdering Sokha does not mean reconciliation with the past, but rather aporetic reconciliation. In fact, despite his confession to his daughter, the nefarious effects of his violent personality subvert any future normalcy inside the family. This is the most subversive element of *The Last Reel*.

The film's reflection on the horrific situation of a KR cadre who betrayed his own family means breaking social taboo and shame. However, keeping the remorseful perpetrator within the family and protecting the secret (the truth remains unknown to the mother and Sophoun's younger brother) become more subversive in retrospect because of the ways the film represents the prevalence of KR ideology, values, and rhetoric in current Cambodian society. In the past, the shift in the positioning of the father as Sothea's savior-turned-husband instead of the man Sothea loved is made possible by the institution of forced marriage and his status as a low-ranking cadre.[136] At present, the colonel's behavior inside and outside his family still exerts power and is violent.

One scene is particularly significant: When the colonel, escorted by an armed soldier, enters the old cinema house in search of his daughter, he

FIGURE 3.7 Colonel Bora at the *stupa* in Kulikar Sotho's *The Last Reel*. Courtesy of Andy Brouwer (Hanuman Films).

sees pre-KR film posters hanging on the wall in the projectionist' booth. Expressing his rage, he tears them to pieces. Though his rage might be attributed to the fact that the poster he destroys is a glamorous portrait of his wife, young Sothea, he says: "I once saw a man have his stomach ripped out and filled with grass. Just because he sang a song from before the revolution." In spite of this ambiguous rage, the next scene—unrelated to unacknowledged guilt feelings—portrays him as a perpetrator, totally trapped by KR indoctrination embodied in his current behavior and rhetoric: When the soldier, who looks like a hit man, sees Vichea entering the cinema, he blindfolds him under the colonel's order, ties his hands behind his back, and takes him to a deserted lot far from the city center. There, when frightened Vichea swears he has no information related to Sophoun's whereabouts, the colonel threatens him by using a highly infamous KR slogan: "If I find out you know anything else . . . *to keep you is no gain.*" This scene, which looks like a typical scene from a crime movie, exposes the KR mentality as having infiltrated every aspect of Cambodian lives and is strongly felt forty years after the genocide. The aporetic reconciliation symbolized by the colonel's family is thus the only available option, acknowledging the situation by which, in spite of admitting that the horror placed inside the family still prevails, its beneath-the-surface tension threatens to erupt.

The Last Reel's excessive style and twisted symmetries and upheavals serve to present two families whose lives are burdened with secrets and deadly betrayals. Moreover, it attests to the power of cinema as a trigger for a drastic change in current Cambodian society. It's the film-within-the-film that forces Sophoun, her mother, her father, and Vichea to confront the secrets they have kept since the war. The film's subversive stance has also to do with symbolic processes—the intimacy of horror enables on one side a literal fratricide (Vichea and Sokha), and on the other a symbolic fratricide (the colonel and Sokha). Moreover, the genre allows for the perpetrator-collaborator to be captured within a mirroring and doubling unstable dynamic, which symbolizes the autogenocide: he is his brother in the imaginary postgenocide life of the cinema (reshooting the last scene). In contrast to the nonfiction corpus that confronted both the Big Perpetrators and the low-ranking ones, representing the tension but proving an inclination toward moral resentment, *The Last Reel* proposes a familial intimate constellation that attests to the enormous

FIGURE 3.8 Horror inside the family, the final scene in Kulikar Sotho's *The Last Reel*. Courtesy of Andy Brouwer (Hanuman Films).

unresolvable difficulties still taking place inside the Cambodian family. Overinvestment in horrific taboos and shame and the compulsion to break them mean, finally, that the aporetic reconciliation tends toward Amérian moral resentment.

Finally, striving to construct Cambodia's national consciousness, both nonfiction and fiction perpetrator cinema advances the possibility of cinematic creation of ethical communities, moving Cambodia toward a culture of accountability. As Stanley Cohen contends,

> The most politically fitting way to acknowledge past injuries and suffering is to rebuild (or build from scratch, if there is no democratic tradition to fall back on) the foundations necessary to maintain the new democracy. Atrocity is neither a concept nor a state of mind, but an institution and a concrete set of social practices . . . but there must be room for "negative" reconstruction: looking back not just to acknowledge, but to undermine the public discourse which allowed for collusion, silence and indifference. Civic education should include a discussion course on linguistic morality. This would scrutinize the public denials from the past: all the techniques of neutralization, rationalizations, excuses, justifications and bystander clichés.[137]

4

GENDERED GENOCIDE

The Female Perpetrator, Forced Marriage, and Rape

PAULINA. So when I heard his voice, I thought the only thing I want is to have him raped, have someone fuck him, that's what I thought, that he should know just once what it is to . . .

But I began to realize that wasn't what I really wanted—something that physical. And you know what conclusion I came to, the only thing I really want?

I want him to confess. I want him to . . . tell me what he did—not just to me, everything, to everybody—and then have him write it out in his own handwriting and sign it and I would keep a copy forever—with all the information, the names and data, all the details. That's what I want.

—ARIEL DORFMAN, *DEATH AND THE MAIDEN*[1]

TRAUMA AND REVOLUTION:
THREE DISPLACEMENTS

The twentieth century has been defined by various scholars (e.g., Shoshana Felman, Cathy Caruth, Annette Wieviorka)[2] as the "century of traumas and (concurrently) a century of theories of trauma."[3] However, as Zygmunt Bauman claims, the twentieth century is also "bound to be recorded in history as the age of revolutions."[4] Given these reflections, it is remarkable that although current research on both trauma and revolution has been flourishing to an unprecedented extent, the relationships between these two fields of inquiry are yet undertheorized.[5] In other words, during the twentieth century, the "great revolutions" (e.g., the Russian Revolution of 1905 and the October Revolution of 1917 against the Tsar, and the German Revolution of 1918–19 against the Kaiser) did not influence the development of trauma theory.[6]

Rather, trauma theories' polemics over gender, beginning with women's hysteria in 1896 and male shell shock during and after World War I, motivated the first cycle of trauma theories, while race horrifically motivated the second, derived in relation to the Holocaust. Thus, analyses of revolutions in Communist regimes (and so-called Third World countries) emphasize the taken-for-granted Eurocentric nature of trauma theory and its disregard of the traumatic element embodied in extreme disruptions of state/state, state/economy, and state/class relationships.[7] These last nexuses in current trauma theory are totally overlooked.[8]

Moreover, both cycles of trauma theory, the one based on gender and the other on race, are characterized by immanent disruptions. The evolution of the first cycle suffers from "episodic amnesia": trauma theory is a field of study that has been discovered and repeatedly abandoned several times over the last hundred years.[9] The second cycle's progression is based on the Holocaust-driven crisis of testimony and the collapse of language in psychoanalysis, literature, the courts, and the writing of history and trauma during the 1990s and afterward (e.g., from Shoshana Felman and Dori Laub, Cathy Caruth, and Dominick LaCapra, up to Agamben).[10]

In contrast to these convoluted and disrupted trajectories, the study of revolution, undeniably a traumatic, unanticipated event—consisting of a series of traumatic happenings in the course of its evolution—has blossomed, unblocked by denial processes typical of postrevolutionary societies. Revolution theory from the first generation of revolution scholars during the 1920s and 1930s through the second (e.g., Samuel Huntington), the third (e.g., Theda Skocpol and Timur Kuran), and up to the fourth generation (e.g., Michael Hardt and Antonio Negri and Jack A. Goldstone), gradually transformed its discussion from events, causes, and structural factors to questions of gender, ethnicity, identity, and ideology.[11] In contrast to trauma theory's evolution, encapsulating mainly the nexus of gender and race, revolution theory has evolved toward an all-encompassing social-cultural consciousness.

I argue that though trauma and revolution are theorized in literature as two separate, dissociable phenomena with apparently unbridgeable and distinct evolutions, the question of their relationship bears special resonance in regard to one of the most incomprehensible genocides of the post-Holocaust twentieth century, the Cambodian genocide, and thus also to the new post-Khmer Rouge (KR) Cambodian cinema. Thus, asking what we can learn from the emergence of the New Cambodian Cinema on postrevolution trauma theory means considering not only the absent nexus (state/state, state/economy, state/class relationships), but also current revolution theory's multifaceted exploration of a panoply of diverse events. Post-KR Cambodian cinema reflects on gender, race, ethnicity, class, economy, identity, and ideology in an unprecedented, taboo-breaking way.

This newness is evidenced primarily in regard to the postgenocide representations of the subject positions of victim and perpetrator. As is well known, the subject positions of the victim, the bystander, and the perpetrator, which are prevalent in trauma studies and its related disciplines (genocide, Holocaust, atrocity, postcolonial, and memory studies), have been entangled and differentiated over and again during the twentieth century, mainly in regard to post-Nazi Germany, post-Apartheid South Africa, and post-Tutsi genocide in Rwanda.[12] In contrast, up to the present day, forty years after the collapse of the Pol Pot regime, neither genocide research on post-KR Cambodia nor cinema trauma research on Cambodian cinema have analyzed these subject positions through a perspective emanating from a non-Western conceptualization of trauma theory or from a fusion of trauma and revolution theories.

I suggest that post-KR cinema enables a new conceptualization of the victim and the perpetrator subject positions (and to a lesser degree also those of the bystander and collaborator). This reconceptualization emanates from the films' representation of the KR regime's enforcement of what I regard as three consecutive (and mostly overlapping) revolutionary displacements: from gender to class, from bourgeois people to the "New People" (that is, from class to class-less), and from a civilian to a KR revolutionary/cadre.[13] These class-dominated displacements transform the conventional definition of victimhood, making gender a temporary, eraseable identity feature under the auspices of the KR's violent imposition of class as the salient and sole identity feature. Referring to class as the major, crucial structure not only enables a connection between the two cycles of trauma theories (based on gender and race), but reflects on a new hierarchy beyond the conventional intersection of gender, class, and race in Western thinking. In this corpus, class becomes a defining and structuring category from which gender derives and upon which its centrality is based. In other words, the multiplicity of social identities drastically transformed during the KR regime is reshaped accordingly in post-KR cinema. The survivor's voice (first- or second-generation) presents both these new identities and a new conception of subalternity. It attempts to assess the agency of victimhood through them, proposing a post-KR historical perspective while simultaneously reflecting on current Cambodia's unstabilized sociopolitical conditions, dominated on one hand by the establishment of the Extraordinary Chambers in the Courts of Cambodia for the Prosecution of Crimes Committed During the Period of Democratic Kampuchea (ECCC),[14] and on the other by the ongoing rule of Hun Sen's (1985–2019) "mirage democracy."[15]

According to Pierre Bourdieu's theory,[16] class analysis cannot be reduced to the analysis of economic relations. His conceptual elaboration of a model of class, linked not exclusively to employment inequalities but to the interplay between economic, social, and cultural capital, allows us to reassert an interest in the classical Weberian problematic of "class formation" through an examination of how the three capitals might combine to generate distinctive class boundaries. In the following, in light of Bourdieu's recognition of social class as a multidimensional construct, with "all the symbolism constitutive of its existence,"[17] I will analyze the three displacements (from gender to class, from bourgeois people to the New People, and from a civilian to a KR revolutionary/cadre) in relation to post-KR Cambodian cinema. The analysis will focus on the major displacement—from gender to class—beginning with the French-Cambodian director Rithy Panh's representation of gender- and class-based victimhood under the KR through the paradigmatic case of Hout Bophana.

I suggest that the New Cinema's breakthrough in representing the KR genocide as a gendered genocide is embodied in the cinematic breaking of almost forty years (1979–2014) of taboo surrounding events of forced marriage and rape,[18] represented mainly in the films *Red Wedding* (*Noces Rouges*, directed by Lida Chan and Guillaume P. Suon and produced by Rithy Panh, Cambodia/France, 2014) and *Three Wheels* (*Kong Bei*, directed by Kavich Neang and mentored by Rithy Panh, Cambodia/France, 2015), among others.[19] The analysis will point to the complex ways class and social class differentiation operate within the genocidal process through forms of degradation, objectification, dehumanization, and destruction of "classed"-based gender.

Moreover, this chapter aims to contribute to a growing body of mainly Cambodian research on gender-based violence (GBV) under the regime, long neglected as a scholarly and legal focus, and—prior to the initial hearings of the ECCC on July 30, 2014—often suppressed in Cambodian public historical discourse about this atrocity. The analysis will also refer to the issues of forced marriage and rape as they were represented through the hearings and the screenings of film clips during the ECCC proceedings in Case No. 002/02,[20] and the upcoming hearings of Case Nos. 003 and 004. I suggest that more than the other crimes against humanity committed by the Pol Pot regime, crimes of forced marriage and rape epitomize the perverse unconscious of the Cambodian revolution. As the scholarly works analyzed in the following claim, this relates to the virtual dissolution of the family unit via near-totalized collective living, the displacement of gender in favor of an ostensibly gender-equal and class-based system, a sudden and rapid change in the female lifecycle, supervision of the population, enslavement of the body, humiliating erasure of individual identity, enforced collaboration, rupturing of the human bond, and exclusion from history.

GENDERING CLASSED HISTORY: RITHY PANH'S ICONIZATION OF BOPHANA

Rithy Panh's oeuvre is built on the survivor's perspective and is deeply indebted to the victims, the dead. It reflects on victimhood as a "classed" subject position, a reflection that is multiformed: First, Panh's films blur the conventional gendered distance between the male director and his female protagonists. The films render the first-generation male director's sharing with the suffering of the films' female social actors (in nonfiction films) and characters (in fiction films, mostly scripted by him). Since class was a much stronger feature in terms of the revolutionary *cogito* than gender,[21] and since both genders were forced to become the New People, reclassification "down" the class hierarchy meant sharing the horrific experience of life lived under the KR. In other words, in this oeuvre, the common gendered opposition (male vs. female) is transcended in order to reflect on a shared "classed" subject position (thus also providing a key insight into transcending the conventional distinction between fiction and nonfiction films in Panh's oeuvre). Blurring differences in order to return to the pre-revolution *cogito* prior to the reduction of gender and its violent displacement into, and subjection to, class, the films constitute an epistemology based on sharing the same (New People) class, regardless of the concrete past gender identity. Post-KR identity is assumed within a symbolic system in which the only apt epistemological position is the survivors' sharing of the past.

The privileging of a post-KR cinematic narrative emanating from and designed by a shared past of suffering from extreme dehumanization is a conspicuous ethical imperative proposed by the survivor seen throughout Panh's work (as director, producer, and mentor of the first generation of filmmakers in post-KR Cambodia). In this act of sharing, Panh's "economy of meaning"[22] builds a fundamental epistemic structure against the conception of female submissiveness, as well as an uncompromising negotiation of new relations to Angkar.[23] These "locations in the space of positions" in "the field of power" might also permit new relations between men and women in the post-KR era.[24]

Second, notwithstanding the reflection on a shared class as a significant experience of cinematic victimhood, I suggest that it is one of Rithy Panh's earliest documentaries, *Bophana, a Cambodian Tragedy* (*Bophana, une tragedie cambodgienne*, France/Cambodia, 1996)[25] that rewrites the history of the Cambodian genocide as first and foremost a women's history. This gendered subject position is unique because in traversing Cambodian official history on and off screen, Panh's film rewrites Cambodian male history as a female history. Thus, the body "totally imprinted by history" becomes its submissive bearer.[26]

By rewriting the history of the Cambodian genocide as a women's history through this pinnacle act of sharing, Rithy Panh's *Bophana* established the renaissance of the New Cinema. Through this film by a first-generation (male) survivor, one twenty-five-year-old woman out of the 1.7 million Cambodian victims became a folk heroine. According to the American journalist Elizabeth Becker, who discovered Bophana's story,[27] Hout Bophana and Ly Sitha were a young couple caught in Cambodia's political turmoil. They had fled their hometown, East Baray, during the early years of the war and become separated. Ly took refuge in a Buddhist monastery to avoid being drafted. Bophana fled to Phnom Penh after being raped by a government soldier and giving birth to a son. She worked at a Western-run charity for women. Each presumed the other dead, until they were reunited after the KR victory. Ly had left the monastery and fought for the KR. Bophana was a near-slave working in the fields near East Baray, "but she kept writing love letters to Ly, signing 'Flower of Dangerous Love,' or as Sita, after the heroine of the *Ramayana*, the Indian epic that teaches the ideal virtues of duty and love in the face of separation and danger."[28] Their forbidden letters—which had been stuffed into her file, the thickest at the infamous detention and execution center Tuol Sleng (S-21)—kept them in touch with each other but were also used by the KR as evidence to justify the couple's imprisonment, torture, and execution there.

Produced two years before Pol Pot's death, *Bophana* revealed a denied, taboo-ized history of abuse and sexual violence. The film turned Bophana, often referred to as the Anne Frank of Cambodia, into an enduring icon of the horrors, of "resistance, courage and dignity,"[29] and of breaking social taboos. Gendering the supremacist, racist, and ethnicist genocidal discourses of history, *Bophana* established the Cambodian narrative by putting together an iconography and positioning agency. Moreover, by capturing and repeatedly filming Bophana's gaze in the photo taken by the perpetrators before her execution (among the hundreds on the memorial wall at the Tuol Sleng Genocide Museum) and extending it through the camera's reflection on a picture of her painted by the artist survivor of Tuol Sleng Vann Nath,[30] Panh pointed to the difference between the perpetrators', the survivors', and the iconic perspectives, as well as highlighted the transcendence of sharing. Following Panh, Guillaume Suon's films *About My Father*, which renders a young woman looking for traces of her dead father and eventually becoming a civil party[31] at the ECCC,[32] and *The Storm Makers* (*Ceux qui amènent la tempête*, France/Cambodia, 2014), about women trafficking, and Davy

Chou's *Golden Slumbers* (*Le sommeil d'or*, France/Cambodia, 2011), about Chou's search for Cambodia's murdered cinema actresses, are but three examples of the New Cinema's documentary films made by male directors but devoted to gendering the Cambodia's history as well as highlighting the transcendence of sharing.

In the absence of founding mothers, this gendered iconization, based on cinema spectatorship, institutional activism (the Bophana Center's ongoing cinematic and cultural projects), as well as the growing popularity of Becker's book about Bophana in Cambodia,[33] made Bophana's icon a "cultural marker." This means, first, a sociocultural acknowledgment of Cambodian cinema's replacing the KR's policy of making the victims invisible and nameless with an act of visibility and naming of the dead. Second, Bophana, as an iconic constellation (validated through viewing, reading, and networking), not only works against the perpetrators' past monopoly but, comprising themes that resonate with the Cambodians' own life experiences, aspirations, and cultural imagination, came to the surface at the folk or popular level, where the cultural power of the State is far from assured. Third, and most importantly, I argue that this symbolic density through iconization became cultural capital that encourages the rapid development of the New Cambodian Cinema. Following Rithy Panh, whom I regard as its founding father, New Cambodian Cinema became devoted to rewriting the Cambodian genocide as a gendered-based history, constituting an epistemological act of sharing.

THE NEW CAMBODIAN CINEMA'S GENDERED GENOCIDE

This chapter will focus on an analysis of the taboo-ized case of gendered genocide, which both is symptomatic of the perpetrator-era phenomenon and reflects it. Through the female victim/female perpetrator encounter, this cinematic activism-driven case portrays new ethics based on closeness to the dead, which, foregrounding embodiment, suggests a new reflection on perpetration as well as on cinema's postgenocide role.

The remarkable renaissance of what I term the New Post-KR Cambodian Cinema is evidenced in recent years through first- and second-generation posttraumatic autobiographical nonfiction, fiction, and short-short films.[34] This corpus' depiction of women has wide-ranging implications in relation to the disclosure of women's history both during the KR dictatorship (1975–79) and for the four decades of its aftermath (1980–2019). Following Rithy Panh's rendering of classed-gendered history, a new wave of women directors deals with issues of past fighting for personal and familial survival, the second generation's search for the silenced story of the first generation and lost love (as in Chhay Bora's *Lost Loves* [Cambodia, 2010]; Kulikar Sotho's *The Last Reel* [Cambodia, 2014];[35] Marina Kem's *Bonne Nuit Papa* [Germany/Cambodia, 2014]; and Kulikar Sotho's *Beyond the Bridge* [UK/Cambodia, 2016]),[36] and the current crisis of modernization that causes destruction of rural communities and the landscape (as in Kalyanee Mam's *A River Changes Course* [Cambodia, 2013]).

However, it is Lida Chan and Guillaume P. Suon's award-winning documentary film *Red Wedding* that stands out:[37] First, in its dealing for the first time with the Cambodian genocide as a gendered genocide, exposing the taboo-ized issue of forced marriage and rape. Though other films like *New Year Baby* (Socheata Poeuv, USA, 2008), *Enemies of the People* (Rob Lemkin and Thet Sambath, UK/Cambodia, 2009), *Camp 32* (Andrew Blogg and Tim Purdie, Australia/Cambodia, 2014), and *Angkar* (Neary Adeline Hay, France/Cambodia, 2017)[38] mentioned the atrocity of forced marriage and its personal and familial consequences, none made it a central topic.

The circumstances of the genocidal forced marriages have been suppressed and covered up for four decades inside and outside Cambodia. In contrast to the revelations made inside Cambodia by both the cinema and the ECCC, and while stories of forced labor, starvation, executions, and the "killing fields" have been etched into the imagination of the international community, even belatedly, the story of gender violence, derived especially in relation to the class of the New People, has remained largely untold.

Second, *Red Wedding* stands out because it is only recently, with the intervention of the ECCC and the assistance of cinema, as will be elaborated later, that the unique Cambodian genocidal form of forced marriage and the subsequent rape it engendered has been gradually recognized as KR official policy. I claim that it differs from all other forms of conflict-, war-, ethnic cleansing-, or genocide-related crimes of sexual violence such as sexual torture and mutilation; forced pregnancy, abortion, and prostitution; sexual slavery; and rape documented in research.[39] Although, as Wood claims, "Scholars have made significant advances in understanding conflict-related sexual violence since the turn of the century,"[40] most of the earlier-mentioned literature on the subject made no reference to a context-dependent difference in the Cambodian case.[41]

Third, *Red Wedding* is unique in world cinema in staging confrontations between first-generation female survivors and their female (and male) genocidal perpetrators. With Holocaust cinema taken as paradigmatic, to the best of my knowledge during the seventy-three years that have passed since the end of World War II, no post-Holocaust film has represented such a confrontation. The few films that somehow come close to this achievement are second-generation mother-daughter-centered documentaries in which the female perpetrator herself is absent as a living person and only present in photographs and the memories of her daughter, who tries to come to terms with this "inheritance" (as in Gesa Knolle and Birthe Templin's *What Remains* [*Was Bleibt*, Germany, 2008] and Simone Bader and Jo Schmeiser's *Love History* [Austria, 2010]),[42] thus inevitably altering the issue of accountability, displacing it into postmemorial shame. The major reason for the gendered gap between the Holocaust and the New Cambodian Cinema is that the nature of the Cambodian genocide is entangled with the establishment of an international tribunal.[43] As I elaborated on in the previous chapters, the autogenocide, in which the KR murdered almost two million of their own people, a quarter of the population, made this confrontation possible. After the fall of the regime, both high- and low-ranking perpetrators continued to live their lives alongside their former victims,[44] and past intimate violence once again turned into daily closeness of members of the same imagined community.[45] The establishment of the ECCC then enabled thousands of witnesses and civil parties to confront the perpetrators, thus affecting the public sphere and the only medium that can stage such a confrontation—cinema. In contrast, in post-Holocaust Europe, for example, as is well known, Jewish communities no longer existed in much of Europe. Jewish survivors refused to return to their pre-Holocaust homes (and when some did return from camps or hiding places, they found that in many cases their homes had been looted or taken over by others).

Fourth, and consequently, *Red Wedding* also stands out for its contribution as a docu-activist act: it was vital in assisting its main protagonist in her petition to be accepted as a civil party in the ECCC.[46] Most importantly, when some of its scenes were later screened during the trials of the former KR leaders Nuon Chea and Khieu Samphan,[47] it was used as an indictment, an evidentiary legal supplement to her testimony. After both leaders were charged with crimes against humanity and sentenced to life imprisonment in 2014 (Case No. 002), the ECCC authorized an additional trial, Case No. 002/02, in which Chea and Samphan faced a charge, among others, over their regime's policy of forced marriage.[48] Thus, the film played a prominent role in the ECCC's legal breakthrough in recognizing the "nationwide regulation of marriage" as a crime among other crimes against humanity.[49]

Fifth, and most importantly, *Red Wedding* proposes a new epistemology, which I regard as typical to the New Cambodian Cinema: Many fiction and nonfiction films present the rice paddies-turned-killing fields in which bodies were unburied and scattered as a major psychoreligious trauma. After the genocide, the survivors' resettlement in these killing fields-turned-rice-paddies reflects, I suggest, on a symbolic necrophagia (the practice of feeding on corpses). The living body (*corpora viva*) and the unburied one (*corpora cadavera*) became entangled within a new "feeding" necrophagic economy that in the post-genocide period entails a new body-soul ethics.[50] In *Red Wedding*, the necrophagic epistemology and the ethics entailed stand at the core of the confrontation with the female perpetrator, as will be described later.

The following section of the chapter will outline the background for discussing the exceptionality of the Cambodian form of forced marriage and rape as a gendered genocidal crime. In the subsequent section, a detailed analysis of *Red Wedding* has a twofold objective: to describe how the meaning of forced marriage and rape is framed by both the cinema and the relevant national and international discourses embodied by the ECCC and the controversies its proceedings caused. The comparison between the cinematic testimony *per se* and the same cinematic testimony transferred into legal testimony in court will reflect on the role of cinema in promoting women's history. The comparison will also put forth the necrophagic ethics, based on the vicissitudes of the body, which stands at the heart of the testimony. Broadening the spectrum of the presentation

of this crime in the New Cambodian Cinema, the next section will analyze Kavich Neang's short drama *Three Wheels*, which presents a mainly
male perspective on the issue. A short analysis of the pioneer six-part television series *Time to Speak Out* (UK/Cambodia, 2016) will reflect on current exposure of the issue through popular broadcasting. Finally, the conclusion will reflect on the unique role of this gendered cinema and its
new ethics in the post-Holocaust post-genocide perpetrator era, suggesting that these intense and persistent first-generation embodied memories
resist remembering and instead continue to haunt the individual and the
collective. Since the emergence of second- and third-generation post-
Holocaust documentary cinema in the West coincides with the emergence of first-generation cinema in Cambodia, we need to take into
account that the latter's first-generation encounter, which might look like
an "already known," is in fact totally unknown and unpredictable in terms
of Western cine-historiography of genocidal trauma and perpetration. It
is only through the Cambodian cinema, I suggest, that we can pave our
way into theorization and comprehension of the first generation's encounter with the perpetrator.

BACKGROUND: FORCED MARRIAGE AND RAPE—AN EXCEPTIONAL GENOCIDAL CRIME

The following review will briefly sketch the main categorizations relating to the subject of forced marriage and marital rape, their historical-
cultural and legal background, and how they developed during the ECCC
proceedings. This will serve to put the films' analysis and the discussion
of the role of post-KR cinema as mediator of KR genocidal sexualized
violence into context. Cambodian cinema's gendering of the genocide,
a major characteristic of this new wave, is conspicuous, along with the
evolution of the ECCC's proceedings toward recognition and investigation of gender crimes. Thus, the following discussion will relate to both
the cinema and the ECCC, reflecting on their representation of the
entanglement of the trauma of the revolution, class, and gender through
the Cambodian case as an exceptional genocidal crime of forced marriage and rape.

BACKGROUND: FORCED MARRIAGE AND RAPE

As Cameron Christensen reminds us,

> The landmark Universal Declaration of Human Rights, adopted by the United Nations General Assembly on December 10, 1948, gave the clearest prohibition of forced marriage. It explicitly states in Article 16: "2. Marriage shall be entered into only with the free and full consent of the intending spouses. 3. The family is the natural and fundamental group unit of society and is entitled to protection by society and the State."[51]

Under the regime of the Communist Party of Kampuchea, the concept of marriage was reconstructed. In September 1977, Pol Pot articulated the party objective of increasing Cambodia's population from seven million to twenty million within ten to fifteen years.[52] By 1978, the death rate in the country was so terrible, and so few children had been born or survived, that the regime decided on a policy of forced population increase. Moreover, the regime wanted to ensure the emergence of the next generation of workers from unions that would naturally provide less family loyalty.[53]

Moreover, Christensen states, "in the past decade, international law has made significant strides in the criminalization and prosecution of forced marriage as a crime against humanity. However, progress has not moved fast enough, and will likely not gain significant traction as a crime against humanity without clarification of what elements constitute the crime, why it is unique, and how it can be prosecuted."[54]

As a law scholar and legal advisor to the Cambodian Defenders Project, Bridgette Toy-Cronin, emphasizing the wide context of jurisprudence of international criminal law, suggests, there is a lacuna in the law because it does not recognize forced marriage as a crime: "If the crime encompasses other conduct within these 'marriages'—for example, rape, slavery, or torture—the jurisprudence will not be enriched but will instead serve the perpetrator's aim of veiling criminal conduct with the term 'marriage.'" Thus, she contends, forced marriage and violence within the marriage are separate offenses that need separate recognition.[55] These suggestions will be reflected upon in the following discussion of the films.

FORCED PREGNANCY AND FORCED IMPREGNATION

Laurence Picq, the French ex-wife of a high-ranking member of Ieng Sary's Ministry of Foreign Affairs,[56] worked as a translator in the B1 compound in Phnom Penh and was close to KR leaders. In her outstanding memoir, *Beyond the Horizon: Five Years with the Khmer Rouge*, she refers to the regime's total engineering of the woman's body (mediated by the team leader, Choeun).[57] She writes,

> The party wanted many children. . . . Choeun kept the register and a note-book on menstruations. Things moved quickly. People presented them-selves as candidates, the party formed couples. The marriages took place in the hours that followed. . . . Marriages were arranged to fall exactly during the woman's most fertile period. There was no place for poetry or senti-ment. Once the woman was pregnant, her husband did not come back.[58]

I regard this eyewitness account as a rare revelation that cannot be found in any of the dozens of scholarly articles and NGO accounts written on the subject.

On June 13, 2016, after three years of discussion (2013–16), the Office of the Co-Investigating Judges of the ECCC published its decision "The Requests for Investigative Action Concerning the Crime of Forced Preg-nancy and Forced Impregnation." The decision includes a discussion of the legality of forced pregnancy as an "other inhumane act" from 1975 to 1979. It made clear that "forced pregnancy was not a crime under the Cam-bodian 1956 Penal Code, which formally still applied from 1975 to 1979. . . . Forced pregnancy was also not criminalized, let alone defined in international instruments codifying the laws of war by 1975. These instruments contained broad protections for individuals against violence, for their honor and family rights, and for the protection of women from rape."[59] In other words, the tribunal decided that it would not investigate forced pregnancy as a distinct crime. This decision also means that forced pregnancy is a crime no international criminal tribunal has yet prose-cuted. On September 16, 2016, the *Phnom Penh Post* reported:

> Civil party lawyer Linda Behnke . . . says the scenario in which forcibly married couples were pressured through spying or threats to consummate

amounted to "forced impregnation." . . . "Forced marriage is a crime against both men and women, whereas forced pregnancy is only against women," Behnke says. "We wanted to make clear that we do not see the child as the harm, because this is a very conflicted situation. Nobody wanted to be pregnant—not because they didn't want children, but because of the conditions."[60]

Based on interviews with survivors, Kasumi Nakagawa, a key figure in the development of the Cambodian National Action Plan to Prevent Violence Against Women (NAPVAW), contributed to the public debate by emphasizing that the KR's all-gendered policy was the outcome of their conception of class. On September 19, 2016, she wrote to the *Phnom Penh Post*:

I would like to assert that "forced pregnancy" within "forced marriage" was not a solely inhuman act against women, but also an inhuman act against men. Men were forced to become the biological father of a child that they might not have wanted to have with their assigned wife. Men's reproductive function was used by the state (KR) without his consent and treated with indignity. . . . In the discourse of "forced pregnancy," the differing impacts between men and women need to be carefully examined from the perspective of gender dynamics. Surely, it is of great importance to acknowledge that women were disproportionately affected by such an inhuman act, as some of my fellow women's rights activists assert, because it was only women that could be forced to carry a pregnancy at the risk of her life under extraordinary hardship. However, such a biological function does not preclude men from having equal reproductive rights or diminish their suffering from the emasculation of their gender roles.[61]

CODE NO. 6 AND RAPE

Rape during the KR regime and the subsequent period of civil war was commonly viewed as a rare occurrence that was unrelated to the context of the conflict. This assumption was based on lack of statistics and Code No. 6, the official KR policy on sexual relations, which prohibited sexual relations between unmarried couples under pain of death for both parties.

Code No. 6 is listed as one of the "Twelve Codes of Conduct of the Combatants," circulated by the KR leadership and setting out norms of discipline expected of all cadres. It was most often paraphrased as the rule against "immoral offenses" and was imposed even on the general population.

The full text of Code No. 6 reads:

6. Never commit any moral misconduct toward women.

In short, never commit any moral misconduct toward women and men. Our honor, revolutionary influence, the clean and dignified culture of our people would be affected if such acts were committed. On the one hand it would affect our people.

On the other hand, and most importantly, if we committed such moral misconduct toward women and men, which is an acutely corrupt element believed to be possessed by enemies of all sorts, we would be easily lured by the enemy. This act is therefore dangerous to us and to the revolution movement. There is no obstacle concerning the present arrangement of marriages, so long as the following principles are adhered to:

First. Each to-be-married individual consents to the marriage; and

Second. It is approved by the collective.

When these principles are followed, there is no reason for anyone to commit moral misconduct toward women and men.[62]

Another factor leading to the persistence of the assumption that sexual violence did not occur under the KR was that most survivors of sexual crimes have been silent about their suffering for almost forty years. In fact, Code No. 6 was less concerned with protecting women from sexual violence by state actors and more concerned with regulating sexual activity as a means of subordinating human relations to the aims of the revolution.[63]

Theresa de Langis argues that Code No. 6 was not primarily, if at all, an antirape policy and therefore does not exonerate senior KR cadre from the sexualized violence committed under their leadership. In her work, de Langis incorporates personal testimonies from survivors and witnesses into the Cambodian Women's Oral History Project and points to a counternarrative: Rather than protect victims, Code No. 6 facilitated the sexual abuse of women; and rather than provide recourse for victims and punishment for perpetrators, it was a disincentive for victims to seek justice, thereby promoting impunity for perpetrators. Linking Code No. 6 to forced marriage and the "enemy policy," recognized by the ECCC as two of the regime's five policies to accomplish its criminal ends (the others being forced movement, collectivization, and persecution of targeted groups based on religion, ethnicity, and race), de Langis suggests that sexualized violence may have played a larger role in the atrocities of that era than previously calculated, with Code No. 6 implicating rather than exculpating senior regime leaders.[64]

BRIEF HISTORY OF THE ECCC PROCEEDINGS ON FORCED MARRIAGE AND RAPE (2009-19)

According to Patrick Hein, "The longheld belief that women were responsible for what happened to them was only challenged in 2009 when civil parties supported by NGOs brought up the issue in public and the office of the coinvestigating judges at the ECCC began to look into forced marriages (of both men and women)."[65] Eventually, the Office of the Co-Investigating Judges at the ECCC included the indictment under the fifth policy of the KR as "regulation of marriage." Following the ECCC's Case No. 001 (which tried Kaing Guek Eav, alias Duch),[66] Melanie Hyde, Emma Palmer, and Sarah Williams emphasized in their report on sexual violence in Cambodia that the abuses perpetrated during the Democratic Kampuchea (DK) regime also had a significant impact on women in myriad ways, including starvation, forced transfers, forced labor (particularly for pregnant women), and separation from children and partners.[67]

Since the ECCC began the proceedings, at the beginning of 2009, the Cambodian Defenders Project has conducted a project on Gender Based Violence (GBV) during the KR regime.[68] It provides legal services to victims of sexual violence, such as rape and forced marriage, and aspires to raise public awareness about sexual violence that occurred during the regime.

Although the ECCC decided only in 2014 that forced marriage and rape were indeed a crime against humanity, the dispute surrounding the issue began during the arrest of Ieng Sary, the DK foreign minister and deputy prime minister, when on August 11, 2009, Ieng was questioned by the civil parties' colawyers for investigative actions about forced marriages and forced sexual relations. Since then, the ECCC has confirmed the prevalence of sexual violence, with the coinvestigating judges in Case No. 002 (against Nuon Chea, and Khieu Samphan, both of whom were sentenced to life imprisonment in August 2014) concluding that it was "clearly established that crimes against humanity of rape were committed in diverse circumstances."[69] The court found that forced marriage was a policy of the Communist Party of Kampuchea, but noted that the nature and implementation of this policy would be addressed only in the follow-up trial against the same accused,[70] that is, in Case No. 002/02.

In the *Tentative Plan for Future Trial of the Remaining Portions of Case 002*, which is annexed to the decision, the Trial Chambers lists the charge of forced marriage in Case 002/03, the third and final subtrial.[71] During 2017, the prosecution requested that these same crimes be part of investigations for upcoming Case Nos. 003 and 004, which, being controversial, have been pending since 2009.[72] Case No. 003 refers to Meas Muth (former KR naval commander), who was initially charged in absentia on March 3, 2015. On December 14, 2015, he appeared in person before the international coinvestigating judge and was charged with further crimes, including forced marriage and rape. Case No. 004 refers to Ao An (former KR Central Zone secretary) and Yim Tith (former acting secretary of the Northwest Zone).[73] Ao An was charged with premeditated homicide and crimes against humanity on March 27, 2015. On March 14, 2016, he was charged with additional crimes, including genocide, forced marriage, and rape. Yim Tith's initial appearance at court was on December 9, 2015, when he was formally charged in the case. As of the beginning of 2019, both cases are not only under investigation, but also the subject of public dispute: the international side of the ECCC's prosecution team has argued that Ao An is responsible for genocide, oversaw more than forty thousand deaths, and should be sent to trial. In contrast, the national investigating judge You Bunleng has refused to sign off on investigations and has vocally opposed Case Nos. 003 and 004 going forward. The deep rift in the prosecution was once again on display when the team released separate summaries of their final submissions to the coinvestigating judges in An's case.[74]

Moreover, Case No. 004/01 refers to Im Chaem (allegedly a former district leader), who was charged by the ECCC in absentia in 2015 with crimes against humanity, including murder, extermination, and enslavement. In 2016, her case as well was severed into Case No. 004/01. It was originally dismissed in February 2016 on the grounds that Chaem was not a senior leader of the regime, and therefore outside the court's mandate to try those "most responsible" for the atrocities committed by the KR. The case has drawn controversy because of the present government's public opposition to it, and here as well, disagreement over whether she should be charged has split the prosecutors' office along national and international lines. The appeal was lodged specifically by the office of the international coprosecutor (Nicholas Koumjian); the national coprosecutor (Chea Leang) was in favor of dismissal. The national investigating judges' opposition to the controversial cases is in line with the views of the government at large, Prime Minister Hun Sen having suggested that trying the cases against Meas Muth, Yim Tith, Ao An, and Im Chaem would plunge the country into civil war.[75] Im Cheam's case was finally dismissed in June 2018.[76]

In other words, these ongoing cases have long been under the shadow of political pressure. However, the broad context is even more complicated. As John Ciorciari and Anne Heindel convincingly argue in their work *Hybrid Justice: The Extraordinary Chambers in the Courts of Cambodia*, the hybridity of the ECCC, which fuses national and international laws, procedures, personnel, and political interests, has added considerably to the challenge of delivering a credible and efficient accountability process. They suggest, "Given the state of Cambodia's judiciary, the ECCC's greatest built-in weakness is that the United Nations has too much involvement to escape responsibility for the Court but too little authority to run it. That has contributed to . . . relatively weak international responses to serious problems that have originated on the Cambodian side."[77]

The ECCC's acute vulnerability to political interference and paralysis is reflected in how the court treats pending cases and, I contend, will be further reflected in the extent of revelations of historical-genocidal truth during the proceedings.

RED WEDDING

Red Wedding, codirected by the second-generation female director Lida Chan and the male director Guillaume Suon, tells the story of Pen Sochan, who at the age of sixteen was forced to marry a much older man, a soldier, whom she had never met. On the wedding night, she was abused, beaten, and raped several times by her husband and later by other KR cadres.[78] Afraid and ashamed to talk about this trauma, Sochan kept silent for thirty years till the ECCC was formed. *Red Wedding* follows her as a civil party, bringing her complaints against the KR leadership, especially female perpetrators, to the ECCC.[79]

From 1979, the fall of the KR regime, to 2014 and the creation of *Red Wedding*, forced marriage and rape were recognized neither as *mens rea* crimes (including the intent to destroy in whole or in part a national, ethnical, religious, or racial group as such), nor as embodying the *chapeau* element (crimes that must have been committed in the context of a widespread or systematic attack against a civilian population and thus are defined as crimes against humanity, distinguished from ordinary crimes).[80] As the opening sequence of the film indicates, during the KR dictatorship, between 1975 and 1979, and especially after 1978, more than 250,000 young women, often aged fourteen or fifteen, were forced into marriages with KR cadres.[81] The circumstances of these forced marriages have been suppressed and covered up for four decades.[82]

The logic operating behind the scenes was completely obscure to those forced into these marriages. Stripped of the fundamental right of choice and consent, girls and young women were instructed to prepare for weddings to men whom they had by and large never met. Throughout the country, people were typically married in mass ceremonies ranging from two to over one hundred couples. According to de Langis et al., who conducted research based on interviews with 106 civil parties to Case No. 002 about their experiences of forced marriage,

> Traditional Khmer weddings were a means to validate and legitimize the union in the eyes of the community, the family, and, for the largely Buddhist population, in the ancestral realm. Traditionally, weddings and marriages were also a way to demonstrate the respect and obedience of children to parents, and both a marriage and the wedding event itself held

spiritual meaning. For Buddhists, this included karmic consequences related to past and future lives.[83]

In contrast, KR marriage ceremonies were not held in accordance with traditional rituals or the participation of monks and family or with respect to the ancestral spirit.[84] They all followed a similar pattern: Couples were provided with new black clothing (the official and only permitted KR outfit) and krama scarves, were stood next to each other or held hands, and were made to make vows to accept each other and to work to achieve the objectives of the Communist Party and the revolution.[85] People were not able to assert their opposition for fear of violence or death. According to testimonies given at the ECCC, "Some people committed suicide either by drowning into the water or poisoning themselves."[86] After a few nights, the couple was totally separated, with each of them located in their own work unit, which was regarded by the regime as the most important social cell, the "new family." In this regard, Laurence Picq's remarks on the new spoken, simplified Khmer language, which was different from the Khmer taught and used before the revolution, are instructive: "The words *husband* and *wife* were abolished in favor of the more general *family*, with its

FIGURE 4.1 The only known wedding photo from the Khmer Rouge period. Courtesy of Documentation Center of Cambodia Archives.

peasant resonance."[87] The transformation of language assumed, of course, a new social behavior.

Forced marriages exploited the age-old Cambodian tradition of arranged marriage in an extremely perverse way.[88] Reflecting on the KR's Newspeak, Pen Sochan said during her testimony as a civil party at the ECCC, "At that time they did not use the word 'marriage' but 'arranged family.'"[89] On the wedding night, KR spies were placed under the raised huts to make sure the marriages were consummated. Refusal often resulted in imprisonment, torture ("refashioning"), or death. Even if the wedding night did not include a gang rape (*bauk*), which it sometimes did, it was exposed to the gang's gaze. The supervised rape, the collective gaze (both felt and embodied), turned KR's forced marriage into one of the worst forms of collective abuse and degradation.

Virginity, previously considered essential prior to marriage, was not highly prized; the young bride's body was turned into a collective one in another form of hard labor. Moreover, binding the victim for life to a person who has committed serious crimes, such as rape, torture, or forcing childbearing, the course of the marriage itself, and "carrying the responsibility of bringing up a child of the marriage, including children from forced pregnancies with a genocidal motive" should be considered essential parts of the crime.[90]

As de Langis et al. suggest,

> Perhaps one of the most radical transformations of the KR regime was the abolition of the family unit, dissolved via near-totalized collective living. Family members were separated by age and gender into work camps, many of the work units mobile. Cooking and eating was communalized; designated nursemaids cared for infants while parents worked; older children lived away from parents with little access or rights to visit. *Angkar* . . . took over the role of parent for all, demanding unwavering and exclusive loyalty.[91]

Patrick Heuveline and Bunnak Poch add,

> The KR's attempt to radically transform Cambodian society included a frontal attack on the family, which it saw as the core institution of social reproduction. Meanwhile, the powerful familial imagery was "recycled"

in describing (1) the intended new society as a one-family society, (2) the higher echelon of the political structure, the *Angkar*, as providing for the people and requiring their allegiance the way parents cared for and exerted their authority over their children, and (3) the political leader Pol Pot as "Brother Number One" among the people, that is, the first-born and, as such, the most respected sibling.[92]

Red Wedding begins with a prologue, taking place at night, in which the protagonist, Pen Sochan, is shown but not heard telling her story to her son. Using merely the light of a candle, he is completing an ECCC form requesting she be accepted as a civil party and describing the suffering she endured and the crimes she witnessed.[93] Then, the editing cuts from an extreme long shot of the countryside landscape in the dark to a high-angle shot of the rice plantations in first daylight; all that is seen is the shadow of a person walking through the water of the rice field. Then, Sochan's voice-over is heard. The uncanny feeling of specters inhabiting the threshold of nighttime/daytime and embodying the immersion of the body and space portends Sochan's initial monologue. We first hear this monologue as a sound bridge over the next few daylight scenes, which show her working in the rice field: "My name is Sochan Pen. I am forty-eight years old. The village where I live is a former Khmer Rouge killing field. When we settled here we were afraid of ghosts, because of the many graves and corpses not yet decomposed. Now, thirty years later, many people have settled here. This place became a simple rice field. But we still call it 'the rice field of ghosts.'"[94]

In a tragic way, this new epistemology based on symbolic necrophagia horrifically embodies the logic of the genocide as an autogenocide: it reenacts "a[n] . . . intimacy, a problematic collusion with the rotting double,"[95] that is, the Cambodian fellow man. Reconstructing the dynamic of sameness and difference perverted by the KR's purity of class, this epistemology's paradoxical nature is embodied in the symbolic reenacting of the abuse of the body extended beyond death. Past threat of annihilation with no trace (*kamtech*) by the Other who is the same, felt mainly by the New People, is transformed into a new psychosocial dynamic in which peasant women's survival in the postgenocide era, as Sochan's testimony attests, is built on their reconstructive capacities to turn the killing fields once again into cultivated fields (*srae*) of the most important crop, rice.

Locked in the aftereffects of the revolution's abuse of the dead, the women paradoxically perform mourning through necrophagic renewal, which "revives" the traces, and Buddhist rituals. This new body-soul ethics, both symbolically aggressive and self-reparative, reflecting less on incorporation of the dead's powers, as most of the literature on totemism and cannibalism describes, and more on the post-autogenocide period's paradoxical situation of survival through and by the dead, determines the entire journey of Sochan—and the spectator—to her past.[96]

However, this symbolic and paradoxical necrophagia has another, non-paradoxical, meaning. As the ethnographer Ann Ivonne Guillou claims, based on her fieldwork, "The Khmer system of mourning and memory is not based on a linear principle, which would suppose that suffering and loss would be gradually lessened by the work of time and rituals of death. It is based on a circular principle that could be called 'switch on/switch off.' During a second phase, the dead burst forth again from time to time into the world of the living."[97] The new form of symbolic necrophagia, I suggest, is indeed based on planting and harvesting according to the cyclicality of nature and soil. Thus, it enables incessant mourning work.

The film's editing enhances the horrific materiality of this new kind of mourning work taking place in the rice-paddy-turned-killing-field. Following Sochan's disembodied voice is a very short black-and-white archival shot of bare feet walking in a space full of bones and skulls while the cry of hawks is heard from the sky above the killing field. Devoid of a body, the bare feet are connected to Sochan's floating voice, the shadow previously represented, and the other covered, invisible workers of the field. This archival insertion combines the fertile green field with the decomposed bodies in an image the spectator is forced to absorb. The new epistemology that incessantly reflects on the proximity of the living and the dead, the visible and the invisible, is constituted by the editing (the shadow, the acousmatic sound bridge, the archive, the two fields).[98] Though we finally know who the owner of this floating voice-over is,[99] a strong feeling of unconscious optics that "hint[s] at the invisible behind and inside the transparently visible" and at "not just the unseen but that which is unavailable to sight,"[100] becomes blurred with many ways of seeing.

I claim that although Britta Sjogren's notion of "between-ness" as the space in which (Western) feminine discourse emerges[101]—e.g., between the film's visuals and the female voice-off, between the woman's voice and her body—might be partially relevant to the "Eastern"-Cambodian presentation of the female genocidal-inured voice, it is not prominent. The film grants Sochan her agential voice to its full through a similar kind of between-ness, but only after and through her confrontations with (mostly female) KR perpetrators and collaborators. Moreover, forcedly affiliated with the New People, a class devoid of basic human rights, Sochan's quest for the truth regarding her "red wedding" becomes neither a process of resubjectivization (conventionally symbolized and analyzed in Western cinema and scholarship through the shift from a floating off-screen voice to an on-screen synchronized one) providing her agency, nor a working-through of her trauma. In contrast to prevailing theorizations of the female voice, body, and trauma,[102] following her repeated confrontations with perpetrators and collaborators, Sochan's posttraumatic resentment-turned-activism, projected onto justice to be dispensed by the ECCC, is the prominent feature of her subjectivity.[103]

Female testimony in *Red Wedding* is heard, thus, through three forms: as a voice-off, mostly through a sound bridge, as Sochan unfolds her story for the spectator; as a synchronized voice, as Sochan tells her friend Chhean (and the spectator) about her traumatic past, followed by Chhean, herself a victim of forced marriage, briefly telling her own story; and as a synchronized posttestimonial voice turned into testimonial activism as Sochan directly confronts several of the perpetrators and collaborators who forced her into marriage and supervised the marital and gang rapes.

These forms mark periods in the testimonial process. Before Sochan discloses her traumatic past, she overcomes a specific kind of covert, unmarked, and unacknowledged forgetting, described by Paul Connerton as "humiliated silence."[104] She also overcomes the shame/anger loop described in the psychoanalyst Helen Lewis's influential analysis of unacknowledged shame from 1971,[105] in which she portrays this loop leading to silence and withdrawal. From Lewis's work, we can detect that an unacknowledged shame is embodied through three stages: masking of the shame with anger; being ashamed of being angry; and reacting to those feelings that create the shame/anger loop. Lewis calls these later reactions— much like Pen Sochan's—"feeling traps," and argues that "this loop may be extended indefinitely."[106] When Sochan applies to the ECCC and confronts the perpetrators, she breaks the loop. *Red Wedding* follows, thus, four consecutive processes: overcoming taboo-ized shame, bearing witness through disclosure of past secrets, confronting the perpetrators, and filing and submitting the complaint.

The film presents a series of four short scenes in which Sochan confronts the low-ranking perpetrators who were in charge of her forced marriage. The first encounter with a perpetrator, a former district chief, appears after a nightmare scene from which Sochan awakens. The nightmare comprises traumatic black-and-white archival material: burned houses; bombing; abandoned children crying; corpses, bones, and skulls spread out in a killing field; and an assembly in which a KR low-ranking leader speaks to his subordinates. The entire nightmare is devoid of sound but is accompanied by the night voices (mainly of crickets) typical of the countryside, symbolizing the ever-intrusive power of the past into Sochan's life in the present, as well as years of suffering from a chronic sleep disturbance (a recognized symptom of PTSD).[107] This nonreplicative dream is a reminder that the sexual abuse was part of a still-felt larger, overwhelming trauma.

It is noteworthy that *Red Wedding* uses this black-and-white footage taken (probably) from the perpetrators' point of view in reverse, as the survivor's posttraumatic symptom: i.e., as recurring psychical experience. The perpetrators' dominated images-turned-collective-memory, of course, accentuate the survivor's feeling of helplessness and catastrophe. However, the question to be asked is if this memorial shift from the perpetrator's mind to the victim's dream separates the subject from her own memories and thus her sense of selfhood. In other words, is this shift part of her multilayered unintentionally internalized memory (similar to the one appearing in the song scene, to be analyzed later, in which Sochan sings the propaganda song she was forced to repeat during the KR regime to the point at which she finds it difficult to recall the lyrics and then the editing fills in where she left off and completes the song through a propagandistic archival scene of young women working in the fields and singing)? Are these two perpetrator-dominated instances (the nightmare's images, the propaganda song) strong indications of her still docile and disciplined body? Do these intrusions of past trauma written on both the nonacoustic and acoustic unconscious nevertheless embody a phase in Sochan's gradual shift from victim to "inner witness," an awakening from an "experiencing I" to a "reflective I" that enables a testimonial narrative?[108] The editing provides the key to understanding these vicissitudes of memory, since the real encounters with the perpetrators take place after the nightmare (and song) scenes.

The first encounter begins with the perpetrator's (an ex-district chief) refusal to be filmed, let alone to admit her guilt. The entire dialogue is shot with a hidden camera:

EX-DISTRICT CHIEF: What do you want to know? I am busy. . . . I've already talked a lot. A lot, including to the media. That's too much for me.

SOCHAN: It's never too much. I'd like to know how it happened.

EX-DISTRICT CHIEF: I've already spoken to the tribunal! I attended the Khmer Rouge trial . . .

SOCHAN: I am frank and I'd like to know. I am a victim of forced marriage. I want to know who decided when you were in charge.

EX-DISTRICT CHIEF: I don't know.

SOCHAN: When you forced people to marry, did the orders come from above or directly from you? That's my question.

EX-DISTRICT CHIEF: I wasn't the chief.

SOCHAN: You were a district chief.

EX-DISTRICT CHIEF: Who said I was a district chief?

SOCHAN: But I know you!

EX-DISTRICT CHIEF: Do you have any proof?

SOCHAN: I don't have any proof. No offense, but I'd like to know . . .

EX-DISTRICT CHIEF: If you came to accuse me, you can leave. That's enough.[109]

The raw power of the clandestine filming of this scene lies not in its predictable outcomes, but in the hidden camera being an extension of Sochan's agency. For the first time in thirty years, not only is Sochan not the one who hides the past, but she turns the former insidious gaze, which inspected and supervised her marriage, upon itself in a form of *sousveillance* (surveillance from below).[110] Capturing the perpetrator's reactions, unaware that she is being observed, turns "backstage" into "front-stage" performance, disclosing the perpetrator's exercising of classed-based domination and social control. The gap between the gaze as a means for tyrannical social control and identifying a crime against humanity becomes conspicuous, though there is of course no reciprocity between the *chhlop* (spies) of *Angkar*, whose carceral gaze culminated in a horrific objectification through gang rape, and the gaze of the hidden camera. Although she is forced to leave, the sheer occurrence of the encounter and the gaze of the hidden camera mean a reversal of power relations for Sochan, enabling her journey to continue so that the next encounter brings more traumatic features to the surface and empowers her testimonial agency.

The loss and dissolution of the boundaries of the body are revealed during Sochan's second duel, which is directed at the ex-head of her working unit (*prothean kang*), who totally ignores her pain and denies her own complicity. Following Sochan's testimony—"This story disgusts me. I feel sorry for my body. I hate my ex-husband. I want to cut off the parts of my body that he touched at that time"[111]—she shows the female perpetrator a photo of stone carvings picturing the gang rape of a woman by KR cadres, as if she were that woman.[112] The carving in stone symbolizes the grave effect of the rape, both as a violent act and as a genocidal sealed-off buried secret. In other words, the body that stands between them in the mise-en-scène is petrified-in-stone. It symbolizes the traumatized body of one of the women as well as the other woman's denial of the body

FIGURE 4.2 An obscene space in Lida Chan and Guillaume P. Suon's *Red Wedding*. Screen shot.

(including her own). Elevating the (traumatized) body as an aporetic mediator for the confrontation apparently reflects on the sameness between the two women's (the survivor's and the perpetrator's) bodies, but in fact confirms the still-violent difference and separateness. Thus, it implicitly both demands a based-on-the-body acknowledgment, refusing its transference to remembering, and defines the female KR leader as a collaborator-perpetrator due to her alienation from the sameness of the body (and future implications of possible acknowledgment of this sameness, such as forced pregnancy and motherhood, keeping the entire trauma secret for the sake of the children born out of the marital or gang rape, and so on).

However, in a paradoxical, tragic way, the personal body engraved with the crime and the anonymous body carved in stone become similar as unseen yet nonerasable proofs. Under Sochan's cry, though the perpetrator does not admit her deeds, she does not deny that the gang rape carved in stone occurred. The camera shares Sochan's pain through its repeated-and-immediately-averted looks at the photo, bearing witness against the

FIGURE 4.3 Gang rape carved in stone in Lida Chan and Guillaume P. Suon's *Red Wedding*. Screen shot.

perpetrator's compassionless alienation from it. The perpetrator's refusal
to be accountable and bear witness to Sochan's testimonial truth and her
continuous denial of the rape's function as a class-based social sexing
might, in fact, be regarded as a second act of perpetration, reexecuted after
thirty years.[113] However, the sheer confrontation and possible future cross-
examination at the ECCC promote Sochan resubjectivization.

Through Sochan's acts analyzed earlier (revealing the secret, imagining two bodies, projecting a self-mutilation that echoes the rape, using
sousveillance as an extension of the self, and presenting the photo), *Red
Wedding* (as well as other films that represent forced marriage) is characterized not only by exposing women's traumatic history and breaking
genocidal taboos, but also by accentuating corporeal memory as a way to
defy remembering. The film's shooting style supports and heightens
Sochan's tormented estrangement from her sixteen-year-old raped body,
as well as its presence in her current identity as reflected not only in the
carved body, but in the next shot as well, after the encounter ends. Here
her figure is shown blurred by the dancing of a bonfire light outside her
house, materialized but alternately vanished by the camera.

Part of remembering and mourning, the film repeatedly presents more
instances of symbolic necrophagia: In another scene, Sochan is seen with
Chhean picking water lilies. The first shots, dominated by the pink and

FIGURE 4.4 Hidden camera and the female perpetrator in *Red Wedding*. Screen shot.

purple colors of both Sochan's clothes and the flowers, almost mislead the spectator into enjoying the visual beauty of the environment. However, this apparent beautification reflects on the fact that the women are working, almost sinking, in an obscene environment, a swamp. The necrophagic, almost necrophilic, immersion in the swamp's water is thus reminiscent of past violent desexualization. Sochan and Chhean's proximity to the space of the utmost objectification, to death, has already been imposed on their bodies during the rape.

The editing connects the water lily scene to a rice field harvest scene. Working in the "rice field of ghosts," where decomposed bodies are still unearthed, Sochan and Chhean are shown reaping rice seedlings with sickles. They sing a propaganda song (mentioned earlier) as an act of memory, which is combined by the editing with a short propaganda clip showing young women during the KR period also reaping rice seedlings with sickles. Reflecting on the silencing of the working women's voice, Sochan and Chhean's song ("We the children we love the Communist Party / With the Party we survive / Life is wonderful, happy and beautiful / A child joining the revolution / With the Party we survive") is completed through a sound bridge by unseen young women who are just heard over the archival scene ("Our love for the Party is boundless / Thanks to the Party we survive / Life is wonderful, happy and beautiful"). Part of the bodily world of the revolution, the women seen in the archive material are silent, their lips do not move. Through the song, Sochan has projected herself into the symbolic space of the past, in which, devoid of autonomous voice and body, body and voice become separated. *Red Wedding* is turned, thus, into a space of gendered manifestations embodied in acts of personal memory, which—using the masculine hegemonic discourse—subverts it with its collective overtones.

Moreover, this reframing tames past violence that is embedded in the archive's feigning of a harmonious and happy agricultural society. As Achille Mbembe claims,

> The best way to ensure that the dead do not stir up disorder is not only to bury them, but also to bury their "remains," the "debris." Archives form a part of these remains and this debris, and that is why they fulfil a religious role in modern societies. But . . . they also constitute a type of sepulchre where these remains are laid to rest. In this act of burial, and

in relation to sepulture, is found the second dimension of the trade between the archive and death. Archiving is a kind of interment, laying something in a coffin, if not to rest, then at least to consign elements of that life which could not be destroyed purely and simply. These elements, removed from time and from life, are assigned to a place and a sepulchre that is perfectly recognisable because it is consecrated: the archives. Assigning them to this place makes it possible to establish an unquestionable authority over them and to tame the violence and cruelty of which the "remains" are capable, especially when these are abandoned to their own devices.[114]

In a horrific paradoxical way, the symbolic violent act of necrophagia, which—taking place in the former-killing-field-turned-rice-paddy—dominates the harvest scenes, is both restrained by the archive's temporal transposition and made all the more "real" because of the false dimension of its propagandistic value. But, most importantly, these scenes establish the geographies of the Cambodian genocide as a chain of spatial tropes in which the rice-paddy-turned-toxic-swamp and the country-transformed-into-a-huge-labor-camp, as is seen in the archive material, become iconic instances of the biopolitical degradation of space and landscape reflecting on the degradation of the woman's body. The essentially necropolitical function of the space in the past highlights the dialectics of inclusion and exclusion, surface and depth, fertility and contagiousness embodied both in the killing fields and in Sochan's body. Her immediate and total responsiveness to the request to sing the propaganda song she had been forced to sing during her youth, to "be there," at the site of perpetration, of course makes past traumatic obedience still present. However, by separating and combining sound and image, the film also depicts a confrontation with what Georges Didi-Huberman calls an "archive of evil" by means of creating counterarchivization.[115]

These scenes prove that Cambodian posttraumatic archive fever challenges the major aporia that Jacques Derrida claims is substantive to the archive as institution—being based on memory as well as the destruction of memory.[116] In these scenes as well, archive fever elevates the opposite impulse—that of corporeal memory, typical of the women's story—by contextualizing the KR's propaganda films, songs, and slogans in a democratic, unpropagandistic framing. Counterarchivization thus reframes the perpetrators' perspective. Realized as well in the picking of the lilies, counterarchivization does not work a priori, as Derrida claims, against itself; rather, it creates an *archiving* archive, an archiving activity designed to keep its ethical impulse in motion. In this regard, counterarchivization challenges submission of both Sochan and the spectator to the Derridean death drive.

Sochan's third confrontation, with the (male) commune chief, ends not only with another denial ("I am not afraid! I am the commune chief!") but with his deputy's, the female perpetrator's, warning as well ("As for you, don't ask too many questions!"). Sochan's resentment-turned-activism is enforced by the Cambodian reality presented in this scene. Although major symbolic acts during the 2000s—like the launching of the first exhibition on forced marriage and the minister of culture's declaration about her personal experience in relation to forced marriage during the KR—gained public attention and recognition,[117] *Red Wedding* shows that thirty years after the genocide, former KR cadres, still interspersed throughout Cambodian society, continue to lead their lives alongside those they had subjugated and whose family members they may have killed, and still exert power. Nevertheless, breaking the horrific intimacy of living together, and after her last futile encounter with her sister-in-law, who was a KR cadre and collaborator, Sochan submits her complaint to the ECCC.

Exposing marital rape, gang rape, and rape assisted by or perpetrated by state actors, Sochan and Chhean's disruptive testimonies,[118] which are given in the name of 250,000 silenced voices, reveal that forced marriages and conjugal relations perpetuated a state-enforced culture of rape and abuse, especially of women, by which sexualized GBV, particularly in marriage, was normalized with impunity via state policy, and thus should be brought to court.[119] Confronting the female perpetrators and submitting her complaint mean disruption of the social death described by the American philosopher Claudia Card. Card, who analyzes the central harm of genocide as a form of "evil," specifically introduces into this context the notion of social death: "The particular evil of genocide . . . is not just physical death, but 'social death,' which can take place even when physical death does not. Social death focuses not on the physical destruction of a group, but it harms the 'social vitality' of the group, the relations of family, community, and intergenerational relations that give meaning to one's identity and links one to both past and future."[120]

After the four encounters with the perpetrators, Sochan breaks her silence and decides to share her story with her daughters as well.[121] The last scene presents her walking in a rice field before the harvest season as an act of reownership of the body. It is a counterpresentation to the body that has undergone hard labor, desexualization, social death, and necrophagic survival.

PEN SOCHAN'S TESTIMONY AT THE ECCC—THE HEARINGS AND THE FILM

ECCC Cases No. 002 (on crimes against humanity) and especially 002/02 (on forced marriage as a crime against humanity) signify a major advancement in international law's gendering of genocides. Kelly Askin concludes the historical overview in her book *War Crimes Against Women: Prosecution in International War Crimes Tribunals* by saying that from 500 BC through the dawn of the twenty-first century history has repeatedly demonstrated that application of the laws of war and attempted utilization of avenues of justice have utterly and completely failed women.[122] Continuing this line of thought, Nicola Henry, who analyzes international war crime trials for victims of wartime sexual violence, claims that "following the Second World War, the Nuremberg and Tokyo tribunals failed to adequately address and prosecute sexual violence, and no victims of rape were called to testify at these proceedings. In comparison, contemporary war crime tribunals have prosecuted sexual violence, rape and enslavement as crimes against humanity, genocide, torture and violations of the laws or customs of war."[123] In this regard, both the unprecedented phenomenon of Cambodian forced marriage (which entails marital rape) and the civil party scheme set new challenges for international humanitarian law and future prosecution and punishing of gender crimes.

Focusing on the Cambodian case, John D. Ciorciari and Anne Heindel emphasize in *Hybrid Justice: The Extraordinary Chambers in the Courts of Cambodia* that the ECCC is the first internationalized mass crimes court to follow the civil law practice of including victims as parties in the proceedings.[124] According to their description, the civil party scheme, one of this court's most notable innovations, both enables victims access to the mechanism of justice and limits the Cambodian government's control of their input into the tribunal. Thus, although a legal aid scheme that includes reparations did not develop under the support of this tribunal, Sochan's testimony (as well as that of other female victims of forced marriage) as a civil party during the hearings of Case No. 002 and especially Case No. 002/02 propelled the process forward in unforeseen and politically unfavorable directions.[125]

In its relation to these cases, *Red Wedding* acquires a unique status, rare in world cinema, that transcends its making as a docu-activist film (meant initially to assist Sochan in her journey to become a civil party) into its becoming a major intervention in legal processes of justice. The film was submitted to the ECCC in 2012 as part of the pretrial evidentiary materials gathered on the subject. However, scenes from the film were presented during Pen Sochan's testimony in court at the request not only of the civil party lawyers, the judges, the president of the Court, and the assistant prosecutor (Andrew Boyle), but also of Nuon Chea's defense counsel (Victor Koppe). Analyzing the relationship between Sochan's testimony during the making of the film and what might be seen, thus, as her posttestimony phase during the hearings, that is, between her cinematic and "legal" testimonial voices, raises the question of what function the film indeed played. First, did the scenes shown by the civil party lawyers support Sochan's efforts to attain agency and master her traumatic past during the hearings? Second, if, as a civil party, Sochan (as well as the other civil parties and witnesses who testified)[126] was truly granted a nonhegemonic, nonpatriarchal space in which she was not revictimized by and through the hearings, what was the film's role in service of Nuon Chea's defense counsel, especially during Sochan's cross-examination?

The scenes shown during the hearings performed contradictory roles: First, they performed as evidence, which—through Sochan's past cinematic testimony—supported and confirmed her current legal one. The scenes presented by the civil party lawyers depict a conversation (which was not included in the final edited version of the film) with the unit chief, "Comrade Om" (as Sochan calls her interpellatively), that proved both Sochan's refusal to marry and her being under grave fear of Om's threats of torture and death. Moreover, they functioned as an emotional active memory that "spoke" as a replacement for Sochan's legal voice. As a revelation of her first self-exposing testimony, beyond juridical processes, the scenes also transcend the contrast between "then" and "now" and thus reinforce the audience's emotional engagement in her story. Moreover, if Nicola Henry's suggestion that, "in criminal trials, the story does not 'belong' to the survivor but rather to the court" is correct, the scenes from *Red Wedding* re-appropriated Sochan's story for her during the trial.[127] They contributed to a discursive competence, resistance, and verbal fortitude, which assisted the production of a narrative that reflected Sochan's experiences, promoted her agency, and addressed her need for closure and healing.

Second, and in contrast, these scenes also could have become evidence against both Sochan's cinematic and legal testimonies, threatening to expose her as an unreliable witness and undermine her credibility and psychological coherence. A "courtroom rape" instigated by Nuon Chea's defense took place much in line with what is described in the huge literature dealing with rape testimony in criminal justice systems, international courts, tribunals, and related institutional discourses (including the research on international courts in former Yugoslavia, Rwanda, and Sierra Leone).[128] The two major debates discussed by this literature—over trauma/fantasy and over consent—are not relevant, of course, to the Cambodian case of forced marriage and marital rape. Nevertheless, when Sochan was asked by the defense about her second husband, whom she married after the fall of the KR regime, a soldier she described as abusive as well, it was in line with this literature's findings on the age-old blaming of the survivor for complicity in her own victimization. I claim that the cross-comparison of Sochan's two marriages above all reveals the tragedy embodied in unending victimization under outstanding but totally distinctive circumstances and that Sochan's second marriage has nothing to do with the crimes committed by Nuon Chea and Khieu Samphan in relation to her first, forced marriage. Since, as Hilary Charlesworth et al., for example, contend, the substantive, procedural, and conceptual dimensions of legal discourse are male defined,[129] *Red Wedding* was used during cross-examination within an adversarial context to create an inherent power imbalance between the female witness and the defense lawyers.

Moreover, when Nuon Chea's defense counsel cross-examined Sochan, the two previously shown scenes (of her talking to Om, the unit chief, and her encounter with her sister-in-law) became the source of wide controversy.[130] The defense showed these clips several times and, based on the English subtitles of the film, claimed that the details given by Sochan and filmed in the movie were inaccurate: "In the clip we hear that you said that your [first] husband wanted to spy after you. Is this true?" The civil party lawyer responded that Sochan's testimony in the film had been translated from Khmer to English and in Khmer "this is not said." Thus, the court asked the defense lawyer to reformulate his question. The clip was shown again, with the court interpreters translating the scene directly from Khmer, confirming that, in contrast to what appears in the English subtitles, Sochan did not say her husband wanted to spy on her.

This intrusion of the Western psyche through its cinematic signifiers into the incompleteness of Sochan's own evolving sexual self-understanding during her testimony in court contaminated the testimonial truth as well as the Cambodian directors' best intentions. Shaping the legal investigation, it revictimized Sochan by violating the trustful fluidity of her memory, almost transforming it into a twisted "gendered legal memory,"[131] and might have prevented her from reinventing her body image through a new and potentially empowering redescription of the trauma.[132] This cross-validation performs ritual dismemberment upon her legal "body image," resulting (as is shown in the video of the hearings) in Sochan's "automatic" responses that follow as she repeats the same answers compulsively, numbingly avoiding some parts of the questions addressed to her by the defense. With her eyes down, probably reexperiencing past traumatic domination, she cries and repeatedly says that she is sick and illiterate and her memory often becomes too weak. She did not feel "worthy of esteem and respect,"[133] and could not recognize how these confusing discourses both explain and apparently attempt to contain the psychological and political forces implicated in the violence of her past.

Thus, although the film preserves its major status as complementary evidence and an emotional force that cannot be ignored, the very premise of a truthful representation provided by a documentary film apparently becomes, due to the Westernization of the testimony, self-contradictory. Though during the first sessions of the hearings the film managed to disentangle the trauma of rape from the tacit violence of a court system, its great transgressive potential to unsettle the maintenance and reproduction of dominant discourses, as well as to curtail their sphere of influence, was disrupted. Calling attention to the complicated ways that cinematic testimonies make meaning in non-Western contexts by carrying more than their indexical traces, the hearings in their entirety show the almost total helplessness of the civil parties at the hands of both Western and local apparatuses, and the domination of epistemological structures deployed by the law. Although *Red Wedding* assisted in exposing a gendered taboo-ized historical truth in and out of Cambodia and forged a connection between the hybrid court and the survivors' community in which it operates, the Westernized apparatus embodied in cinema indeed played an ambiguous, almost hazardous role in this non-Western court.[134]

Although, as Askin contends, "It has taken over twenty-one centuries to acknowledge sex crimes as one of the most serious types of crimes committable, but it appears that this recognition has finally dawned,"[135] Ciorciari and Heindel close their analysis of the civil parties' participation in the ECCC by saying,

In Case 001,[136] many of the relatively small number of civil parties involved were able to participate directly in the proceedings, which appears to have been meaningful and even cathartic for most of the civil parties involved. Since that time, the participation rights of civil parties—and their lawyers—have been reduced in anticipation of the practical realities of accommodating thousands of victims into the Case 002 proceedings. Now participating indirectly and represented as a group, the system is functioning more efficiently, but it is questionable if civil parties in Case 002 are still accorded the rights of "parties" or will have the same quality of experience as those who joined Case 001. Indeed, the primary ECCC lesson for future internationalized courts may be the impracticability of individual civil party participation in mass crimes proceedings.[137]

In this light, Sochan's participation was indeed full, but, as my analysis shows, became both ambiguous and finally uncathartic. However, in her victim impact statement, conveyed at the end of her testimony, Sochan mentioned four main motivations for wanting to bear witness: "To speak for the dead, to tell the world the truth about what happened, to look for justice in the present, and to help prevent future war crimes from occurring."[138]

THREE WHEELS

Kavich Neang's award-winning short drama *Three Wheels*,[139] based on his parents' story,[140] reveals another silenced aspect of the KR forced marriage. As de Langis et al. remind us, "As marriage is a gendered institution— that is, it carries different consequences and meanings for men and women—a gendered analysis is provided to better understand how gender roles and gendered distribution of power informed the experience of forced marriage for husbands and wives in distinct ways, as well as the consequent trauma from these unions."[141] Following this line of thought, Christensen concludes his historical overview of the crime of forced marriage by arguing,

> A better proposed definition for the crime is: forced marriage occurs where an individual or organization confers a status of marriage— regardless of age, gender, or sex—through words, conduct or ceremony, on one or more persons by force or coercion for any amount of time that results in the one forcing, and/or the one being forced to believe that conjugal status has been bestowed. This definition would encompass enough to cover both genders and provide protection against all forms of forced marriage.[142]

In contrast to the violent reality of forced marriage represented in *Red Wedding*, *Three Wheels* adheres to these suggestions. Written, directed, and edited by Neang, the film presents the point of view of the main protagonist, a *tuk-tuk* driver in his late fifties, named Nath (Pho Phanna).[143] Wandering the streets of Phnom Penh on a lonely night, Nath meets a young woman who reminds him of his beloved one from the past. She needs a ride to the central station in order to go to the northern city of Siem Reap, not because she performs there as a dancer (as he presumes), but because she wants to attend her friend's wedding.

During their short ride together, he tells her: "When I saw you, you reminded me of someone I met in the 1960s. She was a dancer. After the fall of Phnom Penh, I didn't know where she was. We lost each other." The camera shows the young woman quickly leaving the *tuk-tuk*, which Nath hardly takes notice of as he continues to talk to her: "Then I met my wife during that time. Do you know how it was?"

The red color—of the *tuk-tuk*, Nath's shirt, and the passenger's dress— dominates the mise-en-scène and delicately combines these elements, reflecting on past lost love and desire. But the young woman, who mysteriously vanishes from the *tuk-tuk* before they get to the station, inspires not only Nath's posttraumatic recollections, but also a future transformation. Returning home after another lonely night's riding the streets, Nath offers his wife (whom he does not call by name, but rather "Hey") to leave Phnom Penh, where they have lived for over forty years. But she refuses.[144]

Their entire conversation is held with no contact whatsoever. His wife is shown behind her mosquito curtain and Nath sits on the floor of their very poor and almost empty one-room apartment. They do not see each other's faces, not because the only light comes from a candle and the electric lights above her mosquito curtain blink due to a power failure, but because of their alienation, which ultimately reveals the unspoken realities of their marriage dating from the KR period.

However, before Nath leaves, his wife has one request: She wants a proper marriage ceremony. Neang presents one scene of the ceremony, which is both metonymical and a replacement for the entire wedding: the taking of wedding photos at a photography studio. The scene begins with seeing the photographer, who addresses the as yet invisible couple, from their point of view. For a few minutes, we see only him taking pictures and hear his instructions and the sound of the camera's clicks: "Please smile. / Smiling is beautiful. / Laugh a little more. / Turn left a bit. / Smile! / Please smile. / Do like that. / When you both smile, it looks great on you." Then the camera shows the couple standing in front of a deep-blue studio curtain that emphasizes their golden ceremonial dresses and the bride's golden belt, massive golden jewelry, and ornamental golden tiara. We look at the couple from the photographer's perspective while he continues to give instructions: "Smile like that. / Look at each other. / Bride, look at the groom. / Look at his face, please. / Groom, look at the bride too. / Look at each other, please. / Look at me."

Bride, look at the groom.

FIGURE 4.5 Acting-out of the trauma of forced marriage in Kavich Neang's *Three Wheels*. Screen shot.

With the shift from showing the couple in extreme long shot to medium close-up, it becomes clear that this "proper" wedding ceremony in fact reenacts the earlier traumatic one, as the two do not touch each other, do not look at each other, and do not smile even once. Though they have lived together some forty years, their performance of couplehood evokes the one imposed on them as total strangers during the KR wedding. Their acting out of the trauma of forced marriage entails what looks like a (failed) performance of a couple's typical romantic gestures, their body language proving they find the photographer's instructions unbearable. Traumatic repetition is realized, thus, in reenacting past feigning and, paradoxically, is displaced into the photographer's incessant repetitive directives: "Please change position! / Face each other. / Put your hands on his shoulders. / Turn your face here. / Come closer. / Bend your neck a bit more and close to him. / Move to the left a bit. / Please move to the left a bit. / A little more. / A little more. / OK. / A little move. / Get closer please. / OK. / Smile." The couple's festive golden dresses, as well as the bride's golden jewelry, ornamental golden tiara, and hair extension, stand in contrast to their "inner (traumatic) theatre," still dominated by past objectification, dehumanization, depersonalization, and fear of death. Do they imagine

Bend your neck a bit more and close to him.

FIGURE 4.6 Posttraumatic dynamics in Kavich Neang's *Three Wheels*. Screen shot.

that looking at the photos will be an act of reconciliation with both their past and the ongoing crisis of couplehood, despite that before the photo shoot they had already decided to terminate a shared future? Is the photo opportunity the only means to rewrite their history, at least through a still picture that (apparently) cannot capture the horrific repetition of post-traumatic dynamics?

The preference for second-generation nonprofessional actors (who were around seventeen or eighteen during the KR regime)[145] and low-key natural lighting of course contribute to the authenticity of Neang's postmemory reflection. However, it is the apartment's location, inside the decrepit White Building housing project in central Phnom Penh, that, I claim, contributes perhaps more than any other element to the atmosphere of the couple's precariousness and (after the wedding ceremony) the wife's uncertain future.[146]

As is well known, following their victory of April 17, 1975, the KR began forcibly evacuating Phnom Penh, the capital, as well as other major cities, relocating more than three million people onto cooperatives and labor camps in neighboring provinces and throughout rural Cambodia. The research that analyzes the city[147] shows that Phnom Penh exemplifies "the most infamous deurbanization of modern times."[148] As major reasons for its urbicide,[149] the research indicates its symbolism as a (presumed) immoral way of life, but also the city's plurality and heterogeneity.[150] AbdouMaliq Simone suggests that "Phnom Penh . . . combines a long-term memory of urban existence with a recent history of having to be remade from scratch after being almost totally evacuated under the KR regime in 1975–79."[151] Taking into account not only this history of the city but also the history of the White Building, *Three Wheels*'s mise-en-scène exposes the neglect of the White Building and the poverty of its residents (the outcome of the forced evacuation and the evacuees' return to the city with no possessions).[152] Thus, the location and the apartment become a metaphor for posttraumatic, collapsing couplehood. Moreover, the slow destruction of the White Building (seen in the dark corridors and the electric system failure) serves as a metaphor for the body stripped of its former identity and "dislocated" into forced marriage.[153]

Filming the White Building, on one hand, presents this unique project, an icon of the city's spatiotemporal layout. On the other, however, it is the White Building—more than any other icon of the city—that symbolizes a second, repetitive, future evacuation exemplifying posttraumatic dynamics. While the film was being made and shortly afterward, a public debate began about either preserving the building or evicting its twenty-five hundred residents and destroying it. Neang—being aware of both options—in fact is already memorializing the building during the shooting and, hinting at this posttraumatic dynamic of a second evacuation, reflects on the tension between the wife's decision to keep the stability of residency (apparently not taking into account the possibility of a second evacuation) and the husband's opposite decision.

In the scene after the photo event, we see Nath's wife pushing her sewing machine to the center of the emptied room. On the wall, one of the wedding photos (in which the retouched image makes the couple look much younger, as if the posttraumatic reenactment of the wedding ceremony is not a reenactment at all, but rather the real event) is hanging. She counts the few banknotes she is left with and sits down to work. A quick cut leads to the final scene, in which Nath is shown on his red motorcycle, without the cart.

Once again displaced (this time by choice), Nath leaves his wife to a similar destiny, yet unknown to her.[154] Since the film's symbolic title refers not only to the *tuk-tuk* left behind, a symbol of Nath's lonely life and unacknowledged search for his lost love, but also to the imaginary trio (Nath, his wife, and his lost love) imposed on them for forty years, the open ending leaves an open question: Does driving on the bridge to what might be a promising future mean leaving the imaginary trio behind as well?[155]

The second marriage ceremony reflects on the uniqueness of *Three Wheels*, which lies in its raising a new social shame in relation to KR's forced marriage—that of the male. I mentioned earlier that the issue of forced marriage was subjected to deliberate concealment and repression for forty years because of the personal silence attached to the trauma and the power still held by former KR in the current Cambodian regime (leading to its deliberate erasure by the government, fear of reprisal by the perpetrators, and fear of social discrimination).[156] Other possible reasons are the scale of the gender crimes in comparison to other genocidal crimes committed by the KR and the social taboo against talking openly about sex.[157] But *Three Wheels* may be raising still another explanation: The gender crimes are not only a so-called "feminine" issue, and therefore considered a nonissue; they relate to men as well. Thus, they also adhere to repression and concealment of the past.

TIME TO SPEAK OUT

In many respects, *Red Wedding* and *Three Wheels*, as well as *Enemies of the People*, *New Year Baby*, and *Camp 32*, paved the way for the emergence of the pioneering six-part television series *Time to Speak Out*,[158] which explores the prevalence of forced marriage and sexual and gendered-based violence during the KR regime. Covering ECCC Case No. 002/02 by presenting some of the important testimonies from witnesses, experts, and civil parties, the first episode presents two male civil parties whose testimonies relate to threats on their lives. The first, Om Oeun, talks about his experience at the ECCC. Back then, he told the tribunal that he was forced to marry a woman whom he did not love and who did not love him, and thus "whenever we stayed together at night, we cried together." He stresses that he was punished and his life was in danger, so he "HAD to do it." The other male civil party, Yos Phal, testified that he was not permitted to marry his fiancé because one of her relatives was "smashed by Angkar," and instead was forced to marry the woman Angkar chose for him. He was told that "if after marriage we could not get along together, the 'Common Practice' in sector 33 would be applied. Pretty women would marry ugly men and uneducated people would marry educated people. The unit chief said if I didn't follow the instruction, I would be killed. For that reason, I followed it through."

In contrast to women's testimonies given to the ECCC, including that of Pen Sochan, the testimonies of male civil parties that were later chosen to be aired as a part of the television series, as these representative examples show, are those featuring male civil parties as victims. Thus, the question is, do the high-ranking KR leaders accused in Case No. 002/02 stand for all the low-ranking perpetrators (mostly KR cadres), and was the victimage of perpetrators during forced marriage eclipsed by their willingness as husbands to commit the crime of marital rape? Moreover, despite the series's general topic, what was not mentioned is no less outstanding. One of the interviewees, Ny Chandy, a lawyer who has worked with the civil parties, explains that, in 1977, Pol Pot announced the policy of increasing the regime's population to twenty million within fifteen years, and that this policy was implemented through regulating marriage. Following his interview, the anchor mentions that the children "would become vital additions to the regime's workforce and revolutionary ranks." That is, although both raise the point that the policy was meant to destroy the family group while still maintaining population growth, neither relate to the huge number of deaths in 1977 as a major reason for this policy!

Finally, I suggest that the written, oral, and visual testimonies on the catastrophe of forced marriage and rape given in *Red Wedding*, as well as *Three Wheels*'s postmemorial reflection (and, to a lesser degree, those heard in *Enemies of the People, Camp 32, Time to Speak Out*, and the streamed videos of the ECCC hearings), contribute to both making visible and unsettling the gendered depictions of genocide. The films show that the gender catastrophe of forced marriage, especially for women, was the result of, and based on, the class catastrophe. As indicated earlier, in terms of chronology, the policy of forced marriage was declared as the Party objective in 1978, three years after the KR took over. Not acknowledging the monstrous number of dead, together with a deep need for new members to carry on the revolution, this policy was based on an already-known dehumanization of the New People, labeled as a class totally devoid of status and privileges. Although these films break the layers of gendered silencing around this specific (classed and sexualized) past violence, I suggest that their major gendered images of the genocide further elaborate the complex relationships between gender and class.

Both *Red Wedding* and *Three Wheels*, I argue, present the gendered breakings of past silences simultaneously with locating past absences. At the core of *Red Wedding* lies the image of the (imagined and anonymous) photo of the gang rape carved in stone, while at the core of *Three Wheels* stands the (falsely performed) image of the wedding ceremony. In both cases, these posttraumatic images reflect the absence of the traumatic events (and their reconstruction or reenactment, respectively); the body (mutilated or decorated, respectively) carries the burden of classed-turned-sexualized-violence. Since the Cambodian genocide has no definitive image beyond heaps of skulls, which are genderless (and the relatively new icon of Bophana), the New Cambodian Cinema's gendering of the genocide further exposes these absences. Presenting the forced-marriage body also raises the question of whether it is possible after forty years to cinematically create a gendered image that can be etched into the imagination of both the Cambodian and the international communities.

CONCLUSION: THE FEMALE PERPETRATOR AND THE GENDER CRIME AS CRIME AGAINST HUMANITY

The analysis of *Red Wedding* has proven, first, the exceptional case of forced marriage and rape among other global, more known forms of gendered genocidal crimes. Second, as a paradigmatic perpetrator documentary, *Red Wedding* has shown that although the New Cambodian Cinema does not as yet succeed in proposing an entire new set of conventions similar to the one developed during the last seventy-three years of the witness era, it indeed sheds new light on the new perpetrator era. The sheer presentation of a first-generation survivor's duel with the perpetrator should be considered, I finally suggest, as a new phase in comprehending the survivor-perpetrator relations characterized by genocide, trauma, trauma cinema, and perpetrator (gendered) studies.

The docu/history-activists, who provided the cinematic stage for this confrontation, later to be completed and rewritten in legal terms by the ECCC, indeed showed that beyond the (female) perpetrators' denial of their accountability, the ongoing confrontation built the survivor's subjectivity, enabled—through the cyclicality of symbolic necrophagia—the mourning of the dead and thus reconnected the Cambodians to their previously banned religiousness, undermined the perpetrators' subject positions as always threatening neighbors, supported new definitions of gender crimes as crimes against humanity, led to a new evidentiary legal level, empowered the subject position of the civil party, and thus built the new ethics of the community.

In this, Cambodian cinema undoubtedly exceeds national cinemas' role in rehabilitation of ethics, especially in Germany and generally in post–World War II Europe.[159] Cambodian cinema's high level of "live" overcoming of amnesia, taboo, and denial of past atrocities marks a suspension of processes of remembering and postmemorialization in favor of direct, first-generation confrontation, corporeal memory, and counterarchivization.

This chapter began by questioning if we are capable of adopting into trauma theory the major insights culled from the twentieth century's traumas of the great revolutions. It is my premise that incorporating revolution into trauma might enrich our understanding of both fields beyond East-West differences. As this chapter's analysis of the Cambodian genocide through the New Cambodian Cinema (and the surrounding *jus cogens* discourses) shows, the Cambodian revolution's horrendous policy of forced marriage and rape, being both a unique and an exemplary test case, turned both female and male subjects into victims of the regime. One of several possible contributions of the Cambodian revolution to trauma theory would be, thus, a reappraisal of gendered subject positions. As a consequence, I would like to add another "obsession" to racism, territorial expansionism, agrarianism, and antiquity, the four ideological "obsessions" animating genocidal violence as identified by the Yale genocide scholar Ben Kiernan.[160] As the case of forced marriage shows, simultaneously imposing violent differentiation and sameness between the sexes is the obsession with gender and sexuality.

However, this obsession is mediated through processes of displacements. The analysis of the cinematic representation of the Cambodian revolution's displacements (from gender to class, from bourgeois people to the New People, and from a civilian to a KR revolutionary/cadre) allows us to appreciate the interplay between the differentiations within this hierarchical society. Completing its subversive stance, this postgenocide cinema proposes (through various means, most notably encounters between the survivors and the perpetrators) an evolution from past hierarchy toward a heterarchical structure based on decentralization of society.

Will Cambodian cinema be able to propel the social evolution embodied in its own critical cultural patterns into social norms, judicial procedures, and the legal system in general? Its cinematic representations politically and culturally charged the idea of class, demonstrating how cinema navigates and negotiates, critiques and essentializes, contains and regulates class in order to expose the taboo-ized processes of class-dependent gender adaptation. In this regard, the perspective of critical class studies proposed by this analysis transcends the old state- and class-based conception of revolution, and points to a much richer and broader epistemology of one of the twentieth century's most undecipherable traumas. As the first generation of survivors and perpetrators is slowly passing away, enabling new frames of thinking and new social-cultural gendered mentality channeled through cinema is crucial for the younger generations.

EPILOGUE

The Era of Perpetrator Ethics

*Saloth Sâr (Pol Pot): "I hate them all, those who haven't the noble cour-
age to hate, / And those who are mere dilettantes in hatred, paying it lip-
service on tiptoe. / O hatred, I shall do you justice. / Hatred, you are
power, you are intelligence. / And I dare proclaim you / The true Sun of
my destiny./ . . . Our next Cambodia, virgin, virile, incorruptible. / One
fine day, beginning tomorrow, / at History's turning point, / . . . In a mag-
nificent slaughter. / . . . And you, Cambodian, my brothers, you are
made / Out of my country's mud, / I'll be your potter, I'll smash you to
bits, / I'll return you to primal matter / And then I'll mold from this clay
a new Khmer people."*

—HÉLÈNE CIXOUS, *THE TERRIBLE BUT UNFINISHED STORY OF NORODOM
SIHANOUK, KING OF CAMBODIA*[1]

 few years after the completion of *Shoah* (France/UK, 1985),
Claude Lanzmann famously wrote:

It is enough to formulate the question in specific terms—Why have the
Jews been killed?—for the question to reveal right away its obscenity.
There is an absolute obscenity in the very project of understanding.
Not to understand is my iron law during all the eleven years of the

production of *Shoah*. I clung to this refusal of understanding as the only possible ethical and at the same time the only possible operative attitude. This blindness was for me the vital condition of creation. Blindness has to be understood here as the purest mode of looking, of the gaze, the only way to not turn away from a reality which is literally blinding.

Hier ist Kein Warum; Primo Levi narrates how the word "Auschwitz" was taught to him by an SS guard. "Here there is no why," Primo Levi was abruptly told upon his arrival at the camp. This law is equally valid for whoever undertakes the responsibility of such a transmission [like that which is undertaken by *Shoah*]. Because the act of transmitting is the only thing that matters, and no intelligibility, that is to say no true knowledge, preexists the process of transmission.[2]

The Lanzmaniann-Levi formulation, as well as Lanzmann's refusal to watch and discuss a film made on the Auschwitz Nazi doctor Eduard Wirths, reflects on Theodor Adorno's famous statement and reinvigorates the debate initiated after World War II and dealt with continuously since then. Focusing on testimony, in the era of testimony this debate connected the problem of the unimaginable and the rejection of the aesthetization of the Holocaust horrors with an (unnoticeable or deliberate) rejection of the perpetrator's image, which was inevitably connected to, and imposed upon, testimonial imagery. The crisis of testimony became, in many respects, entwined with the problematics of the perpetrator's representation (which mostly referred to issues of identification and fascination with Evil, especially in regard to literary representations).[3]

Does perpetrator cinema, despite Claude Lanzmann's and Primo Levi's decrees and while redirecting the "Why" toward the perpetrators, provide an adequate response to the question? Does the Cambodian corpus analyzed in this book, which mostly intertwines the survivors' testimony with the perpetrator's reactions within the "duel documentary," succeed in transcending the boundaries of twentieth-century cinema of testimony in this regard? Or does it, in fact, follow the Lanzmaniann method of showing "How"? Moreover, does the alternative representation of perpetratorhood and victimhood inevitably entail rupturing intergenerational transmission of the testimonies? And lastly, are the perpetrator's representations tangent on the verge of the obscene, that is, do they betray the creed of what I propose to see not only as the transmission elected by

Lanzmann, but as double transmission—first, to the coming generations of the Cambodian people and, second, on another, political level—to the United States and the West?[4]

Perpetrators' representations might be classified according to their initial perspective, the constraints of accessibility, and the style entailed. Two forms of survivors' perspectives from which we can learn about perpetratorhood can be discerned: testimonies given by direct witnesses and those photographed by eyewitnesses, usually third parties. Revealed through the demonstration of suffering and through footage of atrocities, respectively, these indirect representations point more to perpetratorhood than to specific known-in-advance perpetrator figures. In these two cases, it is the scale of the perpetrators' acts that is revealed through the recording of dehumanization and pain. Susie Linfield's claim in relation to photojournalism is insightful in this regard: "Why are photographs so good in making us *see* cruelty? . . . Because photographs bring home to us the reality of physical suffering with a literalness and an irrefutability . . . 'Hunger looks like the man that hunger is killing.'"[5] In the Cambodian films, these are first and foremost the descriptions of perpetratorhood told by the survivors and, further, the video recordings and still photos filmed by the Vietnamese when they first entered the rooms of execution center S-21 in Phnom Penh. They include by-now iconic images like the corpse chained to an iron bed with shackles on its ankles, a vulture pacing at its side. Thus, the "showable" becomes the point of departure for the spectators' assessing of evildoing, more than evildoers, while they simultaneously adopt an exorcizing perspective.

Perpetrators' presentations detected in documentary propaganda films that show both the victims and themselves serve this dual mode of accessibility as well, while the spectators constantly acknowledge their aesthetic of noninnocence and systematic exploitation. Taken by the perpetrators, propaganda films reflect the immediacy of the perpetrators' point of view as well as their (false) ideological rhetoric. In the Cambodian films, this form includes the propagandistic images of the Communist agrarian utopia embodied in clips of hundreds of victims working at building dams and roads, planting or harvesting rice fields, and so on and the hundreds of mug shots of tortured S-21 prisoners prior to their execution. Since the perpetrators are usually unseen in the frame, these are indirect representations of perpetratorhood. In both cases (of false and of administrative representation, respectively), the spectators' look turns into a nonnaïve gaze that deciphers the rhetoric of propaganda or the context of the shooting, examines the conditions of these images' creation, and concurrently breaks the ontological status of the images filmed. Another form of representation that proposes an exactness that allows the identification of the (usually Big) perpetrators is embodied in formal photographs of Khmer Rouge assemblies, military marches, public speeches, and the like. In this regard, in global perpetrator cinema, the perpetrators' self-presentation might become excessively sublimated (as in the highly controversial case of Joshua Oppenheimer's depiction of the Indonesian paramilitary perpetrators of the massacre in the 1960s of alleged communists in *The Act of Killing* [UK/Denmark/Norway, 2012]).[6]

A NEW FORM: THE DUEL TESTIMONY

As I hope my analysis throughout this book proves, the documentary duel provides the spectator with intimacy-driving historical knowledge that transcends the constraints of representation, as well as the problematics indicated earlier. Usually a lengthy process, the duel is not indirect, fantasized, or illusive in regard to perpetratorhood—particularly the perpetrator figure. Despite the lacuna caused by failed accountability, the image of the Big Perpetrator is precise: a real-life figure mostly depicted through its defeat (or upcoming "defeat" at the ECCC trial). I suggest that many images described earlier as *lived archive* taken by the perpetrators (footage of atrocities, propagandistic images of victims, formal presentations, and perpetrators' self-presentations) are repeatedly shown and reframed in the films of most of the directors discussed. In Rithy Panh's oeuvre, for example, such repeated images include the Khmer Rouge's expulsion of city dwellers from Phnom Penh on April 17, 1975, the trails of evacuees on the main roads outside Phnom Penh, and the image of Phnom Penh as a deserted, empty city; the rebellious look of Hout Bophana at S-21; the propagandistic clips of hard labor; and the Khmer Rouge assemblies mentioned earlier. During the past few decades of Panh's filmmaking (beginning in 1989), their reframing is transformative in terms of the Why. In other words, through their repetitive screening the spectators identify their visual (and audial) details, are requested to hypostasize the conditions of cruelty that enabled their creation, and learn to interpret and appropriate meaning as if this were a constant exercise in observation. Through this attentive questioning of the images, they learn to "read" perpetratorhood. Thus, I suggest that the survivor-perpetrator documentary duel, which constantly uses such images as a major dueling strategy, as I showed earlier, presents a new form of testimony. Though it might be cathartic, as in the case of Lida Chan and Guillaume P. Suon's *Red Wedding* (*Noces Rouges*, Cambodia/France, 2012), it is first and foremost anchored in the acts of How and of refutation. Interweaving the Why and the How, the testimony is aimed at repudiation of the perpetrators' reactions of denial: the new form of duel testimony expresses the responsibility of double transmission through the ongoing encounter.

In one of the first scenes of *Angkar*, Neary Adeline Hay's biographical film on the return of her father (Khonsaly Hay) to the village where, as a young man, he was forced to do hard labor, starved, tortured, and survived day-to-day anxiety and near death, the camera shows from a distance a man washing himself in the yard outside a shack. He is filmed from the back, but when the next cut shows his thin wrinkled torso and white-haired, half-bald head in close-up, it is revealed he is probably in his late eighties or early nineties. Sitting on a stool, several times he uses a bowl to take water from a bucket and pour it over his head, scratching his skull. Over his slow climbing of the stairs into the hut, the spectator hears Khonsaly Hay's first question, confirming that the old man, whose name will be revealed only in the film's coda, was a collaborator, a spy (*chhlop*) for Angkar. The next scene, inside the house, shows the survivor and the perpetrator sitting very close to each other on the floor so that the *chhlop* can whisper in Khonsaly Hay's ear the names of some of the killers. After their tête-à-tête about the killings and cannibalism,[7] the conversation is shifted by the survivor to more personal directions:

KHONSALY HAY: So were you at the execution?
THE PERPETRATOR: As I said just now it's the only time I've been at an execution.
KHONSALY HAY: How was he killed?
THE PERPETRATOR: How was he slaughtered? I saw blood spurting . . .
KHONSALY HAY: What did they hit him with?

THE PERPETRATOR: I didn't dare look.

KHONSALY HAY: You're not sure what the weapon was?

THE PERPETRATOR: A pickaxe handle. They also hit him with bamboo sticks.

KHONSALY HAY: Ahmmm

THE PERPETRATOR: They executed him and threw him in the ditch.

Then the editing cuts to a few shots of Khonsaly Hay in another yard in the village, washing himself the same way the collaborator-perpetrator did. Though it is obvious that the conditions in the village do not permit running water and indoor baths, the similarity between the two scenes is appalling. However, in one of the next scenes, an extreme long shot shows Khonsaly Hay walking through the outer environs of the village at the former site of the executions. The spectators hear his voice-over saying: "I don't want to call them Khmer Rouge. In it there is 'Khmer,' and folks associate the Khmer people with this murderous regime. I prefer to talk about 'Communists.' About the 'Angkar.' Because these people are not me, I'm not them. When I hear 'Khmer Rouge,' I'm ashamed."

Later, her father refers to one of the old women in the village as "Mother" and hugs her. Back then she supported him and once risked herself by giving him food (though she finally turned him in). The spectators hear Neary's voice-over saying: "When you spoke about passive resistance, the woman you called Mother, I couldn't understand. For me there were only ever victims and their executioners." Over hazed, almost abstract filming of the water and trees from the perspective of a drone, such that they look like dots, Neary Hay's voice is heard again: "One and a half to three million dead, out of a population of seven million, in three years, eight months, and twenty days. Cambodians killed Cambodians. Like a man killing his brother, so that the shame of it made the whole family keep the crime a secret. This silence, which passes on no memories, is the shame within which I grew up. The silence of a people's collective shame."

These scenes are emblematic of the complexity of the intimacy of horror, shown through the film's staging of the survivor/(low-ranking) perpetrator encounter, but—reflecting in various ways on the autogenocide tragedy of sameness and difference—the scenes' revelation of the How, the low-ranking perpetrator's confession, undoubtedly renders the conflictual views that this complex form of transmission engenders. This begins with

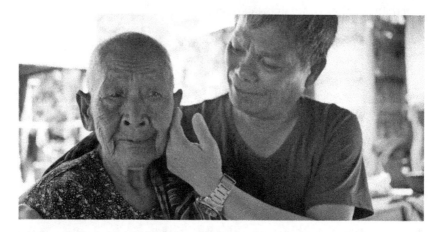

FIGURE E.1 Khonsaly Hay and his perpetrator-mother in *Angkar*. Courtesy of Christophe Audeguis (The Cup of Tea Productions).

the uneasy visual resemblance of the bathing scenes and ends with contrasting meaning-making through the voice-overs. Regardless of the intergenerational tensions, cinema's empowerment of both the survivor and second-generation subjectivities is remarkable. Further, in contrast to other violent contexts, most notably in South Africa after the Truth and Reconciliation Commission, in which the categories of perpetrators and victims were reorganized and mixed, the challenge that the ethics of moral resentment poses, as Neary's voice-over emphasizes, is the sheer differentiation between the victims and the perpetrators in this postgenocide society that refuses any option for reconciliation. In this regard, it is the drone's perspective that is both a hopeful symbolic reminder of Cambodia's beauty in the midst of the violent cruelty rendered and a symbol of the impossibility of the gaze to mediate intelligibility. In other words, the ambiguity of transmission is reflected through the (apparently) "no one's point-of-view" shots. Pointing through cinema's metalanguage to the intergenerational tensions enables the second-generation daughter/filmmaker's moral resentment, repeatedly "Being Then," to become a form of vicarious mourning.

In contrast to the expectations that might arise from the title of this book, as well as from Pol Pot's vehement statement as presented in Cixous's Shakespearean play in the epigraph of this epilogue, Cambodian

FIGURE E.2 Fantasy in *Exile*. Courtesy of Rithy Panh.

perpetrator cinema is first and foremost a cinema of survival that keeps the wound open. Unraveling over forty years of repressed and taboo-ized historical truth, as well as fighting denial and cover-up in the public sphere of this society run by a nondemocratic regime, where ideas and images about the past have not been produced, mediated, reworked, fought over, refashioned into new ideology, or put into collective circulation, and where the "pastness" of the society was very unsettled and unsecured, this becomes a large-scale achievement. It is not only Cambodian cinema's major intervention in legal processes of justice but also docu-activism's unraveling of crimes against humanity like forced marriage and rape that extend the boundaries of collective, corporeal memory. New forms of mourning (such as necrophagic renewal) become, as I have suggested earlier, major forces among various others campaigning for democratization of culture. Finally, on a broader scale, since perpetration is a tragic feature of the human condition, my concluding analysis of what perpetrator studies teaches us not only as a counterdiscipline to victim studies but as a reflection on the complex intertwining of the two disciplines in the twenty-first century reveals the new challenge faced by spectators of the perpetrator era.

NOTES

PREFACE

1. Article 2 of the United Nations' *Convention on the Prevention and Punishment of the Crime of Genocide* defines "genocide" as

   > any of the following acts committed with the intent to destroy, in whole or in part, a national, ethnic, racial or religious group, as such: Killing members of the group; Causing serious bodily or mental harm to members of the group; Deliberately inflicting on the group conditions of life calculated to bring about its physical destruction in whole or in part; Imposing measures intended to prevent births within the group; and forcibly transferring children of the group to another group.

   Quoted in Steven Baum, *The Psychology of Genocide: Perpetrators, Bystanders, and Rescuers* (Cambridge: Cambridge University Press, 2008), 9. This definition was recently adopted by the International Association of Genocide Scholars.

2. Karl D. Jackson, *Cambodia, 1975–1978: Rendezvous with Death* (Princeton, NJ: Princeton University Press, 1989), 3.

ACKNOWLEDGMENTS

1. Raya Morag, "The Survivor-Perpetrator Encounter and the Truth Archive in Rithy Panh's Documentaries," in *Post-1990 Documentary Reconfiguring Independence*, ed. Camille Deprez and Judith Pernin (Edinburgh: Edinburgh University Press, 2015), 97–111.

2. Raya Morag, "Gendered Genocide: New Cambodian Cinema and the Case of Forced Marriage and Rape," *Camera Obscura* 113, no. 1 (2020).

1. DEFINING PERPETRATOR CINEMA

1. Paul Ricoeur and David Pellauer, "Evil, a Challenge to Philosophy and Theology," *Journal of the American Academy of Religion* 53, no. 4 (1985): 645.

2. Rithy Panh and Christopher Bataille, *The Elimination: A Survivor of the Khmer Rouge Confronts His Past and the Commandant of the Killing Fields,* trans. John Cullen (New York: Other Press, 2013), 266.

3. See the introduction to my book *Waltzing with Bashir: Perpetrator Trauma and Cinema* (London: I. B. Tauris, 2013), xiv, which introduces the concept of ethical trauma (in contrast to psychological trauma), in the context of new wars' deliberate targeting of noncombatants. To the best of my knowledge, this is the first elaboration on the shift from the witness to the perpetrator era. See Kara Critchell, Susanne C. Knittel, Emiliano Perra, and Uğur Ümit Üngör, "Editors' Introduction," *Journal of Perpetrator Research* 1, no. 1 (2017): 1. This first issue uses the phrase "era of the perpetrator" without relating to the major role of cinema in promoting perpetrator studies or elaborating any further.

4. For example, Patricio Guzmán, *The Pinochet Case* (*Le cas Pinochet*, France/Chile/Belgium/Spain, 2001), which presents the story of the arrest of Chile's ex-dictator Augusto Pinochet rendered through mainly women victims' testimonies and the following international judicial proceedings to bring him to trial.

5. As Shoshana Felman and Dori Laub claim,

    > The historic trauma of the Second World War, a trauma we consider as the watershed of our times and which . . . [we] come to view not as an event encapsulated in the past, but as a history which is essentially not over, a history whose repercussions are not simply omnipresent (whether consciously or not) in all our cultural activities, but whose traumatic consequences are still actively evolving . . . in today's political, historical, cultural and artistic scene.

    Felman and Laub, *Testimony: Crises of Witnessing in Literature, Psychoanalysis and History* (Leiden, Netherlands: Taylor and Francis, 1992), Kindle location 101–9.

6. Jacques Rancière, "The Ethical Turn of Aesthetics and Politics," in *Aesthetics and Its Discontents,* trans. Steven Corcoran (Cambridge: Polity, 2009), 125.

7. See Ben Kiernan, "Wall of Silence: The Field of Genocide Studies and the Guatemalan Genocide," in *Den Dannede Opprorer Bernt Hagtvet 70 ar* [The educated rebel for Bernt Hagtvust at 70], ed. Nik Brandal and Dag Einar Thorsen (Oslo: Dreyers Forlag, 2016), 169–98.

8. Jean Laplanche, "Time and the Other," in *Essays on Otherness* (New York: Routledge, 1999), 54.

9. A phrase coined by Emmanuel Levinas. See Levinas, *Emmanuel Levinas: Basic Philosophical Writings,* ed. Adriaan T. Peperzak, Simon Critchley, and Robert Bernasconi (Bloomington: Indiana University Press, 2008), 14.

10. As indicated by Critchell et al., "Editors' Introduction," 1.

11. See, e.g., Tristan Anne Borer, "A Taxonomy of Victims and Perpetrators: Human Rights and Reconciliation in South Africa," *Human Rights Quarterly* 25, no. 4 (2003): 1088–116.

12. See, for example, M. C. Brower and B. H. Price, "Advances in Neuropsychiatry of Frontal Lobe Dysfunction in Violent and Criminal Behaviour: A Critical Review," *Journal of Neurology, Neurosurgery, and Psychiatry* 71, no. 6 (2001): 720–26; Angela Scarpa and Adrian Raine, "The Psychophysiology of Antisocial Behavior: Interactions with Environmental Experiences," in *Biosocial Criminology: Challenging Environmentalism Supremacy,* ed. Anthony Walsh and Lee Ellis (Hauppauge, NY: Nova Science, 2003), 209–26; Pauline S. Yaralian and Adrian Raine, "Biological Approaches to Crime Psychophysiology and Brain Dysfunction Positive," in *Explaining Criminals and Crime: Essays in Contemporary Criminological Theory,* ed. Raymond Paternoster and Ronet Bachman (Los Angeles: Roxbury, 2001), 57–72; Alison Abbott, "Into the Mind of a Killer," *Nature* 410 (2001): 296–98; Adrian Raine, D. Phil, Jacqueline Stoddard, Susan Bihrle, and Monte Buchsbaum, "Prefrontal Glucose Deficits in Murderers Lacking Psychosocial Deprivation," *Neuropsychiatry, Neuropsychology, and Behavioral Neurology* 2, no. 1 (1998): 1–7.

13. Binjamin Wilkomirski, *Fragments: Memories of a Wartime Childhood,* trans. Carol Brown Janeway (New York: Schocken, 1996). See John Mowitt, "Trauma Envy," *Cultural Critique* 46 (2000): 272–97.

14. Jonathan Dunnage, "Perpetrator Memory and Memories About Perpetrators," *Memory Studies* 3, no. 2 (2010): 91.

15. In the following chapters I will discuss mainly the perpetrator figure, which is more prevalent in the Cambodian films. As an autogenocide (see analysis in chapter 2), the Cambodian genocide turned collaborators into perpetrators/killers even inside their own families and small agrarian communities because the peasants had been elevated into the preferred class. The most conspicuous figure of the Cambodian collaborator, the spy, is depicted and analyzed through its appearance in specific films.

16. The fantasmatic dimension of fiction films and the blurring of fiction with history need further elaboration that exceeds the scope of this book, which mainly concerns documentaries. However, in order to complete the picture of perpetrator cinema as a global phenomenon, I include here a list of fiction films that gave rise to scholarly as well as popular debates on the issue of perpetrator representation such as Oliver Hirschbiegel's *Downfall* (*Der Untergang,* Germany/Austria/Italy, 2004), on Hitler's last ten days in the bunker; Jutta Bruckner's *Hitler Cantata* (*Die Hitlerkantate,* Germany, 2005), on women who were fans of Hitler; Florian Henckel von Donnersmarck's *The Lives of Others* (*Das Leben der Anderen,* Germany, 2006), a portrayal of a Stasi secret-police agent who begins to care about and protect a couple under his surveillance; Lee Isaac Chung's *Munyurangabo* (Rwanda/USA, 2007), the quest of a teenage boy to kill the soldier who murdered his father in the Rwandan genocide in 1994; Stephen Daldry's *The Reader* (USA/Germany, 2008), about a woman who after many years is revealed to have been a Nazi prison guard being tried for murder; Vladimir Perisic's *Ordinary People* (Serbia/Netherlands/France/Switzerland, 2009), in which the leader of a small military unit in the Balkans sends his ten soldiers to a deserted area where they are

repeatedly ordered to execute prisoners transported in a lorry; Alrick Brown's *Kinyarwanda* (USA/France, 2011), which stages a scene of perpetrators' confessions in a reeducation/forgiveness camp in Rwanda in 1994; Srdan Golubovic's *Circles* (*Krugovi*, Serbia/Germany/France/Croatia/Slovenia, 2012), which intertwines a few subplots that reflect the consequences and implications of an incident that occurred twelve years previously—the beating to death of a Serbian soldier by three of his comrades when he stops them from killing a Muslim kiosk owner in a small town in Bosnia; Roland Joffé's *The Forgiven* (USA, 2017), in which the fictional character of a racist death-squad assassin confronts Forest Whitaker's Archbishop Desmond Tutu in South Africa in the mid-1990s; Jonathan Teplitzky's *Railway Man* (Switzerland/UK/Australia, 2013), in which a middle-aged British man suffering from PTSD (post-traumatic stress disorder) since World War II resulting from torture by a Japanese officer meets his torturer when he visits the Japanese War Museum, housed in a previous torture center, where his torturer is working and is asked for forgiveness; Atom Egoyan's *Remember* (Canada/Mexico/Germany/South Africa, 2015), in which the true identity of a Nazi criminal pretending to be a Jewish survivor is finally revealed; Kai Wessel's *Fog in August* (*Nebel im August*, Germany, 2016), telling the story of a Roma boy who at the mental sanatorium to which he was sent discovers the Nazi euthanasia program and plans to sabotage it.

17.   The prominent films that present perpetrators in the context of the War on Terror are Errol Morris's *The Fog of War: Eleven Lessons from the Life of Robert S. McNamara* (USA, 2003), *Standard Operating Procedure* (USA, 2008), and *The Unknown Known* (USA, 2013); Coco Fusco's *Operation Atropos* (USA, 2006); and Rory Kennedy's *The Ghosts of Abu Ghraib* (USA, 2007). The number of films dealing with the issue of soldiers as perpetrators is huge. Under the umbrella of perpetrator cinema, I chose to include the trend that follows the September 11 attack and extraordinary documentaries that, I suggest, in their presentation of soldiers, transcend both the war film genre and the specific context of the War on Terror, such as Laurent Bécue-Renard's *Of Men and War* (France/Switzerland/USA, 2014). On war films that present this dilemma, see my books *Defeated Masculinity: Post-Traumatic Cinema in the Aftermath of War* (Brussels: Peter Lang, 2009) and *Waltzing with Bashir*. See also Patty Ann Dillon's *There Will Be No Stay* (USA, 2016), which presents the posttraumatic experiences of former soldiers who became prison executioners. When their suffering and that of their families caused by their job became unbearable, they were forced to either continue or pay the price by being stripped of their rank. The experiences expose the difficulties they faced and the many ex-soldiers that committed suicide because of the system's blindness and lack of psychological treatment offered to them.

18.   As part of current media culture that celebrates sensationalism, the number of films that give center stage to mercenaries or perpetrators involved in crime is growing rapidly, especially in the second decade of this century, such as Scott Dalton and Margarita Martinez's *La Sierra* (Columbia/USA, 2005), which describes the veritable civil war battle between paramilitary groups and leftist guerrillas; Gianfranco Rosi's *El Sicario: Room 164* (France/USA, 2010) unfolds the monologues of a Mexican drug cartel killer, masked in a bare hotel room, who details his methods in the drug war; Everardo

González's *Devil's Freedom* (*La libertad del Diablo*, Mexico, 2017) presents accounts and testimonies of killers, soldiers, police, mothers, fathers, and children—all wearing elastic skull-like masks over their heads—on the systemic violence that pervades practically all levels of Mexican society; Salomé Lamas's *No Man's Land* (*Terra de Ninguém*, Portugal, 2012), the confession of sixty-six-year-old Paulo de Figuiriedo on his activities as a mercenary, assassin, and soldier in the Portuguese colonies in Rhodesia, Angola, and Al-Salvador, and in the service of the CIA, mixed with the director's reflections through her voice-over narration; Marc Wiese's *Camp 14: Total Control Zone* (South Korea/Germany, 2012) is based on interviews with a former political prisoner in a North Korean reeducation camp who relates his memories of the camp, where he was born, until his escape at the age of twenty-three, and two ex-guards who live in South Korea; and in Nadav Schirman's *In the Dark Room* (Germany/Finland/Israel/Romania, 2013), the director interviews Magdalena and Rosa Kopp, wife and daughter of the terrorist Carlos, known as "The Jackal," leader of the radical German revolutionary cell during the 1970s. See also Barbet Schroeder's *Terror's Advocate* (*L'avocat de la terreur*, France, 2007), which interviews Jacques Vergès, the controversial lawyer and former Free French Forces guerrilla, on his career and mind-set. From the 1960s till the 2000s he defended bombers, kidnappers, rebels, and other unpopular figures, such as the Nazi war criminal Klaus Barbie and the Holocaust denier Roger Garaudy.

19. Recent films that deal with the ambiguous subject position of *Capos* and *Zonderkommandos*, collaborators who were forced to work in what Primo Levi called "the gray zone," include Tim Blake Nelson's *The Grey Zone* (USA, 2001); Dany Setton and Tor Ben-Mayor's *Kapo* (Israel, 1999); Claude Lanzmann's *The Last of the Unjust* (*Le dernier des injustes*, France/Austria, 2013); and László Nemes's fiction film *Son of Saul* (*Saul fia*, Hungary, 2015). Recent fiction films in which the collaborator figure is not the main protagonist include, among many others, Stefan Ruzowitzky's *The Counterfeiters* (*Die Fälscher*, Austria/Germany, 2007), Ferenc Török's *1945* (Hungary, 2017), Pawel Pawlikowski's *Ida* (Poland/Denmark/France/UK, 2015), Vincent Perez's *Alone in Berlin* (UK/France/Germany, 2016), and Adrian Sitaru's *Illegitimate* (*Ilegitim*, Romania/Poland/France, 2016). An analysis of collaborator films exceeds the scope of this book.

20. Morag, *Waltzing with Bashir*, 19–20, 130–31.

21. Daniel. J. Goldhagen, *Hitler's Willing Executioners* (New York: Vintage, 1997).

22. Dori Laub and Susanna Lee, "Thanatos and Massive Psychic Trauma: The Impact of the Death Instinct on Knowing, Remembering, and Forgetting," *Journal of American Psychoanalytic Association* 51, no. 2 (2003): 438.

23. I suggest that in contrast to victims' testimony, perpetrators confess their accounts, which I regard as the relevant mode for describing their ethical response.

24. James E. Young, "Holocaust Documentary Fiction: The Novelist as Eyewitness," in *Writing and the Holocaust*, ed. Berel Lang (New York: Holmes and Meier, 1988), 209.

25. Barbara Harff and Ted Robert Gurr, "Toward Empirical Theory of Genocides and Politicides: Identification and Measurement of Cases Since 1945," *International Studies Quarterly* 32, no. 3 (1988): 370.

26. Rudolph J. Rummel, *Statistics of Democide: Genocide and Mass Murder Since 1900*, annotated ed. (Münster, Germany: LIT Verlag, 1998).

27. Andreas Huyssen, "Present Pasts: Media, Politics, Amnesia," *Public Culture* 12, no. 1 (2000): 22.

28. Winner of the Avner Shalev Yad Vashem Chairman's Award at the Jerusalem International Film Festival, 2014.

29. The recordings are the first known documents in which a high-ranking German member of the Nazi government speaks of the ongoing extermination of the Jews in extermination camps. They demonstrate that the German government planned and carried out the Holocaust.

30. Stefan Ruzowitzky's *The Counterfeiters*.

31. Quentin Tarantino's *Inglourious Basterds* (Germany/USA, 2009); Giulio Ricciarelli's *Labyrinth of Lies* (*Im Labyrinth des Schweigens*, Germany, 2014).

32. Uli Edel's *The Baader Meinhof Complex* (*Der Baader Meinhof Komplex*, Germany/France/Czech Republic, 2008).

33. Desbois founded an organization aimed at locating the sites of mass graves of Jewish victims of the Einsatzgruppen in the former Soviet republics and the Eastern bloc.

34. Dominick LaCapra, *Writing History, Writing Trauma* (Baltimore: Johns Hopkins University Press, 2001), 125.

35. *Depth Two*, which premiered at Berlinale Forum in 2016, is Glavonić's first feature-length documentary. So far, it has been screened at more than fifty festivals, winning twenty awards, including the main awards at the Festival dei Popol; Open City Documentary Festival's Dokufest (the Kosovo-based documentary festival); and ZagrebDox, where it won the Big Stamp Award for Best Film in Regional Competition.

36. The Suva Reka massacre was the mass murder of Kosovan Albanian civilians committed by Serbian police officers on March 26, 1999, in Suva Reka, Kosovo, during the NATO bombings of Yugoslavia in 1999. There were forty-eight victims, including fourteen under the age of fifteen. One woman survived the massacre. The victims were locked inside a pizzeria into which two hand grenades were thrown. The bodies of the victims were later transported to Serbia and buried in mass graves near a police facility at Batajnica, near Belgrade. The investigation into the Suva Reka massacre started three years after the mass graves in Serbia had been discovered. After a three-year trial, a war crimes court found four former Serbian policemen guilty of the massacre and sentenced them to up to twenty years in prison. Suva Reka is the first war crimes case in Serbia related to mass graves discovered after Slobodan Milošević's ouster in 2000.

37. The original meaning of the word *acousmêtre* dates back to the Greek philosopher Pythagoras, who is believed to have tutored his students from behind a curtain "so that the sight of the speaker wouldn't distract them from the message." Michel Chion, *The Voice in Cinema*, trans. Claudia Gorbman (1982; New York: Columbia University Press, 1999), 19.

38. Chion, 23.

39. Moreover, marked after Shoshana Felman and Dori Laub launched the field of literary trauma studies with their seminal work *Testimony: Crises of Witnessing in Literature,*

Psychoanalysis and History, published in 1992, claiming that the twentieth century was "an era of testimony," their theorization (as well as praxis) was later expanded, in 1998, in Annette Wieviorka's *The Era of the Witness*, which analyzes the changing historical and social conditions under which testimony has been produced, circulated, and received, and under which the survivor's authority as a witness has been consolidated. Toward the end of 1970s, after the scandalous broadcast of the television miniseries *The Holocaust* in Germany, the United States, and France, it became clear, as Wieviorka suggests, that the systematic recollections of audiovisual testimonies should begin. Though the efforts to bear witness in diaries, chronicles, and unpublished manuscripts began in the earliest stages of the genocide, in the postwar period the meaning of testimony remained largely personal. The Eichmann trial (1961–62), claims Wieviorka, conferred on the witnesses the social identity of survivor and transformed them into bearers of history. See Felman and Laub, *Testimony*, and Wieviorka, *The Era of the Witness*, trans. Jared Stark (Ithaca, NY: Cornell University Press, 2006).

40. As early as 1943, Arnold Zweig's book *The Axe of Wandsbek* (*Das Beil von Wandsbek*), adapted to film in 1951 by Falk Harnack, challenged the reader with ethical questions in regard to the ordinary perpetrator, a poor butcher turned into a Nazi executioner. See also my analysis of the New German Cinema and especially Rainer Werner Fassbinder's oeuvre in my book *Defeated Masculinity*. See also, for example, this list of fictional texts that featured Holocaust perpetrator-narrators: Robert Merle's novel *Death Is My Trade* (published in the French original [*La mort est mon m'tier*] in 1952 and in English translation in 1954), which is a fictionalized rendering of the autobiography of Rudolf Höss, the infamous commandant of Auschwitz; Romain Gary's *The Dance of Genghis Cohn* (published in the original French [*La Danse de Gengis Cohn*] in 1967 and in English translation in 1968), a comic novel narrated by a dybbuk—the soul of a Jew who perished in the Holocaust—who inhabits the body of the SS officer who murdered him; Ian MacMillan's *Village of a Million Spirits: A Novel of the Treblinka Uprising* (1999), which contains a number of homodiegetic narrators, including an SS guard and a Ukrainian auxiliary guard. See also Erin McGlothlin, "Empathetic Identification and the Mind of the Holocaust Perpetrator in Fiction: A Proposed Taxonomy of Response," *Narrative*, 24, no. 3 (2016): 271. According to McGlothlin, a fictional first-person narrative of a Nazi perpetrator was published in 1971.

41. Cathy Caruth's influential work is also literary-based, although part of her theorization of trauma is based on another prominent film (Alan Resnais and Marguerite Duras's *Hiroshima Mon Amour* [France/Japan, 1959]). See Caruth, *Unclaimed Experience: Trauma, Narrative and History* (Baltimore: Johns Hopkins University Press, 1996).

42. And, to a lesser extent, an imaginary staging of this encounter format in fiction cinema.

43. Dramatic representations of the survivor-perpetrator battle can be discerned in theater (as in Ariel Dorfman's *Death and the Maiden* [New York: Penguin, 1994]), but, among other differences, they lack the authenticity and immediacy of real events, as well as the ideology entailed.

44. The meaning of *The Gate*'s French title is "the time for confession." It was coproduced by Rithy Panh and shot on location with nonprofessional actors. However, besides a few scenes that contribute to the realist depiction of the previously literary-described events (the poor and hungry peasants at M-13, the headquarters of M-13 inside the jungle, and the evacuation of the French Embassy), it does not provide any new insight into the issue.

45. François Bizot, *The Gate*, trans. Euan Cameron (New York: Knopf, 2003); and Bizot, *Facing the Torturer: Inside the Mind of a War Criminal*, trans. Charlotte Mandell and Antoine Audouard (London: Rider, 2012). The latter book includes the comments Duch wrote at Bizot's request on the original memoir while in prison, sent to Bizot in 2008. Most are clarifications of small details. At the end of his letter to Bizot, Duch accepts responsibility "for all the crimes that were perpetrated there (at M-13), for which I have the most painful remorse" (148). I find this declaration totally disconnected from his emotional and practical reaction in the fifteen pages that precede it (133–48).

46. As the head of the government's internal security branch (Santebal), Duch oversaw the Tuol Sleng (S-21) prison camp, where approximately fourteen thousand prisoners were held for interrogation and torture, after which the vast majority of them were executed. He was the first KR leader to be tried by the ECCC. He was convicted of crimes against humanity, murder, and torture and sentenced to thirty years' imprisonment. On February 2, 2012, the ECCC extended his sentence to life imprisonment.

47. "The 'S' . . . stood for *sala*, or 'hall,' while '21' was the code number assigned to *santebal*, a Khmer compound term that combines the words *santisuk* (security) and *nokorbal* (police). 'S-21,' and *santebal*, were names for Democratic Kampuchea's security police," a special branch of the KR in charge of internal security and running prison camps. David P. Chandler, "Songs at the Edge of the Forest: Perceptions of Order in Three Cambodian Texts," in *Facing the Cambodian Past: Selected Essays, 1971–1994* (Chiang Mai, Thailand: Silkworm, 1996), 3. In his memoir, Rithy Panh indicates that the word *santebal* was used instead of the traditional word *nokorbal*: "The KR used many terms I didn't recognize. Frequently these were invented words based on existing ones; they mixed up sounds and meanings in disconcerting ways." Panh and Bataille, *Elimination*, 52.

48. Also known as Democratic Kampuchea. It was the government founded when KR forces defeated the US-backed Khmer Republic of Lon Nol in 1975. It existed until 1979. See Cambodia Tribunal Monitor, "Khmer Rouge History," www.cambodiatribunal.org/history/cambodian-history/khmer-rouge-history/. According to the anthropologist Peg LeVine, "The KR insisted that the country be known in Western languages as Kampuchea . . . which means 'born from *Kambu*' (and is a legendary figure in Indian mythology). The name is connected to past mythology written in Sanskrit from a story linked to marriage." LeVine, *Love and Dread in Cambodia: Weddings, Births, and Ritual Harm Under the Khmer Rouge* (Singapore: National University of Singapore Press, 2010), 38, 38n3.

49. The ECCC is a special Cambodian court, often called the Khmer Rouge Tribunal or the Cambodia Tribunal, set up in 2006 pursuant to an agreement from 2003 between

Cambodia and the United Nations to prosecute high-level KR leaders. It is funded by international support provided by the UN Assistance to the Khmer Rouge Trials (UNA-KRT). This hybrid tribunal aims at prosecuting crimes against humanity and was set up "to bring to trial senior leaders and those most responsible for crimes committed during the time of Democratic Kampuchea, also known as the KR regime, which lasted from 17 April 1975 to 6 January 1979." The ECCC only has the authority to prosecute two categories: senior leaders of former Democratic Kampuchea and individuals deemed "to be most responsible for grave violations of national and international law." See ECCC, "Introduction to the ECCC," www.eccc.gov.kh/en/about-eccc/introduction.

50. Alexander Laban Hinton, *Man or Monster: The Trial of a Khmer Rouge Torturer* (Durham, NC: Duke University Press, 2016).

51. Nicknamed "the butcher," Ta Mok replaced Pol Pot as chief of the outlawed guerrilla group after Pol Pot's death in 1998. See chapter 2, notes 16 and 44.

52. Following their victory of April 17, 1975, the KR began forcibly evacuating Phnom Penh, the capital (as well as other major cities), relocating more than three million people onto cooperatives and labor camps in neighboring provinces and throughout rural Cambodia. Under their order, all foreigners were gathered at the French Embassy and the nearby compound and were not allowed to leave.

53. Duch had disappeared in 1979. Taking on the identity of Hang Pin, he presented himself as a schoolteacher and was working with American refugee aid organizations. See Nic Dunlop, *The Lost Executioner: The Story of Comrade Duch and the Khmer Rouge* (London: Bloomsbury, 2005), esp. 217–78.

54. The title might refer also to the French Embassy gate, which under the storm of the KR invasion and takeover had been blocked against locals who once assisted the United States and other foreign institutions in the hope they would get asylum and protection if necessary.

55. In *Facing the Torturer*, Bizot writes,

> My own ordeal concealed no glory, no revelation, and my release was tainted with the shame of returning without my two companions. At the time, victims were not warned about possible trauma—not to protect them from it, but to lessen its violence. And in fact, the shock didn't really hit me until thirty years later when I learned that Lay and Son had been executed.

Bizot, *Facing the Torturer*, 40. Bizot was seventy-one years old during the writing of this book.

56. Annette Wieviorka, "The Witness in History," *Poetics Today* 27, no. 2 (2006): 389.

57. "The Fortunoff Archive currently holds more than 4,400 testimonies, which are comprised of over ten thousand recorded hours of videotape. Testimonies were produced in cooperation with thirty-seven affiliated projects across North America, South America, Europe, and Israel, and each project maintains a duplicate collection of locally recorded videotapes." Yale University Library, Fortunoff Video Archive for Holocaust Testimonies, https://web.library.yale.edu/testimonies/about.

58. Wieviorka, "Witness in History," 388. Wieviorka relates to ghetto archives, diaries, personal chronicles, manuscripts, and the like.

59. On the distinction between the victim's testimony and the perpetrator's uncathartic confession, see Morag, *Waltzing with Bashir*. Zygmunt Bauman, for example, contends, "The problem of the guilt of the Holocaust perpetrators has been by and large settled and with the passage of time lost a good deal of its urgency and political edge, the one being remaining question is the innocence of all the rest—not least innocence of ourselves." Bauman, *Modernity and the Holocaust*, 2nd ed. (1989; Ithaca, NY: Cornell University Press, 2011), 223–24.

60. Morag, *Waltzing with Bashir*.

61. This work is being carried out by both the Bophana Audiovisual Center, cofounded in late 2006 by leu Pannakar and Rithy Panh, and by the Documentation Center of Cambodia (DC-Cam), established in 1994 by the US Congress through the Cambodian Genocide Justice Act, which provided grants to Yale University's Cambodian Genocide Program. In 1997 it became an independent nongovernmental organization. See also Jan Krogsgaard and Thomas Weber Carlsen's film *Voices of Khmer Rouge* (Denmark, 2011).

62. The ECCC is the first court trying international mass crimes that provides an opportunity for victims to participate directly in the trial proceedings as "civil parties." Individuals who can demonstrate that they have suffered physical, material, or psychological injury as a direct consequence of at least one of the crimes prosecuted before the ECCC may apply to become a civil party. Civil parties have rights such as to choose a legal representative, to request the investigation of alleged crimes, and to request the judges ask specific questions of the witnesses and the accused. See ECCC, "Who Is Eligible to Become a Civil Party?," www.eccc.gov.kh/en/victims-support/civil-party -information. See also *Brother Number One* by Annie Goldson and Peter Gilbert (New Zealand, 2011).

63. This term refers especially to Brother nos. 1–3 (Pol Pot, Nuon Chea, and Khieu Samphan) (see in the following analysis), but also to Kaing Guek Eav, nicknamed Duch. As will be elaborated on, though he was not a senior leader in the Communist Party, his position as the head of the infamous execution center S-21, to which Pol Pot sent not only the low-ranking people regarded as the regime's opponents, but also members of the KR leadership, made Duch a high-ranking perpetrator similar to the Brothers. This status gained more symbolic power after Duch became the first high-ranking KR leader to be tried. See chapter 1, note 46, on Duch.

64. As most of the films that present clips from the trial (such as Guillaume P. Suon's *About My Father*) show. See also John D. Ciorciari and Anne Heindel, *Hybrid Justice: The Extraordinary Chambers in the Courts of Cambodia* (Ann Arbor: University of Michigan Press, 2014); Hinton, *Man or Monster*.

65. See an analysis of the film in chapter 2.

66. Besides Wiesenthal, out of the list of best-known Nazi hunters (Tuviah Friedman, Serge and Beate Klarsfeld, Ian Sayer, Yaron Svoray, Elliot Welles, and Efraim Zuroff), only Friedman and Welles were Holocaust survivors. None of the hunters was a filmmaker.

In the West, Nazi-hunting films are a genre (which includes award-winning films such as the Giulio Ricciarelli's recently made German submission for the Academy Award for Best Foreign Language Film, *Labyrinth of Lies*, and Atom Egoyan's *Remember* [Canada/Mexico/Germany/South Africa, 2015], nominated for Canadian Best Motion Picture).

67. Directors who are members of the second and third generations assume both identities— of filmmakers and of those who suffer from intergenerational transmission of the trauma—but their docu-activism is far from that of the Cambodian directors in every respect, even though they also sometimes invest considerable efforts in production. This is the case, for example, of the second-generation German director Michael Verhoeven in his film *Human Failure* (*Menschliches Versagen*, Germany, 2008), which deals with the formal methods the Nazis used to take control of Jewish property. As the film proves, Verhoeven faced many difficulties gaining access to the tax files (containing compulsory reports by the Jewish population on all their possessions), when over and again he was blocked by the authorities, who preferred this information not be publicized.

68. The difference between the Cambodian films that present an encounter and the non-Cambodian films that render the past in various other ways is conspicuous. See, for example, Janet Gardner's *Lost Child: Sayon's Story* (USA/Cambodia, 2012); Adrian Maben's *Pol Pot Mystery* (*Le mystère de Pol Pot*, France, 2001), *Comrade Duch: Welcome to Hell* (*Camarade Duch Bienvenue en Enfer*, UK, 2011), and *Comrade Duch: The Bookkeeper of Death* (France/UK/USA, 2011); Jean Baronnet's *Behind the Gate* (France, 2003); Arthur Dong's *The Killing Fields of Dr. Haing S. Ngor* (USA, 2015); and Jan Krogsgaard and Thomas Weber Carlsen's *Voices of Khmer Rouge*, a forty-three-hour media installation that contains thirty personal narratives by former low-ranking KR cadres about their lives, ideologies, and experiences during the thirty-three-year-long civil war in Cambodia.

69. See Panh and Bataille, *Elimination*, 33–34. Hereafter cited parenthetically in the text.

70. Panh's dedication is embodied in the production of over fourteen fiction and documentary films relating mainly to Cambodia (or reflecting on the region's history seen chiefly through the colonizers' point of view, as in the archive-based *France Is Our Mother Country* [*La France est notre patrie*, Cambodia/france, 2015]), in the founding of the Bophana Archive Center for collecting past testimonies, and in the education of a new generation of Cambodian filmmakers.

71. Rithy Panh is not successful in extracting an admission from Duch regarding the taking of prisoners' blood in S-21. It is obvious that in light of his trial the (highly conscious) high-ranked perpetrator would not incriminate himself by taking full responsibility. In contrast, the low ranked do confess, mostly because they know they will not be tried, though they too do not take full responsibility.

72. Randall Collins, *Violence: A Micro-Sociological Theory* (Princeton, NJ: Princeton University Press, 2009), 218.

73. Felman and Laub, *Testimony*, Kindle location 155.

74. Primo Levi, *If This Is a Man*, trans. Stuart Woolf (New York: Orion, 1959). Similarly, in *Auschwitz and After*, Charlotte Delbo speaks of two selves, her Auschwitz self and her post-Auschwitz self (though she simultaneously devotes the last chapters to her dead camp friends, as if they were alive). Delbo, *Auschwitz and After*, trans. Rosette C. Lamont (1985; New Haven, CT: Yale University Press, 1995).

75. Geoffrey Hartman, "The Humanities of Testimony: An Introduction," *Poetics Today* 27, no. 2 (2006): 257.

76. See also Jan van den Berg and Willem Van de Put's documentary film *Deacon of Death* (Netherlands), winner of the Golden Calf for Best Feature-Length Documentary at the 2004 Netherlands Film Festival, made in the period prior to the ECCC. Though the director is not Cambodian, the film represents the survivor Sok Chea, a woman in her thirties, as she confronts Karoby, the man she witnessed killing her family and others in their village when she was a child. Karoby has never been brought to trial and still lives in the village of Khum Tap Piem, where the atrocities took place. With the assistance of a friend, Sok Chea, still afraid of retaliation against her family, finally dares to confront him in the pagoda where the killings took place thirty years previously. Karoby, currently working in the village as a traditional healer and a "deacon of death" during cremations, does not confess, but finally admits before her and a local Buddhist monk that the killings did take place.

77. Ervin Staub, *The Roots of Evil: The Origins of Genocide and Other Group Violence* (Cambridge: Cambridge University Press, 1992), 7, 191.

78. See an analysis of the film in chapter 2.

79. Jean Améry, *At the Mind's Limits: Contemplations by a Survivor on Auschwitz and Its Realities*, trans. Sidney Rosenfeld and Stella P. Rosenfeld (1966; Bloomington: Indiana University Press, 1980). My thanks to Rithy Panh for recommending I read Jean Améry.

80. See, in contrast, the revenge in the scene showing the lynching of the KR cadre in Angelina Jolie's fiction film *First They Killed My Father* (Cambodia/USA, 2017), based on Loung Ung's autobiographical novel *First They Killed My Father: A Daughter of Cambodia Remembers* (New York: Harper Perennial, 2000).

81. Améry, *At the Mind's Limits*, xxi, emphasis in the original.

82. For a definition of the terms *resentment* and *ressentiment* and a discussion of the difference between them, see chapter 3.

83. Aleida Assmann, "Two Forms of Resentment: Jean Améry, Martin Walser and German Memorial Culture," *New German Critique* 90 (2003): 123–33; Arne Johan Vetlesen, "A Case for Resentment: Jean Améry Versus Primo Levi," *Journal of Human Rights* 5 (2006): 27–44; Jeffrey K. Olick, "From Theodicy to *Ressentiment*: Trauma and the Ages of Compensation," in *The Politics of Regret: On Collective Memory and Historical Responsibility* (New York: Routledge, 2007), 153–73; Magdalena Zolkos, "Jean Améry's Concept of Resentment at the Crossroads of Ethics and Politics," *European Legacy* 12, no. 1 (2007): 23–38; Thomas Brudholm, *Resentment's Virtue: Jean Améry and the Refusal to Forgive* (Philadelphia: Temple University Press, 2008).

84. The TRC was established in South Africa in 1995 and began its work in 1996. It continued through 1998 and then was extended until 2002.

85. Alain Badiou, *Ethics: An Essay on the Understanding of Evil*, trans. Peter Hallward (1993; New York: Verso, 2001); Chantal Mouffe, *The Democratic Paradox* (New York: Verso, 1999); Mouffe, "Which World Order: Cosmopolitan or Multipolar?," *Ethical Perspectives* 15, no. 4 (2008): 453–67; Alenka Zupančič, *Ethics of the Real: Kant, Lacan* (London: Verso, 2000); and Slavoj Žižek, *For They Know Not What They Do: Enjoyment as a Political Factor*, 2nd ed. (New York: Verso, 2002).

86. Joan Tronto, *Moral Boundaries: A Political Argument for an Ethic of Care* (New York: Routledge, 1994); Tronto, *Caring Democracy: Markets, Equality, and Justice* (New York: New York University Press, 2013); Fiona Robinson, *Globalizing Care: Ethics, Feminist Theory, and International Relations* (Boulder, CO: Westview, 1999); Robinson, "Exploring Social Relations, Understanding Power, and Valuing Care: The Role of Critical Feminist Ethics in International Relations Theory," in *Ethics and International Relations*, ed. Hakan Seckinelgin and Hideaki Shinoda, 56–80 (Basingstoke, UK: Palgrave, 2001); Virginia Held, *The Ethics of Care: Personal, Political, Global* (New York: Oxford University Press, 2006); Held, "Military Intervention and the Ethics of Care," *Southern Journal of Philosophy* 46 (2008): 1–20; Jess Kyle, "Protecting the World: Military Humanitarian Intervention and the Ethics of Care," *Hypatia* 28 (2013): 257–73.

87. Tronto, *Moral Boundaries*, 3, 127.

88. Held, "Ethics of Care," 71. See my elaboration on these discourses in Raya Morag, "Blood Relations and Nonconsensual Ethics: Israeli Intifada Documentaries," *Post Script* 36, nos. 2–3 (2018): 75–85.

89. Améry, *At the Mind's Limits*, 72.

90. Assmann, "Two Forms of Resentment," 124–25.

91. In this film, based on *Elimination*, Panh describes the unbearable situation of his father as an intellectual under the KR in very similar terms to those of Améry in his essay "At the Mind's Limits" on the situation of the intellectual in the concentration camp (in *Mind's Limits*, 1–20). See Panh and Bataille, *Elimination*, especially 61–62. For a later depiction of his autobiography, see Panh's installation-based *Exile* (*Exil*, France, 2016).

92. See Panh and Bataille, *Elimination*, 245–46.

93. Susan Rubin Suleiman coined the term *1.5 generation* to define the blurred generational boundaries and highlight the interest in the persona of the child survivor. She distinguishes between "children 'too young to remember' (infancy to around three years old); children 'old enough to remember but too young to understand' (approximately age four to ten); and children 'old enough to understand but too young to be responsible' (approximately age eleven to fourteen)." She claims: "By responsible, I mean having to make choices (and to act on those choices) about their own or their family's actions in response to catastrophe." Suleiman, "The 1.5 Generation: Thinking About Child Survivors and the Holocaust," *American Imago* 59, no. 3 (2002): 283. Most of the directors whose films are mentioned here, including Panh and Hay, were child-survivors. Thus, according to Suleiman's distinction, they belong neither to the first nor to the second generation, but to the 1.5 generation.

94. During the KR dictatorship, between 1975 and 1979, and especially after 1978, more than five hundred thousand young women were forced into marriages, often with KR

cadres. The circumstances of these forced marriages have been suppressed and covered up for four decades. See chapter 4 for an analysis of the films that represent this exceptional form of gendered genocide.

95.   As the filmmaker told me, her father stayed at the village and met his former acquaintances, and from time to time she joined them with a small video camera. It was just the two of them, with no extra film crew. Nothing could be planned in advance (personal conversation via Skype on August 17, 2018).

96.   All orders were issued in the name of Angkar Padevoat, the Revolutionary Organization, literally, in Khmer, "The Organization." See an example of the instructions on using the terms *Angkar* and *Party* signed by Pol Pot in Henri Locard, *Pol Pot's Little Red Book: The Sayings of Angkar* (Chaing Mai, Thailand: Silkworm, 2004), 100–101.

97.   See Michelle Vachon, "Love, Life and Loss During the Pol Pot Regime," *Cambodia Daily*, March 17, 2014, www.cambodiadaily.com/archives/love-life-and-loss-during-the-pol-pot-regime-54314.

98.   One of the most popular KR slogans, meant to serve as a warning and referred to in many films and written memoirs, says: "The Angkar has [the many] eyes of the pineapple." See Locard, *Little Red Book*, 112–13.

99.   See the analysis of this phenomenon in chapter 3.

100. See the epilogue.

101. In our personal conversation, the director told me that the atmosphere was similar to that felt in Lars Von Trier's *Dogville* (Netherlands/Denmark/UK/France/Finland/Sweden/Germany/Italy/Norway, 2003). Moreover, a young man showed up and told her he would disclose all the truth and tell her "who did what," but when she came to the meeting they had set, he had disappeared. Personal conversation via Skype on August 17, 2018.

102. Rancière, "The Ethical Turn," 126.

103. Rancière, 110.

2. POST-KHMER ROUGE CAMBODIAN CINEMA

1.   Haing S. Ngor with Roger Warner, *Survival in the Killing Fields* (1987; New York: Basic, 2003), 258, emphases in the original.

2.   For a historical review of the Cambodian film industry, including the influence of King Nordom Sihanuk as a filmmaker, see, for instance, Poppy McPherson, "Cambodia: Dawn of a New Cinematic Golden Era," *Diplomat*, March 6, 2015, https://thediplomat .com/2015/03/cambodiadawn-of-a-new-cinematic-golden-era/; and Bun Y. Ung, "Cambodian Film Industry: A Paradox to Glorious Revival," *Cambodian Communication Review* (2016): 35–43. For a documentary film on the golden age of Cambodian cinema between 1960 and 1975, see Davy Chou's *Golden Slumbers* (*Le sommeil d'or*, France/Cambodia, 2012), with the participation of directors Yvon Hem and Liv Sreng and the actress Dy Saveth.

3. In comparison, the takeover of the German film industry after World War II by the American film industry, for instance, lasted through the 1950s and into the early 1960s, until the signing in 1962 of the Oberhausen Manifesto by a collective of West German directors. They declared their Year Zero and the future emergence of a new wave of non-Nazi German cinema, later to be known as the New German Cinema.

4. I am not referring here to Adam Smith's conceptualization of the virtues of resentment for civic society and thus his definition of moral resentment, but to the Amérian attitude based on—and referring to—the post-Holocaust standing, which I see as highly relevant to postgenocide Cambodia, as will be elaborated later. See Smith, *The Theory of Moral Sentiments*, ed. Ryan Patrick Hanley (1790; New York: Penguin, 2009).

5. See Cambodia Tribunal Monitor, "Khmer Rouge History," www.cambodiatribunal.org/history/cambodian-history/khmer-rouge-history/.

6. See chapter 1, note 49, about the ECCC.

7. *Die Mörder sind unter uns* is the title of the 1946 German film by Wolfgang Staudte.

8. Cowritten with the French novelist Christopher Bataille in 2013. Rithy Panh and Christopher Bataille, *The Elimination: A Survivor of the Khmer Rouge Confronts His Past and the Commandant of the Killing Fields*, trans. John Cullen (New York: Other Press, 2013), 110–11.

9. Shoshana Felman and Dori Laub, *Testimony: Crises of Witnessing in Literature, Psychoanalysis and History* (New York: Routledge, 1992); Cathy Caruth, *Unclaimed Experience: Trauma, Narrative and History* (Baltimore: Johns Hopkins University Press, 1996); Annette Wieviorka, *The Era of the Witness*, trans. Jaren Stark (Ithaca, NY: Cornell University Press, 2006); Dominick LaCapra, *Writing History, Writing Trauma* (Baltimore: Johns Hopkins University Press, 2001); Marianne Hirsch, *Family Frames: Photography, Narrative and Postmemory* (Cambridge, MA: Harvard University Press, 1997).

10. For example, Mahmood Mamdani, "Amnesty or Impunity? A Preliminary Critique of the Report of the Truth and Reconciliation Commission of South Africa (TRC)," *Diacritics* 32, nos. 3–4 (2002): 32–59; Anne Borer, "A Taxonomy of Victims and Perpetrators: Human Rights and Reconciliation in South Africa," *Human Rights Quarterly* 25, no. 4 (2003): 1088–116; Stef Craps, *Postcolonial Witnessing: Trauma out of Bounds* (Basingstoke, UK: Palgrave Macmillan, 2012).

11. For example, Martha Minow, *Breaking the Cycles of Hatred: Memory, Law, and Repair*, ed. Nancy L. Rosenblum (Princeton, NJ: Princeton University Press, 2002); Michael Mann, "Communist Cleansing," in *The Dark Side of Democracy: Explaining Ethnic Cleansing* (Cambridge: Cambridge University Press, 2005), 318–52; Jens Meierhenrich, "Varieties of Reconciliation," *Law and Social Inquiry* 33, no. 1 (2008): 195–231.

12. Jean Améry, *At the Mind's Limits: Contemplations by a Survivor on Auschwitz and Its Realities*, trans. Sidney Rosenfeld and Stella P. Rosenfeld (1966; Bloomington: Indiana University Press, 1980), 70–72.

13. Khamboly Dy, *A History of Democratic Kampuchea, 1975–1979* (Phnom Penh: DC-Cam, 2007).

14. Ieng Sary was a cofounder and senior member of the KR. He was a member of the Central Committee of the Communist Party of Kampuchea, led by Pol Pot, and served in the government of Democratic Kampuchea from 1975 to 1979 as foreign minister and deputy prime minister. He was known as "Brother Number Three," third in command after Pol Pot and Nuon Chea.

15. Hun Sen, a former KR commander, has been the prime minister of Cambodia since 1985 and president of the Cambodian People's Party (CPP). He is a dictator who assumed authoritarian power in Cambodia using violence, intimidation, and corruption. From 1979 to 1986 and again from 1987 to 1990 he served as Cambodia's foreign minister. Born Hun Bunal, he changed his name to Hun Sen in 1972, two years after joining the KR.

16. Ta Mok was held in custody while awaiting his war crimes trial until his death in 2006.

17. Regional KR leaders who were defendants in Case 003 and Case 004.

18. Nuon Chea, "Brother Number 2," was the chief ideologist of the KR and prime minister of Democratic Kampuchea; Khieu Samphan, "Brother Number 4," was Cambodia's head of state.

19. From the launching of the ECCC in early July 2006 until 2016, Duch (Case 001) was the first and only defendant to be sentenced for crimes against humanity. Ieng Thirith was excused from her trial. She later died (see chapter 2, note 61), following her husband Ieng Sary. Proceedings for Case 002 began in 2011, but it took six years to convict the remaining former senior KR officials Nuon Chea and Khieu Samphan. The cost of the ten years of work for these three convictions was $260 million dollars.

20. Stanley Cohen, *States of Denial: Knowing About Atrocities and Suffering* (Cambridge: Polity, 2001), 147.

21. See also Jean Baronnet's *Behind the Gate* (*Derrière le portail*, France, 2003); and Adrian Maben's *Pol Pot Mystery* (*Le mystère de Pol Pot*, France, 2001), *Comrade Duch Welcome to Hell* (*Camarade Duch Bienvenue en Enfer*, 2011), and *Comrade Duch: The Bookkeeper of Death* (France/UK/USA, 2011). To the best of my knowledge, the only film on Saloth Sar, known as Pol Pot (general secretary of the Communist Party of Kampuchea and the prime minister of Democratic Kampuchea from 1976 to 1979), was made by a French director, Adrian Maben. This film, not part of the New Cambodian Cinema, and Maben's two films on Duch were all made for French television as historical-chronological films.

    In this book I refer to coproduced films as Cambodian films only if they were shot in Cambodia.

22. The corpus of perpetrator cinema includes as well films like Rithy Panh's *S21: The Khmer Rouge Death Machine* (*S21, la machine de mort Khmère rouge*, Cambodia/France, 2003), in which the director interviews low-ranking perpetrators such as S-21 detention and execution center guards.

23. Norodom Sihanouk became the King of Cambodia in 1941. After the Second World War, in 1953, he secured Cambodian independence from France. In 1955, he abdicated the throne and governed Cambodia under one-party rule as prime minister. Officially neutral in foreign relations, in practice he was closer to the communist bloc. A military coup in 1970 initiated by the general Lon Nol ousted him and paved the way for

the US-backed Khmer Republic. Sihanouk fled to China and North Korea, there form-
ing a government-in-exile and resistance movement. In 1975, his support of the KR
movement allowed his return to Cambodia as the KR figurehead head of state. Although
initially supportive of the KR, his relations with them declined and in 1976 he resigned
and was placed under house arrest until 1979, when Vietnamese forces overthrew the
KR. Sihanouk went into exile again and in 1981 formed a resistance party. In 1991, peace
accords were signed, and in 1993, the United Nations Transitional Authority in Cambodia (UNTAC) organized general elections. A coalition government, jointly led by his
son Norodom Ranariddh and Hun Sen, was subsequently formed. In 1993, Sihanouk
was reinstated as Cambodia's head of state and King. In 2004, he abdicated again and
his son Norodom Sihamoni was elected his successor.

24.   I propose this last term as more adequate to the Cambodian context than the prevailing categorization in genocide studies, which differentiates between the perpetrator and
the bystander.

25.   Karnavas, Ieng Sary's international colawyer, said via email to a journalist,

> If she [Helen Jarvis] has made those comments and if she is an unrepentant
> Marxist-Leninist with views that are antithetical to the founding laws and prin-
> ciples of the Cambodian Judicial System, then, at a minimum, the inevitable
> perception that will arise whenever she is called upon to make an important or
> difficult decision is that she is promoting her revolutionary agenda.

See Robbie Corey Boulet, "Attacks on Jarvis Multiply," *Phnom Penh Post,* June 8, 2009,
www.phnompenhpost.com/national/attacks-jarvis-multiply; Elena Lesley, "Jarvis'
Leninist Ties Under Fire," *Phnom Penh Post,* June 3, 2009, www.phnompenhpost.com
/krt-talk/jarvis-leninist-ties-under-fire.

26.   See the *Phnom Penh Post*'s series of articles on the Jarvis Debate during June 2009, i.e.,
Youk Chhang, "Jarvis's Citizenship Not at Issue," June 22, 2009, www.phnompenhpost
.com/national/jarviss-citizenship-not-issue; Bethany Murphy, "Jarvis Wrong Choice for
Victims' Unit," June 22, 2009, www.phnompenhpost.com/national/jarvis-wrong
-choice-victims-unit; Georgia Wilkins, "KR Victims Question Jarvis's Politics," June 19,
2009, www.phnompenhpost.com/national/kr-victims-question-jarviss-politics; and
Robbie Corey Boulet, "Nationality and the Jarvis Debate," June 12, 2009, www
.phnompenhpost.com/national/nationality-and-the-jarvis-debate.

Samdech Vibol Panha Sok An was a Cambodian academic and politician. In 1980,
An served as personal secretary to the deputy prime minister and minister of foreign
affairs Hun Sen. He was deputy prime minister and minister for the office of the
Council of Ministers from 2004 until his death in 2017, as well as a member of Parlia-
ment for Takéo and a member of the Central Committee of the Cambodian People's
Party.

27.   See Thierry Cruvellier, *The Master of Confessions: The Making of a Khmer Rouge Torturer,* trans. Alex Gilly (New York: Ecco, 2014), 74–76.

28.   See chapter 1, notes 46 and 47, about Duch.

29. "Your Honour, my remorse does exist and it has progressed. . . . Personally, I know that my feeling of remorse for the criminal acts I committed at S-21 has evolved. . . . And when the two psychological experts gave their testimony, I appealed to them for advice. I asked them to counsel me about what I could do to make the world see me as a human being once again. For that is where my remorse lies." See Transcript (KH) of 2 September 2009 [p. 66, lines 5–11; p. 66, line 23, to p. 67, line 5], in ECCC, "Compilation of Statements of Apology Made by Kaing Guek Eav Alias Duch During the Proceedings 31 March 2009," www.eccc.gov.kh/en/document/court/corrected1compilation-statements -apology-made-kaing-guek-eav-alias-duch-during, p. 15.

30. At the end of the film, Roux, dismissed by Duch for "lack of confidence," admits that he feels Duch has betrayed him. Silke Studzinsky, who represents Civil Parties Group 2, said Kar Savuth's remarks amounted to "a slap in the face of the civil parties and, I dare to say, all victims of the regime," adding that her clients were "shocked" and "stunned" at the request for Duch's release. See Robbie Corey Boulet, "Duch Defence Split on Verdict," *Phnom Penh Post*, November 27, 2009, www.phnompenhpost.com /national/duch-defence-split-verdict.

    See also Alexander Laban Hinton's observation at the court, in which, after one of the testimonies, Duch concluded "his remarks as he had begun by addressing the President 'with respect' (*ti korop, daoy korop*). They were the words he used to address his superiors in S-21 confession annotations." See Hinton, *The Justice Facade: Trials of Transition in Cambodia* (Oxford: Oxford University Press, 2018), 200, Kindle edition.

31. Hinton observes the tension Duch raised within the group of civil parties who attended the hearings. For instance, he says, "One of the first signs of this tension was a petition submitted by twenty-eight civil parties, including Bou Meng, requesting that Duch cease gesturing disrespectfully toward the civil parties." See Hinton, *Justice Facade*, 194. Bou Meng was a survivor of Toul Sleng.

32. See John D. Ciorciari and Anne Heindel, introduction to *Hybrid Justice: The Extraordinary Chambers in the Courts of Cambodia* (Ann Arbor: University of Michigan Press, 2014).

33. See PopulationPyramid.net, "Population Pyramids of the World from 1950–2100, Cambodia," www.populationpyramid.net/cambodia/2017. See also a list of sources in United Nations, Department of Economic and Social Affairs, Population Division, *World Population Prospects: The 2015 Revision, World Population 2015 Wallchart, ST/ ESA/SER.A/378*, https://esa.un.org/unpd/wpp/Publications/.

34. Duch is not considered a Big Perpetrator like Pol Pot and "Brother Numbers 2–5," but, being Pol Pot's chief executioner and the first to stand trial by the ECCC, he became the symbol of the high-ranking perpetrators.

35. See chapter 1, note 62, about civil parties.

36. Adrian Maben's three-part made-for-TV series includes one episode titled *Pol Pot Mystery*. Although it is one of a very few (mostly made-for-TV) efforts to portray the biography of Pol Pot, it does not include a survivor-perpetrator confrontation. The film provides an historical overview that includes scenes from Nate Thayer's exclusive interview with Pol Pot and scenes from his death.

37. For example, Alexander Laban Hinton, "Justice and Time at the Khmer Rouge Tribunal: In Memory of Vann Nath, Painter and S-21 Survivor," *Genocide Studies and Prevention: An International Journal* 8, no. 2 (2014): 7–17; Hinton, *Man or Monster: The Trial of a Khmer Rouge Torturer* (Durham, NC: Duke University Press, 2016); Ciorciari and Heindel, *Hybrid Justice*; Helen Jarvis, "'Justice for the Deceased': Victims' Participation in the Extraordinary Chambers in the Courts of Cambodia," *Genocide Studies and Prevention: An International Journal* 8, no. 2 (2014): 19–27; Cruvellier, *The Master*; Cathy J. Schlund-Vials and Samuel Martínez, "Interrogating the Perpetrator: Violation, Culpability and Human Rights," *International Journal of Human Rights* 19, no. 5 (2015): 549–54.

38. The ECCC has provided the opportunity for some four thousand victims to play a direct role as civil parties. See Jarvis, "'Justice.'"

39. This vulnerability was acknowledged at a very early stage by the ECCC's first international coprosecutor, Robert Petit, who said: "In the end, the victims of the KR got the tribunal that Hun Sen and his allies, including other former KR throughout the regime, wanted." Petit, "Lawfare and International Tribunals: A Question of Definition? A Reflection on the Creation of the Khmer Rouge Tribunal," *Case Western Reserve Journal of International Law* 43, no. 1 (2010): 197. Petit served as a coprosecutor from 2006 to 2009. See also the discussion about Pen Sochan's participation as a civil party in chapter 4.

40. The term *Pol Potism* was coined by Ben Kiernan. See Kiernan, "Myth, Nationalism and Genocide," *Journal of Genocide Research* 3, no. 2 (2001): 92. See Cruvellier, *The Master*, 71. Jean Améry, for instance, writes: "No matter how terrible Communism may at times appear, it still symbolizes an idea of man, whereas Hitler-Fascism was not an idea at all, but depravity." Améry, *Mind's Limits*, 31.

41. See *Khmers Rouges Amers*, www.brunocarette.com/films/khmers-rouges-amers. The film was selected for the 2008 Paris Festival International du Grand Reportage d'Actualite (FIGRA). It is the result of sixteen years of investigation and took seven years to produce.

42. In a conversation I had with Sien Meta in Phnom Penh on July 8, 2014, the director expressed his disappointment over the limited options for screening the film in Cambodia and the censorship that blocks any possibility of future productions.

43. Ponnary was married to Pol Pot from 1956 to 1979. By 1975, if not earlier, Ponnary was growing increasingly disturbed, the result of the onset of schizophrenia. She became extremely paranoid and was convinced the Vietnamese were trying to assassinate her and her husband. Pol Pot divorced her in 1979 after the Vietnamese invasion and took a second wife. Ponnary died in Pailin on July 1, 2003.

44. Born Chhit Choeun and nicknamed "the butcher," Ta Mok replaced Pol Pot as chief of the outlawed guerrilla group after Pol Pot's death in 1998. In a speech made after Pol Pot's body was unceremoniously burned, Ta Mok denigrated him: "Nobody killed or poisoned Pol Pot. Now he is finished, he has no power and no rights any longer. He is nothing more than cow dung. Actually, cow dung is more useful because it can be used as a fertilizer." See AP Archive, "Cambodia: General Ta Mok Gives Reaction to Death

of Pol Pot," YouTube, www.youtube.com/watch?v=x7kO8v-lWSo. Unlike other surviving KR leaders, Ta Mok did not strike a deal to surrender or defect to the government. He was captured along the Thailand-Cambodian border by the Cambodian army and arrested in 1999. He was charged with crimes against humanity in 2002, four years prior to his death.

45. Ian Harris, "Cambodian Buddhism After the Khmer Rouge," in *Cambodian Buddhism: History and Practice* (Honolulu: University of Hawaii Press, 2005); describing the restoration of Buddhism after the fall of the KR, Harris claims that in the early 1980s "the KR had begun a shift in their position on Buddhism" (199), but he hardly relates to isolated KR communities outside Hun Sen's or the defectors' circles, like Pailin and especially Anlong Veng. See also Erik Davis, *Deathpower: Buddhism's Ritual Imagination in Cambodia* (New York: Columbia University Press, 2015), 7. The Dhammayietra movement march of 1997 "entered the Khmer Rouge strongholds of the northwest. On reaching Pailin, the marchers were greeted by Ieng Sary, Y Chhien, the town's mayor, and other important KR defectors" (Davis, 209, quoting *The Cambodia Daily*, April 21, 1997).

46. At Chuor Phnom Kravanh, which is an extension of the Kardamom Mountains.

47. David P. Chandler, "Songs at the Edge of the Forest: Perceptions of Order in Three Cambodian Texts," in *Facing the Cambodian Past: Selected Essays, 1971–1994* (Chiang Mai, Thailand: Silkworm, 1996), 2; Erik W. Davis, "Imaginary Conversations with Mothers About Death," in *At the Edge of the Forest: Essays on Cambodia, History, and Narrative in Honor of David Chandler*, ed. Anne Ruth Hansen and Judy Ledgerwood (Ithaca, NY: Cornell Southeast Asia Program Publications, 2008), 221–28.

48. The New People, sometimes called "April 17 people," is the KR term that described the new class of civilian Cambodians that, broadly speaking, included anyone who was from an urban area and thus impure, perverted by Western ideas: the middle class, intellectuals, and artists. It also included ethnic minorities and any other social stratum defined by the regime's heterophobia as an enemy. Being deported from the cities to the countryside on April 17, 1975, they were made a new people, in contrast to the class of peasants from rural areas who were considered the privilege class of Old People (Base/Ancient People), pure and unstained by what the KR regarded as the corruption of capitalistic city life.

49. Henri Lefebvre, *The Production of Space*, trans. Donald Nicholson-Smith (1974; Malden, MA: Blackwell, 1991), 85.

50. Lefebvre, 85. Since November 13, 2007, the day Ieng Sary was arrested by the ECCC, his son Ieng Vuth has served as a deputy governor in Pailin. Other family members also hold prominent positions in the Pailin municipality. See Erika Kinetz and Yun Samean, "ECCC Arrests the 'Untouchable' Ieng Sary," *Cambodia Daily*, November 13, 2007, www.cambodiadaily.com/archives/eccc-arrests-the-untouchable-ieng-sary-61623.

51. See Pascale-Anne Brault and Michael Naas, "To Reckon with the Dead: Jacques Derrida's Politics of Mourning," in *The Work of Mourning*, by Jacques Derrida (Chicago: University of Chicago Press, 2003), 3.

52. See Encyclopedia.com, "Khieu Ponnary (1920–2003)," www.encyclopedia.com/women /dictionaries-thesauruses-pictures-and-press-releases/khieu-ponnary-1920-2003; Elizabeth Becker, "Khieu Ponnary, 83, First Wife of Pol Pot, Cambodian Despot," *New York Times*, July 3, 2003, www.nytimes.com/2003/07/03/world/khieu-ponnary-83-first -wife-of-pol-pot-cambodian-despot.html?mcubz=02003.

53. Based on three years of field research (from 2006 to 2009) in crematoriums around Phnom Penh, Erik W. Davis analyzes the contemporary Buddhist death rituals in Cambodia from an ethnographic perspective. In describing the typical Cambodian funeral, he stresses the importance of moving the corpse in ways that prevent the return of the deceased, binding of the corpse with rope, and cremation—all of which are represented in the film. See Davis, *Deathpower*, 42–81.

54. See *Phnom Penh Post*, "Filmmaker Aims to Show the KR Tragedy from All Angles," February 17, 2009, www.phnompenhpost.com/lifestyle/filmmaker-aims-show-kr -tragedy-all-angles.

55. Marshal Lon Nol led the military coup of 1970 against Prince Norodom Sihanouk and became the self-proclaimed president of the US-backed Khmer Republic, ruling until 1975. After the KR took power, he fled to the United States, and remained there until his death in 1985.

56. Bruno Carette claims in an interview on the film,

> Then, it became apparent that revisiting Cambodia's past through the eyes of the KR could bring new elements for a better understanding of history. But we investigated as journalists—not as prosecutors, lawyers or judges. We tried to work objectively. . . . Actually, after receiving the agreement from the KR to talk, we couldn't do anything other than listen to them and be honest. I'm not saying that I believe everything that they have said, but I tried to do my job as a journalist. Our film is neither an accusation nor a defense.

See *Phnom Penh Post*, "Filmmaker."

57. The directors interviewed Khieu Samphan twice, around six hours each time. See a short interview of Neth Pheaktra with Carette on the film in *Phnom Penh Post*, "Filmmaker." Other ex-KR interviewees include Long Norin, former head of protocol under Khieu Samphan; Mey Mak, executive officer in charge of Phnom Penh airport; and Sann Chheng, Pol Pot's radio officer.

58. As Tom Fawthrop and Helen Jarvis claim in regard to the 2003 election campaign, both candidates came from the ranks of the KR. The victorious Cambodian People's Party (CPP) candidate Y Chhiem was Pol Pot's bodyguard and later became a KR general in command of the Pailin Zone. After the defections led by Ieng Sary in 1996, he was appointed governor of Pailin. The rival candidate from the Sam Rainsy Party was Ven Dara. Fawthrop and Jarvis, *Getting Away with Genocide? Elusive Justice and the Khmer Rouge Tribunal* (London: Pluto Press, 2004), 138. On Y Chhiem's removal from this position in 2014 due to allegations of corruption and his new job as deputy chief of Prime Minister Hun Sen's cabinet, see Meas Sokchea, "Federal Job Awaits Pailin Chief Accused

of Corruption," *Phnom Penh Post*, November 5, 2014, www.phnompenhpost.com /national/federal-job-awaits-pailin-chief-accused-corruption.

59. My emphases.

60. During her interview, Laurence Picq describes the trap she naively stepped into: following her husband; being tempted to leave China, where the family was part of the diplomatic milieu; and joining the Cambodian revolution in order to "rebuild the nation." However, when she arrived in Phnom Penh in 1971 with her daughters their passports were confiscated so they would not be able to leave the country. She refers to this experience as emblematic of her new life in the "Stone Age period." See her autobiographical book *Beyond the Horizon: Five Years with the Khmer Rouge*, trans. Patricia Norland (New York: St. Martin's, 1989), written after her return to France. See chapter 2, note 14, about Ieng Sary.

61. My emphasis. Laurence Picq mentions the unawareness of Ieng Thirith, minister of social affairs from October 1975 until the fall of the KR in 1979 and the wife of Ieng Sary (foreign minister and deputy prime minister in the 1975–79 government of Democratic Kampuchea). She is considered the most infamous female perpetrator among the party leaders. In November 2007, five years before the case against her was suspended, she was placed in pre-trial detention by the ECCC; in September 2010, due to dementia, she was found unfit to stand trial for crimes against humanity, grave breaches of the 1949 Geneva Conventions, and genocide. In November 2012, the proceedings against her were stayed and she was released. She died on August 22, 2015, at the age of eighty-three from complications of Alzheimer's.

62. See Cohen, *States of Denial*, 42–43.

63. See Picq, *Beyond the Horizon*, 215.

64. Son Sen, a member of the Central Committee of the Communist Party from 1974 to 1992, was minister of national defense. He oversaw the Party's security apparatus, including the Santebal secret police and S-21. Sen was married to Yun Yat, who became the Party's minister of education and information. Along with the rest of his family, he was killed at the order of Pol Pot during a factional split in the KR in 1997.

65. Cruvellier, *The Master*, 187.

66. Cruvellier, 182–83.

67. The term *acharya* is most often said to include the root *char* or *charya* (conduct).

68. Quoted in Erik W. Davis, "Treasures of the Buddha: Imagining Death and Life in Contemporary Cambodia," PhD diss., University of Chicago, 2009, 76–78, https://search .proquest.com/docview/305062096?pq-origsite=gscholar. Davis quotes from Li Sovira's *Vidhi Dhvoe Punya Khmoca* (2002), which deals with funeral ceremonies in the nineteenth and twentieth centuries.

69. Quoted in Davis, *Treasures*, 77.

70. Davis, 77.

71. See chapter 1, note 96, on *Angkar*. See also Michelle Vachon, "Love, Life and Loss During the Pol Pot Regime," *Cambodia Daily*, March 17, 2014, www.cambodiadaily.com /archives/love-life-and-loss-during-the-pol-pot-regime-54314. For example, see the following lines taken from the song "The Dazzling Victory of 17 April!": "Long live the

dazzling victory of 17 April! / More grandiose, more meaningful than the Angkor era!... / A gigantic, a glorious, a prodigious Leap Forward!" Henri Locard, *Pol Pot's Little Red Book: The Sayings of Angkar* (Chaing Mai, Thailand: Silkworm, 2004), 42–43. See also the Maoist-inspired slogan "Through rapid development, our country must surpass the Angkor period" (73).

In his memoir, Rithy Panh writes:

> The flag of Democratic Kampuchea ... bears not a hammer and sickle but an image of the great temple of Angkor. "For more than thousand years, the Khmer people have lived in utter destitution and the most complete discouragement.... If our people were capable of building Angkor Wat, then they are capable of doing anything." (Pol Pot, in a speech broadcast on the radio)

See Panh and Bataille, *Elimination*, 24.

72. "The democratic project had produced a mirage on the Mekong, an illusion of Western democratic forms behind which the country operated much as it always had. The mirage was everywhere. It hung over Cambodia's courts and parliament." See Sebastian Strangio, *Hun Sen's Cambodia* (New Haven, CT: Yale University Press, 2014), xiv.

73. Henry F. Smith notes,

> From a historical point of view, the Oxford English Dictionary (1971) indicates that around the year 900 CE the verb to forgive meant simply to give, as in to give one's love. Thus in its etymological roots it was an active form. It was not until 300 years later that it came to mean to give up, as in to give up or let go of resentment, indicating that there was a gradual historical trend toward viewing forgiveness as a passive process or description of something that is not felt, as in "to cease to feel resentment."

Smith, "Leaps of Faith: Is Forgiveness a Useful Concept?," *International Journal of Psychoanalysis* 89, no. 5 (2008): 924.

74. As Damien Short indicates, there have been at least twenty-one official truth commissions established around the world since 1974 (though they have received different names). Short, "Reconciliation and the Problem of Internal Colonialism," *Journal of Intercultural Studies* 26, no. 3 (2005): 267–82.

75. Ervin Staub, "Genocide and Mass Killing: Origins, Prevention, Healing and Reconciliation," *Political Psychology* 21, no. 2 (2000): 367–82; John Borneman, "Reconciliation After Ethnic Cleansing: Listening, Retribution, Affiliation," *Public Culture* 14, no. 2 (2002): 281–304, Ernesto Verdeja, "Derrida and the Impossibility of Forgiveness," *Contemporary Political Theory* 3, no. 1 (2004): 23–47; Short, "Reconciliation and Internal Colonialism"; Andrew Schaap, "Reconciliation as Ideology and Politics," *Constellations* 15, no. 3 (2008): 249–64; Meierhenrich, "Varieties of Reconciliation"; Jeffrey K. Olick, "Time for Forgiveness: A Historical Perspective," in *Considering Forgiveness*, ed. Aleksandra Wagner with Carin Kuoni and Matthew Buckingham (New York: Vera List

Center for Art and Politics, 2009), 85–92; Ann Rigney, "Reconciliation and Remembering: (How) Does It Work?," *Memory Studies* 5, no. 3 (2012): 251–58; and Eve Monique Zucker, "Trauma and Its Aftermath: Local Configurations of Reconciliation in Cambodia and the Khmer Rouge Tribunal," *Journal of Asian Studies* 72, no. 4 (2013): 793–800.

76. Quoted in Short, "Reconciliation and Internal Colonialism," 268.

77. Roteberg in Short, 268–70.

78. Emphasis in the original. Short is referring to Minow in "Reconciliation and Internal Colonialism," 268. According to Short, "South Africa's TRC stated that it was 'concerned not so much with punishment as with correcting imbalances, restoring broken relationships/with healing, harmony and reconciliation' (TRC Final Report: Chapter 1: 36, 5: 70)" (268).

79. Borneman, "Reconciliation After Ethnic Cleansing," 282, emphasis in the original. Hereafter cited parenthetically in the text.

80. Rigney, "Reconciliation and Remembering," 253.

81. Rigney, 256.

82. Schaap, "Reconciliation as Ideology," 249.

83. Schaap, 249, emphasis in the original.

84. Olick, "Time for Forgiveness," 87.

85. Jeffrey K. Olick, "The Value of Regret? Lessons from and for Germany," in *The Politics of Regret: On Collective Memory and Historical Responsibility* (New York: Routledge, 2007), 144.

86. Undoubtedly Olick's choice of focusing on the *politics* of regret is meant to overcome the major gap between Derrida's pure forgiveness, which Derrida himself calls a "hyperbolic," excessive, ethical vision of forgiveness, and "the reality of a society at work in pragmatic processes of reconciliation." See Jacques Derrida, "On Forgiveness," in *On Cosmopolitanism and Forgiveness*, trans. Mark Dooley and Michael Hughes (New York: Routledge, 2001), 51.

87. Derrida, "On Forgiveness," 32–33. Hereafter cited parenthetically in the text.

88. See Verdeja's critique of Derrida. In contrast to Derrida, Verdeja separates between the act and the actor, the agent, arguing that the moral transformation undergone by perpetrators separates them from the act of perpetration. Moreover, he claims, without reasoning, that unconditional forgiveness obliterates the memory. Verdeja, "Derrida."

3. PERPETRATORHOOD PARADIGMS

1. Nancy L. Rosenblum, introduction to *Breaking the Cycles of Hatred: Memory, Law, and Repair*, by Martha Minow, commentaries ed. Nancy L. Rosenblum (Princeton, NJ: Princeton University Press, 2002), 18.

2. Annemarie Prins, *Breaking the Silence: A New Cambodian Play* (script) (Phnom Penh, Cambodia: DC-Cam, 2009).

3. The film has been shown in Cambodia, but according to Susan Needham, Karen Quintiliani, and Robert Lemkin, the filmmakers could not get a permit from government

officials to show it in theaters. Instead, it premiered at Meta House, an NGO in Phnom Penh. See Needham, Quintiliani, and Lemkin, "The Space of Sorrow: A Historic Video Dialogue Between Survivors and Perpetrators of the Cambodian Killing Fields," *International Journal of Human Rights* 19, no. 5 (2015): 645. The film is shown frequently at the Bophana Centre in Phnom Penh.

4. Rob Lemkin, the British director/producer, is Sambath's codirector, cowriter, cocinematographer, and coproducer on *Enemies*. As the nephew of Raphael Lemkin, Rob Lemkin was probably drawn to this subject because of his ancestry. He joined Sambath's ten-year project after seven years. The film won more than twenty awards, including a special Sundance Jury Prize. It was shortlisted for the Academy Award for Best Documentary Feature in 2011. In 2012, the film won an Emmy Award for Outstanding Investigative Journalism (Long Form). In June 2011, the US-based International Center for Journalists announced that Thet Sambath was the recipient of its Knight International Journalism Award for career achievement.

5. Khoun joined the KR military wing in 1970. After the KR victory in 1975, he became a military intelligence commissar in the northwest zone and was assigned to investigate cooperatives from 1976 to 1978. He oversaw the killing of soldiers from the previous regime, suspect ethnic minorities, and deportees from the eastern zone. Briefly arrested in 1979 for mass murder but released for lack of evidence, since 1979 he has lived as a peasant farmer in northwest Cambodia. Suon joined the KR military wing in 1970. In 1975 he became militia commander of a cooperative in northwest Cambodia and worked in killing units controlled by Khoun. Since 1979, he has lived as a peasant farmer in northwest Cambodia. See *Enemies of the People*, "Offical [sic] Movie Page," www .enemiesofthepeoplemovie.com/Press/DownloadPressKit.

6. "Sister Em" joined the KR political wing in 1973 and worked as a district chief in northwest Cambodia from 1975 to 1979. In that role she was responsible for ordering the deaths of many thousands of suspected enemies of the party. She now lives and works under an assumed name elsewhere in Cambodia, where she is a senior politician in local government. See *Enemies of the People*, "Offical [sic] Movie Page." Toward the end of the film, Sambath introduces Khoun and Suon to Nuon Chea and the three talk about the history of which they were each a lethal part; however, Chea's KR rhetoric constantly blocks Khoun's and Suon's questions in regard to the responsibility of KR leaders.

7. For an autobiographical account of cannibalism, see also Loung Ung, *First They Killed My Father: A Daughter of Cambodia Remembers* (New York: Harper Perennial, 2000). On testimony on cannibalism in security centers given during Case No. 002/02 at the ECCC, see George Wright and Kuch Naren, "Cannibalism, Khmer Rouge and Horrors of War," *Cambodia Daily*, April 25, 2014, www.cambodiadaily.com/news/cannibalism -khmer-rouge-and-horrors-of-war-82653. On the testimony of a victim from the Cham Muslim minority given at the ECCC, see Erin Handley, "Chams Recall Horror Inflicted by Angkar," *Phnom Penh Post*, March 1, 2016, www.phnompenhpost.com/national /chams-recall-horror-inflicted-angkar.

8. Jan van den Berg and Willem van de Put's documentary film *Deacon of Death* (Netherlands, 2004) begins with the testimony of a survivor, Sok Chea, who was a young child

during the KR period. She related seeing a person with his belly slashed in order to remove his liver. Knowing that the perpetrators killed all possible witnesses to this crime, she ran away. At present, during her confrontation with Karoby, the low-ranking perpetrator who killed her father, she tells him she knows that "they used human livers ... to make a drink with gallbladder and alcohol." Alexander Laban Hinton claims that Cambodian cannibalism (especially eating the liver and gallbladder and drinking bile) has been recorded since the fourteenth century and through the KR period into the early 1990s. In contrast to the frying of a liver, which according to Hinton symbolizes decontamination and is enhanced by communal eating, the gall-bladder transforms the eaters/drinkers into another mode of being and could drive them to madness. Hinton, "Anthropologies of the Khmer Rouge, Part II: Genocidal Bricolage," paper presented at the Genocide Studies Program Seminar, Yale University, New Haven, CT, September 17, 1998.

9.   Sigmund Freud, *Totem and Taboo*, 2nd ed., trans. James Strachey (1913; New York: Routledge, 2001).

10.   Shirley Lindenbaum, "Thinking About Cannibalism," *Annual Review of Anthropology* 33 (2004): 478.

11.   Gananath Obeyesekere, in Lindenbaum, "Thinking About Cannibalism," 485.

12.   For an elaboration on the Cambodian classicide, see Michael Mann, *The Dark Side of Democracy: Explaining Ethnic Cleansing* (Cambridge: Cambridge University Press, 2005), 342–52.

13.   In Panh's film *Duch, Master of the Forges of Hell*, Duch says: "The KR word *kamtech* has its own meaning. It doesn't only mean kill, it means kill and leave no trace, to reduce to ashes, so that nothing left remains." In another scene, which Panh places near the end of the film, while describing the KR's violation of all former traditions of mourning, notification of the victim's family, burial, and so on, he says: "*Kamtech* means to destroy the name, the image, the body, everything."

14.   On September 19, 2007, Chea was arrested at his home in Pailin and flown to the KR Tribunal in Phnom Penh. On August 7, 2014, the court convicted him of crimes against humanity and sentenced him to life imprisonment.

15.   During the Sundance postscreening Q and A session (on January 27, 2010), Sambath claimed that he sincerely forgives Nuon Chea, opposes the endless violence inherent in revenge, prefers a face-to-face dialogue with the perpetrators, and hopes for a reconciliation, "so we can stop the killing in future generations."

16.   During the Sundance postscreening Q and A session (on January 27, 2010), Lemkin said: "The film was requested by the Court because of primary, significant information ... by the investigator, ... the prosecutor, ... and Brother Number 2 defense lawyers, ... all three of them." On the dispute over the tapes and Sambath and Lemkin's appearance as witnesses, see, for instance, ECCC, "Nuon Chea's Response to the Co-Prosecutors' Request to Call THET Sambath (2-TCW-885) as a Priority Witness," www.eccc.gov.kh/en/document/court/nuon-cheas-response-co-prosecutors-request-call-thet-sambath-2-tcw-885-priority; www.eccc.gov.kh/sites/default/files/documents/courtdoc/2015-01-27%2016%3A13/E335_1_EN.PDF; ECCC, "Order On Co-Prosecutors' Request for

Investigative Action Regarding Interviews of NUON Chea, and the Film 'Enemies of the People,'" www.eccc.gov.kh/en/document/court/order-co-prosecutors-request-investigative-action-regarding-interviews-nuon-chea-and; ECCC, "Order on Investigative Request Regarding the Film 'Enemies of the People,'" www.eccc.gov.kh/sites/default/files/documents/courtdoc/D344_1_EN.pdf; ECCC, "Co-Prosecutors' Response to Nuon Chea's Response to Questions on the Supreme Court Chamber's Additional Investigation Into Footage in the Possession of Filmmakers Rob Lemkin and Thet Sambath," www.eccc.gov.kh/en/document/court/co-prosecutors-response-nuon-cheas-response-questions-supreme-court-chambers; see Sambath and Lemkin's response at *Phnom Penh Post Blogspot*, "Documentary Film Co-Producer Defends Dealing with Tribunal," April 21, 2010, http://khmernz.blogspot.com/2010/04/documentary-film-co-producer-defends.html.

17. Gina Chon and Sambath Thet, *Behind the Killing Fields: A Khmer Rouge Leader and One of His Victims* (Philadelphia: University of Pennsylvania Press, 2010).

18. See the special edition of the DVD, which includes additional features: deleted scenes (such as Nuon Chea on his early years); Q and A sessions filmed during the postpremieres of the film at Sundance and at Phnom Penh; short films (*Looking for Vorn*, UK/Cambodia, 2009), in which Sambath follows, in vain, the traces of his dead brother and *One Day at Po Chrey: Anatomy of a Massacre* (UK, 2012), two scenes of which were shown at the ECCC 2013 hearings; and a video conference organized by Sambath and filmed outside Cambodia in which Khoun and Suon talked with members of the Cambodian refugee community in Long Beach, CA, in the United States. During a talk after the Phnom Penh's premiere, Lemkin characterized their filmmaking as done "in a non-adversarial spirit." He defined Sambath's work as an emblem of "dispassionate neutrality," "subtlety of approach," and "balanced."

19. See Bridget di Certo, "KRT: When Art Becomes Evidence," *Phnom Penh Post*, December 23, 2011, www.phnompenhpost.com/national/krt-when-art-becomes-evidence. On May 16, 2015, after Chea's verdict, Sambath said in an interview: "I don't see the current court is going the right way. Even if this court sentences Nuon Chea or other KR leaders to their whole lives in prison, it's useless because the KR tribunal does not summon . . . the people that were involved like the current leaders in the government and other former KR." See George Wright, "Journalist Again Asked to Testify at Tribunal," *Cambodia Daily*, May 16, 2015, www.cambodiadaily.com/archives/journalist-again-asked-to-testify-at-tribunal-83784.

20. Chon and Sambath, *Behind the Killing Fields*, 164–65.

21. Chon and Sambath, 166.

22. John Pilger and David Munro's *Year Zero: The Silent Death of Cambodia* (UK, 1979) was probably the first international film to present Pol Pot's horrors to the West, though *The Killing Fields* was the first to reach wide global audiences as a result of being awarded three Academy Awards.

23. In contrast to *Enemies*, for which Sambath began his quest in around 1999, *The Killing Fields* covers the period between August 7, 1973, and October 9, 1979. Most of Joffé's fiction film is rendered through the point of view of the *New York Times*

foreign correspondent Sydney Schanberg (Sam Waterston), and only part of it is rendered through that of Dith Pran (Dr. Haing S. Ngor). For Ngor's biography, based on his autobiography, archival footage, clips from *The Killing Fields* (such as the invasion to Phnom Penh), and animation, see Arthur Dong's documentary film *The Killing Fields of Dr. Haing S. Ngor* (USA, 2015). The film includes dramatic footage of Duch testifying at the ECCC that Pol Pot ordered the murder of Haing Ngor because of his role in *The Killing Fields*. However, to my mind, the film fails to delve more deeply into Ngor's personality, life, or tragic undeciphered death. See also Ngor's memoir with Roger Warner, *Survival in the Killing Fields* (1987; New York: Basic, 2003).

24. Jens Meierhenrich, "Varieties of Reconciliation," *Law and Social Inquiry* 33, no. 1 (2008): 209.

25. I refer particularly to moral emotions.

26. Manfred S. Frings, introduction to *Ressentiment*, by Max Scheler, trans. Lewis B. Coser and William W. Holdheim (1914; Milwaukee, WI: Marquette University Press, 2010), 4. Hereafter cited parenthetically in the text.

27. Thomas Brudholm, *Resentment's Virtue: Jean Amery and the Refusal to Forgive* (Philadelpha: Temple University Press, 2008), Kindle location 2582.

28. Aleida Assmann, "Two Forms of Resentment: Jean Améry, Martin Walser and German Memorial Culture," *New German Critique* 90 (2003): 123–33; Arne Johan Vetlesen, "A Case for Resentment: Jean Améry Versus Primo Levi," *Journal of Human Rights* 5 (2006): 27–44; Jeffrey K. Olick, "From Theodicy to *Ressentiment*: Trauma and the Ages of Compensation," in *The Politics of Regret: On Collective Memory and Historical Responsibility* (New York: Routledge, 2007), 153–73; Brudholm, *Resentment's Virtue*; Magdalena Zolkos, "Jean Améry's Concept of Resentment at the Crossroads of Ethics and Politics," *European Legacy* 12, no. 1 (2007): 23–38; Stefano Tomelleri, *Ressentiment: Reflections on Mimetic Desire and Society* (East Lansing: Michigan State University Press, 2015).

29. Friedrich Wilhelm Nietzsche, *On the Genealogy of Morals*, 1st ed., trans. Douglas Smith (1887; New York: Oxford University Press, 2009).

30. Nietzsche, 22.

31. Frings, "Introduction," 4, emphasis in the original.

32. Frings, 5–6, emphasis in the original.

33. Brudholm, *Resentment's Virtue*, Kindle location 1262–78.

34. Max Scheler, *Ressentiment*, trans. Lewis B. Coser and William W. Holdheim (1914; Milwaukee, WI: Marquette University Press, 2010), 23–25, emphases in the original. Beyond Scheler's emphasizing that the core of Christian ethics has not grown on resentment, but rather on "bourgeois morality," he tries to comprehend what *ressentiment* can contribute to our understanding of certain individual and historical *moral judgments* and of entire moral systems. It goes without saying that genuine moral value judgments are never based on *ressentiment*. . . . Nietzsche is wrong in thinking that genuine morality springs from *ressentiment* (45).

35. Scheler analyzes various types such as the woman, the old aged, the "mother-in-law," and compares them to active types, which are not in danger of being subject to *ressentiment*, such as the criminal and the soldier.

36. Especially Améry, *Radical Humanism: Selected Essays*, ed. and trans. Sidney Rosenfeld and Stella P. Rosenfeld (Bloomington: Indiana University Press, 1984); and Améry, *On Suicide: A Discourse on Voluntary Death*, trans. John D. Barlow (1976; Bloomington: Indiana University Press, 1999).

37. Rithy Panh and Christopher Bataille, *The Elimination: A Survivor of the Khmer Rouge Confronts His Past and the Commandant of the Killing Fields*, trans. John Cullen (New York: Other Press, 2013), 97.

38. A continuation of his film practice, the Bophana Audiovisual Resource Centre in Phnom Penh, launched by Panh, is working on training a new generation of filmmakers after the mass murder of the previous generation of filmmakers, actors, and actresses. In addition, it archives AV material relating to the KR period and beyond. See www .bophana.org.

39. Jean Améry, *At the Mind's Limits: Contemplations by a Survivor on Auschwitz and Its Realities*, trans. Sidney Rosenfeld and Stella P. Rosenfeld (1966; Bloomington: Indiana University Press, 1980), xxiii.

40. See D. G. Myers, "Jean Améry: A Biographical Introduction," http://dgmyers.blogspot .com/p/jean-amery-biographical-introduction.html.

41. Vetlesen, "A Case for Resentment," 40. The author compares the attitudes of the two "barracks mates" who became Auschwitz survivors, suggesting that "Levi's disagreement with fellow survivor Améry over resentment is not primarily an intellectual dispute or a discourse on morality. It is an occasion for Levi's fight against himself, within himself" (40), a highly speculative claim in regard to Levi that I find unconvincing.

42. Améry, *Mind's Limits*, 64. I suggest that Brudholm's work to a certain degree still reflects the age-old inclination of psychological discourse against resentment. Brudholm, for example, is hopeful that Améry's resentments can be welcomed into the reconciliatory process. Though Magdalena Zolkos reads Améry's resentments as disrupting "the very discourse of 'normalization'" that reconciliation tends toward (in "Jean Améry's Concept of Resentment," 27), she claims that, "on the one hand, resentment invokes the desire for the reversal of time and for the undoing of wrongs. It thus bears a certain family resemblance to Nietzsche's and Scheler's ressentiment as it remains inherently affixed to the past, haunted by the past, immobilized by it" (29). In my view, this suggestion misses the existential state revealed in Améry's position as a victim, his own reflection on the regression in time, and the evolution of his ideas in the collection, which, as noted, was written chronologically and not according to its subjects.

43. This is the reason for his objection to Arendt's observations that were made "through the glass cage." See Améry, *Mind's Limits*, 15. Hereafter Améry's text is cited parenthetically in the text.

44. See Améry's insightful reflection on revenge: "My conviction that loudly proclaimed readiness for reconciliation by Nazi victims can only be either insanity and indifference

to life or the masochistic conversion of a suppressed *genuine* demand for revenge" (Améry, 71).

45. Hinton, "Anthropologies," and Hinton, "Begrudgement, Reconciliation, and the Khmer Rouge," *Searching for the Truth* (Khmer version), *A Magazine of the Documentation Center of Cambodia* 20 (August 2001), www.d.dccam.org/Tribunal/Analysis/Begrud gement_Reconciliation.htm.

46. Améry, *Mind's Limits*, 77.

47. Leo Kuper, *The Prevention of Genocide* (New Haven, CT: Yale University Press, 1985).

48. Israel W. Charny, "A Classification of Denials of the Holocaust and Other Genocides," in *The Genocide Studies Reader*, ed. Samuel Totten and Paul R. Bartrop (New York: Routledge, 2009), 518–37.

49. Danien Short, "Reconciliation and the Problem of Internal Colonialism," *Journal of Intercultural Studies* 26, no. 3 (2005): 267–82.

50. John Borneman, "Reconciliation After Ethnic Cleansing: Listening, Retribution, Affiliation," *Public Culture* 14, no. 2 (2002): 281–304.

51. Ann Rigney, "Reconciliation and Remembering: (How) Does it Work?," *Memory Studies* 5, no. 3 (2012): 251–58.

52. Jacques Derrida, "On Forgiveness," in *On Cosmopolitanism and Forgiveness*, trans. Mark Dooley and Michael Hughes (1966; New York: Routledge, 2001), 32.

53. Améry, *Mind's Limits*, 77.

54. Which became the Tuol Sleng Genocide Museum in 1980.

55. "First I went to see the torturers in their homes. I spoke to them. I tried to persuade them. Then I filmed them in the very places where their acts had been committed. I often paid someone to take their place in the fields because a shoot could require several days. I gave them room and board. . . . I want to make them draw near and feel the truth, to punctuate the small lies and refute the big ones" (in Panh and Bataille, *Elimination*, 7).

56. See Deirdre Boyle, "Trauma, Memory, Documentary: Re-Enactment in Two Films by Rithy Panh (Cambodia) and Garin Nugroho (Indonesia)," in *Documentary Testimonies: Global Archives of Suffering*, ed. Bhaskar Sarkar and Janet Walker (New York: Routledge, 2010), 155–72.

57. A term coined by Herbert Kelman and V. Lee Hamilton. Quoted in David Chandler, *Voices from S-21: Terror and History in Pol Pot's Secret Prison* (Berkeley: University of California Press, 1999), 137.

58. See, for instance, the detailed "confession" at S-21 of Chum Mey (one of only seven known survivors) from November 6, 1978, translated by Rich Arant and published in Mey's memoir. Mey's main forced inventions had to do with the destruction of equipment and machines that belonged to Angkar and planning a coup throughout the country. Chum Mey with Documentation Center of Cambodia, *Survivor: The Triumph of an Ordinary Man in the Khmer Rouge Genocide*, trans. Sim Sorya and Kimsory Sokvisal (Phnom Penh: Documentation Center of Cambodia, 2012), 77–100.

59. See Raya Morag, *Waltzing with Bashir: Perpetrator Trauma and Cinema* (London: I. B. Tauris, 2013), 14–21.

60. Dori Laub, "Bearing Witness, or the Vicissitudes of Listening," in *Testimony: Crises of Witnessing in Literature*, ed. Shoshana Felman and Dori Laub (New York: Routledge, 1992), 59–60.

61. Morag, *Waltzing with Bashir*, 14–21.

62. All quotations are taken from the film.

63. Panh and Bataille, *Elimination*, 91.

64. Panh and Bataille, 1.

65. Nic Dunlop, *The Lost Executioner: The Story of Comrade Duch and the Khmer Rouge* (London: Bloomsbury, 2005), 5.

66. Panh and Bataille, *Elimination*, 7.

67. Duch was arrested in 2010. See Dunlop, *Lost Executioner*, 11–13, 254–78, written before Duch's trial. The book follows Duch's life trajectory through major turning points.

68. Duch, represented by the Cambodian lawyer Kar Savuth and the French lawyer François Roux, appealed his provisional detention by the ECCC, based on the more than eight years he had spent in Cambodian military detention before trial. The appeal was unsuccessful. On February 2, 2012, the ECCC increased his sentence to life imprisonment. See Padraic J. Glaspy, "Justice Delayed—Recent Developments at the Extraordinary Chambers in the Courts of Cambodia," *Harvard Human Rights Journal* 21, no. 1 (2008): 143–54, http://heinonline.org/HOL/Page?handle=hein.journals/hhrj21&div=9&g_sent=1&collection=journals.

69. The questions are not heard, but are very much present because of the documents, as will be described later.

70. In his memoir, Rithy Panh writes: "Starting with the first day . . . I brought along material to show to Duch: I'd copied fifty of the Angkar's slogans, one on each of fifty pages. I asked him to pick out one. Some were threatening, others enigmatic, and still others poetic but cold. . . . I want to understand the nature of the crime, not to establish a cult of memory." Panh and Bataille, *Elimination*, 72–74.

71. This term was coined by Adam Crawford in "Temporality in Restorative Justice: On Time, Timing and Time-Consciousness," *Theoretical Criminology* 19, no. 4 (2015): 470.

72. Améry, *Mind's Limits*, 71.

73. Améry, 71.

74. Panh and Bataille, *Elimination*, 82.

75. Panh and Bataille, 71.

76. According to Chandler, roughly forty-three hundred accounts were found in S-21. These texts, in which the prisoners admitted to counterrevolutionary crimes, range from a single page to several hundred. Chandler, *Voices from S-21*, 1–13.

77. "Duch's neatly written queries and annotations, often in red ink, appear on hundreds of confessions. They frequently correct and denigrate what prisoners confessed, suggest beating and torture." Chandler, 22.

78. As Christopher R. Browning contends, "The men who carry out 'atrocity by policy' are in a different state of mind." Browning, *Ordinary Men: Reserve Police Battalion 101 and the Final Solution in Poland* (1992; New York: HarperCollins, 1998), 161.

79. The love story between Bophana and her husband and her subversive stand against the KR and her torturers in S-21 became one of Panh's major symbols. See Panh's film *Bophana: A Cambodian Tragedy* (1996).

80. Panh and Bataille, *Elimination*, 261.

81. Borrowed from the Latin *nunc* (now) and *stāns* (staying, remaining).

82. Stanley Cohen, *States of Denial: Knowing About Atrocities and Suffering* (Cambridge: Polity, 2001), 80.

83. Améry, *Mind's Limits*, 68.

84. See Bill Nichols, "Documentary Reenactment and the Fantasmatic Subject," *Critical Inquiry* 35, no. 1 (2008): 78; and Nichols, "The Voice of Documentary," *Film Quarterly* 36, no. 3 (1983): 17–30.

85. Jacques Derrida, *The Work of Mourning*, ed. Pascale-Anne Brault and Michael Nass (Chicago: University of Chicago Press, 2001), 159.

86. Jacques Derrida, *The Gift of Death* (Chicago: University of Chicago Press, 1995), 41.

87. He played Monsieur Jo in Panh's *The Sea Wall* (*Un barrage contre le Pacifique*, France/Cambodia/Belgium, 2008).

88. The narration was written by Panh (with Bataille).

89. Hannah Arendt, *Eichmann in Jerusalem: A Report on the Banality of Evil* (1963; New York: Penguin, 2006), 69.

90. In *Elimination*, Panh writes, "Overnight I become 'new people,' or (according to an even more horrible expression) an 'April 17.' . . . The history of my childhood is abolished. Forbidden. From that day on, I, Rithy Panh, thirteen years old, have no more history, no more family, no more emotions, no more thoughts, no more unconscious. . . . What a brilliant idea, to give a hated class a name full of hope: '*new people.*'" Panh and Bataille, *Elimination*, 23, emphasis in the original.

91. Arjun Appadurai, *Fear of Small Numbers: An Essay on the Geography of Anger* (Durham, NC: Duke University Press. 2006), 1–13.

92. Améry, *Mind's Limits*, 81.

93. Bophana's image appears in many of Rithy Panh's films. As he said in an interview on January 19, 2014: "Yes, but in fact, if you watch my film, all [my other] films also—I put Bophana inside the film somewhere. Some people know who she is. Some people just know her as a victim. . . . I think that one day people will identify her. It is just like *un homage*, a tribute to her." See Yuan-Kwan Chan, "A Rithy Panh Interview: *The Missing Picture* and Cambodian Cinema," www.meniscuszine.com/articles/2014011927208/a -rithy-panh-interview-the-missing-picture-and-cambodian-cinema.

94. Améry, *Mind's Limits*, 68–69.

95. Panh and Bataille, *Elimination*, 113.

96. Alessandra Lemma, "The Many Faces of Lying," *International Journal of Psychoanalysis* 86, no. 3 (2005): 738.

97. Panh and Bataille, *Elimination*, 114.

98. Panh and Bataille, 186.

99. For the use of this term, see Achille Mbembe. Though I disagree with his political per-
    spective, I find his definition of political counterspheres a productive one. Mbembe,
    "Necropolitics," *Public Culture* 15, no. 1 (2003): 11–40.

100. See, for instance, Janet Gardner's documentary film *Lost Child: Sayon's Journey* (USA/
     Cambodia, 2013), which tells the story of a child-soldier kidnapped by the KR at age
     six and later adopted by an American family. Unable to recall his traumatic memories,
     he returns to Cambodia and finds his remaining brothers. Verifying that they are his
     lost family through DNA tests, he also discovers that they survived because they
     belonged to the KR.

101. Panh and Bataille, *Elimination*, 245–46.

102. The film, produced by Rithy Panh, won the Jury Award at FEMI 2012 and the Special
     Jury Award at the Festival Internacional de Cino Politico (FICIP), Buenos Aires, Argen-
     tina, 2013.

103. Houy describes the transfer of victims to Choeung Ek and their slaughter in Rithy
     Panh's *S21* as well. The killing field image is prevalent in the new Cambodian cinema
     (it appears as well in Arthur Dong's documentary film *The Killing Fields of Dr. Haing S.
     Ngor*). Mass graves containing 8,895 bodies were discovered at Choeung Ek after the
     fall of the KR regime. Currently, Choeung Ek is a memorial marked by a Buddhist *stupa*
     filled with more than five thousand human skulls that are shown through its acrylic
     glass sides. See Helen Jarvis, "Mapping Cambodia's 'Killing Fields,'" in *Matériel Cul-
     ture: The Archaeology of Twentieth-Century Conflict*, ed. Colleen M. Beck, William
     Gray Johnson, and John Schofield (New York: Routledge, 2002), 91–102. For a current
     discussion regarding the ethics of exhumation see Erin Handley, "The Ethics of Exhu-
     mation," *Phnom Penh Post*, January 5, 2017, www.phnompenhpost.com/post-weekend
     /ethics-exhumation.

104. Georges Didi-Huberman, *Images In Spite of All: Four Photographs from Auschwitz*,
     trans. Shane B. Lillis (Chicago: University of Chicago Press, 2008), 80–81, emphases in
     the original.

105. Didi-Huberman, 87.

106. Didi-Huberman, 90.

107. Robert Jay Lifton, *The Nazi Doctors: Medical Killing and the Psychology of Genocide*
     (1986; New York: Basic, 2000); and Cohen, *States of Denial*.

108. "By the start of the Duch trial, ninety-three people had brought suit as civil parties,
     most of whom were family members of people who had been killed at S-21. They were
     represented by fifteen lawyers." Alexander Laban Hinton, *Man or Monster: The Trial
     of a Khmer Rouge Torturer* (Durham, NC: Duke University Press, 2016), 63.

109. After reading out loud an extensive list of Mam Nai's academic achievements, Judge
     Sylvia Cartwright asked why one of the most intelligent people at Tuol Sleng was not
     aware of how the prison worked. "In principle . . . I was only mindful about my duties,"
     Mam Nai said. He claimed he had not known that all Tuol Sleng prisoners were pre-
     sumed guilty and he told Judge Jean-Marc Lavergne that his only regret was "that [Cam-
     bodia] was invaded" by America and Vietnam. Judge Lavergne then asked if he knew

what the words "no fear" meant in English, and Mam Nai responded that he did not. "In that case, I have no further questions, Lavergne replied." See Georgia Wilkins, "S-21 Deputy Denies Torture," *Phnom Penh Post*, July 15, 2009, www.phnompenhpost .com/national/s-21-deputy-denies-torture.

110. Asian International Justice Initiative, "Duch on Trial." Reports and videos from the Khmer Rouge Tribunal, a cooperative project of the East-West Center and the University of California, Berkeley, War Crimes Study Center, 2012.

111. See the description of the coprosecutor Bill Smith's criticism of the defense and the court on this issue in Hinton, *Man or Monster*, esp. 204–12, and his discussion of the conflict between Man Nai and the survivor Bou Meng, who is convinced that evidence of Mam Nai's lies is demonstrated by the intervention of *neak ta* in a car accident. ("*Neak ta* is the local guardian spirits sometimes said to be the spirit of the founding ancestors of the village, who are nevertheless feared and to whom offerings are made. When offended or disrespected, *neak ta*, including the *neak ta* found in Cambodian court complexes, may inflict sickness or hardship." Alexander Laban Hinton, *The Justice Facade: Trials of Transition in Cambodia* [Oxford: Oxford University Press, 2018], 181–82.) In their critical perspective on Duch's trial, Ciorciari and Haindel do not comment on the Mam Nai example, though they devote considerable discussion to what they term "blending civil and common law procedures." See John D. Ciorciari and Anne Heindel, *Hybrid Justice: The Extraordinary Chambers in the Courts of Cambodia* (Ann Arbor: University of Michigan Press, 2014), Kindle location 2608; Thierry Cruvellier, *The Master of Confessions: The Making of a Khmer Rouge Torturer*, trans. Alex Gilly (New York: Ecco, 2014), 222. See also Cruvellier's analysis of the Phung Ton case on pages 227–318, which includes his belief regarding the tears of both Duch and Mam Nai. See also his remarks on Duch, such as "The morning's discussion of Professor Phung Ton left him shattered" (232).

112. The Supreme Court Chamber of the ECCC (SCC) ruled that Duch's cooperation with the court was "incomplete, selective and opportunistic," and that he "spent almost the entire time given to him for his final statements seeking to minimize his responsibility . . . while his reference to remorse and apology was limited to a few sentences." See Hinton, *Man or Monster*, 258.

113. See Hinton's remarks on the trial's dynamic in relation to Duch's lawyers, the civil parties, the civil parties' lawyers, and prominent witnesses like Mam Nai in Hinton, esp. 184–242.

114. Shoshana Felman, *The Juridical Unconscious: Trials and Trauma in the Twentieth Century* (Cambridge, MA: Harvard University Press, 2002), 165.

115. See chapter 2, note 18, on Khieu Samphan.

116. See Cohen, *States of Denial*, esp. 76–116.

117. Cohen, 103, emphases in the original.

118. Khieu Samphan wrote a doctoral dissertation in economics at the Sorbonne in 1959 that foreshadowed the radical agrarian nightmare to come. See Khieu Samphan, "Cambodia's Economy and Problems of Industrialization," in *Underdevelopment in Cambodia*, trans. Laura Summers, *Indochina Chronicle* 51–52 (1976): 1–27, www.scribd.com/doc

3. PERPETRATORHOOD PARADIGMS   223

/58800629/Underdevelopment-in-Cambodia-by-Khieu-Samphan#scribd: "The concrete strategies of transition appear above all as those of *self-reliance*. Self-reliance, which must be understood on different levels, and which must democratically respect the true popular social groups which constitute the nation: the village, the region, . . . the state. . . . Self-conscious, autonomous development is therefore objectively necessary."

119. Dori Laub, "Listening to My Mother's Testimony," *Contemporary Psychoanalysis* 51, no. 2 (2015): 195.

120. Laub, 196.

121. Cohen, *States of Denial*, 238–39.

122. See Melanie Kline, quoted in Claudia Frank, "On the Reception of the Concept of the Death Drive in Germany: Expressing and Resisting an 'Evil Principle?'" *International Journal of Psychoanalysis* 96 (2015): 430–31.

123. As Nicola Henry claims, "Full justice goes beyond criminal trials. . . . Full justice involves the identification of missing bodies, the return of property, reparations, apologies, economic and social security, safety, stability and community reintegration, as well as the arrest and prosecution of war criminals." Nicola Henry, "Witness to Rape: The Limits and Potential of International War Crimes Trials for Victims of Wartime Sexual Violence," *International Journal of Transitional Justice* 3 (2009): 134.

124. Felman, *Juridical Unconscious*.

125. Dominick LaCapra, *Writing History, Writing Trauma* (Baltimore: Johns Hopkins University Press, 2001).

126. Meierhenrich, for instance, devotes considerable argumentation against what he calls "conceptual stretching" of the notion of reconciliation in scholarship. See Meierhenrich, "Varieties of Reconciliation."

127. Both Khieu Samphan in *Bitter Khmer Rouge* (France/Cambodia, 2007) and Duch in *Duch, Master of the Forges of Hell* admit that they saw *S21: The Khmer Rouge Death Machine*.

128. The film won the Spirit of Asia Award at the 2014 Tokyo Film Festival. It has been submitted by the Cambodia Oscar Selection Committee (COSC) for the Best Foreign-Language Film category for the 88th Academy Awards. The director told me that it was screened first in the International Film Festival in Cambodia in 2014, and then for six weeks in three cinema houses in Phnom Penh and one cinema house in Siem Reap. Most of the spectators were members of the old generation (personal conversation via Skype, November 26, 2017). Against this background, it is important to indicate the proliferation of the horror genre and popular comedies, which attests as well to unresolved tensions. This phenomenon, which is beyond the scope of this book, appears in other contexts in world cinema, such as post–World War II Japanese cinema, with its abundance of sci-fi horror films replete with body mutations, and post–World War II German cinema, with its defeated males, convoluted sexuality, and deformed families. See Raya Morag, *Defeated Masculinity: Post-Traumatic Cinema in the Aftermath of War* (Brussels: Peter Lang, 2009).

129. For example, Thomas Elsaesser, "Tales of Sound and Fury: The Family Melodrama," *Monogram* 4 (1972): 2–15; Peter Brooks, *The Melodramatic Imagination: Balzac, Henry*

James, Melodrama, and the Mode of Excess (New Haven, CT: Yale University Press, 1976); Linda Williams, "'Something Else Besides a Mother': 'Stella Dallas' and the Maternal Melodrama," *Cinema Journal* 24, no. 1 (1984): 2–27; and Williams, "Melodrama Revised," in *Refiguring American Film Genres*, ed. Nick Browne (Berkeley: University of California Press, 1998), 42–88; Christine Gledhill, "Rethinking Genre," in *Reinventing Film Studies*, ed. Christine Gledhill and Linda Williams (London: Arnold, 2000), 221–43; and Gledhill, "The Melodramatic Field: An Investigation," in *Home Is Where the Heart Is: Studies in Melodrama and the Woman's Film*, ed. Christine Gledhill (London: BFI, 1987), 5–39; and E. Ann Kaplan, "Melodrama, Cinema and Trauma," *Screen* 42, no. 2 (2001): 201–5; and Kaplan, "Ann Kaplan Replies to Linda Williams's '"Something Else Besides a Mother": "Stella Dallas" and the Maternal Melodrama,'" *Cinema Journal* 24, no. 2 (1985): 40–43. More recently, Ben Singer takes up the issue in *Melodrama and Modernity: Early Sensational Cinema and Its Contexts* (New York: Columbia University Press, 2001).

130. This is the local term for a gang member who is not considered a gangster. A kind of a playboy, he is relatively rich, with options for buying a gun. (Thanks to Kulikar Sotho for this information.)

131. The cinema scenes were shot in the Golden Temple Cinema in Battambang, built in the early 1960s and one of the few cinema houses not totally destroyed during the KR period. It still stands abandoned today. As the director told me, the people who live around the cinema are those who lived there long ago. They worked in the cinema before the war and returned to it after. For example, Mr. Saran, the projectionist, worked in the cinema his entire life (personal correspondence, February 13, 2018). See also Harriet Fitch Little and Vandy Muong, "Relics of Cambodia's Cinematic Golden Age," *Phnom Penh Post*, December 19, 2014, www.phnompenhpost.com/post-weekend/relics -cambodias-cinematic-golden-age.

132. Dy Saveth starred in over one hundred Cambodian films throughout the 1960s and 1970s until the communist takeover in 1975, and has starred in films from 1993 to the present. In 2011, she appeared in the Davy Chou's documentary *Golden Slumbers* (*Le sommeil d'or*, France/Cambodia).

133. See Jarvis, "Mapping Cambodia's 'Killing Fields,'" 97–98. As the author indicates, since Buddhism was restored as the official religion of Cambodia, *stupas* have been built in various *wats* around the country. In Trapeang Sva, Tonle Bati, a new *stupa* was built in 1999.

134. The script was written by Ian Masters, who, together with Kulikar Sotho, is also a coproducer.

135. During my conversation with Kulikar Sotho (on November 26, 2017), the director told me that she was a very young child during the KR regime, and that her mother refused to talk about the past until the film's premiere. In many respects, her mother's silence for thirty-five years was her reason for making the film. In the film's final titles we read: "*The Last Reel* is dedicated to my father Om Channy and my mother Ang Seantho and a love that could not be extinguished by the cruelty of the KR." See the discussion of the term *1.5 generation* in chapter 1.

136.   See the discussion of forced marriage in chapter 4.

137.   Cohen, *States of Denial*, 239–40.

4. GENDERED GENOCIDE

1.   Ariel Dorfman, *Death and the Maiden* (New York: Penguin, 1994), 40–41.

2.   Shoshana Felman, *The Juridical Unconscious: Trials and Traumas in the Twentieth Century* (Cambridge, MA: Harvard University Press, 2002); Cathy Caruth, *Unclaimed Experience: Trauma, Narrative and History* (Baltimore: Johns Hopkins University Press, 1996); Annette Wieviorka, *The Era of the Witness*, trans. Jared Stark (Ithaca NY: Cornell University Press, 2006).

3.   Felman, *Juridical Unconscious*, 1.

4.   Zygmunt Bauman, "A Revolution in the Theory of Revolutions?," *International Political Science Review* 15, no. 1 (1994): 15.

5.   The term *revolution* means in this context "fundamental change in the social order brought about in a short period of time through a massive shift in people's expressed political views." See Timur Kuran, "Sparks and Prairie Fires: A Theory of Unanticipated Political Revolution," *Public Choice* 61, no. 1 (1989): 42. Analyzing the dynamics involved in major revolutions, and especially what Kuran regards as some theories' false claim regarding the inevitability and thus the predictability of revolutions, he contends that the magnitude and speed of the revolutionary process come as an enormous surprise precisely because the masses had been concealing their growing frustrations.

6.   The effects of World War I, destroying one of Europe's oldest monarchies, gave rise to the political phenomenon of socialist dictatorship—the Russian Revolution of 1917. See Jonathan Smele, "War and Revolution in Russia 1914–1921," October 3, 2011, www.bbc .co.uk/history/worldwars/wwone/eastern_front_01.shtml.

7.   See Stef Craps, *Postcolonial Witnessing: Trauma out of Bounds* (New York: Palgrave Macmillan, 2015). As Stanley Aronowitz suggests, class as a socioeconomic category has been disappearing from postindustrial, postcapitalist societies since shortly after the middle of the twentieth century, replaced by "the politics of subalternity." This shift is related to various post–World War II changes, among them the rise of welfare programs as well as the growth of a global capitalist economy, which diminished the role of the nation-state and shifted attention to smaller subject-groups, or minorities, like women, blacks, LGBT communities, and so on. The concurrent spread of various intellectual trends, like postcolonialism and postmodernism, provided important theoretical justifications for the political shift from class to identity at the dawn of the twenty-first century. Aronowitz, *The Politics of Identity* (New York: Routledge, 1992), ix, 8. There has recently been renewed interest in class as a meaningful category in the current world of advanced capitalism. See, e.g., June Deery and Andrea Press, eds., *Media and Class: TV, Film, and Digital Culture* (New York: Routledge, 2017).

8.   A huge range of other events that claim our attention as examples of revolution, ranging from the communist transformations of nation in the first part of the twentieth

century to the collapse of communist regimes and the chaotic revolutionary wars in Africa at its end, and up to the Islamic fundamentalist revolutions and the "Arab Spring" in the second decade of the twenty-first century, have still left no mark on trauma theory. In tandem, twenty-first-century ethnoreligious struggles as major factors shaping the twenty-first century's revolutions are still at their inception in terms of influencing current conceptualizations of trauma theory.

9. As Judith Herman-Lewis claims in *Trauma and Recovery* (New York: Basic, 1992), 22–23.

10. Shoshana Felman and Dori Laub, *Testimony: Crises of Witnessing in Literature, Psychoanalysis and History* (New York: Routledge, 1992); Caruth, *Unclaimed Experience*; Felman, *Juridical Unconscious*; Dominick LaCapra, *Writing History, Writing Trauma* (Baltimore: Johns Hopkins University Press, 2001); Giorgio Agamben, *State of Exception*, trans. Kevin Attell (Chicago: University of Chicago Press, 2005). Current post-9/11 trauma debates focus mainly on ethnicity and embrace the disruptive nature of the "race cycle."

11. Samuel P. Huntington, *Political Order in Changing Societies* (1968; New Haven, CT: Yale University Press, 2006); Theda Skocpol, *States and Social Revolutions: A Comparative Analysis of France, Russia, and China* (New York: Cambridge University Press, 1979); Kuran, "Sparks and Prairie Fires," 42; Michael Hardt and Antonio Negri, *Empire* (Cambridge, MA: Harvard University Press, 2000); Jack A. Goldstone, "Toward a Fourth Generation of Revolutionary Theory," *Annual Review of Political Science* 4 (2001): 139–87; for an analysis of developments in sociological theorizing about revolution, see John Foran, "Theories of Revolution Revisited: Toward a Fourth Generation?," *Sociological Theory* 11, no. 1 (1993): 1–20.

12. The bystander-perpetrator-victim triangle, mainly constituted by Raul Hilberg in *Perpetrators, Victims, Bystanders: The Jewish Catastrophe, 1933–1945* (New York: Harper Perennial, 1993) is the most common model referred to in the huge literature on genocide and its aftermath. On the entanglement and differentiation of these seemingly entitative social categories/subject positions, see, for instance, LaCapra's reflection on victims, perpetrators, and the Goldhagen debate in *Writing History*; Zygmunt Bauman's analysis of the situation in which some individuals occupied all three roles in *Modernity and the Holocaust*, 2nd ed. (1989; Ithaca, NY: Cornell University Press, 2011); Tristan Anne Borer's new taxonomy of victims and perpetrators following the TRC trials in "A Taxonomy of Victims and Perpetrators: Human Rights and Reconciliation in South Africa," *Human Rights Quarterly* 25, no. 4 (2003): 1088–116; and Ben Kiernan, *Blood and Soil: A World History of Genocide and Extermination from Sparta to Darfur* (New Haven, CT: Yale University Press, 2007).

13. See chapter 2, note 48, explaining the term *New People*.

14. See chapter 1, note 48, on Democratic Kampuchea. More than twenty-eight thousand people followed the proceedings of Duch's trial (Case No. 001); an unprecedented number of 103,724 people attended the trial of Nuon Chea and Khieu Samphan (Case No. 002), when they were found guilty of crimes against humanity committed between

April 17, 1975, and December 1977 and sentenced to life imprisonment. See ECCC, "Key Events," www.eccc.gov.kh/en/keyevents.

15. See Sebastian Strangio, *Hun Sen's Cambodia* (New Haven, CT: Yale University Press, 2014).

16. Pierre Bourdieu, "The Social Space and the Genesis of Groups," *Theory and Society* 14, no. 6 (1985): 723–44; Bourdieu, "What Makes a Social Class? On the Theoretical and Practical Existence of Groups," *Berkeley Journal of Sociology* 32, no. 1 (1987): 1–17; Bourdieu, "Social Space and Symbolic Power," *Sociological Theory* 7, no. 1 (1989): 14–25.

17. Bourdieu, "Social Space and the Genesis," 742.

18. "Following the definition used by recent international war crimes tribunals, by *rape* I mean the coerced (under physical force or threat of physical force against the victim or a third person) penetration of the anus or vagina by the penis or another object, or of the mouth by the penis." Elisabeth Jean Wood, "Variation in Sexual Violence During War," *Politics and Society* 34, no. 3 (2006): 308. Wood refers to UNESCO, *Contemporary Forms of Slavery: Systematic Rape, Sexual Slavery and Slavery-Like Practices During Armed Conflict*, E/CN.4/Sub.2/1998/13 (New York: United Nations, 1998); and Human Rights Watch, *"We'll Kill You if You Cry": Sexual Violence in the Sierra Leone Conflict* (New York: Human Rights Watch, 2003).

19. The first post-KR film class in contemporary Cambodia was established by Rithy Panh. It included eight students, whom Panh has mentored. Five of them have finished their films: Yos Katank, Chan Lida, Neang Kavich, Chhoun Sarin, and Sao Sopheak.

20. Case No. 002/02 refers to the second trial against Khieu Samphan and Nuon Chea, in which additional charges from the Closing Order in Case No. 002 were heard.

21. At least till 1978, when the forced marriages began. But even then, class determined the crime.

22. See Luce Irigaray, ed., *The Irigaray Reader* (Oxford: Blackwell, 1991), 133.

23. See chapter 1, note 94, on forced marriage.

24. Bourdieu, "Social Space and Symbolic Power," 16.

25. See the translation of the film script, the first appearance in print of a documentary by Panh in Rithy Panh, "Bophana: A Cambodian Tragedy," *Manoa* 16, no. 1 (2004): 108–26.

26. Michel Foucault, "Nietzsche, Genealogy, History," in *Language, Counter-Memory, Practice: Selected Essays and Interviews*, ed. Donald F. Bouchard (Ithaca, NY: Cornell University Press, 1977), 148.

27. Elizabeth Becker, who was a war correspondent, retrieved the file from the thousands discovered at S-21. A decade later she publicized it in her book *When the War Was Over: Cambodia's Revolution and the Voices of its People* (New York: Simon and Schuster, 1986). Rithy Panh adapted the story to the screen. Youk Chhang, a survivor and the director of the Documentation Center of Cambodia (DC-CAM), translated *When the War Was Over* into Khmer in 2005:

We settled on an image for the book jacket. Not Pol Pot, or Lon Nol, the Cambodian leader he defeated, or any of the other men who sent the soldiers to battle in those endless wars. Instead, the cover shows an image of the minor character who promised her husband she would stay with him to the end and then return to Cambodia as a ghost and "win total revenge."

The chapter devoted to Bophana's story was published as a separate book, but was printed only in Cambodia. See Becker, *Bophana: Love in the Time of the Khmer Rouge* (Phnom Penh: Cambodia Daily Press, 2010).

28. Elizabeth Becker, "Minor Characters," *New York Times*, August 28, 2005, www.nytimes .com/2005/08/28/books/review/minor-characters.html?_r=0.

29. See the history of the Bophana Center, established by Rithy Panh, at Bophana Audiovisual Resource Center, http://bophana.org/. Youk Chhang also translated *The Diary of Anne Frank* into Khmer. As he told me during a personal conversation at DC-CAM (Phnom Penh, July 8, 2014), it is compulsory reading in every school in Cambodia.

30. Vann Nath died in 2011, at the age of sixty-five. He received the prestigious Lillian Hellman/Hammett Award, which recognizes courage in the face of political persecution— which he faced during the KR regime.

31. See chapter 1, note 62, on civil parties.

32. See an analysis of the film in chapter 3.

33. In 2005, during her visit to Cambodia, Becker was astonished to discover that her little book *Bophana* was sold all over Cambodia.

34. One Dollar Project, Bophana Center.

One Dollar is a participatory web documentary initiated by Rithy Panh. The . . . filmmakers . . . focus their portraits on the daily lives of men and women who fight for every dollar they make, every day, and provide them an opportunity to share their personal experiences with a global audience. What does a day's work mean? What effort does a woman make in order to earn a dollar? What does she buy with this bit of money? What does she do when the prices of basic goods increase? Does she struggle to eat, to find shelter, to send her children to school, to take care of herself, to remain standing? How much money does she need to make to earn respect?

See http://onedollar.bophana.org/en/. Eight short-short films out of sixteen from this project were made by women directors.

35. Kulikar Sotho is the first Cambodian woman to direct a narrative feature since Ung Kanthouk (*10,000 Regrets* [*Mouy Mern Alai*, Cambodia, 1970s]).

36. This list includes the work of scriptwriter Loung Ung. See chapter 1, note 80, and chapter 3.

37. Both directors belong to the new generation of Cambodian cinema mentored by Rithy Panh, who also produced this film. Among the eight film students who attended Rithy Panh's first workshop, designed as a replacement for pre-KR film schools, only Lida

Chan was a woman director. The film won many awards, among them for Best Mid-Length Documentary at the International Documentaries Film Festival, Amsterdam (IDFA), 2013, and the Special Jury Award in Human Rights, Human Dignity International Film Festival (Burma), under the patronage of Aung San Suu Kyi (2013).

38. Both *Enemies of the People* and *Camp 32* were made by second-generation male directors and mention the issue of forced marriage: In *Enemies of the People*, the protagonist, Sambath, tells his family history during the KR regime. After his father was tortured and killed, his mother was forced to marry a KR cadre. "She cried a lot but the militia man told her that if she would refuse, her entire family will be killed. She got pregnant, lost a lot of blood during the delivery of the baby, and died." When finally, after four years of once-a-week meetings, he tells Nuon Chea about his parents, Nuon Chea asks him if this was a forced marriage. (See my analysis of the film in chapter 3.) In *New Year Baby* and *Camp 32*, forced marriage is mentioned even more briefly than in *Enemies of the People*. *Camp 32* focuses on a survivor's search for his lost childhood in a labor camp he cannot locate. *Angkar* was made by a second-generation female director who discovers late in her life that she was born out of a forced marriage. (See my analysis of the film in chapter 1.) See also *Phnom Penh Post*, "Marriage Under the Khmer Rouge," n.d., www.phnompenhpost.com/post-weekend /marriage-under-khmer-rouge-documentary-series. Three short films of four minutes each appear on this website; the second and third films include brief wedding scenes. The *Phnom Penh Post* talked to victims, to lawyers participating in tribunal proceedings, and to experts on forced marriage.

39. For example, John Borneman, "Reconciliation After Ethnic Cleansing: Listening, Retribution, Affiliation," *Public Culture* 14, no. 2 (2002): 281–304; Catharine A. MacKinnon, "Rape, Genocide, and Women's Human Rights," *Harvard Women's Law Journal* 17 (1994): 5–16; MacKinnon, "Defining Rape Internationally: A Comment on *Akayesu*," *Columbia Journal of Transitional Law* 44, no. 3 (2006): 940–47; Neha Jain, "Forced Marriage as a Crime Against Humanity: Problems of Definition and Prosecution," *Journal of International Criminal Justice* 6 (2008): 1013–32; Wood, "Variation in Sexual Violence," 307–41; Wood, "Sexual Violence During War: Variation and Accountability," in *Collective Crimes and International Criminal Justice: An Interdisciplinary Approach*, ed. Alette Smeulers (Antwerp: Intersentia, 2010), 295–322; Wood, "Conflict-Related Sexual Violence and the Policy Implications of Recent Research," *International Review of the Red Cross* 894 (2014): 457–78; Karen G. Weiss, "Too Ashamed to Report: Deconstructing the Shame of Sexual Victimization," *Feminist Criminology* 5, no. 3 (2010): 286–310; Paul Kirby, "How Is Rape a Weapon of War? Feminist International Relations, Modes of Critical Explanation and the Study of Wartime Sexual Violence," *European Journal of International Relations* 19, no. 4 (2012): 797–821.

40. Wood, "Conflict-Related," 458.

41. See, for example, the use of the term *forced marriage* to describe the "bush wife" in Sierra Leone: " 'Forced marriages . . . involved the abduction and detention of women by AFRC troops. . . . The . . . rebels exercised control over the sexuality, movement and labour of their 'wives.' The use of the term 'wife' . . . was a mark of ownership over the

victim." Jain, "Forced Marriage," 1017. The author does not relate to the specific form of rape in the Cambodian case.

42. In *What Remains*, the families of the victim and the perpetrator do not meet and are interrelated only through the editing. In both films, in contrast to the Cambodian films, the Germans can seemingly depict only intergenerational and inner dialogues.

43. And other genocides such as Rwanda, Sierra Leone, and former Yugoslavia.

44. "Ieng Sary moved back to Phnom Penh in the late 1990s, having defected to the government and having been pardoned by King Norodom Sihanouk. . . . To most outsiders, permitting Ieng Sary to quietly return to the capital was akin to allowing Joseph Goebbels . . . or other Nazi leaders to move back into their Berlin homes after World War II. But Cambodians find it utterly unremarkable that a KR leader lived openly among them for years." Joel Brinkley, "Cambodia's Curse: Struggling to Shed the Khmer Rouge's Legacy," *Foreign Affairs* 88, no. 2 (2009): 113–14.

45. The specific guilt-ridden code of silence in Germany was, of course, different. Suffice to mention here that the trials (especially the Auschwitz and the Majdanek ones) were the most important forum for such an encounter for Germany. In his documentary film from 1984 *The Trial (Der Prozess Eine Darstellung des Majdanek—Verfahrens in Düsseldorf)*, for example, Eberhard Fechner interviewed perpetrators, victims, judges, and attorneys during the six-year Majdanek trial and, since filming was not permitted, later fabricated a cinematic conversation between them through editing. In Rwanda, Sierra Leone, and former Yugoslavia, for example, the nature of the genocide/ethnic cleansing was also different from Cambodia because the parties involved did not belong to the same ethnic origin or religious belief, as was true in Cambodia. Though the genocide in Cambodia entailed killings of minorities like the Cham, their percentage in the population did not alter the fact that autogenocide was dominant.

46. In Case No. 002, described later, 61 percent of civil party applicants were female. Forced marriage complainants now constitute the second largest group of civil parties.

47. See chapter 2, note 18, on Nuon Chea and Khieu Samphan.

48. Nuon Chea died on August 4, 2019, before the conclusion of Case No. 002/02.

49. See the ECCC Press Release Closing Statements in Case 002/02, June 2017: www.eccc .gov.kh/sites/default/files/media/Press%20Release%20Closing%20Statements%20 in%20Case%20002-02%20Conclude%20English.pdf.

50. In his memoir, Rithy Panh testifies about KR policy: "Behind the hospital . . . the KR quickly planted green beans . . . and pumpkins on the covered graves. . . . Decomposing corpses make excellent fertilizer, as implied in the Angkar slogan. . . . When I found pieces of pumpkin in my soup, I felt nauseated. I could feel their roots plunging into soil sown with bones." See Rithy Panh and Christophe Bataille, *The Elimination: A Survivor of the Khmer Rouge Confronts His Past and the Commandant of the Killing Fields* (New York: Other Press, 2013), 188–89. See also Loung Ung's description of Phnom Penh in 1979 in her autobiographical novel: "Though the palm trees are heavy with fruit, I see no people climbing to get it. People say the Khmer Rouge buried corpses next to them and now the palm milk is pink like thin blood and the fruit tastes like human

flesh." Ung, *First They Killed My Father: A Daughter of Cambodia Remembers* (New York: HarperPerennial, 2000), 218.

51. Cameron Christensen, "Forced Marriage at the Cambodian Crossroads: ECCC Can Develop a New Crime Against Humanity," *Brigham Young University Law Review* 6 (2016): 1827.

52. At the beginning of *Red Wedding*, we listen to Pol Pot's declaration of this goal, heard over a black-and-white clip of a propaganda film.

53. See GBV under the Khmer Rouge, Information Platform. "Forced Marriage," http://gbvkr.org/gender-based-violence-under-khmer-rouge/facts-and-figures/forced-marriage/. Describing the history of these cases, the author indicates that the first mention that forced marriage could be a crime against humanity came in 2001 during the International Criminal Tribunal for former Yugoslavia (ICTY). Forced marriages were never prosecuted at the International Criminal Tribunal for Rwanda. The Special Court for Sierra Leone (SCSL) addressed forced marriage in three cases between 2008 and 2009, with varying, contradictory interpretations of the crime.

Despite these advances, feminist activists and others have critiqued these tribunals for being inconsistent in their efforts to adequately investigate and prosecute crimes of sexual and gender-based violence. See, e.g., Susana SáCouto, "Victim Participation at the International Criminal Court and the Extraordinary Chambers in the Courts of Cambodia: A Feminist Project?," *Michigan Journal of Gender and Law* 18, no. 2 (2012): 297–359.

Wood addresses the questions of why sexual violence is often higher in wartime than in peacetime and why the frequency and form of sexual violence vary across conflicts and across groups in a given conflict. She analyzes documents and statistics in various cases, among them the massive rapes of German girls and women by Russian soldiers, the so-called "comfort women" in Nanjing during World War II, and sexual slavery (mostly in detention facilities) as a prominent form of sexual violence in the conflict in former Yugoslavia in the early 1990s. She indicates that, in Sierra Leone, "In some cases [girls and women] . . . underwent forced marriage with a particular person. Of the internally displaced women who suffered sexual assault, thirty-three percent of the respondents were abducted, fifteen percent were forced to serve initially as sexual slaves, and nine percent were forced to marry a captor." Wood, "Variation in Sexual Violence," 315.

> In some cases, an armed group engages in sexual violence against civilian members of its own community, or its own combatants, as when such targets are suspected of collaborating with the enemy. However, the most prevalent form of selective violence against collaborators in civil wars is homicide, particularly in certain zones of war in which an army is in control but not dominant. Why some armies deploy sexual violence to control and punish collaborators while others do not remains unexplained. (327)

See also MacKinnon's elaboration on "the definitional (consent vs. coercion) debate" in "Defining Rape," 954.

54. Christensen, "Forced Marriage," 1826.

55. Bridgette A. Toy-Cronin, "What Is Forced Marriage? Towards a Definition of Forced Marriage as a Crime Against Humanity," *Columbia Journal of Gender and Law* 19, no. 2 (2010): 544. See also Erin Handley and Kong Meta, "Forced Pregnancy: Crime but No Punishment?," *Phnom Penh Post*, September 16, 2016, www.phnompenhpost.com/post -weekend/forced-pregnancy-crime-no-punishment.

56. See chapter 2, note 14, on Ieng Sary.

57. In a letter dated October 4, 1996, to the *Phnom Penh Post*, Picq openly addresses Ieng Sary's crimes against humanity. She refers to Ieng Sary's advancement of the concept of "property-personality," which, I suggest, has a special gender resonance. See Laurence Picq, Comment: My Life under Ieng Sary: "Crying Against the Shame and Horror," October 4, 1996, www.phnompenhpost.com/national/comment-my-life-under -ieng-sary-crying-against-shame-horror. During the next few months, Picq's letter was followed by many letters to and replies from the editors in what Ieng Sary called the "Laurence Picq Affair."

58. Laurence Picq, *Beyond the Horizon: Five Years with the Khmer Rouge*, trans. Patricia Norland (New York: St. Martin's, 1989), 122.

59. See pages 9–10 in ECCC, "Consolidated Decision on the Requests for Investigative Action Concerning the Crime of Forced Pregnancy and Forced Impregnation," www .eccc.gov.kh/sites/default/files/documents/courtdoc/2016-06-15%2017:17/D301_5_ REDACTED_EN.PDF.

60. See Handley and Meta, "Forced Pregnancy."

61. See *Phnom Penh Post*, letter to the editor, "An Inhuman Act Against Men and Women," September 19, 2016, www.phnompenhpost.com/analysis-and-op-ed/inhuman-act -against-men-and-women; see also Kasumi Nakagawa, "Gender-Based Violence During the Khmer Rouge Regime: Stories of Survivors from the Democratic Kampuchea (1975–1979)," in *Asia Pacific Year Book of International Humanitarian Law*, 2nd ed. (Phnom Penh, Cambodia, 2008), 1–30. This work was first presented at the 14th Asian Law Institute ASLI Conference on May 2017 (personal correspondence with Nakagawa on November 6, 2017). Nakagawa, who speaks and reads Khmer, testified at the ECCC as an expert, based on the earlier-mentioned book she wrote and other accounts, including on forced pregnancy.

62. Quoted in Theresa de Langis, "'This Is Now the Most Important Trial in the World': A New Reading of Code #6, the Rule Against Immoral Offenses Under the Khmer Rouge Regime," *Cambodia Law and Policy Journal* 3 (2014): 64–65. She states that the Code was translated by an independent professional translation company based on an electronic scan of the original in Khmer from the DC-CAM archives (65n13). Theresa de Langis is a senior expert on women's human rights in conflict and postconflict settings, with a focus on the Asia-Pacific region. She has been based in Phnom Penh since 2012 and engaged in advocacy efforts to raise awareness of sexual violence crimes under the KR regime within the ECCC and more generally.

63. See GBV under the Khmer Rouge, Information Platform, "Welcome," http://gbvkr.org.

64. de Langis, "This Is Now," 61–78. The Closing Order of Case 002/19-9-2007-ECCC-OCIJ, 157 (September 15, 2010) listed the five policies. See also the short film *The Khmer Rouge Rice Fields: The Story of Rape Survivor Tang Kim* (Rachana Phat and Youk Chhang, Cambodia, 2004). This documentary relates the story of Tang Kim and her constant struggle to come to terms with the past. She and eight other newlywed women were told by the KR that they would be taken to live with their soldier husbands, but instead were sent to a rice field near the village and raped. She claims that because they were destined to be executed, the soldiers raped them. She ran away and during the following years changed her name several times and moved from place to place in fear of being identified. After the fall of the regime, she became a Buddhist nun.

> Reportedly, there were many women who were raped repeatedly; thus, they were not murdered after being raped. In particular, young women who were "new people" were targeted for repeated rape. KR high ranking officers who hold a huge power in local governance were reported to abuse their power and raped young women whom they liked.

Nakagawa, "Gender-Based Violence," 21.

65. Patrick Hein, "The Multiple Pathways to Trauma Recovery, Vindication, and National Reconciliation in Cambodia," *Asian Politics and Policy* 7, no. 2 (2015): 202.

66. See chapter 1, note 46, on Duch.

67. See Melanie Hyde, Emma Palmer, and Sarah Williams, "Transformative Reparations for Sexual and Gender-Based Violence at the Extraordinary Chambers in the Courts of Cambodia," *Australian Human Rights Centre and the Asian International Justice Initiative* (2014), 7, www.eastwestcenter.org/sites/default/files/filemanager/Research_ Program/Politics_Governance_and_Security/AIJI/Reparations%20Workshop%20 Report.pdf.

68. See the collected testimonies in Duong Savron, *The Mystery of Sexual Violence Under the Khmer Rouge Regime* (Cambodian Defenders Project, 2011), 1–56. http://gbvkr.org /wp-content/uploads/2013/01/Mystery_of_Sexual_Violence_during_KR_ENG-web .pdf.

69. ECCC, *Prosecutor v Nuon Chea, Ieng Sary, Khieu Samphan, Ieng Thirith*, Case 002, Closing Order, at [1426].

70. Hein, "Multiple Pathways," 203. The research conducted by Theresa de Langis, Judith Strasser, Thida Kim, and Sopheap Taing was based on interviews with 106 civil parties to Case No. 002 about their experience of forced marriage under the KR regime. de Langis et al., *"Like Ghost Changes Body": A Study on the Impact of Forced Marriage Under the Khmer Rouge Regime* (Cambodia: Transcultural Psychosocial Organization, 2014).

71. It reads as follows:

> In their *Decision on Severance of Case 002 following Supreme Court Chamber Decision of 8 February 2013* issued on 26 April 2013, the Trial Chamber of the

ECCC rules that forced marriage charges will not be included in the first sub-trial of Case 002/01 for the following reasons: Inclusion of offences concerning forced marriage and rape in addition confront particular issues, some of which stem from their manner of incorporation into the Case 002 Closing Order, which binds the Trial Chamber. Their inclusion also remains subject to the resolution of various legal challenges concerning the exact nature of the crimes alleged. (paragraph 160, 69)

GBV under the Khmer Rouge, Information Platform, "Prosecution of GBV Under KR," http://gbvkr.org/gender-based-violence-under-khmer-rouge/prosecution-of-gbv-under-kr/.

72. See *Phnom Penh Post*, "Team at Odds Over Ao An Case," *Phnom Penh Post*, September 1, 2017, www.phnompenhpost.com/national/team-odds-over-ao-case.

73. Now a wealthy businessman, Tith is married to Ong Ken, sister of the deceased high-ranking Khmer Rouge leader Ta Mok. See Erin Handley and Chhay Channya, "Chaem Cleared at KRT, to the Regret of Survivors," *Phnom Penh Post*, February 23, 2017, www.phnompenhpost.com/national/chaem-cleared-krt-regret-survivors.

74. "Team at Odds," *Phnom Penh Post*.

75. Alessandro Marazzi Sassoon, "Khmer Rouge Tribunal Severs Im Chaem from Case 004," February 16, 2016, www.phnompenhpost.com/national/khmer-rouge-tribunal-severs-im-chaem-case-004.

76. See ECCC, "The Pre-Trial Chamber Issues Its Considerations on the International Co-Prosecutor's Appeal Against the Co-Investigating Judges' Closing Order Having Dismissed the Case Against IM Chaem," www.eccc.gov.kh/en/articles/pre-trial-chamber-issues-its-considerations-international-co-prosecutors-appeal-against-co.

77. John D. Ciorciari and Anne Heindel, *Hybrid Justice: The Extraordinary Chambers in the Courts of Cambodia* (Ann Arbor: University of Michigan Press, 2014).

78. As de Langis et al. suggest in "'This Is Now,'" (13): "KR forced marriages may have been unique in compelling husbands to rape their wives as a means of securing their own survival." They claim,

> The research suggests that forced marriage was one of the contributing factors to increased domestic abuse (in a context of continued civil conflict and mobilization of husbands) and high rates of desertion, polygamy, remarriage, and female-headed households following the fall of the regime. . . . Many of the forced marriages that remained intact are reported as dysfunctional, with more than half (52.9 percent) in the survey sample reporting spousal abuse. (4)

Moreover, "Forced marriages after the fall of the regime contributed to radical shifts in gender roles and responsibilities" (17).

See similar conclusions on gender-based violence on the web platform supported by Transcultural Psychosocial Organization (TPO) Cambodia, the ECCC, and the Cambodian Defenders Project (CDP):

The state took control of the institution of marriage. This practice not only reflected the KR ideology of the ruling party taking the place of parents as guardians, but it further entrenched already established notions of gender inequality by imposing the duty of sexual obedience and confining the roles of women to being child-bearers. These notions still continue to this day.

79. See chapter 2, notes 19 and 61, about Ieng Thirith. Among the civil parties are more women than men. In both criminal cases submitted to the ECCC—Case No. 001 and Case No. 002—the majority of civil parties have been female: In Case No. 001, 69 percent of total applicants were female and in Case No. 002 61 percent. Forced marriage parties now constitute the second largest group of civil parties at the ECCC—780 out of a total of 3,866 parties. At least 474 of these civil parties are direct victims. See Hein, "Multiple Pathways," 203.

80. See Guénaël Mettraux, "Crimes Against Humanity in the Jurisprudence of the International Criminal Tribunals for the Former Yugoslavia and for Rwanda," *Harvard International Law Journal* 43, no. 1 (2002): 244.

81. The *Phnom Penh Post* claimed that half a million people had been forced into marriages by the KR. See *Phnom Penh Post*, "Marriage Under the Khmer Rouge."

82. The historian David Chandler suggests that oral transmission of edifying sayings, rhymes, and proverbs was deeply rooted in Cambodian culture. In Henri Locard, *Pol Pot's Little Red Book: The Sayings of Angkar* (Chaing Mai, Thailand: Silkworm, 2004), xiii. The Angkar sayings assembled by Locard include a section referring to male-female relations. Locard states,

> Before marrying, the Party repeated there were three conditions to be met. He lists the relevant slogans: "1. You can choose your spouse yourself. 2. *Angkar* endorses [your partner]. 3. If you don't obey *Angkar*'s discipline, you will be sent to a study session for a time." According to his interpretations of these slogans, "Young people had to accept a partner chosen by the Party and at the same time convince themselves that it was their own personal choice." (265–67)

83. De Langis et al., "This Is Now," 11.

84. See Peg LeVine, *Love and Dread in Cambodia: Weddings, Births, and Ritual Harm Under the Khmer Rouge* (Singapore: National University of Singapore Press, 2010), 25. LeVine argues that Cambodians experienced "cultural genocide" under the KR due to the absence of cultural rights to call forward the ancestral realm during forced marriage ceremonies. Although some parts of her anthropological works on marriage and birth are fascinating, I find that her findings lack sufficient analysis and theorization to shed light on the rituals she describes. Because of her book, LeVine also appeared in the ECCC as an expert witness on the issue of forced marriage. (See Case No. 002/02, hearing days 239 and 240.)

85. See GBV Under the Khmer Rouge, "Forced Marriage."

86. ECCC, "Forced Marriage," from the Case No. 002 Closing Order, Clause No. 849, www
     .eccc.gov.kh/en/node/33817.

87. Emphases in the original. See Picq, *Beyond the Horizon*, 35. Trudy Jacobson indicates
     that the correct way husbands and wives had to call each other was *mit p'dai* (comrade
     husband) and *mit prapuan* (comrade wife). See Jacobson, *Lost Goddesses: The Denial
     of Female Power in Cambodian History* (Copenhagen: Nias, 2008), 223. I find her
     description of the sexual violence during marriage to be very minor.

88. On the concept of traditional arranged marriage, see Patrick Heuveline and Bunnak
     Poch, "Do Marriages Forget Their Past? Marital Stability in Post-Khmer Rouge Cam-
     bodia," *Demography* 43, no. 1 (2006): 99, www.ncbi.nlm.nih.gov/pmc/articles
     /PMC3930764/. See also the fiction film *Day in the Country* (Matthew Robinson, Cam-
     bodia, 2015), which deals with arranged marriage within two high-middle-class fami-
     lies in contemporary Phnom Penh but does not refer to the past. The film was screened
     at the Cambodia International Film Festival in 2015.

89. See her testimony at ECCC, Mrs. PEN Sochan, Session 4, day 239, October 12, 2016,
     www.eccc.gov.kh/en/witness-expert-civil-party/mrs-pen-sochan. See summary at
     ECCC, "Case 002 Witnesses, Experts and Civil Parties"—Mrs. Pen Sochan, www.eccc
     .gov.kh/en/witnesses/119.

90. Toy-Cronin, "What Is Forced Marriage," 585.

91. De Langis et al., *"Like Ghost Changes Body,"* 19.

92. See Heuveline and Poch, "Do Marriages Forget." Based on qualitative and quantitative
     data, the first nationally representative survey, the CDHS 2000, interviewed a sample of
     15,351 women aged fifteen to forty-nine (Cambodia Demographic and Health Survey
     2000, https://dhsprogram.com/pubs/pdf/FR124//FR124.pdf). To this first quantitative
     assessment of the prevalence of forced marriage under the KR, the authors added their
     analyses of the MIPopLab focus group discussions.

93. See an example of the form at ECCC, "Practice Direction 02/2007/Rev. 1: Victim Par-
     ticipation," www.eccc.gov.kh/sites/default/files/legal-documents/PD_Victims_Partic-
     ipation_rev1_En.pdf.

94. According to Jacobsen, the major crisis in relation to female power took place in the
     colonial period (the French occupation in the nineteenth century). Jacobsen, *Lost God-
     desses*. During the KR period, the rice paddy became an open mass grave. In this
     regard, I suggest, the necrophilic change of the soil, an ongoing symbol of the Cam-
     bodian female body, violently reflects on the cultural conception of femininity. There
     is no commentary at all in the film, only the voices of Sochan, her friend Chhean, and
     those she is speaking with.

95. Reza Negarestani, "The Corpse Bride: Thinking with *Nigredo*," in *Collapse*, vol. 4, ed.
     Robin Mackay (Falmouth: Urbanomic, 2008), 135.

96. For a discussion of the current controversies in Cambodia in regard to cremation, see
     Julie M. Fleischman, "Working with the Remains in Cambodia: Skeletal Analysis and
     Human Rights After Atrocity," *Genocide Studies and Prevention: An International Jour-
     nal* 10, no. 2 (2016): 121–30.

97. Anne Yvonne Guillou, "An Alternative Memory of the Khmer Rouge Genocide: The Dead of the Mass Graves and the Land Guardian Spirits [*Neak ta*]," *South East Asia Research* 20, no. 2 (2012): 218.

98. "The etymology of the modern Khmer word 'grave' [*phnor*] is the old Khmer word 'monticle' [*vnur*] where the *neak ta* [guardian spirits] live." See Guillou, 222n56. This etymology further reflects the reality of twenty thousand killing fields embodying the KR's anti-Buddhist policy.

99. The term *floating voice-over* was coined in Britta Sjogren, *Into the Vortex: Female Voice and Paradox in Film* (Urbana: University of Illinois Press, 2006), 9.

100. See the analysis of Walter Benjamin's well-known phrase "unconscious optics," in Marianne Hirsch, *Family Frames: Photography, Narrative, and Postmemory* (Cambridge, MA: Harvard University Press, 1997), 118.

101. Sjorgren, *Into the Vortex*, 8–15.

102. Mary Anne Doane, "The Voice in the Cinema: The Articulation of Body and Space," *Yale French Studies* 60 (1980); Kaja Silverman, "Disembodying the Female Voice," in *Re-Vision: Essays in Feminist Film Criticism*, ed. Mary Ann Doane, Patricia Mellencamp, and Linda Williams, 131–49, American Film Institute Monograph Series 3 (Frederick, MD: University Publications of America, 1984); Silverman, *The Acoustic Mirror: The Female Voice in Psychoanalysis and Cinema* (Bloomington: Indiana University Press, 1988); Caruth, *Unclaimed Experience*; Hirsch, *Family Frames*; Sjogren, *Into the Vortex*.

103. Since 2011, the Victims Support Section of the ECCC, the Cambodian Defenders Project, and the Transcultural Psychosocial Organization are jointly implementing the project "Women and Transitional Justice in Cambodia":

> The aim of the project is to ensure the engagement of female survivors in the transitional justice process addressing gross human rights violations and mass crimes committed under the KR. . . . Women, in particular Gender-Based Violence survivors, are encouraged to fully exercise their rights to truth, justice and reparations, which are inherent in transitional justice.

See http://vss.eccc.gov.kh/.

104. Paul Connerton, "Seven Types of Forgetting," *Memory Studies* 1, no. 1 (2008): 67. Connerton emphasizes the collective dimension of the silencing phenomenon:

> In the collusive silence brought on by a particular kind of collective shame there is detectable both a desire to forget and sometimes the actual effect of forgetting. Confronted with a taboo, people can fall silent out of terror or panic or because they can find no appropriate words. We cannot, of course, infer the fact of forgetting from the fact of silence. Nevertheless, some acts of silence may be an attempt to bury things beyond expression and the reach of memory; yet such silencings, while they are a type of repression, can at the same time be a form of

survival, and the desire to forget may be an essential ingredient in that process of survival. (68)

It is remarkable that women broke this type of forgetting. As Connerton suggests regarding the anonymous war diary *A Woman in Berlin*,

> It was published in English translation in 1954, and translated into Norwegian, Italian, Danish, Japanese, Spanish, French and Finnish; but it was a further five years before the German original found a publisher, and then only in Switzerland. The German readership reacted to the book with neglect, silence or hostility, for it broke the taboo of post-war amnesia. German women were supposed not to talk about the rapes, nor about sexual collaboration for the sake of survival in the post-war period, as if this dishonoured German men who were supposed to have somehow defended them. Only in the late 1980s did a younger generation of German women encourage their mothers and grandmothers to speak of their wartime experiences. (69)

105. Quoted in Thomas J. Scheff, "Shame and the Social Bond: A Sociological Theory," *Sociological Theory* 18, no. 1 (2000): esp. 93–95.

106. See Lewis, in Scheff, "Shame." He suggests, "Apparently each emotion in the sequence is brief, but the loop can go on and on. This proposal suggests a new source of protracted conflict" (95).

107. See, e.g., Joanne L. Davis, Patricia Byrd, Jamie L. Rhudy, and David C. Wright, "Characteristics of Chronic Nightmares in a Trauma-Exposed Treatment-Seeking Sample," *Dreaming* 17, no. 4 (2007): 187–88.

108. See Dana Amir, "The Inner Witness," *International Journal of Psychoanalysis* 93 (2012): 879.

109. The scene with the hidden camera was shot in Veal Veang. In a personal conversation (on December 17, 2014), Lida Chan, the film director, told me that the mobile cinema, which screens films made by the new generation of Cambodian directors in rural Cambodia, avoids screening *Red Wedding* in Pen Sochan's village in the Pursat province because the Veal Vent/Veang district, also located in Pursat Province, was until 1998 one of the last remaining strongholds of the KR and is still populated by its cadres, including the former district chief, who participated in Pen Sochan's forced marriage. The ex-KR district chief moved to Veal Veang after 1979. During the KR period, she lived in the same village as the protagonist (Boeung Chhouk, commune of Kna Totoeung, Bakan district, and "Drifting Bodhi" Pursat province).

110. On *sousveillance*, see Margaret Kohn, "Unblinking: Citizens and Subjects in the Age of Video Surveillance," *Constellations* 17, no. 4 (2010): 580–81.

111. Sochan testified that after the rape by her husband "I was bleeding for more than one month." See Andrew Nachemson, "Civil Parties Challenge Expert Witness Over Forced Marriage," *Phnom Penh Post*, October 13, 2016, www.phnompenhpost.com

/national/civil-parties-challenge-expert-witness-over-forced-marriage. See also ECCC, "Mrs. PEN Sochan," www.eccc.gov.kh/en/witness-expert-civil-party/mrs-pen-sochan.

112. Discovered in a province near Pursat, they are reminiscent of ancient carvings found in Cambodian temples from the ninth century, evidence that stone carvings are part of an old Khmer tradition.

113. Monique Plaza writes, *"Rape is an oppressive act exercised by a (social) man against a (social) woman. . . . It is very sexual in the sense that it . . . opposes men and women: it is social sexing which underlies rap."* In Ann J. Cahill, "Foucault, Rape, and the Construction of the Feminine Body," *Hypatia* 15, no. 1 (2000): 45, emphases in the original.

114. Achille Mbembe, "The Power of the Archive and Its Limits," in *Refiguring the Archive*, ed. Carolyn Hamilton et al. (Boston: Academic, 2002), 22.

115. Georges Didi-Huberman, *Images in Spite of All: Four Photographs from Auschwitz*, trans. Shane B. Lillis (Chicago: University of Chicago Press, 2008), 98.

116. Jacques Derrida, "Archive Fever: A Freudian Impression," *Diacritics* 25, no. 2 (1995): 9–16.

117. On March 1, 2016, the culture minister Phoeung Sakona said during the opening of the first exhibition on forced marriage under the KR that she herself escaped a potential forced marriage, that after she heard of a male comrade who had taken an interest in her, she did her best to make herself appear unappealing before asking to go to the front line. The exhibition was on display at S-21. See Anadolu Agency, "In Cambodia, Stories of Forced Marriage Go on Display," http://aa.com.tr/en/culture-arts-lifestyle/in-cambodia-stories-of-forced-marriage-go-on-display/529675.

In 2017, Victims Support Section (VSS) conducted the first mobile exhibition, "Forced Marriage During the Khmer Rouge Regime," and intergenerational dialogue. A second mobile exhibition was conducted from November 30 to December 1, 2017, in Siem Reap province with the objectives of (1) letting participants know the victims' suffering and the consequences of forced marriage, (2) improving victims' participation by encouraging them to join intergenerational dialogue and share their experiences about forced marriage with the young generation, and (3) raising youth and public awareness of GBV during the KR regime and encouraging them to participate in the struggle against the current gender issues and to offer empathy to victims. See ECCC, "Mobile Exhibition on 'Forced Marriage During the Khmer Rouge Regime' and Intergenerational Dialogue," www.eccc.gov.kh/en/articles/mobile-exhibition-forced-marriage-during-khmer-rouge-regime-and-intergenerational-dialogue.

118. And those of the other four victims of forced marriage and rape who shared their stories with the directors and are listed in the "thanks" section that ends the film.

119. Hyde, Palmer, and Williams argue in "Transformative Reparations" that

sexual violence continues to be a problem in Cambodia today, with a 2013 United Nations (UN) Report finding that 20.4 percent of men admitted to having perpetrated rape. That report also found relatively high rates of gang rape compared to other regional countries. Moreover, more than forty percent of men who admitted to rape had never faced legal consequences for their crimes. There is therefore both a critical need for more research to understand the links between the DK period and sexual and gender-based violence today, and an opportunity for the ECCC to respond meaningfully to these crimes in a way that recognizes the ongoing nature of violence against women in Cambodia. (7)

120. Claudia Card, "Genocide and Social Death," *Hypatia* 18, no. 1 (2003): 63–79. Orlando Patterson used the notion of social death in his major work, *Slavery and Social Death*. Quoted in Robin May Schott, "War Rape, Natality and Genocide," *Journal of Genocide Research* 13, nos. 1–2 (2011): 10.

121. In the film's earlier version, her talk with her daughters appears after the wedding ceremony of Sochan's older daughter. However, it was cut from the final version, emphasizing Sochan's loneliness, as in the last scene of the film she walks through the rice field of ghosts.

122. Kelly Askin, "Prosecuting Wartime Rape and Other Gender-Related Crimes Under International Law: Extraordinary Advances, Enduring Obstacles," *Berkeley Journal of International Law* 21 (2003): 289.

123. Nicola Henry, "Witness to Rape: The Limits and Potential of International War Crimes Trials for Victims of Wartime Sexual Violence," *International Journal of Transitional Justice* 3 (2009): 115.

124. "The International Criminal Tribunals for the former Yugoslavia and Rwanda (ICTY and ICTR) and the hybrid Special Court for Sierra Leone (SCSL) provided a role for victims only as simple witnesses." Ciorciari and Heindel, *Hybrid Justice*, Kindle location 4556–57.

125. Sochan testified at court from October 12, 2016 (date no. 239 of the court's hearings) till October 13, 2016 (date no. 240). The video recordings of the hearings are available in Khmer, French, and English as video streaming at the ECCC website. See www.eccc .gov.kh/en/witness-expert-civil-party/mrs-pen-sochan.

126. More specifically,

Six hundred and sixty-four (664) civil parties were declared admissible with regards to the policy of the regulation of marriage, since the alleged crimes described in the application were considered as being more likely than not to be true.... These civil parties have provided sufficient elements tending to establish prima facie personal harm as a direct consequence of the crime of forced marriage.

See Louise Thirion, "Trial Chamber Heard Evidence on Forced Marriage and Rape," February 9, 2016, www.eccc.gov.kh/en/blog/2016/09/02/trial-chamber-heard-evidence -forced-marriage-and-rape.

127. Henry, "Witness to Rape," 125.

128. Linda Alcoff and Laura Gray, "Survivor Discourse: Transgression or Recuperation?," *Signs* 18, no. 2 (1993): 260–90; Kelly D. Askin, conclusion to *War Crimes Against Women: Prosecution in International War Crimes Tribunals* (Cambridge MA: Nijhoff, 1997);

Laura Hengehold, "Remapping the Event: Institutional Discourses and the Trauma of Rape," *Signs* 26, no. 1 (2000): 189–214; Wendy Larcombe, "The 'Ideal' Victim v Successful Rape Complainants: Not What You Might Expect," *Feminist Legal Studies* 10 (2002): 131–48; Christoph Schiessl, "An Element of Genocide: Rape, Total War, and International Law in the Twentieth Century," *Journal of Genocide Research* 4, no. 2 (2002): 197–210; Askin, "Prosecuting"; Julie Mertus, "Shouting from the Bottom of the Well: The Impact of International Trials for Wartime Rape on Women's Agency," *International Feminist Journal of Politics* 6, no. 1 (2004): 110–28; Henry, "Witness to Rape"; Schott, "War Rape."

129. Quoted in Henry, "Witness to Rape," 122.
130. This happened during Session 2 (day no. 240, October 13, 2016). See www.eccc.gov.kh/en/witness-expert-civil-party/mrs-pen-sochan.
131. See Campbell, in Henry, "Witness to Rape," 132.
132. As Hengehold stresses in "Remapping," 197.
133. Henry, "Witness to Rape," 121.
134. Finally, during her victim impact statement Sochan said: "I have never had a happy life. . . . I have no more to say but one question to put to the accused. Mr. President I would like to ask the accused the question: Why people who we did not know each other were matched up to get married? What was it for? . . . Why they did such things to us?"

  Since January 1, 2015, Nuon Chea has invoked his right to remain silent. He was not present at court during Pen Sochan's testimony, but listened from afar because of poor health.
135. Askin, "Prosecuting," 349.
136. The Duch Case.
137. Ciorciari and Heindel, *Hybrid Justice*, Kindle locations 5125–28.
138. The quoted list was compiled by the Tribunal's Victim and Witnesses Section in former Yugoslavia and is similar to her words. See Henry, "Witness to Rape," 119.
139. The film won the Youth Jury Award at the Singapore International Film Festival. In an interview, Neang said:

  Taxi Driver, a film by American filmmaker Martin Scorsese in 1976, was my first inspiration to make this film, and then *In the Mood for Love*, a film by Hong Kong filmmaker Wong Kar-wai in 2000, and finally *Xiao Wu* (*Unknown Pleasures*), a film by Chinese filmmaker Jia Zhangke in 1997. Stylistically, with my experience so far in documentary, I want to bring this "verisimilitude" to a fictional situation and use an observational and detached "vérité" style to express my ideas.

  See Anti-Archive, www.antiarchive.com/threewheels.html.
140. This information is based on a personal conversation I had with the director on July 10, 2014, in Phnom Penh, and our correspondence via email from April 29 to May 30, 2016. Ian Masters is the writer and script advisor.
141. de Langis et al., "*'Like Ghost Changes Body,'*" 23.

142. Christensen, "Forced Marriage," 1839.

143. A three-wheeled motorized vehicle used as a taxi.

144. The music assists in this process as well. The first song to be heard is a KR song called "17, April," and later songs are from the 1960s and 1970s ("Skol Ros Cheat Sne" and "Pel Mek Sro Pum") and deal with "one-sided love" and the man's realization that "even though how hard I try, still cannot win."

145. See also a short interview with Neang at Indiegogo, "The Project: What Is It About?," www.indiegogo.com/projects/tuc-tuc-a-short-film-by-kavich-neang.

146. Designed by the Cambodian architect Lu Ban Hap and the Russian architect Vladimir Bodiansky, the White Building project (originally known as the Municipal Apartments) was part of the ambitious Bassac River Front cultural complex in central Phnom Penh. Since Phnom Penh's population tripled from 370,000 to one million between 1953 and 1970, the building's inauguration in 1963 was the first attempt to offer a multistory modern urban lifestyle to lower- and middle-class Cambodians. After the forced evacuation of Phnom Penh during the regime of 1975–79, some former residents returned to the neighborhood and the community grew again. For many in Phnom Penh, the White Building, housing more than twenty-five hundred residents, was perceived as an irregular community, cloaked in stigma associated with poverty, drugs, sex work, petty crime, dangerous construction, and poor sanitation. The White Building was also one of the city's most vibrant communities, whose residents included classical dancers, master musicians, skilled craftspeople, cultural workers, civil servants, and street vendors. See White Building, "About the White Building," www.whitebuilding.org/en/page/about_the_white_building.

147. Kevin McIntyre, "Geography as Destiny: Cities, Villages and Khmer Rouge Orientalism," *Comparative Studies in Society and History* 38, no. 4 (1996): 730–58; Martin Shaw, "New Wars of the City: Relationships of 'Urbicide' and 'Genocide,'" in *Cities, War, and Terrorism: Towards an Urban Geopolitics*, ed. Stephen Graham (Malden, MA: Blackwell, 2004), 141–53; James A. Tyner, "Imagining Genocide: Anti-Geographies and the Erasure of Space in Democratic Kampuchea," *Space and Polity* 13 (2009): 9–20; James A. Tyner, Samuel Henkin, Savina Sirik, and Kimsroy Sokvisal, "Phnom Penh During the Cambodian Genocide: A Case of Selective Urbicide," *Environment and Planning A* 46 (2014): 1873–91.

148. Ryan Bishop and Gregory Clancey, "The City-as-Target, or Perpetuation and Death," in Graham, *Cities, War,* 63.

149. The deliberate targeting and total destruction of urban environments.

150. Bishop and Clancey likewise describe the forcible evacuation of Phnom Penh as "the most infamous deurbanization of modern times" (in Tyner et al., "Phnom Penh," 1873). Brown noted that "public buildings such as schools, colleges, and hospitals were emptied and left derelict. Libraries were scattered. Factories, houses, shops, and valuable infrastructure were abandoned" (in Tyner et al., "Phnom Penh," 1888).

151. AbdouMaliq Simone, "The Politics of the Possible: Making Urban Life in Phnom Penh," *Singapore Journal of Tropical Geography* 29 (2008): 188. Simone analyzes the ways in which, in contrast to the prevalent assumption that low-income residents lack the

capacity to give shape to the urban system beyond an efficacy related to their own limited survival needs, the residents of the White Building, as a large low-income housing tract, collaborate to maximize their access to resources and opportunities. See also Kavich Neang's short film *A Scale Boy* (Cambodia, 2010).

152. See, for example, the short film *Don't Know Much About ABC* (directed by Norm Phanith and Sok Chanrado, Cambodia, 2016), which presents a group of homeless persons living in the White Building. Rithy Panh shot two films in the White Building, emphasizing the uniqueness of the location: *One Evening After the War* (*Un soir après la guerre*, France/Cambodia/Switzerland/Belgium, 1998) and *Paper Cannot Wrap Ember* (*La papier ne peut pas envelopper la braise*, France, 2007).

153. According to Chandler, the KR used the phrase "Phnom Penh—the great prostitute on the Mekong" in their propaganda (in McIntyre, "Geography," 755).

154. In July 2017, two years after the premiere of *Three Wheels*, the almost five hundred families still living in the project were moving out; the building was to be replaced by a twenty-one-story mixed-use development.

155. Referring to long-term consequences and ramifications, Beini Ye claims, "The Khmer Rouge regime, through their policy of separating children from their parents, husbands from their wives, sisters from their brothers, and generally severing the bonds of family at all levels, also destroyed the survivors' strongest support network." Ye, "Forced Marriages as Mirrors of Cambodian Conflict Transformation," *Peace Review* 23, no. 4 (2011): 473. "It is no surprise that, in the context of a family whose very creation was forced and which in many cases has a history of violence, conflicts and violence between family members often results. Without dialogue and confrontation with the past, these can lead to the intergenerational transmission of these problems" (474). In this light, the character of Solei as male prostitute in Davy Chou's *Diamond Island* (Cambodia/France/Germany/Qatar/Thailand, 2016) as well as the phenomenon of Cambodian trafficking in Guillaume Suon's documentary film *The Storm Makers* (*Ceux qui amènent la tempête*, France/Cambodia, 2014) have particular meaning.

156. Nakagawa's work is based on findings from research into gender crimes during the KR regime. The first study was conducted in 2006 by the Cambodian Defenders Project (CDP), a human rights NGO based in Phnom Penh. Initial interviews were carried out first by targeting fifteen hundred people who had been over ten years old during the KR regime. Then one hundred people were selected for the purpose of documenting their personal stories about gender crimes of the time. The author claims that in

> the Cambodian culture . . . the victims of sexual violence are pressured to remain silent for fear of discrimination from the society. . . . Further, the Cambodian proverb *"men are god while women are white cloth,"* indicates their general perception that women who lose their virginity have no value or women who are sexually abused are given least value by the Cambodian society. In addition, women are encouraged to keep silent to such sexual violence in order to maintain family reputation because once outsiders know that a daughter is raped or sexually abused, her whole family would be targeted for a criticism and

discrimination. Finally, during the KR regime, family members of the victims of these violent crimes kept silent for fear of reprisal by the perpetrator. These factors combined have contributed to these untold stories.

Nakagawa, "Gender-Based Violence," 10, emphasis in the original.

157. Nakagawa, 29.

158. Matthew Robinson is the executive producer. The six episodes were shown weekly on Cambodia's top TV channels MyTV and CTN. The scale of this book does not permit further elaborations on this TV series. See also the radio program on "Women Under the Khmer Rouge Regime": monthly broadcasts of call-in shows on FM 102 look at various aspects of women's experience in conflict, including GBV, psychosocial consequences, and participation at the ECCC. See GBV Under the Khmer Rouge, Information Platform, "Outreach and Advocacy." http://gbvkr.org/activities/outreach-and-advocacy/.

159. See, e.g., Raya Morag, *Defeated Masculinity: Post-Traumatic Cinema in the Aftermath of War* (Brussels: Peter Lang, 2009).

160. See Kiernan, *Blood and Soil*, 605. See also Michael Mann's analysis, which emphasizes what he calls classicide but totally ignores gender. Mann, "Communist Cleansing," in *The Dark Side of Democracy: Explaining Ethnic Cleansing* (Cambridge: Cambridge University Press, 2005), 320.

EPILOGUE

1. Hélène Cixous, *The Terrible but Unfinished Story of Norodom Sihanouk, King of Cambodia*, trans. Juliet Flower MacCannell, Judith Pike, and Lollie Groth (1985; Lincoln: University of Nebraska Press, 1994), first epoch, act 1, scene 1, lines 15–16.

2. Claude Lanzmann, "The Obscenity of Understanding: An Evening with Claude Lanzmann," in *Trauma Explorations in Memory* (Baltimore: Johns Hopkins University Press, 1995), 204. The quotation is taken from Shoshana Felman's introduction to Lanzmann's appearance before the Western New England Institute for Psychoanalysis (WNEIPA) in April 1990. Lanzmann refused to watch a film made on the Nazi doctor Eduard Wirths and devoted his entire presentation to explaining this refusal. As Lanzmann explains, "This quotation was excerpted from a short text that I wrote in a recent issue of a psychoanalytic magazine in France, which is called *La Nouvelle Revue de Psychanalyse*. It was a special issue devoted to the topic of evil, 'Le Mal'" (205–6).

3. According to Susan Rubin Suleiman, "A few fiction films have also attempted to suggest, if not downright represent, the subjectivity of perpetrators. One thinks of the 'mirror-scene' depicting the sadistic camp commander Amon Goeth in a moment of self-doubt in Steven Spielberg's film *Schindler's List* (USA, 1993), or of Oliver Hirschbiegel's more extended recent attempt to portray Joseph Goebbels and Hitler as full-edged characters in *Der Untergang* (*Downfall*, Germany/Austria/Italy, 2004), but again, these are exceptions rather than the rule." Suleiman, "When the Perpetrator

Becomes a Reliable Witness of the Holocaust: On Jonathan Littell's *Les bienveillantes*," *New German Critique* 36, no. 1 (2009): 1–2. See also Erin McGlothlin, "Empathetic Identification and the Mind of the Holocaust Perpetrator in Fiction: A Proposed Taxonomy of Response," *Narrative* 24, no. 3 (2016): 251–75.

4. The United States assisted General Lon Nol's coup in 1970 against Prince Norodom Sihanouk, and, as most historians dealing with the subject observe, the American carpet bombing of Cambodia assisted in the Khmer Rouge's takeover. Moreover, both the United States and other Western countries turned a blind eye to the Pol Pot regime and allowed the Khmer Rouge to hold their seat in the United Nations until 1982.

5. Emphasis in the original. Susie Linfield, "Photojournalism and Human Rights," in *The Cruel Radiance: Photography and Political Violence* (Chicago: University of Chicago Press, 2010), 39.

6. See, for example, Joram Ten Brink and Joshua Oppenheimer, eds., *Killer Images: Documentary Film, Memory and the Performance of Violence* (London: Wallflower, 2012); Brad Simpson, "*The Act of Killing* and the Dilemmas of History," *Film Quarterly* 67, no. 2 (2013): 10–13; Janet Walker, "Referred Pain: *The Act of Killing* and the Production of a Crime Scene," *Film Quarterly* 67, no. 2 (2013): 14–20; Bill Nichols, "Irony, Cruelty, Evil (and a Wink) in *The Act of Killing*," *Film Quarterly* 67, no. 2 (2013): 25–29; Homay King, "Born Free? Repetition and Fantasy in *The Act of Killing*," *Film Quarterly* 67, no. 2 (2013): 30–36, especially her description of the film as a taboo breaker in the Indonesian public sphere; and Irene Lusztig, "The Fever Dream of Documentary: A Conversation with Joshua Oppenheimer," *Film Quarterly* 67, no. 2 (2013): 50–56.

7. See the film's analysis in the chapter 1.

FILMOGRAPHY

2 or 3 Things I Know About Him (*2 oder 3 Dinge, die ich von ihm weiß*). Directed by Malte Ludin. Germany, 2005.

1945. Directed by Ferenc Török. Hungary, 2017.

10,000 Regrets (*Mouy Mern Alai*). Directed by Ung Kanthouk. Cambodia, 1970s.

The Act of Killing. Directed by Joshua Oppenheimer; Christine Cynn; and anonymous. UK/Denmark/Norway, 2012.

About My Father. Directed by Guillaume P. Suon. Cambodia, 2010.

Alone in Berlin. Directed by Vincent Perez. UK/France/Germany, 2016.

Angkar. Directed by Neary Adeline Hay. France/Cambodia, 2018.

As We Forgive. Directed by Laura Waters Hinson. USA, 2010.

The Axe of Wandsbek (*Das Beil von Wandsbek*). Directed by Falk Harnack. Germany, 1951.

The Baader Meinhof Complex (*Der Baader Meinhof Komplex*). Directed by Uli Edel. Germany/France/Czech Republic, 2008.

Behind the Gate (*Derrière le portail*). Directed by Jean Baronnet. France, 2003.

Behind the Walls of S-21: Oral Histories from Tuol Sleng Prison. Directed by Doug Kass. Cambodia, 2007.

Beyond the Bridge. Directed by Kulikar Sotho. UK/Cambodia, 2016.

Bitter Khmer Rouge (*Khmers Rouges Amers*). Directed by Bruno Carette and Sien Meta. France/Cambodia, 2007.

Bonne Nuit Papa. Directed by Marina Kem. Germany/Cambodia, 2014.

Bophana, a Cambodian Tragedy (*Bophana, une tragédie cambodgienne*). Directed by Rithy Panh. France/Cambodia, 1996.

Breaking the Silence—Sexual Violence Under the Khmer Rouge. Directed by Lov Sophea. Cambodia, 2017.

Brother Number One. Directed by Annie Goldson and Peter Gilbert. New Zealand, 2011.

Camp 14: Total Control Zone. Directed by Marc Wiese. South Korea/Germany, 2012.

Camp 32. Directed by Andrew Blogg and Tim Purdie. Australia/Cambodia, 2014.

Circles (Krugovi). Directed by Srdan Golubovic. Germany/Serbia/France/Croatia/Slovenia, 2012.

Comrade Duch: The Bookkeeper of Death. Directed by Adrian Maben. France/UK/USA, 2011.

Comrade Duch, Welcome to Hell (Camarade Duch, bienvenue en enfer). Directed by Adrian Maben. UK, 2011.

The Counterfeiters (Die Fälscher). Directed by Stefan Ruzowitzky. Austria/Germany, 2007.

Day in the Country. Directed by Matthew Robinson. Cambodia, 2015.

Deacon of Death. Directed by Jan Van den Berg and Willem Van de Put. Netherlands, 2004.

The Decent One (Der Anständige). Directed by Vanessa Lapa. Austria/Israel/Germany, 2014.

Depth Two (Dubina dva). Directed by Ognjen Glavonić. Serbia/Serbia and Montenegro, 2016.

Devil's Freedom (La libertad del Diablo). Directed by Everardo González. Mexico, 2017.

Diamond Island. Directed by Davy Chou. Cambodia/France/Germany/Qatar/Thailand, 2016.

Dogville. Directed by Lars Von Trier. Netherlands/Denmark/UK/France/Finland/Sweden/Germany/Italy/Norway, 2003.

Don't Know Much About ABC. Directed by Norm Phanith and Sok Chanrado. Cambodia, 2016.

Downfall (Der Untergang). Directed by Oliver Hirschbiegel. Germany/Austria/Italy, 2004.

Duch, Master of the Forges of Hell (Duch, le maître des forges de l'enfer). Directed by Rithy Panh. France/Cambodia, 2011.

El Sicario: Room 164. Directed by Gianfranco Rosi. France/USA, 2010.

Enemies of the People: A Personal Journey Into the Heart of the Killing Fields. Directed by Rob Lemkin and Thet Sambath. UK/Cambodia, 2009.

Exile (Exil). Directed by Rithy Panh. France, 2016.

First They Killed My Father. Directed by Angelina Jolie. Cambodia/USA, 2017.

Fog in August (Nebel im August). Directed by Kai Wessel. Germany, 2016.

The Fog of War: Eleven Lessons from the Life of Robert S. McNamara. Directed by Errol Morris. USA, 2003.

The Forgiven. Directed by Roland Joffé. UK, 2017.

France is Our Mother Country (La France est notre patrie). Directed by Rithy Panh. Cambodia/France, 2015.

The Gate (Le temps des aveux). Directed by Régis Wargnier. France/Cambodia/Belgium, 2014.

A German Life (Ein deutsches Leben). Directed by Christian Krönes, Olaf S. Müller, Roland Schrotthofer, and Florian Weigensamer. Austria, 2016.

Ghosts of Abu Ghraib. Directed by Rory Kennedy. USA, 2007.

Golden Slumbers (Le sommeil d'or). Directed by Davy Chou. France/Cambodia, 2012.

The Grey Zone. Directed by Tim Nelson Blake. USA, 2001.

Hiroshima Mon Amour. Directed by Alain Resnais. France/Japan, 1959.

Hitler Cantata (Die Hitlerkantate). Directed by Jutta Brückner. Germany, 2005.

Human Failure (Menschliches Versagen). Directed by Michael Verhoeven. Germany, 2008.

Ida. Directed by Pawel Pawlikowski. Poland/Denmark/France/UK, 2013.

If That's So, Then I'm a Murderer! (. . . dann bin ich ja ein Mörder!). Directed by Walter Manoschek. Austria, 2012.

Illegitimate (*Ilegitim*). Directed by Adrian Sitaru. Romania/Poland/France, 2016.

Inglourious Basterds. Directed by Quentin Tarantino. Germany/USA, 2009.

In the Dark Room. Directed by Nadav Schirman. Germany/Finland/Israel/Romania, 2013.

Kapo. Directed by Dan Setton and Tor Ben-Mayor. Israel, 1999.

The Khmer Rouge and the Man of Non-Violence (*Le Khmer rouge et le non-violent*). Directed by Bernard Mangiante. France/Cambodia, 2011.

The Khmer Rouge Rice Fields: The Story of Rape Survivor Tang Kim. Directed by Rachana Phat and Youk Chhang. Cambodia, 2004.

The Killing Fields. Directed by Roland Joffé. UK, 1984.

The Killing Fields of Dr. Haing S. Ngor. Directed by Arthur Dong. USA, 2015.

Kinyarwanda. Directed by Alrick Brown. USA/France, 2011.

Labyrinth of Lies (*Im Labyrinth des Schweigens*). Directed by Giulio Ricciarelli. Germany, 2014.

La Sierra. Scott Dalton and Margarita Martinez. Columbia/USA, 2005.

The Last of the Unjust (*Le dernier des injustes*). Directed by Claude Lanzmann. France/Austria, 2013.

The Last Reel. Directed by Kulikar Sotho. Cambodia, 2014.

The Lives of Others (*Das Leben der Anderen*). Directed by Florian von Donnersmarck. Henckel. Germany, 2006.

Looking for Vorn. Directed by Thet Sambath. UK/Cambodia, 2009.

The Look of Silence (*Senyap*). Joshua Oppenheimer. Denmark/Indonesia/Finland/Norway/UK/Israel/France/USA/Germany/Netherlands, 2014.

Lost Child: Sayon's Journey. Directed by Janet Gardner P. USA/Cambodia, 2013.

Lost Loves. Directed by Chhay Bora. Cambodia, 2010.

Love History (*Liebe Geschichte*). Directed by Simone Bader and Jo Schmeiser. Austria, 2010.

The Missing Picture (*L'image manquante*). Directed by Rithy Panh. Cambodia/France, 2013.

Munyurangabo. Directed by Lee Isaac Chung. Rwanda/USA, 2007.

The Murderers Are Among Us (*Die Mörder sind unter uns*). Directed by Wolfgang Staudte. Germany, 1946.

My Neighbor, My Killer (*Mon voisin, mon tueur*). Directed by Anne Aghion. USA/France, 2009.

New Year Baby. Directed by Socheata Poeuv. USA, 2006.

No Man's Land (*Terra de Ninguém*). Directed by Salomé Lamas. Portugal, 2012.

Of Men and War. Directed by Laurent Bécue-Renard. France/Switzerland/USA, 2014.

One Day at Po Chrey: Anatomy of a Massacre. Directed by Thet Sambath. UK, 2012.

One Evening after the War (*Un soir après la guerre*). Directed by Rithy Panh. France/Cambodia/Switzerland/Belgium, 1998.

Operation Atropos. Directed by Coco Fusco. USA, 2006.

Ordinary People. Directed by Vladimir Perisic. Serbia/Netherlands/France/Switzerland, 2009.

Paper Cannot Wrap Ember (*La papier ne peut pas enveloper la braise*). Directed by Rithy Panh. France, 2007.

The Pinochet Case (*Le cas Pinochet*). Directed by Patricio Guzmán. France/Chile/Belgium/Spain, 2001.

Pol Pot Mystery (*Pol Pot et les Khmers rouges: Le mystère de Pol Pot*). TV mini-series. Directed by Adrian Maben. France, 2001.

Radical Evil (*Das radikal Böse*). Directed by Stefan Ruzowitzky. Germany/Austria, 2013.

The Railway Man. Directed by Jonathan Teplitzky. Switzerland/UK/Australia, 2013.

The Reader. Directed by Stephen Daldry. USA/Germany, 2008.

Red Wedding (*Noces Rouges*). Directed by Lida Chan and Guillaume P. Suon. Cambodia/France, 2012.

Remember. Directed by Atom Egoyan. Canada/Mexico/Germany/South Africa, 2015.

A River Changes Course. Directed by Kalyanee Mam. Cambodia, 2013.

S21: The Khmer Rouge Death Machine (*S21: la machine de mort Khmère rouge*). Directed by Rithy Panh. Cambodia/France, 2003.

A Scale Boy. Directed by Kavich Neang. Cambodia, 2010.

Schindler's List. Directed by Steven Spielberg. USA, 1993.

The Sea Wall (*Un barrage contre le Pacifique*). Directed by Rithy Panh. France/Cambodia/Belgium, 2008.

Shoah. Directed by Claude Lanzmann. France/UK, 1985.

Son of Saul (*Saul fia*). Directed by László Nemes. Hungary, 2015.

Standard Operating Procedure. Directed by Errol Morris. USA, 2008.

The Storm Makers (*Ceux qui amènent la tempête*). Directed by Guillaume Suon. France/Cambodia, 2014.

Survive: In the Heart of Khmer Rouge Madness (*L'important c'est de rester vivant*). Directed by Roshane Saidnattar. France, 2009.

Terror's Advocate (*L'avocat de la terreur*). Directed by Barbet Schroeder. France, 2007.

There Will Be No Stay. Directed by Patty Ann Dillon. USA, 2016.

Three Wheels (*Kong Bei*). Directed by Kavich Neang. Cambodia/France, 2015.

Time to Speak Out. TV mini-series. Produced by Olivier Van Bockstael. UK/Cambodia, 2016.

The Unknown Known. Directed by Errol Morris. USA, 2013.

Voices of Khmer Rouge. Directed by Jan Krogsgaard and Thomas Weber Carlsen. Denmark, 2011.

The Waldheim Waltz (*Waldheims Walzer*). Directed by Ruth Beckermann. Austria, 2018.

War Child. Directed by Christian Karim Chrobog. USA, 2008.

What Remains (*Was Bleibt*). Directed by Gesa Knolle and Birthe Templin. Germany, 2008.

Wrong Elements. Directed by Jonathan Littell. France/Belgium/Germany, 2016.

Year Zero: The Silent Death of Cambodia. Directed by David Munro. UK, 1979.

BIBLIOGRAPHY

Abbott, Alison. "Into the Mind of a Killer." *Nature* 410 (2001): 296–98.

Agamben, Giorgio. *State of Exception*. Translated by Kevin Attell. Chicago: University of Chicago Press, 2005.

Alcoff, Linda, and Laura Gray. "Survivor Discourse: Transgression or Recuperation?" *Signs* 18, no. 2 (1993): 260–90.

Améry, Jean. *At the Mind's Limits: Contemplations by a Survivor on Auschwitz and Its Realities*. Translated by Sidney Rosenfeld and Stella P. Rosenfeld. Bloomington: Indiana University Press, 1980. First published 1966.

——. *On Suicide: A Discourse on Voluntary Death*. Translated by John D. Barlow. Bloomington: Indiana University Press, 1999. First published 1976.

——. *Radical Humanism: Selected Essays*. Edited and translated by Sidney Rosenfeld and Stella P. Rosenfeld. Bloomington: Indiana University Press, 1984.

Amir, Dana. "The Inner Witness." *International Journal of Psychoanalysis* 93 (2012): 879–96.

Anadolu Agency. "In Cambodia, Stories of Forced Marriage Go on Display." http://aa.com.tr /en/culture-arts-lifestyle/in-cambodia-stories-of-forced-marriage-go-on-display/529675.

Anti-Archive. *Three Wheels*. www.antiarchive.com/threewheels.html.

AP Archive. "Cambodia: General Ta Mok Gives Reaction to Death of Pol Pot." YouTube. www .youtube.com/watch?v=x7kO8v-lWSo.

Appadurai, Arjun. *Fear of Small Numbers: An Essay on the Geography of Anger*. Durham, NC: Duke University Press, 2006.

Arendt, Hannah. *Eichmann in Jerusalem: A Report on the Banality of Evil*. New York: Penguin, 2006. First published 1963.

Aronowitz, Stanley. *The Politics of Identity*. New York: Routledge, 1992.

Asian International Justice Initiative. "Duch on Trial." Reports and videos from the Khmer Rouge Tribunal, a cooperative project of the East-West Center and the University of

California, Berkeley War Crimes Study Center, 2012. http://forum.eastwestcenter.org /Khmer-Rouge-Trials/tag/kaing-guek-eav//.

Askin, Kelly D. Conclusion to *War Crimes Against Women: Prosecution in International War Crimes Tribunals*. Cambridge, MA: Nijhoff, 1997.

——. "Prosecuting Wartime Rape and Other Gender-Related Crimes Under International Law: Extraordinary Advances, Enduring Obstacles." *Berkeley Journal of International Law* 21 (2003): 288–349. doi:10.15779/Z384D2S.

Assmann, Aleida. "Two Forms of Resentment: Jean Améry, Martin Walser and German Memorial Culture." *New German Critique* 90 (2003): 123–33.

Badiou, Alain. *Ethics: An Essay on the Understanding of Evil*. Translated by Peter Hallward. New York: Verso, 2001. First published 1993.

Baum, Steven. *The Psychology of Genocide: Perpetrators, Bystanders, and Rescuers*. Cambridge: Cambridge University Press, 2008.

Bauman, Zigmunt. *Modernity and the Holocaust*. 2nd ed. Ithaca, NY: Cornell University Press, 2011. First published 1989.

——. "A Revolution in the Theory of Revolutions?" *International Political Science Review* 15, no. 1 (1994): 15–24.

Becker, Elizabeth. *Bophana: Love in the Time of the Khmer Rouge*. Phnom Penh: Cambodia Daily Press, 2010.

——. "Khieu Ponnary, 83, First Wife Of Pol Pot, Cambodian Despot." *New York Times*, July 3, 2003. www.nytimes.com/2003/07/03/world/khieu-ponnary-83-first-wife-of-pol-pot-cam bodian-despot.html?mcubz=0.

——. "Minor Characters." *New York Times*, August 28, 2005. www.nytimes.com/2005/08/28 /books/review/minor-characters.html?_r=0.

——. *When the War Was Over: Cambodia's Revolution and the Voices of Its People*. New York: Simon and Schuster, 1986.

Bishop, Ryan, and Gregory Clancey. "The City-as-Target, or Perpetuation and Death." In *Cities, War, and Terrorism: Towards an Urban Geopolitics*, edited by Stephen Graham, 54–74. Malden, MA: Blackwell, 2004.

Bizot, François. *Facing the Torturer: Inside the Mind of a War Criminal*. Translated by Charlotte Mandell and Antoine Audouard. London: Rider, 2012.

——. *The Gate*. Translated by Euan Cameron. New York: Knopf, 2003.

Bophana Audiovisual Resource Center. www.bophana.org.

Borer, Tristan Anne. "A Taxonomy of Victims and Perpetrators: Human Rights and Reconciliation in South Africa." *Human Rights Quarterly* 25, no. 4 (2003): 1088–116.

Borneman, John. "Reconciliation After Ethnic Cleansing: Listening, Retribution, Affiliation." *Public Culture* 14, no. 2 (2002): 281–304.

Boulet, Robbie Corey. "Attacks on Jarvis Multiply." *Phnom Penh Post*, June 8, 2009. www .phnompenhpost.com/national/attacks-jarvis-multiply.

——. "Duch Defence Split on Verdict." *Phnom Penh Post*, November 27, 2009. www.phnompen hpost.com/national/duch-defence-split-verdict.

——. "Nationality and the Jarvis Debate." *Phnom Penh Post*, June 12, 2009. www.phnompen hpost.com/national/nationality-and-jarvis-debate.

——. "The Social Space and the Genesis of Groups." *Theory and Society* 14, no. 6 (1985): 723–44.

Bourdieu, Pierre. "Social Space and Symbolic Power." *Sociological Theory* 7, no. 1 (1989): 14–25.

——. "What Makes a Social Class? On the Theoretical and Practical Existence of Groups." *Berkeley Journal of Sociology* 32, no. 1 (1987): 1–17.

Boyle, Deirdre. "Interviewing the Devil: Interrogating Masters of the Cambodian Genocide." In *A Companion to Contemporary Documentary Film*, edited by Alexandra Juhasz and Alisa Lebow, 506–23. Hoboken, NJ: Wiley Blackwell, 2014.

——. "Trauma, Memory, Documentary: Re-Enactment in Two Films by Rithy Panh (Cambodia) and Garin Nugroho (Indonesia)." In *Documentary Testimonies: Global Archives of Suffering*, edited by Bhaskar Sarkar and Janet Walker, 155–72. New York: Routledge, 2010.

Brault, Pascale-Anne, and Michael Naas, eds. "To Reckon with the Dead: Jacques Derrida's Politics of Mourning." In *The Work of Mourning*, by Jacques Derrida, 1–30. Chicago: University of Chicago Press, 2003.

Brinkley, Joel. "Cambodia's Curse: Struggling to Shed the Khmer Rouge's Legacy." *Foreign Affairs* 88, no. 2 (2009): 113–14.

Brooks, Peter. *The Melodramatic Imagination: Balzac, Henry James, Melodrama, and the Mode of Excess.* New Haven, CT: Yale University Press, 1976.

Brower, M. C., and B. H. Price. "Advances in Neuropsychiatry of Frontal Lobe Dysfunction in Violent and Criminal Behaviour: A Critical Review." *Journal of Neurology, Neurosurgery, and Psychiatry* 71, no. 6 (2001): 720–26.

Browning, Christopher R. *Ordinary Men: Reserve Police Battalion 101 and the Final Solution in Poland.* New York: Harper Collins, 1998. First published 1992.

Brudholm, Thomas. *Resentment's Virtue: Jean Améry and the Refusal to Forgive.* Philadelphia: Temple University Press, 2008.

Cahill, Ann J. "Foucault, Rape, and the Construction of the Feminine Body." *Hypatia* 15, no.1 (2000): 43–63.

Cambodia Demographic and Health Survey 2000. https://dhsprogram.com/pubs/pdf/FR124//FR124.pdf.

Cambodia Tribunal Monitor. "Khmer Rouge History." www.cambodiatribunal.org/history/cambodian-history/khmer-rouge-history/.

Card, Claudia. "Genocide and Social Death." *Hypatia* 18, no.1 (2003): 63–79.

Caruth, Cathy. *Unclaimed Experience: Trauma, Narrative and History.* Baltimore: Johns Hopkins University Press, 1996.

Chan, Yuan-Kwan. "A Rithy Panh Interview: *The Missing Picture* and Cambodian Cinema." www.meniscuszine.com/articles/2014011927208/a-rithy-panh-interview-the-missing-picture-and-cambodian-cinema.

Chandler, David P. "Songs at the Edge of the Forest: Perceptions of Order in Three Cambodian Texts." In *Facing the Cambodian Past: Selected Essays, 1971–1994*, 76–99. Chiang Mai, Thailand: Silkworm, 1996.

——. *Voices from S-21: Terror and History in Pol Pot's Secret Prison.* Berkeley: University of California Press, 1999.

Charny, Israel W. "A Classification of Denials of the Holocaust and Other Genocides." In *The Genocide Studies Reader*, edited by Samuel Totten and Paul R. Bartrop, 518–37. New York: Routledge, 2009.

Chhang, Youk. "Jarvis's Citizenship Not at Issue." *Phnom Penh Post*, June 22, 2009. www .phnompenhpost.com/national/jarviss-citizenship-not-issue.

Chion, Michel. *The Voice in Cinema*. Translated by Claudia Gorbman. New York: Columbia University Press, 1999. First published 1982.

Chon, Gina, and Sambath Thet. *Behind the Killing Fields: A Khmer Rouge Leader and One of His Victims*. Philadelphia: University of Pennsylvania Press, 2010.

Christensen, Cameron. "Forced Marriage at the Cambodian Crossroads: ECCC Can Develop a New Crime Against Humanity." *Brigham Young University Law Review* 2015, no. 6 (2016): 185–46.

Ciorciari, John D., and Anne Heindel. *Hybrid Justice: The Extraordinary Chambers in the Courts of Cambodia*. Ann Harbor: University of Michigan Press, 2014.

Cixous Hélène. *The Terrible but Unfinished Story of Norodom Sihanouk, King of Cambodia*. Translated by Juliet Flower MacCannell, Judith Pike, and Lollie Groth. Lincoln, NE: University of Nebraska Press, 1994. First published in 1985.

Cohen, Stanley. *States of Denial: Knowing About Atrocities and Suffering*. Cambridge: Polity, 2001.

Collins, Randall. *Violence: A Micro-Sociological Theory*. Princeton, NJ: Princeton University Press, 2009.

Connerton, Paul. "Seven Types of Forgetting." *Memory Studies* 1, no.1 (2008): 59–71.

Craps, Stef. *Postcolonial Witnessing: Trauma Out of Bounds*. Basingstoke, UK: Palgrave Mac-Millan, 2012.

Crawford, Adam. "Temporality in Restorative Justice: On Time, Timing and Time-Consciousness." *Theoretical Criminology* 19, no. 4 (2015): 470–90.

Critchell, Kara, Susanne C. Knittel, Emiliano Perra, and Uğur Ümit Üngör. "Editors' Introduction." *Journal of Perpetrator Research* 1, no. 1 (2017): 1–27.

Cruvellier, Thierry. *The Master of Confessions: The Making of a Khmer Rouge Torturer*. Translated by Alex Gilly. New York: Ecco, 2014.

Davis, Erik W. *Deathpower: Buddhism's Ritual Imagination in Cambodia*. New York: Columbia University Press, 2015.

——. "Imaginary Conversations with Mothers About Death." In *At the Edge of the Forest: Essays on Cambodia, History, and Narrative in Honor of David Chandler*, edited by Anne Ruth Hansen and Judy Ledgerwood, 221–28. Ithaca, NY: Cornell Southeast Asia Program Publications, 2008.

——. "Treasures of the Buddha: Imagining Death and Life in Contemporary Cambodia." PhD diss., University of Chicago, 2009. ProQuest. https://search.proquest.com/docview /305062096?pq-origsite=gscholar.

Davis, Joanne L., Patricia Byrd, Jamie L. Rhudy, and David C. Wright. "Characteristics of Chronic Nightmares in a Trauma-Exposed Treatment-Seeking Sample." *Dreaming* 17, no. 4 (2007): 187–98.

Deery, June, and Andrea Press, eds. *Media and Class: TV, Film, and Digital Culture*. New York: Routledge, 2017.

de Langis, Theresa. "'This Is Now the Most Important Trial in the World': A New Reading of Code #6, the Rule Against Immoral Offenses Under the Khmer Rouge Regime." *Cambodia Law and Policy Journal* 3 (2014): 61–78.

de Langis, Theresa, Judith Strasser, Thida Kim, and Sopheap Taing. *"Like Ghost Changes Body": A Study on the Impact of Forced Marriage Under the Khmer Rouge Regime.* Cambodia: Transcultural Psychosocial Organization (TPO), 2014.

Delbo, Charlotte. *Auschwitz and After.* Translated by Rosette C. Lamont. New Haven, CT: Yale University Press, 1995. First published in 1965.

Derrida, Jacques. "Archive Fever: A Freudian Impression." *Diacritics* 25, no. 2 (1995): 9–16.

——. *The Gift of Death.* Chicago: University of Chicago Press, 1995.

——. "On Forgiveness." In *On Cosmopolitanism and Forgiveness*, translated by Mark Dooley and Michael Hughes, 25–60. New York: Routledge, 2001.

——. *The Work of Mourning.* Edited by Pascale-Anne Brault and Michael Nass. Chicago: University of Chicago Press, 2001.

di Certo, Bridget. "KRT: When Art Becomes Evidence." *Phnom Penh Post*, December 23, 2011. www.phnompenhpost.com/national/krt-when-art-becomes-evidence.

Didi-Huberman, Georges. *Images In Spite of All: Four Photographs from Auschwitz.* Translated by Shane B. Lillis. Chicago: University of Chicago Press, 2008.

Doane, Mary Anne. "The Voice in the Cinema: The Articulation of Body and Space." *Yale French Studies* 60 (1980): 33–50.

Dorfman, Ariel. *Death and the Maiden.* New York: Penguin, 1994.

Dunlop, Nic. *The Lost Executioner: The Story of Comrade Duch and the Khmer Rouge.* London: Bloomsbury, 2009.

Dunnage, Jonathan. "Perpetrator Memory and Memories About Perpetrators." *Memory Studies* 3, no. 2 (2010): 91–94.

Dy, Khamboly. *A History of Democratic Kampuchea, 1975–1979.* Phnom Penh: DC-Cam, 2007.

ECCC. "Case 002 Witnesses, Experts and Civil Parties"—Mrs. Pen Sochan. www.eccc.gov.kh/en/witnesses/119.

——. "Compilation of Statements of Apology Made by Kaing Guek Eav Alias Duch During the Proceedings 31 March 2009." www.eccc.gov.kh/en/document/court/corrected1compilation-statements-apology-made-kaing-guek-eav-alias-duch-during.

——. "Consolidated Decision on the Requests for Investigative Action Concerning the Crime of Forced Pregnancy and Forced Impregnation." www.eccc.gov.kh/sites/default/files/documents/courtdoc/2016-06-15%2017:17/D301_5_REDACTED_EN.PDF.

——. "Co-Prosecutors' Response to Nuon Chea's Response to Questions on the Supreme Court Chamber's Additional Investigation Into Footage in the Possession of Filmmakers Rob Lemkin and Thet Sambath." www.eccc.gov.kh/en/document/court/co-prosecutors-response-nuon-cheas-response-questions-supreme-court-chambers.

——. "Forced Marriage." From the Case No. 002 Closing Order, Clause No. 849. www.eccc.gov.kh/en/node/33817.

——. "Key Events." www.eccc.gov.kh/en/keyevents.

——. "Introduction to the ECCC." www.eccc.gov.kh/en/about-eccc/introduction.

——. "Mobile Exhibition on 'Forced Marriage During the Khmer Rouge Regime' and Intergenerational Dialogue." www.eccc.gov.kh/en/articles/mobile-exhibition-%E2%80%9Cforced -marriage-during-khmer-rouge-regime%E2%80%9D-and-intergenerational-dialogue.

——. Mrs. PEN Sochan. Session 4, day 239, October 12, 2016. www.eccc.gov.kh/en/witness -expert-civil-party/mrs-pen-sochan.

——. "Nuon Chea's Response to the Co-Prosecutors' Request to Call THET Sambath (2-TCW-885) as a Priority Witness." www.eccc.gov.kh/en/document/court/nuon-cheas -response-co-prosecutors-request-call-thet-sambath-2-tcw-885-priority; www.eccc.gov.kh /en/document/court/nuon-cheas-response-co-prosecutors-request-call-thet-sambath-2 -tcw-885-priority; www.eccc.gov.kh/sites/default/files/documents/courtdoc/2015-01-27%20 16%3A13/E335_1_EN.PDF.

——. "Order on Co-Prosecutors' Request for Investigative Action Regarding Interviews of Nuon Chea, and the Film 'Enemies of the People.'" www.eccc.gov.kh/en/document/court /order-co-prosecutors-request-investigative-action-regarding-interviews-nuon-chea -and.

——. Order on Investigative Request Regarding the Film 'Enemies of the People.'" www.eccc .gov.kh/sites/default/files/documents/courtdoc/D344_1_EN.pdf.

——. "Practice Direction 02/2007/Rev. 1: Victim Participation." www.eccc.gov.kh/sites /default/files/legal-documents/PD_Victims_Participation_rev1_En.pdf.

——. "Press Release. Closing Statements in Case 002/02 Conclude." www.eccc.gov.kh/sites /default/files/media/Press%20Release%20Closing%20Statements%20in%20Case%20002 -02%20Conclude%20English.pdf.

——. "The Pre-Trial Chamber Issues Its Considerations on the International Co-Prosecutor's Appeal Against the Co-Investigating Judges' Closing Order Having Dismissed the Case Against IM Chaem." www.eccc.gov.kh/en/articles/pre-trial-chamber-issues-its -considerations-international-co-prosecutors-appeal-against-co.

——. Prosecutor v Nuon Chea, Ieng Sary, Khieu Samphan, Ieng Thirith. Case 002, Closing Order, at 1426.

——. Session 4, day 239, October 12, 2016. www.eccc.gov.kh/en/witness-expert-civil-party /mrs-pen-sochan.

——. "Who Is Eligible to Become a Civil Party?" www.eccc.gov.kh/en/victims-support/civil -party-information.

Elsaesser, Thomas, "Tales of Sound and Fury: The Family Melodrama," Monogram 4 (1972): 2–15.

Encyclopedia.com. "Khieu Ponnary (1920–2003)." www.encyclopedia.com/women/dictionaries -thesauruses-pictures-and-press-releases/khieu-ponnary-1920-2003.

Enemies of the People. "Offical [sic] Movie Page." www.enemiesofthepeoplemovie.com/Press /DownloadPressKit.

Fassin, Didier, and Richard Rechtman. The Empire of Trauma: An Inquiry Into the Condition of Victimhood. Translated by Rachel Gomme. Princeton, NJ: Princeton University Press, 2009.

Fawthrop, Tom, and Helen Jarvis. Getting Away with Genocide? Elusive Justice and the Khmer Rouge Tribunal. London: Pluto, 2004.

Felman, Shoshana. *The Juridical Unconscious: Trials and Trauma in the Twentieth Century.* Cambridge, MA: Harvard University Press, 2002.

Felman, Shoshana, and Dori Laub. *Testimony: Crises of Witnessing in Literature, Psychoanalysis and History.* Leiden, Netherlands: Taylor and Francis, 1992.

Fleischman, Julie M. "Working with the Remains in Cambodia: Skeletal Analysis and Human Rights after Atrocity." *Genocide Studies and Prevention: An International Journal* 10, no. 2 (2016): 121–30.

Foran, John. "Theories of Revolution Revisited: Toward a Fourth Generation?" *Sociological Theory* 11, no. 1 (1993): 1–20.

Foucault, Michelle. "Nietzsche, Genealogy, History." In *Language, Counter-Memory, Practice: Selected Essays and Interviews,* edited by Donald F. Bouchard, 139–64. Ithaca, NY: Cornell University Press, 1977.

Frank, Claudia. "On the Reception of the Concept of the Death Drive in Germany: Expressing and Resisting an 'Evil Principle'?" *International Journal of Psychoanalysis* 96 (2015): 425–44.

Freud, Sigmund. *Totem and Taboo.* 2nd ed. Translated by James Strachey. New York: Routledge, 2001. First published 1913.

Frings, Manfred S. Introduction to *Ressentiment,* by Max Scheler, 1–18. Translated by Lewis B. Coser and William W. Holdheim. Milwaukee, WI: Marquette University Press, 2010. First published 1914.

GBV Under the Khmer Rouge. Information Platform. "Forced Marriage." http://gbvkr.org /gender-based-violence-under-khmer-rouge/facts-and-figures/forced-marriage/.

——. Information Platform. "Outreach and Advocacy." http://gbvkr.org/activities/outreach -and-advocacy/.

——. Information Platform. "Prosecution of GBV under KR." http://gbvkr.org/gender-based -violence-under-khmer-rouge/prosecution-of-gbv-under-kr/.

——. Information Platform. "Welcome." http://gbvkr.org.

Glaspy, Padraic J. "Justice Delayed—Recent Developments at the Extraordinary Chambers in the Courts of Cambodia." *Harvard Human Rights Journal* 21, no. 1 (2008) 143–54. http:// heinonline.org/HOL/Page?handle=hein.journals/hhrj21&div=9&g_sent=1&collection=j ournals.

Gledhill, Christine. "The Melodramatic Field: An Investigation." In *Home Is Where the Heart Is: Studies in Melodrama and the Woman's Film,* edited by Christine Gledhill, 5–39. London: BFI, 1987.

——. "Rethinking Genre." In *Reinventing Film Studies,* edited by Christine Gledhill and Linda Williams, 221–43. London: Arnold, 2000.

Goldhagen, Daniel J. *Hitler's Willing Executioners.* New York: Vintage, 1997.

Goldstone, Jack A. "Toward a Fourth Generation of Revolutionary Theory." *Annual Review of Political Science* 4 (2001): 139–87.

Greenfield, Daniel M. "The Crime of Complicity in Genocide: How the International Criminal Tribunals for Rwanda and Yugoslavia Got It Wrong, and Why It Matters." *Journal of Criminal Law and Criminology* 98, no. 3 (2008): 921–52.

Grünfeld, Fred, and Wessel Vermeulen. "Failures to Prevent Genocide in Rwanda (1994), Sre-
brenica (1995), and Darfur (Since 2003)." *Genocide Studies and Prevention: An International
Journal* 4, no. 2 (2009): 221–37.

Guillou, Anne Yvonne. "An Alternative Memory of the Khmer Rouge Genocide: The Dead of
the Mass Graves and the Land Guardian Spirits (*Neak ta*)." *South East Asia Research* 20,
no. 2 (2012): 207–26.

Handley, Erin. "Chams Recall Horror Inflicted by Angkar." *Phnom Penh Post*, March 1, 2016.
www.phnompenhpost.com/national/chams-recall-horror-inflicted-angkar.

——. "The Ethics of Exhumation." *Phnom Penh Post*, January 5, 2017. www.phnompenhpost
.com/post-weekend/ethics-exhumation.

Handley, Erin, and Chhay Channyda. "Chaem Cleared at KRT, to the Regret of Survivors."
Phnom Penh Post, February 23, 2017. www.phnompenhpost.com/national/chaem-cleared
-krt-regret-survivors.

Handley, Erin, and Kong Meta. "Forced Pregnancy: Crime but No Punishment?" *Phnom Penh
Post*, September 16, 2016. www.phnompenhpost.com/post-weekend/forced-pregnancy
-crime-no-punishment.

Hardt, Michael, and Antonio Negri. *Empire*. Cambridge, MA: Harvard University Press,
2000.

Harff, Barbara, and Ted Robert Gurr. "Toward Empirical Theory of Genocides and Politicides:
Identification and Measurement of Cases Since 1945." *International Studies Quarterly* 32,
no. 3 (1988): 359–71.

Harris, Ian. "Cambodian Buddhism After the Khmer Rouge." In *Cambodian Buddhism: History and Practice*, 190–224. Honolulu: University of Hawaii Press, 2005.

Hartman, Geoffrey. "The Humanities of Testimony: An Introduction." *Poetics Today* 27, no. 2
(2006): 249–60.

Hein, Patrick. "The Multiple Pathways to Trauma Recovery, Vindication, and National Reconciliation in Cambodia." *Asian Politics and Policy* 7, no. 2 (2015): 191–211.

Held, Virginia. *The Ethics of Care: Personal, Political, Global*. New York: Oxford University
Press, 2006.

——. "Military Intervention and the Ethics of Care." *Southern Journal of Philosophy* 46
(2008): 1–20.

Hengehold, Laura. "Remapping the Event: Institutional Discourses and the Trauma of Rape."
Signs 26, no. 1 (2000): 189–214.

Henry, Nicola. "Witness to Rape: The Limits and Potential of International War Crimes Trials for Victims of Wartime Sexual Violence." *International Journal of Transitional Justice*
3 (2009): 114–34.

Herman-Lewis, Judith. *Trauma and Recovery*. New York: Basic, 1992.

Heuveline, Patrick, and Bunnak Poch. "Do Marriages Forget Their Past? Marital Stability in
Post-Khmer Rouge Cambodia." *Demography* 43, no. 1 (2006): 99–125. www.ncbi.nlm.nih
.gov/pmc/articles/PMC3930764/.

Hilberg, Raul. *Perpetrators, Victims, Bystanders: The Jewish Catastrophe, 1933–1945*. New York:
HarperPerennial, 1993.

Hinton, Alexander Laban. "Anthropologies of the Khmer Rouge, Part II: Genocidal Bricolage." Paper presented at the Genocide Studies Program Seminar, Yale University, New Haven, CT, September 17, 1998.

——. "Begrudgement, Reconciliation, and the Khmer Rouge." *Searching for the Truth* (Khmer version), *A Magazine of the Documentation Center of Cambodia* 20 (2001). www.d.dccam .org/Tribunal/Analysis/Begrudgement_Reconciliation.htm.

——. "Justice and Time at the Khmer Rouge Tribunal: In Memory of Vann Nath, Painter and S-21 Survivor." *Genocide Studies and Prevention: An International Journal* 8, no. 2 (2014): 7–17.

——. *The Justice Facade: Trials of Transition in Cambodia.* Oxford: Oxford University Press, 2018.

——. *Man or Monster: The Trial of a Khmer Rouge Torturer.* Durham, NC: Duke University Press, 2016.

Hirsch, Marianne. *Family Frames: Photography, Narrative and Postmemory.* Cambridge, MA: Harvard University Press, 1997.

Human Rights Watch. *"We'll Kill You if You Cry": Sexual Violence in the Sierra Leone Conflict.* New York: Human Rights Watch, 2003.

Huntington, Samuel P. *Political Order in Changing Societies.* New Haven, CT: Yale University Press, 2006. First published 1968.

Huyssen, Andreas. "Present Pasts: Media, Politics, Amnesia." *Public Culture* 12, no. 1 (2000): 21–38.

Hyde, Melanie, Emma Palmer, and Sarah Williams. "Transformative Reparations for Sexual and Gender-Based Violence at the Extraordinary Chambers in the Courts of Cambodia." Australian Human Rights Centre and the Asian International Justice Initiative (2014), 7. www.eastwestcenter.org/sites/default/files/filemanager/Research_Program/Politics_ Governance_and_Security/AIJI/Reparations%20Workshop%20Report.pdf.

Indiegogo. "The Project: What Is It About?" www.indiegogo.com/projects/tuc-tuc-a-short-film -by-kavich-neang.

Irigaray, Luce, ed. *The Irigaray Reader.* Oxford: Blackwell, 1991.

Jackson, Karl D. *Cambodia, 1975–1978: Rendezvous with Death.* Princeton, NJ: Princeton University Press, 1989.

Jacobsen, Trudy. *Lost Goddesses: The Denial of Female Power in Cambodian History.* Copenhagen: Nias, 2008.

Jain, Neha. "Forced Marriage as a Crime Against Humanity: Problems of Definition and Prosecution." *Journal of International Criminal Justice* 6 (2008): 1013–32.

Jarvis, Helen. " 'Justice for the Deceased': Victims' Participation in the Extraordinary Chambers in the Courts of Cambodia." *Genocide Studies and Prevention: An International Journal* 8, no. 2 (2014): 19–27.

——. "Mapping Cambodia's 'Killing Fields.' " In *Matériel Culture: The Archaeology of Twentieth-Century Conflict*, edited by Colleen M. Beck, William Gray Johnson, and John Schofield, 91–102. New York: Routledge, 2002.

Jaspers, Karl. *The Question of German Guilt.* New York: Capricorn, 1961. First published 1947.

Kaplan, E. Ann. "Ann Kaplan Replies to Linda Williams' 'Something Else Besides a Mother: "Stella Dallas" and the Maternal Melodrama.'" *Cinema Journal* 24, no. 2 (1985): 40–43.

——. "Melodrama, Cinema and Trauma." *Screen* 42, no. 2 (2001): 201–5.

Khmers Rouges Amers. www.brunocarette.com/films/khmers-rouges-amers.

Kiernan, Ben. *Blood and Soil: A World History of Genocide and Extermination from Sparta to Darfur*. New Haven, CT: Yale University Press, 2007.

——. "Myth, Nationalism and Genocide." *Journal of Genocide Research* 3, no. 2 (2001): 92.

——. "Wall of Silence: The Field of Genocide Studies and the Guatemalan Genocide." In *Den Dannede Opprorer Bernt Hagtvet 70 ar (The Educated Rebel for Bernt Hagtvust at 70)*, edited by Nik Brandal and Dag Einar Thorsen, 169–98. Oslo: Dreyers Forlag, 2016.

Kinetz, Erika, and Yun Samean. "ECCC Arrests the 'Untouchable' Ieng Sary." *Cambodia Daily*, November 13, 2007. www.cambodiadaily.com/archives/eccc-arrests-the-untouchable-ieng -sary-61623.

King, Homay. "Born Free? Repetition and Fantasy in *The Act of Killing*." *Film Quarterly* 67, no. 2 (2013): 30–36.

Kirby, Paul. "How Is Rape a Weapon of War? Feminist International Relations, Modes of Critical Explanation and the Study of Wartime Sexual Violence." *European Journal of International Relations* 19, no. 4 (2012): 797–821.

Kohn, Margaret. "Unblinking: Citizens and Subjects in the Age of Video Surveillance." *Constellations* 17, no. 4 (2010): 572–88.

Kuper, Leo. *The Prevention of Genocide*. New Haven, CT: Yale University Press, 1985.

Kuran, Timur. "Sparks and Prairie Fires: A Theory of Unanticipated Political Revolution." *Public Choice* 61, no. 1 (1989): 41–74.

Kyle, Jess. "Protecting the World: Military Humanitarian Intervention and the Ethics of Care." *Hypatia* 28 (2013): 257–73.

LaCapra, Dominick. "Historical and Literary Approaches to the 'Final Solution': Saul Friedländer and Jonathan Littell." *History and Theory* 50 (2011): 71–97.

——. *History and Memory After Auschwitz*. Ithaca, NY: Cornell University Press, 1998.

——. *Writing History, Writing Trauma*. Baltimore: Johns Hopkins University Press, 2001.

Lanzmann, Claude. "The Obscenity of Understanding: An Evening with Claude Lanzmann." In *Trauma Explorations in Memory*, edited by Cathy Caruth, 200–20. Baltimore: Johns Hopkins University Press, 1995.

Laplanche, Jean. "Time and the Other." In *Essays on Otherness*, 234–59. London: Routledge, 1999.

Larcombe, Wendy. "The 'Ideal' Victim v Successful Rape Complainants: Not What You Might Expect." *Feminist Legal Studies* 10 (2002): 131–48.

Laub, Dori. "Bearing Witness, or the Vicissitudes of Listening." In *Testimony: Crises of Witnessing in Literature*, edited by Shoshana Felman and Dori Laub, 57–74. New York: Routledge, 1992.

——. "Listening to My Mother's Testimony." *Contemporary Psychoanalysis* 51, no. 2 (2015): 195–215.

Laub, Dori, and Susanna Lee. "Thanatos and Massive Psychic Trauma: The Impact of the Death Instinct on Knowing, Remembering, and Forgetting." *Journal of American Psychoanalytic Association* 51, no. 2 (2003): 433–63.

Lefebvre, Henri. *The Production of Space*. Translated by Donald Nicholson-Smith. Malden, MA: Blackwell, 1991. First published 1974.

Lemma, Alessandra. "The Many Faces of Lying." *International Journal of Psychoanalysis* 86, no. 3 (2005): 737–53.

Lesley, Elena. "Jarvis' Leninist Ties Under Fire." *Phnom Penh Post*, June 3, 2009. www .phnompenhpost.com/krt-talk/jarvis-leninist-ties-under-fire.

Levi, Primo. *If This Is a Man*. Translated by Stuart Woolf. New York: Orion, 1959.

Levinas, Emmanuel. *Emmanuel Levinas: Basic Philosophical Writings*. Edited by Adriaan T. Peperzak, Simon Critchley, and Robert Bernasconi. Bloomington: Indiana University Press, 2008.

LeVine, Peg. *Love and Dread in Cambodia: Weddings, Births, and Ritual Harm Under the Khmer Rouge*. Singapore: National University of Singapore Press, 2010.

Lifton, Robert Jay. *The Nazi Doctors: Medical Killing and the Psychology of Genocide*. New York: Basic, 2000. First published 1986.

Lindenbaum, Shirley. "Thinking About Cannibalism." *Annual Review of Anthropology* 33 (2004): 475–98.

Linfield, Susie. "Photojournalism and Human Rights." In *The Cruel Radiance: Photography and Political Violence*, 33–62. Chicago: University of Chicago Press, 2010.

Little, Harriet Fitch, and Vandy Muong. "Relics of Cambodia's Cinematic Golden Age." *Phnom Penh Post*, December 19, 2014. www.phnompenhpost.com/post-weekend/relics-cambodias -cinematic-golden-age.

Locard, Henri. *Pol Pot's Little Red Book: The Sayings of Angkar*. Chaing Mai, Thailand: Silkworm, 2004.

Lusztig, Irene. "The Fever Dream of Documentary: A Conversation with Joshua Oppenheimer." *Film Quarterly* 67, no. 2 (2013): 50–56.

MacKinnon, Catharine A. "Defining Rape Internationally: A Comment on *Akayesu*." *Columbia Journal of Transitional Law* 44, no. 3 (2006): 940–47.

——. "Rape, Genocide, and Women's Human Rights." *Harvard Women's Law Journal* 17 (1994): 5–16.

Mamdani, Mahmood. "Amnesty or Impunity? A Preliminary Critique of the Report of the Truth and Reconciliation Commission of South Africa (TRC)." *Diacritics* 32, nos. 3–4 (2002): 32–59.

Mann, Michael. "Communist Cleansing." In *The Dark Side of Democracy: Explaining Ethnic Cleansing*, 318–52. Cambridge: Cambridge University Press, 2005.

——. *The Dark Side of Democracy: Explaining Ethnic Cleansing*. Cambridge: Cambridge University Press, 2005.

Mbembe, Achille. "Necropolitics." *Public Culture* 15, no. 1 (2003): 11–40.

McGlothlin, Erin. "Empathetic Identification and the Mind of the Holocaust Perpetrator in Fiction: A Proposed Taxonomy of Response." *Narrative* 24, no. 3 (2016): 251–75.

McIntyre, Kevin. "Geography as Destiny: Cities, Villages and Khmer Rouge Orientalism." *Comparative Studies in Society and History* 38, no. 4 (1996): 730–58.

McPherson, Poppy. "Cambodia: Dawn of a New Cinematic Golden Era." *Diplomat*, March 6, 2015. https://thediplomat.com/2015/03/cambodiadawn-of-a-new-cinematic-golden-era/.

Meierhenrich, Jens. "Varieties of Reconciliation." *Law and Social Inquiry* 33, no. 1 (2008): 195–231.

Mertus, Julie. "Shouting from the Bottom of the Well: The Impact of International Trials for Wartime Rape on Women's Agency." *International Feminist Journal of Politics* 6, no. 1 (2004): 110–28.

Mettraux, Guénaël. "Crimes Against Humanity in the Jurisprudence of the International Criminal Tribunals for the Former Yugoslavia and for Rwanda." *Harvard International Law Journal* 43, no. 1 (2002): 237–316.

Mey, Chum. Documentation Center of Cambodia. *Survivor: The Triumph of an Ordinary Man in the Khmer Rouge Genocide.* Translated by Sim Sorya and Kimsory Sokvisal, 77–100. Phnom Penh: Documentation Center of Cambodia, 2012.

Minow, Martha. *Breaking the Cycles of Hatred: Memory, Law, and Repair.* Commentaries edited by Nancy L. Rosenblum. Princeton, NJ: Princeton University Press, 2002.

Morag, Raya. "Blood Relations and Nonconsensual Ethics: Israeli Intifada Documentaries." *Post Script* 36, nos. 2–3 (2018): 75–85.

——. *Defeated Masculinity: Post Traumatic Cinema in the Aftermath of War.* Brussels: Peter Lang, 2009.

——. "The Survivor-Perpetrator Encounter and the Truth Archive in Rithy Panh's Documentaries." In *Post-1990 Documentary Reconfiguring Independence,* edited by Camille Deprez and Judith Pernin, 97–111. Edinburgh: Edinburgh University Press, 2015.

——. *Waltzing with Bashir: Perpetrator Trauma and Cinema.* London: I. B. Tauris, 2013.

Mouffe, Chantal. *The Democratic Paradox.* New York: Verso, 1999.

——. "Which World Order: Cosmopolitan or Multipolar?" *Ethical Perspectives* 15, no. 4 (2008): 453–67.

Mowitt, John. "Trauma Envy." *Cultural Critique* 46 (2000): 272–97.

Murphy, Bethany. "Jarvis Wrong Choice for Victim's Unit." *Phnom Penh Post,* June 22, 2009. www.phnompenhpost.com/national/jarvis-wrong-choice-victims-unit.

Myers, D. G. "Jean Améry: A Biographical Introduction." http://dgmyers.blogspot.com/p/jean -amery-biographical-introduction.html.

Nachemson, Andrew. "Civil Parties Challenge Expert Witness Over Forced Marriage. *Phnom Penh Post,* October 13, 2016. www.phnompenhpost.com/national/civil-parties-challenge -expert-witness-over-forced-marriage.

——. "Khmer Rouge Tribunal Sets Date for Hearing on Chaem's Dismissal." *Phnom Penh Post,* November 14, 2017. www.phnompenhpost.com/national/khmer-rouge-tribunal-sets -date-hearing-chaems-dismissal-0.

Nakagawa, Kasumi. "Gender-Based Violence During the Khmer Rouge Regime: Stories of Survivors from the Democratic Kampuchea (1975–1979)." In *Asia Pacific Year Book of International Humanitarian Law,* 2nd ed., 1–30. Phnom Penh, Cambodia, 2008.

Needham, Susan, Karen Quintiliani, and Robert Lemkin. "The Space of Sorrow: A Historic Video Dialogue Between Survivors and Perpetrators of the Cambodian Killing Fields." *International Journal of Human Rights* 19, no. 5 (2015): 628–47.

Negarestani, Reza. "The Corpse Bride: Thinking with *Nigredo*." In *Collapse,* vol. 4, edited by Robin Mackay, 129–61. Falmouth, UK: Urbanomic, 2008.

Ngor, Haing, with Roger Warner. *Survival in the Killing Fields.* New York: Basic, 2003. First published 1987.

Nichols, Bill. "Documentary Reenactment and the Fantasmatic Subject." *Critical Inquiry* 35 (2008): 78.

———. "Irony, Cruelty, Evil (and a Wink) in *The Act of Killing*." *Film Quarterly* 67, no. 2 (2013): 25–29.

———. "The Voice of Documentary." *Film Quarterly* 36 (1983): 17–30.

Nietzsche, Friedrich Wilhelm. *On the Genealogy of Morals.* 1st ed. Translated by Douglas Smith. New York: Oxford University Press, 2009. First published 1887.

Olick, Jeffrey K. "From Theodicy to *Ressentiment*: Trauma and the Ages of Compensation." In *The Politics of Regret: On Collective Memory and Historical Responsibility*, 153–73. New York: Routledge, 2007.

———. "Time for Forgiveness: A Historical Perspective." In *Considering Forgiveness*, edited by Aleksandra Wagner with Carin Kuoni and Matthew Buckingham, 85–92. New York: Vera List Center for Art and Politics, 2009.

One Dollar. http://onedollar.bophana.org/en/.

Panh, Rithy. "Bophana: A Cambodian Tragedy." *Manoa* 16, no. 1 (2004): 108–26.

Panh, Rithy, and Christopher Bataille. *The Elimination: A Survivor of the Khmer Rouge Confronts His Past and the Commandant of the Killing Fields.* Translated by John Cullen. New York: Other, 2013.

Petit, Robert. "Lawfare and International Tribunals: A Question of Definition? A Reflection on the Creation of the Khmer Rouge Tribunal." *Case Western Reserve Journal of International Law* 43, no. 1 (2010): 189–99.

Phnom Penh Post. "Filmmaker Aims to Show the KR Tragedy from All Angles." February 17, 2009. www.phnompenhpost.com/lifestyle/filmmaker-aims-show-kr-tragedy-all-angles.

———. "Im Chaem Defence Slams Prosecution's Summation." February 14, 2017. www .phnompenhpost.com/national/im-chaem-defence-slams-prosecutions-summation.

———. Letter to the editor. "An Inhuman Act Against Men and Women." September 19, 2016. www.phnompenhpost.com/analysis-and-op-ed/inhuman-act-against-men-and-women.

———. "Marriage Under the Khmer Rouge." www.phnompenhpost.com/post-weekend /marriage-under-khmer-rouge-documentary-series. n.d.

———. "Team at Odds Over Ao An Case." *Phnom Penh Post*, September 1, 2017. www .phnompenhpost.com/national/team-odds-over-ao-case.

Phnom Penh Post Blogspot. "Documentary Film Co-Producer Defends Dealing with Tribunal." April 21, 2010. http://khmernz.blogspot.com/2010/04/documentary-film-co-producer -defends.html.

Picq, Laurence. *Beyond the Horizon: Five Years with the Khmer Rouge.* Translated by Patricia Norland. New York: St. Martin's, 1989.

———. Comment: My Life Under Ieng Sary: "Crying Against the Shame and Horror." October 4, 1996. www.phnompenhpost.com/national/comment-my-life-under-ieng-sary-crying -against-shame-horror.

PopulationPyramid.net. "Population Pyramids of the World from 1950–2100, Cambodia." www.populationpyramid.net/cambodia/2017.

Prins, Annemarie. *Breaking the Silence: A New Cambodian Play* (script). Phom Phen, Cambodia: DC-Cam, 2009.

Raine, Adrian, D. Phil, Jacqueline Stoddard, Susan Bihrle, and Monte Buchsbaum. "Prefrontal Glucose Deficits in Murderers Lacking Psychosocial Deprivation." *Neuropsychiatry, Neuropsychology and Behavioral Neurology* 2, no. 1 (2003): 1–7.

Rancière, Jacques. "The Ethical Turn of Aesthetics and Politics." In *Aesthetics and Its Discontents*, translated by Steven Corcoran, 109–32. Cambridge: Polity, 2009.

Ricoeur, Paul, and David Pellauer. "Evil, a Challenge to Philosophy and Theology." *Journal of the American Academy of Religion* 53, no. 4 (1985): 635–48.

Rigney, Ann. "Reconciliation and Remembering: (How) Does it Work?" *Memory Studies* 5, no. 3 (2012): 251–58.

Robinson, Fiona. "Exploring Social Relations, Understanding Power, and Valuing Care: The Role of Critical Feminist Ethics in International Relations Theory." In *Ethics and International Relations*, edited by Hakan Seckinelgin and Hideaki Shinoda, 56–80. Basingstoke, UK: Palgrave, 2001.

——. *Globalizing Care: Ethics, Feminist Theory, and International Relations*. Boulder, CO: Westview, 1999.

Rosenblum, Nancy L. Introduction to *Breaking the Cycles of Hatred: Memory, Law, and Repair*, by Martha Minow, 1–13. Commentaries edited by Nancy L. Rosenblum. Princeton, NJ: Princeton University Press, 2002.

Rothberg, Michael. "Between Auschwitz and Algeria: Multidirectional Memory and the Counterpublic Witness." *Critical Inquiry* 33, no. 1 (2006): 158–84.

——. *Traumatic Realism: The Demands of Holocaust Representation*. Minneapolis: University of Minnesota Press, 2000.

Rummel, Rudolph J. *Statistics of Democide: Genocide and Mass Murder Since 1900*. Münster, Germany: LIT Verlag, 1998. Annotated edition.

SáCouto, Susana. "Victim Participation at the International Criminal Court and The Extraordinary Chambers in the Courts of Cambodia: A Feminist Project?" *Michigan Journal of Gender and Law* 18, no. 2 (2012): 297–359.

Samphan, Khieu. "Cambodia's Economy and Problems of Industrialization." In *Underdevelopment in Cambodia*, translated by Laura Summers, *Indochina Chronicle*, nos. 51–52. Berkeley: Indochina Resource Center, 1976. www.scribd.com/doc/58800629/Underdevelopment-in-Cambodia-by-Khieu-Samphan#scribd.

Sassoon, Alessandro Marazzi. "Khmer Rouge Tribunal Severs Im Chaem from Case 004." *Phnom Penh Post*, February 16, 2016. www.phnompenhpost.com/national/khmer-rouge-tribunal-severs-im-chaem-case-004.

Savron, Duong. *The Mystery of Sexual Violence Under the Khmer Rouge Regime*. Cambodian Defenders Project (2011): 1–56. http://gbvkr.org/wp-content/uploads/2013/01/Mystery_of_Sexual_Violence_during_KR_ENG-web.pdf.

Scarpa, Angela, and Adrian Raine. "The Psychophysiology of Antisocial Behavior: Interactions with Environmental Experiences." In *Biosocial Criminology: Challenging Environmentalism Supremacy*, edited by Anthony Walsh and Lee Ellis, 209–26. Hauppauge, NY: Nova Science, 2003.

Schaap, Andrew. "Reconciliation as Ideology and Politics." *Constellations* 15, no. 3 (2008): 249–64.

Scheff, Thomas J. "Shame and the Social Bond: A Sociological Theory." *Sociological Theory* 18, no. 1 (2000): 84–99.

Scheler, Max. *Ressentiment*. Translated by Lewis B. Coser and William W. Holdheim. Milwaukee, WI: Marquette University Press, 2010. First published 1914.

Schiessl, Christoph. "An Element of Genocide: Rape, Total War, and International Law in the Twentieth Century." *Journal of Genocide Research* 4, no. 2 (2002): 197–210.

Schlund-Vials, Cathy J., and Samuel Martínez. "Interrogating the Perpetrator: Violation, Culpability and Human Rights." *International Journal of Human Rights* 19, no. 5 (2015): 549–54.

Schott, Robin May. "War Rape, Natality and Genocide." *Journal of Genocide Research* 13, nos. 1–2 (2011): 5–21.

Shaw, Martin. "New Wars of the City: Relationships of 'Urbicide' and 'Genocide.'" In *Cities, War, and Terrorism: Towards an Urban Geopolitics*, edited by Stephen Graham, 141–53. Malden, MA: Blackwell, 2004.

Short, Damien. "Reconciliation and the Problem of Internal Colonialism." *Journal of Intercultural Studies* 26, no. 3 (2005): 267–82.

Silverman, Kaja. *The Acoustic Mirror: The Female Voice in Psychoanalysis and Cinema*. Bloomington: Indiana University Press, 1988.

——. "Disembodying the Female Voice." In *Re-Vision: Essays in Feminist Film Criticism*, edited by Mary Ann Doane, Patricia Mellencamp, and Linda Williams, 131–49. American Film Institute Monograph Series 3. Frederick, MD: University Publications of America, 1984.

Simone, AbdouMaliq, "The Politics of the Possible: Making Urban Life in Phnom Penh." *Singapore Journal of Tropical Geography* 29 (2008): 188.

Simpson, Brad. "*The Act of Killing* and the Dilemmas of History." *Film Quarterly* 67, no. 2 (2013): 10–13.

Singer, Ben. *Melodrama and Modernity: Early Sensational Cinema and Its Contexts*. New York: Columbia University Press, 2001.

Sjogren, Britta. *Into the Vortex: Female Voice and Paradox in Film*. Urbana: University of Illinois Press, 2006.

Skocpol, Theda. *States and Social Revolutions: A Comparative Analysis of France, Russia, and China*. New York: Cambridge University Press, 1979.

Smele, Jonathan. "War and Revolution in Russia, 1914–1921." October 3, 2011. www.bbc.co.uk /history/worldwars/wwone/eastern_front_01.shtml.

Smith, Adam. *The Theory of Moral Sentiments*. Edited by Ryan Patrick Hanley. New York: Penguin, 2009. First published 1790.

Smith, Henry F. "Leaps of Faith: Is Forgiveness a Useful Concept?" *International Journal of Psychoanalysis* 89, no. 5 (2008): 919–36.

Sokchea, Meas. "Federal Job Awaits Pailin Chief Accused of Corruption." *Phnom Penh Post*, November 5, 2014. www.phnompenhpost.com/national/federal-job-awaits-pailin-chief -accused-corruption.

Staub, Ervin. "Genocide and Mass Killing: Origins, Prevention, Healing and Reconciliation." *Political Psychology* 21, no. 2 (2000): 367–82.

——. *The Roots of Evil: The Origins of Genocide and Other Group Violence.* Cambridge: Cambridge University Press, 1992.

Strangio, Sebastian. *Hun Sen's Cambodia.* New Haven, CT: Yale University Press, 2014.

Suleiman, Susan Rubin. "The 1.5 Generation: Thinking About Child Survivors and the Holocaust." *American Imago* 59, no. 3 (2002): 277–95.

——. "When the Perpetrator Becomes a Reliable Witness of the Holocaust: On Jonathan Littell's *Les bienveillantes.*" *New German Critique* 36, no. 1 (2009): 1–19.

Ten Brink, Joram, and Joshua Oppenheimer, eds. *Killer Images: Documentary Film, Memory and the Performance of Violence.* London: Wallflower, 2012.

Thirion, Louise. "Trial Chamber Heard Evidence on Forced Marriage and Rape." February 9, 2016. www.eccc.gov.kh/en/blog/2016/09/02/trial-chamber-heard-evidence-forced-marriage-and-rape.

Tomelleri, Stefano. *Ressentiment: Reflections on Mimetic Desire and Society.* East Lansing: Michigan State University Press, 2015.

Toy-Cronin, Bridgette A. "What Is Forced Marriage? Towards a Definition of Forced Marriage as a Crime Against Humanity." *Columbia Journal of Gender and Law* 19, no. 2 (2010): 539–90.

Tronto, Joan. *Caring Democracy: Markets, Equality, and Justice.* New York: New York University Press, 2013.

——. *Moral Boundaries: A Political Argument for an Ethic of Care.* New York: Routledge, 1994.

Tyner, James A. "Imagining Genocide: Anti-Geographies and the Erasure of Space in Democratic Kampuchea." *Space and Polity* 13, no. 1 (2009): 9–20.

Tyner, James A., Samuel Henkin, Savina Sirik, and Kimsroy Sokvisal. "Phnom Penh During the Cambodian Genocide: A Case of Selective Urbicide." *Environment and Planning A* 46 (2014): 1873–91.

UNESCO. *Contemporary Forms of Slavery: Systematic Rape, Sexual Slavery and Slavery-Like Practices During Armed Conflict*, E/CN.4/Sub.2/1998/13. New York: United Nations, 1998.

Ung, Bun Y. "Cambodian Film Industry: A Paradox to Glorious Revival." *Cambodian Communication Review* (2016): 35–43.

Ung, Loung. *First They Killed My Father: A Daughter of Cambodia Remembers.* New York: HarperPerennial, 2000.

United Nations. Department of Economic and Social Affairs, Population Division, World Population Prospects: The 2015 Revision, World Population 2015 Wallchart, *ST/ESA/SER.A/378.* https://esa.un.org/unpd/wpp/Publications/.

Vachon, Michelle. "Love, Life and Loss During the Pol Pot Regime." *Cambodia Daily*, March 17, 2014. www.cambodiadaily.com/archives/love-life-and-loss-during-the-pol-pot-regime-54314.

Verdeja, Ernesto. "Derrida and the Impossibility of Forgiveness." *Contemporary Political Theory* 3, no. 1 (2004): 23–47.

Vetlesen, Arne Johan. "A Case for Resentment: Jean Améry Versus Primo Levi." *Journal of Human Rights* 5 (2006): 27–44.

Victims Support Section (VSS). "Forced Marriage During the Khmer Rouge Regime and Intergenerational Dialogue." www.eccc.gov.kh/en/articles/mobile-exhibition-%E2%80%9Cforced-marriage-during-khmer-rouge-regime%E2%80%9D-and-intergenerational-dialogue.

Walker, Janet "Referred Pain: *The Act of Killing* and the Production of a Crime Scene." *Film Quarterly* 67, no. 2 (2013): 14–20.

Weiss, Karen G. "Too Ashamed to Report: Deconstructing the Shame of Sexual Victimization." *Feminist Criminology* 5, no. 3 (2010): 286–310.

White Building. "About the White Building." www.whitebuilding.org/en/page/about_the_white_building.

Wieviorka, Annette. *The Era of the Witness.* Translated by Jared Stark. Ithaca, NY: Cornell University Press, 2006.

——. "The Witness in History." Translated by Jared Stark. *Poetics Today* 27, no. 2 (2006): 385–97.

Wilkins, Georgia. "KR Victims Question Jarvis's Politics." *Phnom Penh Post*, June 19, 2009. www.phnompenhpost.com/national/kr-victims-question-jarviss-politics.

——. "S-21 Deputy Denies Torture." *Phnom Penh Post*, July 15, 2009. www.phnompenhpost.com/national/s-21-deputy-denies-torture.

Wilkomirski, Binjamin. *Fragments: Memories of a Wartime Childhood.* Translated by Carol Brown Janeway. New York: Schocken, 1996.

Williams, Linda. "Melodrama Revised." In *Refiguring American Film Genres*, edited by Nick Browne, 42–88. Berkeley: University of California Press, 1998.

——. "'Something Else Besides a Mother': 'Stella Dallas' and the Maternal Melodrama." *Cinema Journal* 24, no. 1 (1984): 2–27.

Wood, Elisabeth Jane. "Conflict-Related Sexual Violence and the Policy Implications of Recent Research." *International Review of the Red Cross* 894 (2014): 457–78.

——. "Sexual Violence During War: Variation and Accountability." In *Collective Crimes and International Criminal Justice: An Interdisciplinary Approach*, edited by Alette Smeulers, 295–322. Antwerp: Intersentia, 2010.

——. "Variation in Sexual Violence During War," *Politics and Society* 34, no. 3 (2006): 307–41.

Wright, George. "Journalist Again Asked to Testify at Tribunal." *Cambodia Daily*, May 16, 2015. www.cambodiadaily.com/archives/journalist-again-asked-to-testify-at-tribunal-83784.

Wright, George, and Kuch Naren. "Cannibalism, Khmer Rouge and Horrors of War." *Cambodia Daily*, April 25, 2014. www.cambodiadaily.com/news/cannibalism-khmer-rouge-and-horrors-of-war-82653.

Yale University Library. Fortunoff Video Archive for Holocaust Testimonies. https://web.library.yale.edu/testimonies/about.

Yaralian, Pauline S., and Raine Adrian. "Biological Approaches to Crime Psychophysiology and Brain Dysfunction Positive." In *Explaining Criminals and Crime: Essays in Contemporary Criminological Theory*, edited by Raymond Paternoster and Ronet R. Bachman, 57–72. Los Angeles: Roxbury, 2001.

Ye, Beini. "Forced Marriages as Mirrors of Cambodian Conflict Transformation." *Peace Review* 23, no. 4 (2011): 469–75.

Young, James E. "Holocaust Documentary Fiction: The Novelist as Eyewitness." In *Writing and the Holocaust*, edited by Berel Lang, 204–14. New York: Holmes and Meier, 1988.

Žižek, Slavoj. *For They Know Not What They Do: Enjoyment as a Political Factor.* 2nd ed. New York: Verso, 2002.

Zolkos, Magdalena. "Jean Améry's Concept of Resentment at the Crossroads of Ethics and Politics." *European Legacy* 12, no. 1 (2007): 23–38.

Zucker, Eve Monique. "Trauma and Its Aftermath: Local Configurations of Reconciliation in Cambodia and the Khmer Rouge Tribunal." *Journal of Asian Studies* 72, no. 4 (2013): 793–800.

Zupančič, Alenka. *Ethics of the Real: Kant, Lacan.* London: Verso, 2000.

INDEX